W9-BXN-158

Brief Contents

The Academic Writer

A BRIEF GUIDE

LISA EDE

Oregon State University

BEDFORD/ST. MARTIN'S

Boston · New York

For Bedford/St. Martin's

Developmental Editor: Kristin Bowen
Production Editor: Bernard Onken
Production Supervisor: Andrew Ensor
Senior Marketing Manager: Karita dos Santos
Art Director: Lucy Krikorian
Text Design: Anne Carter
Copy Editor: Alice Vigliani
Indexer: Kirsten Kite
Photo Research: Robin Raffer
Cover Design: Donna Dennison
Composition: Pine Tree Composition, Inc.
Printing and Binding: R.R. Donnelley & Sons Company

President: Joan E. Feinberg
Editorial Director: Denise B. Wydra
Editor in Chief: Karen S. Henry
Director of Development: Erica T. Appel
Director of Marketing: Karen Melton Soeltz
Director of Editing, Design, and Production: Marcia Cohen
Managing Editor: Shuli Traub

Library of Congress Control Number: 2007934444

Manufactured in the United States of America.

2 1 0 9 8
f e d c

For information, write: Bedford/St. Martin's, 75 Arlington Street, Boston, MA 02116   (617-399-4000)

ISBN-10: 0-312-45192-X
ISBN-13: 978-0-312-45192-9

Acknowledgments

Acknowledgments and copyrights appear at the back of the book on pages 365–66, which constitute an extension of the copyright page.

To my students
and
(of course)
to Gregory

Preface

Today's world is not the world of 1985, the year I began work on the first edition of *Work in Progress: A Guide to Academic Writing and Revising.* Students now learn the importance of the writing process, especially of invention and revision, throughout their education. While students will always need to be reminded of the value of attention to process, other questions and concerns have become pressing. What is the role of traditional print texts, for instance, in a world that increasingly favors visual and multimedia presentations? How can students strengthen their conventional academic writing skills while also developing their ability to employ multimedia and other forms of communication? As composition courses evolve to include more academic assignments, how can students think critically and effectively evaluate the abundance of sources they can access online? In a world of YouTube, Facebook, MySpace, and other social media, what role does and should traditional print communication play? Does writing really *matter* anymore?

A Reenvisioned Text

Once I was able to formulate this last question, I realized that I needed to undertake a major revision of *Work in Progress*, one that addresses the situations of students and teachers in the twenty-first century, not the late twentieth century. The textbook before you is the result of this radical revision. Its new title, *The Academic Writer: A Brief Guide*, signals my effort to place the situation and demands of academic writers at the conceptual center of my textbook. In working on *The Academic Writer*, I attempted to focus on the kinds of writing that students in college do *now*, using contemporary digital and online as well as traditional print technologies.

This emphasis is reflected in the organization of this new textbook. Part I, "Writing Matters: Writing and Rhetoric in the Twenty-First Century," provides the foundation for the book. Particularly central to the discussion in these chapters are two concepts: that of the rhetorical situation and of writing as design. Increasingly, scholars of rhetoric and writing argue that the most productive way to envision the act of composing texts is as design. *The Academic Writer* draws upon this research, and it does so in a clear, user-friendly manner. This discussion creates bridges between students' self-sponsored writing on such social networks as Facebook and MySpace (where they literally design self-representations) and the writing they undertake as college students.

Part II of *The Academic Writer*, "Writing in College," focuses, as its title suggests, on the demands that contemporary students face. Analysis, argument, and research are central to academic writing, and this section provides chapters on each of these topics, as well as a new chapter on writing in the disciplines. Part III, "Practical Strategies for Reading and Writing," provides concise, reference-friendly advice for students on reading, invention, planning, drafting, document design, and revision.

Even though *The Academic Writer* has been radically rethought and updated, it continues to reflect the assumptions, strategies, and practices of earlier editions of *Work in Progress*. The longer and harder I thought about the new challenges and opportunities that contemporary writers face, the more I found myself returning to the rhetorical tradition. What could the age-old rhetorical tradition have to say to twenty-first-century students? Well, as it turns out, it has *a lot* to say. After all, some of the most important concepts in western rhetoric were formulated in Greece during the fifth century B.C.E., a time when the Greeks were in the midst of a transition from an oral to an alphabetic/manuscript culture. This was also a time when principles of democracy were being developed. In Athens — an early limited democracy — citizens met in the Assembly to make civic and political decisions; they also served as jurors at trials. Those arguing for or against an issue or person made public speeches in the Assembly. Because each case varied, rhetoricians needed to develop flexible, situation-oriented strategies designed to achieve specific purposes.

Rather than providing "rules" about how texts should be organized and developed, rhetoric encourages those composing texts to draw on their commonsense understanding of communication — an understanding they have developed as speakers, listeners, writers and readers — to make local, situated decisions about how they can best communicate in specific situations. A rhetorical approach to communication encourages writers to think in terms of *purpose* and *effect*. In this regard, the rhetorical approach in this book encourages writers to think — and act — like problem solvers. This book offers tools students can use in any writing situation, designed to help students negotiate the demands they face as academic writers and, later, as citizens and workers. In its discussion of rhetoric and of the rhetorical situation, *The Academic Writer* shows students how best to respond to a particular writing challenge — whether they are writing an essay exam, designing a PowerPoint presentation, or posting to their personal blog.

I have tried to make *The Academic Writer* as brief (and hence inexpensive) and student-friendly as possible. It respects students and speaks to them in a language they understand. It is a practical guide to the essentials of academic writing and research that is easy to use either alone or along with a collection of readings or handbook. I hope that readers of *The Academic Writer* will agree that this textbook values the knowledge of teachers and is thus flexible and open to multiple pedagogical approaches. It invites teachers — as peers — to ground their pedagogy in current research on the teaching of writing.

Features

Focus on Applying Commonsense Rhetorical Questions. *The Academic Writer*'s easy-to-understand guidelines enable students to make effective choices as they write. Students learn the questions they need to ask to understand any writing situation in terms of the writer, reader, text, and medium. With each new project they tackle throughout college, students can make effective choices by asking the rhetorically grounded questions presented in Chapter 3, "Analyzing Rhetorical Situations."

"Thinking Rhetorically" icons appear throughout the book, highlighting important strategies and rhetorical advice that students can apply to their own writing. These icons also call attention to examples where student writers effectively analyze and respond to their rhetorical situation.

thinking
rhetorically

Essential Help for Writing in the Disciplines. Responding to changes in first-year writing courses and new attention to writing across the curriculum, *The Academic Writer* offers students essential help for their academic work, with examples throughout the book. The **seventeen model student essays** and documents taken from a variety of academic disciplines provide excellent examples of the kinds of writing students are asked to do in first-year courses and beyond. Many examples are annotated to help students understand the expectations of faculty in diverse disciplines. Chapter 7, "Writing in the Disciplines: Making Choices as You Write," helps students gain a rhetorical understanding of the reasons the conventions of writing vary in the humanities, sciences, social sciences, and business. This chapter introduces students to the kinds of writing they can expect to do after they complete first-year writing and demonstrates how they can draw upon their understanding of the rhetorical situation as they do so.

Attention to Writing as Design. The concept of the rhetorical situation provides a particularly effective and powerful bridge to the world of visual texts and multimedia. Today's students need to know how to employ *all* the resources available to them: words, images, designs, and media. A unique first chapter, "Writing as Design: A Rhetorical Process for Composing Texts," compares writing and design, reminding students that communication is central to both activities. Whether you are designing or writing a text, you are essentially doing the same thing: figuring out how to present your content in the most effective manner. This chapter shows students how to apply the knowledge they already have—gathered in all their experiences communicating, online and off—to the writing they will do in college. Further, it helps them develop the confidence and rhetorical sensitivity they need to succeed as academic writers.

Up-to-date Help for Conducting Academic Research. Chapter 6, "Doing Research: Joining the Scholarly Conversation," provides help students need to effectively evaluate, incorporate, and document print and online sources. The appendix, "Writers' References," includes up-to-date MLA and APA documentation advice. The appendix's Source Maps feature step-by-step, visual advice on documentation, offering annotated instructions and examples for citing print and electronic materials.

Practical Advice on Analyzing Texts and Constructing Effective Arguments. Chapter 4, "Analyzing Texts and Contexts," helps students develop the strong analytic skills that are essential to academic writing; Chapter 5, "Making and Supporting Claims," guides students to design carefully reasoned academic arguments. The rhetorical approach of these chapters enables students to develop an insider's understanding of the conventions that characterize academic writing.

Quick-reference Advice on Reading, Invention, Planning, Drafting, Revising, and Designing. The chapters in Part III, "Practical Strategies for Reading and Writing," give strategies, tips, and examples that are easy for students to apply in their own writing processes. The illustrated chapter on using visuals and design elements, along with attention throughout the book to media and visual literacy, helps students write both traditional print and visually rich texts effectively.

Also included is an extended case study of a student writer, following one assignment through each stage of the writing process. Drafts of this student's work—from informal invention activities and multiple drafts leading to a final essay—appear throughout Part III of the book.

Supplements

Instructor's Notes for The Academic Writer. Written by Lisa Ede and Suzanne Clark, and designed to complement and support *The Academic Writer*, the manual offers multiple course plans, practical advice on teaching, tips for working with each chapter in the text, and sample assignments. (ISBN-10: 0-312-45245-4; ISBN-13: 978-0-312-45245-2)

The following resources are available for packaging with *The Academic Writer*.

i·claim visualizing argument.   This innovative CD-ROM offers a new way to see argument, with six tutorials, an illustrated glossary, and more than seventy multimedia arguments for analysis. (package ISBN-10: 0-312-48563-8; ISBN-13: 978-0-312-48563-4)

i·cite visualizing sources.   This CD-ROM brings research to life through an animated introduction, four tutorials, and hands-on source practice. (package ISBN-10: 0-312-48562-x; ISBN-13: 978-0-312-48562-7)

Writing across the Curriculum Package.   This handy collection of quick reference cards helps students work with sources—a key academic skill in any discipline—using MLA, APA, Chicago, or CSE style. Each card provides clear advice on choosing evidence and integrating sources alongside up-to-date documentation models for the most common types of sources. (package ISBN-10: 0-312-48403-3; ISBN-13: 978-0-312-48403-3)

Acknowledgments

Before I wrote *The Academic Writer*, acknowledgments sometimes struck me as formulaic or conventional. Now I recognize that they are neither; rather, acknowledgments are simply inadequate to the task at hand. Coming at the end of a preface—and hence twice marginalized—acknowledgments can never adequately convey the complex web of interrelationships and collaborations that make a book like this possible. I hope that the people whose support and assistance I acknowledge here not only note my debt of gratitude but also recognize the sustaining role that they have played, and continue to play, in my life and in my work.

I would like to begin by thanking my colleagues at the Center for Writing and Learning at Oregon State University. I could accomplish little in my teaching, research, and administration without the support and friendship of Dennis Bennett, Wayne Robertson, and Jeanna Towns. They, along with our writing assistants, have taught me what it means to collaborate in a sustaining, productive fashion. Others in the OSU English department, my second academic home, supported me while I wrote and revised this text. I am indebted to my colleagues Chris Anderson, Vicki Tolar Burton, Anita Helle, and Sara Jameson for their friendship and their commitment to writing.

I have dedicated this book to my students, and I hope that it in some way reflects what *they* have taught me over the years. I also owe a great debt of gratitude to another friend and teacher, Suzanne Clark, who from the first edition of *Work in Progress* has worked with me on the instructor's manual. Suzanne's thoughts and ideas continue to inform the instructor's manual for *The Academic Writer*. Thanks to Suzanne, and to Judy Voss and Rae Guimond, who also assisted with work on this important project.

I also wish to acknowledge the students whose writing appears in this text. I am particularly grateful to Daniel Stiepleman, whose writing appears throughout Part III of this book, providing students with an extended example of successful academic writing in action.

Colleagues and students play an important role in nurturing any project, but so do those who form the intangible but indispensable community of scholars that is one's most intimate disciplinary home. Here, it is harder to determine who to acknowledge; my debt to the composition theorists who have led the way or "grown up" with me is so great that I hesitate to list the names of specific individuals here for fear of omitting someone deserving of credit. I must, however, acknowledge my friend and frequent coauthor Andrea Lunsford, who writes with me even when I write alone. Andrea generously allowed me to reprint material from *The St. Martin's Handbook*, Sixth Edition, in the appendix of this text, and for that I thank her as well.

I would also like to thank the many dedicated teachers of composition I have worked and talked with over the years. By their example, comments, suggestions, and questions, they have taught me a great deal about the teaching of writing. A number of writing instructors took time from their teaching to look carefully at the sixth edition of *Work in Progress*, as well as drafts of this new book. Their observations and suggestions have enriched and improved *The Academic Writer*. These reviewers include the following instructors: Jeffrey Andelora, Mesa Community College; Niky R. Bean, Mid Michigan Community College; Shannon Carter, Texas A&M–Commerce; Michael Brooks Crye, Mesa Community College; Deborah Coxwell Teague, Florida State University; Allison Detmer Carpenter, Northampton Community College; Laurie L. Esler, Southern Wesleyan University; Christina Fisanick, Xavier University; Jennifer Forsyth, Kutztown University; Jeanne Guerin, Sierra College; Kimberly Harrison, Florida International University; Larry M. Lake, Messiah College; David B. Levy, Sacred Heart University; Martha Marinara, University of Central Florida; Susan K. Miller, Mesa Community College; Lori A. Paige, Westfield State College; Linda K. Parkyn, Messiah College; Doreen Piano, University of New Orleans; Ronald L. Pitcock, Texas Christian University; Harvey Solganick, LeTourneau University; Laura Steinert, Mesa Community College; Donna Strickland, University of Missouri–Columbia; James G. Van Belle, Edmonds Community College; Patricia Ventura, Spellman College; Patricia Webb, Arizona State University; and Jacqueline Wheeler, Arizona State University.

Special thanks go to Dana Ferris at California State University, Sacramento; Ilona Leki at University of Tennessee, Knoxville; and Yazmín Lazcano and Jaime Armin Mejía of Texas State University, who helped me develop and improve the boxed suggestions for multilingual writers.

I wish to thank the dedicated staff of Bedford/St. Martin's. Any textbook is an intensely collaborative effort, and I count myself particularly fortunate in having had Kristin Bowen as the senior editor on this project. Reenvisioning and reinbodying a textbook with as long a history as *Work in Progress* is a difficult task, to put it mildly. I have valued Kristin's commitment, expertise, and insight from start to finish of this project, and I am sure *The Academic Writer* is a better book as a result. At various moments Anne Leung played a key role in the development of this text, as did Ellen Kuhl. I feel fortunate indeed to have been able to work with such an experienced and knowledgeable team. In addition, I want to thank project editor Bernie Onken, whose patient attention to detail proved especially valuable, and marketing manager Karita dos Santos, whose guidance was invaluable.

Finally, I want to (but cannot adequately) acknowledge the support of my husband, Gregory Pfarr, whose passionate commitment to his own creative endeavors, and our life together, sustains me.

Lisa Ede

Contents

PART II

Writing in College

PART III

Practical Strategies for
Reading and Writing

Writing as Design: A Rhetorical Process for Composing Texts

What does it mean to be a writer in the twenty-first century? In a media-saturated world where visual images surround us, how much does writing still matter? How has the increasing emphasis on the visual — and the availability of digital and online media — influenced the communicative practices of ordinary people like you and me? One need only visit Flickr, the popular online photo-sharing space, to notice the power that images hold for many people. While drafting this chapter, for instance, I typed "black labs" into Flickr's search engine and discovered that 5,507 photos of this popular breed were posted on this site. Clearly, black lab owners are using Flickr to communicate how much they love their dogs. Words still play a role in this communication, for the photos cataloged in Flickr include such titles as "Happy Black Lab," "Black Labs, Rainy Day," and "Black Lab in Truck." On Flickr, however, visual images are clearly more important than the words that accompany them (see p. 2).

As a medium, photographs are not new. People have been sharing photographs ever since the process was developed. Long before people posted photos of recent vacations on Flickr or iPhoto, many mailed postcards of famous sites they visited to friends — usually to just a few close friends. Of course, the Web has changed all that, and people are increasingly posting words and images online. In the month since I drafted the previous paragraph, for instance, the number of photos of black labs posted on Flickr rose from 5,507 to 6,548.

When it was first invented, the Internet wasn't a very friendly place for the ordinary communicator. But with the development of the Web and user-friendly software programs, the situation has changed dramatically. Now just about anyone with a computer and Internet access can establish a visually rich presence on the Web. On social-networking sites such as Facebook and MySpace, on video-sharing sites like YouTube, and on many blogs, images, video clips, and audio clips can be at least as important as the written text.

Flickr Search Results Page

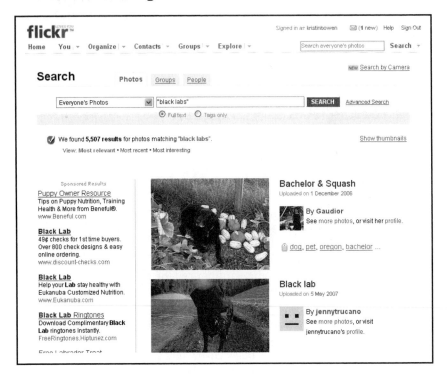

Reproduced 2007 by Yahoo! Inc. YAHOO! and the image with permission of Yahoo! Inc. YAHOO! logo is a trademark of Yahoo! Inc.

Written language has hardly lost its power, however. If you have ever visited the commercial Web site Amazon.com, you know that customer reviews are featured prominently on this site. You may not realize, however, just how many people contribute customer reviews to Amazon. On the same day that I searched for photos of black labs on Flickr, I visited Amazon.com and clicked on *Harry Potter and the Sorcerer's Stone,* the first novel in J. K. Rowling's Harry Potter series (see p. 3). Even though Amazon.com offers no monetary incentive for customer reviewers, I found 5,269 reviews of the novel posted on this site. In the month since that time, twenty-five additional reviews have appeared. Considering that Rowling has published six more novels in this series, and that her first novel came out in 1998, this is a clear indication of how powerful the desire can be to share one's thoughts with others via the Web.

As this example demonstrates, the written word still very much matters. In fact, in a developed country like the United States, those with access to computers and online technologies are writing more than ever before, and in more diverse venues and media. Many students, for instance, switch back and forth from academic writing and reading to instant messaging, commenting

Amazon Customer Review for *Harry Potter and the Sorcerer's Stone*

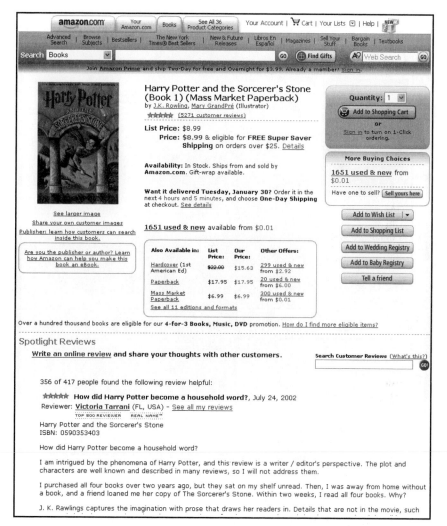

on blogs, checking their Facebook profiles, and so on. The design, or look, of texts is also increasingly important. In their day-to-day writing, ordinary people are now integrating the visual and the verbal—and they are turning to new media to share their words and thoughts. In that regard, consider the extraordinary popularity of podcasts, blogs, and social-networking sites.

How can writers and readers best understand the opportunities and challenges that they face as communicators in the twenty-first century? Which aspects of our contemporary moment are unique? Which reflect shared experience over time? These are particularly important questions for

Student MySpace Page

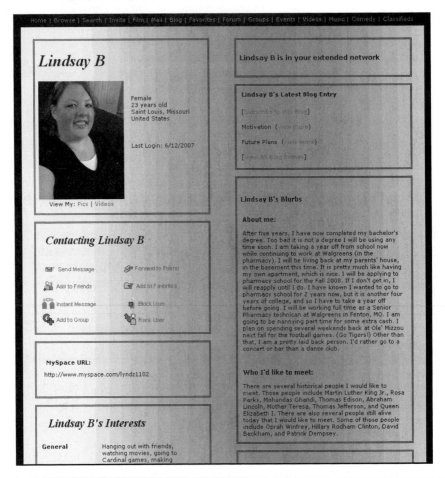

college students to ask. If you're a traditional-age student, you've grown up with the Web. You take sites like YouTube, Flickr, and MySpace for granted. You're probably more comfortable manipulating images and texts at your computer than many of your instructors are. But how might this knowledge of online communication apply to the writing you will do in college?

You may think that the writing you do for fun is irrelevant (and maybe even harmful) when you are writing for your classes. While it's true that you wouldn't compose an essay for a history class the way you text message a friend, the ability to draw upon all the knowledge you have gained about communication can help you negotiate new writing situations. This chapter—and this textbook—will show you how you can draw upon *all* your experiences as a writer, reader, speaker, and listener to meet the demands of academic writing. Gaining a better understanding of the rhetorical tradition and of rhetorical sensitivity will play an important role in this process. (You will read more about both of these terms shortly; these concepts are central to much of the discussion in this book.) Because of rapid changes in the technologies of communication, it is important that you first understand the impact of these developments for writers and readers.

Understanding the Impact of Communication Technologies on Writing

One helpful way to understand this impact is to consider the history of the printed text. For centuries in western Europe, the only means of producing texts was to copy them, as scribes did in the Middle Ages. For this reason, a limited number of manuscripts were created. Few private individuals owned manuscripts, and fewer people could read them. In 1440, Johannes Gutenberg invented the printing press. Thanks to its ability to reproduce multiple copies of texts, over time the printing press dramatically increased the availability of the written word. The rise of printing also tended, however, to de-emphasize the role of visual elements in mass-produced texts. For several centuries after the printing press was developed, there were few illustrated books because the technologies for printing words and images differed. In the 1800s, it again became possible to print high-quality illustrated texts. Since that time, readers of the mass media have come to expect increasingly sophisticated combinations of words and images.

The history of individually produced texts differs from that of the mass media. Until the invention of the typewriter in 1868, writers handwrote their texts. The typewriter enabled writers to produce texts much more efficiently, and with carbon paper they could even make a limited number of copies. But typewriters were designed to produce written text only. Writers could manipulate spacing and margins, and they could underline words and phrases— but that was about it.

The development of the personal computer, and of sophisticated software programs for writing, design, and image manipulation, changed all that. Today ordinary people can compose texts that have most if not all of the features of mass-produced documents. Anyone with a computer and access to the Internet has a wide range of options for including visual elements in a text or for experimenting with media other than traditional print. An art history student who's convinced that graffiti represents an important genre of contemporary art could write an academic essay making this argument. But she could also develop a PowerPoint presentation or create a podcast to make her point. If this student has an ongoing interest in graffiti art, she might even host a blog on this subject.

|||||||||||||||||||||||||||||||||||||||||||||||||||||||||||||||||||||||||||||||||||||||||||

FOR EXPLORATION

Take some time to think about—and list—all the kinds of writing that you do. Obviously, you'll want to include such traditional print and handwritten texts as essays, class notes, letters, and shopping and "to do" lists. You'll also want to inventory the many forms of online writing that you do, such as instant messaging, posting or commenting on blogs, and writing reviews on Amazon.com or other sites. Are design elements and visual images more important to some kinds of writing that you do than to others?

Now turn your attention to the media you use to write. In writing essays for your classes, do you first brainstorm and write rough drafts in pencil or pen and then revise at your computer, or do you write entirely on your computer or laptop—or do you switch back and forth, depending on the project and situation? When you write at the computer, how many programs do you typically have open, and how often do you move back and forth from, say, the Web, email, or instant messaging as you compose? If you have a PDA (personal digital assistant) or cell phone, does it play a role in your writing? Have you ever taken a photograph on your phone and incorporated it into another text—an informal email or a formal essay, for instance?

Take a few more minutes to reflect about what you have written. What insights have you gained from this reflection?

|||||||||||||||||||||||||||||||||||||||||||||||||||||||||||||||||||||||||||||||||||||||||||||

The ability to compose in diverse media and to integrate visual and textual elements represents an exciting opportunity for writers—but opportunity can also bring difficulties and dilemmas. Consider the art history student writing an essay on graffiti as art. Should she follow the traditional conventions of academic writing? If she did, she would double-space her essay and choose a readable font that doesn't call attention to itself (like 12 point Times New Roman). If she's using headings, she might make them bold; she might also import some photographs. But in general her essay would look and read much like one written twenty, or fifty, years ago.

Suppose, however, that this student's assignment gives her more freedom than this. Perhaps in addition to writing a traditional academic essay on graffiti this student is preparing an oral presentation using PowerPoint, and her instructor has encouraged her and other students to view this assignment as an opportunity to be creative. She would still need to communicate her basic points in a clear and understandable way. She might, however, manipulate fonts and spacing to create a more urban and edgy feel to her presentation. While she would hardly want to use an unusual font like the graffiti-style Brooklyn Kid throughout her PowerPoint presentation, she might employ it at strategic points for emphasis and to evoke the graffiti she's writing about (see p. 7). She might also choose and arrange her images

PowerPoint Slides from a Student Oral Presentation

Settings for GRAFFITI

→ **Subways eliminated in late 1980s as most popular venue**

→ **Moved above ground to walls and buildings**

→ **Freight trains took art across continent**

Fig. 3. New York train graffiti. Steve Zabel. 1980. Collection of Joe Testagrose.15 Feb. 2007 <http://www.nycsubway.org/articles/history-nycta1980s.html>.

Tools for GRAFFITI

→ **Paint cans using custom spray nozzles**

→ **Keith Haring's work with chalk**

Fig. 4. Caps. @149st.com. 15 Feb. 2007 <http://www.at149st.com/tools3.html>.

→ **Markers and stickers**

→ **Posters applied with glue**

Fig. 5. Rio from The Death Squad graffiti crew in New York. @149st.com. 15 Feb. 2007 <http://at149st.com/tds.html>.

in prominent or unusual ways. Her goal? To create the kind of "in your face" feel that characterizes much graffiti.

How can this student decide on the best way to convey her ideas and meet her professor's expectations? Obviously, she can discuss the assignment with her teacher. But such consultations aren't always possible. Moreover, this student will eventually have a job where she will be required to compose and take responsibility for other important texts — from reports to Web sites, brochures, and memos. In many instances, she will have to make decisions about these texts' visual and other design elements, and the medium in which the writing will appear.

Like others who value writing and recognize its importance, this student needs to develop the ability to respond effectively to a variety of writing situations. She needs to know, in other words, how to make effective *choices* as a writer — and she needs to do so in the context of the demands and opportunities that twenty-first-century writers face.

Writing, Rhetoric, and Design

thinking rhetorically

One of the most powerful resources this student, and other writers, can draw upon is one of the oldest fields of study in Western culture: rhetoric. Rhetoric was formulated by such Greek and Roman rhetoricians as Isocrates (436–338 B.C.E.), Aristotle (384–322 B.C.E.), Cicero (106–43 B.C.E.), and Quintilian (35–96 C.E.). Originally developed to meet the needs of speakers, rhetoric came to be applied to written texts as well.

When you think rhetorically, you consider the ways in which words and images are used to engage — and sometimes to persuade — others. Writers who think rhetorically apply their understanding of human communication in general, and of written texts in particular, to the decisions that will enable effective communication within a specific situation.

A rhetorical approach to writing encourages you to consider four key elements of your situation:

- Your role as a *writer* who has (or must discover) something to communicate

- One or more *readers* with whom you would like to communicate

- The *text* you create to convey your ideas. We are used to thinking of texts as comprised of words, but increasingly texts may include images and other graphics, such as charts, graphs, and borders.

- A *medium* (print text, PowerPoint presentation, poster, brochure, report, video clip, blog, etc.) that makes this communication possible

The relationship among these elements is dynamic. Writers compose texts to express their meaning, but readers are equally active. Readers don't simply decipher the words on the page; they draw on their own experiences and expectations as they read. As a student, for instance, you read your economics textbook differently than you read the comics or a popular novel. You also know that the more experience you have reading certain kinds of writing—textbooks in your major, or the sports or financial pages of the newspaper, for example—the more you will get out of them.

Rhetoric is a practical art that helps writers make effective choices within specific rhetorical situations. You'll learn more about the rhetorical situation in Chapter 3. For now, you simply need to know that when you analyze your rhetorical situation, you consider each of the four elements of rhetoric: writer, reader, text, and medium. Let's return to the student who wants to write an essay on graffiti as art. To analyze her situation, she would first consider her own situation as a writer. As a student in a class, how much freedom does she have?

In academic writing, this question leads immediately to the second element of the rhetorical situation: the reader. In academic writing, the reader is primarily the teacher, so the student would want to consider the nature of her assignment—how open it is, what statement (if any) the teacher has provided about format, expectations, and so on. But she would also want to draw upon her general understanding of writing in the humanities. Instructors in the humanities often favor a conservative approach to academic writing, so while this student might use headings and images in her research paper, her safest bet would be to focus primarily on the clear and logical development of her ideas.

This student has considerably more flexibility in approaching her Power-Point presentation. The nature of this part of her assignment is less demanding and more open than that of traditional academic writing. Moreover, instructors and students alike expect that those composing PowerPoint presentations will take full advantage of this medium. Even here, though, the student will want visual and design elements to enhance, rather than detract from, the expression of her ideas. She would never want her goal of creating an urban, edgy look for her presentation to interfere with its content.

In this example, the student's teacher has specified the media she should use: a print essay and an oral presentation using PowerPoint slides. For this reason, constructing a blog or creating a video clip would be an inappropriate response to the assignment. In a different situation, employing one or both of these media might be not only appropriate but effective. If this student were writing an honors thesis on graffiti as art, for instance, she might well create a blog to express and explore her ideas during the year that she worked on this major project. At her thesis defense, she might share relevant blog posts and comments with her committee via a new PowerPoint presentation. She might also show film clips of interviews with graffiti artists.

As this example indicates, a rhetorical approach to writing encourages you to think in practical, concrete ways about your situation as a writer. It's no accident that rhetoric takes this approach to communication. The discipline of rhetoric was originally developed to meet the needs of the citizens of Athens, who, in their limited democracy, met to make civic and political decisions and also served as jurors. Those arguing for or against an issue or person made public speeches in the Assembly. Because each case varied, rhetoricians needed to develop flexible, situation-oriented strategies designed to achieve specific purposes.

thinking rhetorically

Rather than providing rules about how texts should be organized and developed, rhetoric encourages those composing texts to draw on their commonsense understanding of communication to decide how best to communicate in specific situations. A rhetorical approach to communication encourages writers to think in terms of purpose and effect. In this regard, a rhetorical approach to writing encourages writers to think and act like problem solvers.

When you think and act like a problem solver, you use skills that have much in common with those in the contemporary profession of design. There are many kinds of design — from industrial design to fashion design — but graphic design is closely allied with writing. In fact, with the development of the Web and of such software programs as Adobe Photoshop and PowerPoint, the visual and textual are becoming increasingly interconnected.

Communication is central to both writing and graphic design. In both cases, if writers and graphic designers want to do more than simply express themselves — if they want to have an impact on readers and viewers — they must be attentive to the needs, interests, and situations of their audience. In both cases, writers and designers work in specific situations, with varying degrees of freedom. In some instances — a student writing a lab report, or a graphic designer creating a logo for a new firm — they are constrained in significant ways, as lab reports and logos are clearly defined and limited genres. In other situations, they have more freedom. Both writers and graphic designers have an increasing number of media options, including digital and online media.

When faced with a new project, both writers and graphic designers know they can't draw on a previous one-size-fits-all solution. Although they can benefit from their previous experience, with each new project they must consider all aspects of their situation.

Composing — and Designing — Texts

Why emphasize the similarities between writing and graphic design? Given ongoing developments in communication technologies, conventional distinctions between these two creative activities seem less and less relevant. While it is true that in the humanities the most traditional forms of academic writing emphasize words over images and other elements of design, increasingly student writers — like all writers — are integrating the visual and verbal in texts. Writing and design share other similarities as well. In his influential book *How Designers Think*, Bryan Lawson lists the essential characteristics of design. These characteristics apply, Lawson argues, to all kinds of design, from product design to graphic design.

- Design problems are open-ended and cannot be fully specified.
- The design process is endless.
- There is no infallibly correct process of design.
- The process involves finding as well as solving problems.
- Design inevitably involves subjective value judgments.
- Design is a persuasive activity that is concerned with what might, could, and should be.
- Designers work in the context of a need for action.

Just as you have developed a good deal of knowledge about writing via your experiences as a writer, reader, speaker, and listener, so too have you developed considerable knowledge about design. If you've ever decorated a dorm room or apartment, for instance, you've engaged in the process of design. When you set up a blog or a Facebook or MySpace page, you also make decisions about design. As you read the following discussion of the similarities between writing and design, think about a recent experience where you planned the look of a space, whether virtual or real.

Writing and design are both creative acts that occur within a complex system of opportunities and constraints. Unless you are filling out a form, any act of writing is open-ended. For example, when you begin work on an essay about the advantages and disadvantages of the new smoking ban in your town's bars and restaurants, you can't know what you will write until you undertake considerable research and reflection. Once you develop a position on this topic, you must still discover the best way to develop and support your position as you compose.

Like design, the writing process is potentially endless in the sense that there is no objective or absolute way to determine when a project is complete. Rare is the writer or designer who thinks, "What I've just created is perfect; I couldn't improve it if I tried." Instead, writers and designers often call a halt to their process for pragmatic reasons. They may have a deadline, or they may feel they've spent as much time as they should, or they may know they've reached the limits of a fixed budget for a design project. Indeed, the open-ended nature of writing and design is typical of activities that require creativity.

Precisely because writing and design are creative processes, there is no infallibly correct process that writers and designers can follow. The more experienced writers and designers are, the better able they are to determine what strategies are appropriate for any particular task. But each time they work on a new project, they must consider their project, situation, purpose, medium, and audience.

As they do so, designers and writers do not just solve problems; they find, or create, them. This may sound intimidating at first. "I don't want to find problems," you might think. "I'm a busy student—I need to solve problems quickly and efficiently." Here's the rub: Often you can't do the latter until you do the former. Let's return to the example of organizing your dorm room. Say that you and your roommate are frustrated because your room is always a mess. There's just not enough storage space, so rather than put clothes and other items away in already-packed closets and chests, you leave them out everywhere.

To address this problem, you have to go beyond the general recognition that you need more storage space to pinpoint the problem more specifically. After reading an online version of a local newspaper feature on organizing and redecorating dorm spaces (see p. 13), you recognize that you have used up all obvious storage space. As a result, you and your roommate realize that you must work with the unused space under your beds and on the bottom half of your closet. Once you've identified the crux of your problem, you can address it. So you take measurements and head to the local discount store to look for inexpensive storage units that will best fit your space. You've solved your storage problem by finding, or creating, it. The better you are at finding your problem, the better you will be at addressing it.

The same is true of writing and of design. In fact, the ability to create complex and sophisticated problems is one feature that distinguishes experienced from inexperienced writers and designers. Imagine, for instance, that two students in the same political science class have been asked to write an essay on the current debate over their state's mandated prison sentences for drug offenders. One student thinks, "The easiest way to approach this assignment is to figure out what my teacher believes and say that." The other student thinks, "This is a complex issue, and I've always had complicated responses to it. I'm going to use this assignment to see if I can develop a clearer sense of my beliefs." In so doing, each student in effect finds, or creates, the problem that he will solve in his writing.

As this example suggests, both design and writing involve subjective value judgments. The first student wants to get his assignment done as easily and quickly as possible; his motivation is external—do the assignment and get a good grade. The second student also wants to get a good grade, but he approaches the assignment as an opportunity for genuine learning. When these students' teacher reads their essays, there will be an element of subjectivity in his or her response as well. As every student knows, two teachers reading the same essay might give that essay different grades. Similarly, the members of a firm's team evaluating potential logos will have differing re-

Design Advice for Organizing Dorm Space

denverpost.com

| Home | News | Politics | Sports | Business | Entertainment | Style | Opinion | Outdoors | Travel |

Weather | Traffic | Gas Prices | Broncos | Blogs | Obits | Contact | **Lotto:** 7 13 14 19 20 40 | **Powerball:** 7 10 25 32 41 (22) pp-2

🖉 Subscribe / Customer Care   PDF Electronic Edition   RSS Web Feeds   ✉ Email Newsletters   Se

room

🖨 Print ✉ Email

Five tips for making the most of your too-small dorm room

Article Last Updated: 08/09/2006 11:22:22 PM MDT

(CLICK TO ENLARGE)

Six out of 10 college students feel their college dorm room is uncomfortably small, according to dormbuys.com. The website surveyed nearly 450 college students to glean their tips for maximizing space. Here are their top five suggestions for uncramping the classic cinderblock box:

1. Loft your bed. Elevating the bed off the floor can free up the space beneath for other necessities. (Note: Not all colleges allow lofting, so check with your school first.) A second-best alternative is to bunk the dorm room beds.

2. Use a bed shelf. Shelves that attach to the post or rail of college beds eliminate the need for a space-reducing nightstand.

3. Stay organized. Plastic, mesh or wicker storage boxes can hold clothes, linens, DVDs, video games, books or shoes. Specially designed storage boxes that fit under the bed or in any size closet work best in small dorm rooms.

4. Buy small furniture. Large, bulky couches can make a small feel even smaller. Students now can choose from small, trendy dorm-specific furniture. Foam-filled chairs, mini-futons and rocker chairs are among the most popular.

5. Condense your closet. College closets fill up fast. Use hangers that can hold more than one item, add extra

sponses to them. This subjectivity can be frustrating, but it's a fact of life for both writers and designers.

The potential for diverse responses is a reminder that both writing and design are persuasive activities. They both occur in the context of a need for action. As a result, writers and designers are always making decisions about what might, could, and should be. Writers do this when they develop an argument or complete an analysis. Designers do this when they determine which of the many logos they've created they will present to their clients.

Because both writing and design are concerned with what might, could, and should be, these activities bring ethical obligations. In the case of designers, the obligations involve the responsibility to do the best work possible for their clients. Writers also have responsibilities, though they may be less obvious. For example, students writing in response to an academic assignment need to complete their assignment by the date it is due. How well they complete the assignment depends in part on their ability and understanding—but commitment to the project is also central, as it is in design. Once they graduate and embark on careers, the context of a need for action for these student writers will become even stronger. Because workplace writing is pragmatic and goal-oriented, strong writing skills can make the difference between an adequate and a highly successful career—just as they can make the difference among poor, adequate, and superior grades in college.

Both writing and design offer individuals the opportunity to make a difference in the world. Someone who redesigns and in so doing improves the comfort and mobility of wheelchairs, for instance, will improve the quality of life of all who rely upon this vehicle. It's easy to think of writers who have made a difference in the world—both positively (e.g., the signers of the Declaration of Independence) and negatively (e.g., Hitler's *Mein Kampf*). Yet there are other, less visible but still important examples of the power that writing can hold to effect economic, social, political, and cultural change. Writing is one of the most important ways that students can become members of a disciplinary or professional community. In order to gain full authority—to be recognized as a professional civil engineer—engineering students need to learn not only how to plan, design, construct, and maintain structures. They must also learn to write like civil engineers—and if you didn't already realize it, engineers do a lot of on-the-job writing. Writing not only plays a key role in most careers, but it also represents an important way that citizens express their views and advocate for causes (see the poster on p. 15). Think of the role that blogs now play in politics and in public affairs. In these and other ways, writing provides an opportunity for ordinary people to shape the future of local, regional, and national communities.

FOR EXPLORATION

Write for five or ten minutes in response to this question: What has this discussion of the connections between writing and design helped you to better understand about written communication?

FOR COLLABORATION

Bring your response to the preceding Exploration to class and meet with a group of peers. Appoint someone to record your discussion, and then take turns sharing your writing. (Your teacher may ask you to summarize, rather than to read, what you've written.) Be sure that your reporter includes as many people's ideas as possible. Be prepared to share your discussion with the class.

Poster Advocating for a Cause

Developing Rhetorical Sensitivity

Experienced graphic designers and writers understand that they must draw on all their resources when they compose. From their prior reading and viewing, they learn about what makes texts work. (Remember, texts include not only the written word but also images and graphics.) They analyze their own situations, think about the purpose and goals of particular projects—the meaning they wish to communicate, their reasons for composing—and consider their audience. They explore their own ideas, challenging themselves to express their ideas as clearly and carefully as possible. They play with words, phrases, images, and other graphic elements to make their work stylistically effective. And they take advantage of such computer and online resources as word processing, image editing, and spreadsheet programs, as well as specialized programs for their particular areas of interest. In all of these activities, experienced writers and designers practice *rhetorical sensitivity*.

Designers and writers practice rhetorical sensitivity when they explore the four elements of rhetoric—writer, reader, text, medium—in the context of specific situations. The student writing about graffiti art drew upon her rhetorical sensitivity in determining how best to respond to her assignment. She realized that as a student writing for a class she was constrained in significant ways and that her reader's (i.e., teacher's) expectations, as indicated in the assignment, were crucial to her decision making. In considering the two texts she was composing, a research paper and an oral presentation using PowerPoint slides, this student understood that the textual conventions governing the former are more conservative than those governing the latter, and that differences in media—print text versus PowerPoint—reinforce this distinction. As a result of her analysis, this student realized that she had more freedom to experiment with visual elements of design in her PowerPoint presentation than in her research paper.

thinking
rhetorically

In order to respond to her assignment, this student consciously explored her rhetorical situation. Writers and designers are particularly likely to do this when they undertake new or demanding tasks. At other times, this kind of analysis is unconscious and takes the form of rhetorical common sense. In your daily life, you already practice considerable rhetorical sensitivity. As you make decisions about how to interact with others, you naturally (if unconsciously) draw on your commonsense understanding of effective communication. Imagine, for instance, that you're preparing to interview for a job. Though you might not think of it this way, everything that you do before and during the interview is an effort to design a successful experience. Every decision that you make—what to wear, how to act, what to say during the interview—reflects your rhetorical sensitivity. Much of your attention will focus on how to present yourself best, but you also recognize the importance of being well prepared and of interacting effectively with your interviewers. If you are smart, you will consider the specific situation for which you are applying. Someone applying for a position as a bank teller might dress and act differently than someone applying for a job as a salesperson in a store that specializes in clothes for teenagers and young adults. Successful applicants know that all they do—the way they dress, present themselves, respond to questions, and interact with interviewers—is an effort to communicate their strengths and persuade the interviewers to employ them.

> **NOTE FOR MULTILINGUAL WRITERS**
>
> It is more challenging to "read" a rhetorical situation when you are new to the context. You may find it helpful to consult your teacher or class-mates, asking specific questions in order to better understand the rhetorical situation for a particular assignment.

You also employ rhetorical sensitivity when you "read" contemporary culture. As a consumer, for instance, you're bombarded with advertisements urging you to purchase various products or services. How you respond to these ads will depend primarily on how you read them. Wise consumers know that ads are designed to persuade, and they learn ways to read them with a critical eye (even as they appreciate, say, a television commercial's humor or a magazine ad's design). You read other aspects of contemporary culture as well. Much of the time, you may do so for entertainment: While watching sports or other programs on television, for instance, your primary goal may be to relax and enjoy yourself. If you find the plot of a detective show implausible or the action of the Monday night football game too slow, you can easily click to a more interesting program.

At times, however, you may take a more critical, distanced perspective on such forms of popular culture as television, music, and magazines. After arguing with a friend about whether 50 Cent advocates homophobia and violence, you may watch his videos with a careful eye, comparing him with other hip-hop acts. When you compare different musicians' lyrics, type of dress, and movements, you're considering the ways in which these groups appeal to and communicate with their audience. Though you probably wouldn't have used this term to describe your viewing, you're analyzing the *rhetoric* of their performances.

Writers and designers who think rhetorically understand that writing and reading do not occur in a vacuum. The language you grow up speaking, the social and cultural worlds you inhabit, and the technologies available to you—these and other factors all influence how you communicate. Even people who have grown up in American culture may find that the writing they do in college differs considerably from the language they use in their everyday lives. The United States is, after all, a country of many ethnic groups, languages, and dialects. The language that feels comfortable and natural to you when you speak with your family and friends may differ considerably from that required in academic reading and writing assignments.

Like life, writing involves negotiation. When you prepare for a job interview, you must decide how much to modify your everyday way of dressing to

|||||||||||||||||||||||||||||||||||||||||||||||||||||||||||||||||||||||||||||||||||||||||||||||

FOR EXPLORATION

Here are two promotional pieces for Dove soaps and lotions, part of their "Campaign for Real Beauty." The ad and Web campaigns, according to the Dove Web site, are "intended to serve as a starting point for societal change and act as a catalyst for widening the definition and discussion of beauty."

Advertisement for Dove

Dove Marketing Web Site for the Campaign for Real Beauty

After reading the ad and Web page carefully, respond in writing to these questions:

1. Bryan Lawson argues that design always involves persuasion, or the effort to specify what "might, could, and should be." What are these two ads trying to persuade readers to believe?

2. How do the designers of the ad and Web page use words, images, and graphics to make this point? Do some of these elements seem more important than others? Why?

thinking rhetorically

3. In what ways do the ad and Web page reinforce Lawson's observation that design involves "subjective value judgments"? Do they, for instance, rely upon culturally sanctioned stereotypes? If they do, how do these stereotypes reinforce their message?

4. In what ways do these promotional pieces demonstrate rhetorical sensitivity on the part of those who created them?

||||||||||||||||||||||||||||||||||||||||||||||||||||||||||||||||||||||||||||||||||||

meet the demands of the situation. Similarly, when you write—whether in college, at work, or for civic or other activities—you must consider the expectations of others. At times it can be difficult to determine, let alone meet, these expectations. In your first weeks at a new job, for instance, you probably felt like the new kid on the block. Gradually, however, you became sensitive to your coworkers' expectations. Likewise, as a college student you may at times feel like a new writer on the block. Both *The Academic Writer* and your composition course will help you build on the rhetorical sensitivity that you already have, so you can use all the resources available to you to meet the demands of writing in the twenty-first century.

NOTE FOR MULTILINGUAL WRITERS

If you learned to write in a language other than English, you may sometimes feel frustrated when teachers ask you to adapt to the conventions of academic writing in the United States. You may feel that you are being asked to stop speaking and writing in a way that feels natural to you. In fact, you are not alone facing this challenge; students educated solely in the United States may also have limited experience with academic writing conventions.

Although conflicts sometimes occur between first or home languages and those you use in school, your goal as a writer should not be to abandon your first or home language. Instead, as you become more fluent in the conventions of standard written English, you should try to develop a rhetorical sensitivity that allows you to write effectively in both languages and communities.

||||||||||||||||||||||||||||||||||||||||||||||||||||||||||||||||||||||||||||||||||||

FOR THOUGHT, DISCUSSION, AND WRITING

1. Take a few moments to reflect on your understanding of the terms *rhetoric* and *rhetorical sensitivity*. You may find it helpful to recall an incident in your daily life when you were called on to demonstrate rhetorical sensitivity. Write a paragraph describing this incident. Then write a paragraph or so stating your current understanding of these terms. Finally, write one or two questions that you still have about *rhetoric* and *rhetorical sensitivity*.

2. Write an essay in which you describe and reflect upon the many kinds of writing that you do and the role that visual and design elements play in your writing. After writing the essay, create a text that uses words, images, and (if you like) graphics to convey the ideas you discuss in your essay. You can use any mix of photographs, drawings, text, or other material that will help others understand your experience.

3. Interview two or three students in your current or prospective major to learn more about writing in this field. Ask these students the following questions:

   What kinds of writing are students required to do in classes in this field?

   How would they characterize the role of images and other graphic elements in this writing? What role, if any, do multimedia play in their writing?

   How is their writing evaluated by their professors?

   What advice about writing would they give to other students taking classes in this discipline?

   Your instructor may ask you to report the results of these interviews to the class. Your instructor may also ask you to write an essay summarizing and reflecting on the results of your interview.

||||||||||||||||||||||||||||||||||||||||||||||||||||||||||||||||||||||||||||||||||||

Understanding the Writing Process

Writing is hardly a mysterious activity, yet many people seem to think that those who write well possess a magical power or talent. According to this view, people are either born with the ability to write well or not, and those who do write well find writing easy. They just sit down, and the words and ideas begin to flow.

Interestingly, people often feel the same way about those who work with images and graphics, whether they're designers or artists. They believe that these individuals have a gift that enables them to create vivid and compelling designs, paintings, or other aesthetic objects. They don't understand that designers and artists, like writers, study their craft for many years. What some would call talent might more aptly be characterized as interest, motivation, and commitment.

Successful writers and designers know that their skills take time to mature. They also know that to develop their skills they must look for opportunities to practice them. As they do so, they reflect on the strengths and limitations not only of the products they produce but also of the processes they use to create them. As a result, successful writers and designers develop strategies to cope with the complexities of writing and design, and thus to experience the satisfaction of a job well done.

Reflecting on Your Experiences as a Writer

Here are two essays, one by a student writer, Mary Ellen Gates, and one by a professor of English, Burton Hatlen. In different ways, Gates and Hatlen discuss what it means to be a writer and comment on their own development as writers. They also each make the point that, as Hatlen says, "writing is a craft, which can be learned by anyone willing to work at it." As you read their essays, ask yourself to what extent your own assumptions about writing and experiences as a writer resemble theirs. How are they different? See if you can recall specific experiences, such as those Gates and Hatlen describe in their essays, that played a critical role in your development as a writer or your understanding of writing.

A Writer Is Formed

MARY ELLEN GATES

The woman at the front of the room hardly resembled my idea of an English teacher. Her raggedy undershirt, heavy flannel jacket, disheveled pants, and braided, stringy hair gave her the appearance of having just returned from a backcountry expedition.

"My name is Harriet Jones," she said, "and this is English 111."

This was my introduction to college writing. Ten students had enrolled in this beginning composition class at Islands Community College. Like most of my classmates, I was returning to education after a period in the work force. I had spent one year at Western Washington University but had avoided writing classes. I discovered later, when I sent for my transcripts to apply to Oregon State University, that I had withdrawn from a writing course at Western. I have no memory of this. Did I drop it the first day, or did I struggle with an essay or two before giving up?

At any rate, I went to Alaska that summer to work in the seafood canneries. It was a trip I had planned with two friends during my senior year in high school. I expected to return to college in the fall with thousands of dollars in my bank account. The work was miserable, but I fell in love with remote Sitka, and I stayed. Time passed with adventures enough to fill a novel. I eventually landed a job I really wanted at Northern Lights Natural Foods, a small, family-owned natural foods store. That job inspired me to take a nutrition course at the community college. I realized during the course that some biology would help me understand nutrition, so I took biology the following semester. I began to consider a career in nutrition, which led me to apply to the Department of Foods and Nutrition at OSU. I wasn't ready to leave Sitka, however; I would work one more year and take a few more classes on the side.

That is how I came to be sitting in Ms. Jones's class, preparing myself for a relationship with an English grammar handbook. We were to respond to short stories, an exercise which in my experience was limited to junior high school book reports. Although I have always been an avid reader, I had given little thought to characters, conflicts, plots, and settings. So those early essays were on topics that did not interest me. I had never heard of a comma splice either, but Ms. Jones assured us that any paper containing one would be promptly rewarded with an F grade. I would agonize over blank pages, afraid to begin, afraid of saying the wrong thing, afraid of committing some technical error. I somehow managed to fill up the pages and hand in those early essays. Fortunately, Ms. Jones encouraged us to revise after she had graded our papers.

It turned out that she was also very willing to talk with us about writing. I discovered that this formidable woman was actually a caring, humorous person. The writing did not instantly become easier, though. During the second term, we worked on longer papers that required some research. We also did in-class assignments such as freewriting and essay exams. By the end of the term, I had finally become comfortable with putting my ideas on paper.

The year with Ms. Jones was great preparation for my studies at OSU. I learned the importance of editing my work and following conventions. I gained confidence in stating my views. I also learned that teachers are human and that most of them enjoy discussing projects with students outside of class.

In thinking about my history as a writer for this essay, I realized that I have always been a writer—even when I felt unconfident and out of practice. Letters to aunts, uncles, and grandparents were my earliest writings outside of schoolwork, and they have been the main link between my parents' families on the East Coast and my nuclear family here in the Northwest. These letters followed a set format for years:

Dear Aunt _____ (or Grandma),

How are you? I am fine. Thank you for the _____ _____ .

                       Love,
                       Mary Ellen

My letters have matured with me, and I consider them a sort of journal except that I mail this journal off in bits and pieces instead of keeping it to read later. My letters describe what I have been doing, how I feel about things, and what I plan to do. When I lived in Alaska, letters were my link to family and friends in Washington.

Another early writing experience was an expanded form of passing notes in school. A friend and I wrote notes to each other that often went on for pages, much of it nonsense and gossip. We would work on these packets for days before exchanging them. Now I can see that we were flexing and developing our writing muscles as well as building our friendship through the sharing of ideas.

Currently, I write the newsletter for a club I belong to, an activity I volunteered for to gain experience and to stay involved with writing. I would like to combine writing with nutrition as a career. (I considered a major in journalism, but I have a strong desire to learn everything I can about nutrition.) I would like to help people improve their health by sharing this knowledge with them. I still think of myself as someone who is going to write someday. But I have been writing because I wanted to ever since I learned how.

✳ bedfordstmartins.com/academicwriter
To read an essay that Mary Ellen Gates wrote after reflecting further on technology and how it has affected her writing in the years since she wrote the essay above, click on **Chapter 2** *and then* **Readings.**

Writing Is a Craft That Can Be Learned, Not an Effortless Outpouring by Geniuses

BURTON HATLEN

A writer—that's what I would be when I grew up. I made that decision in 1952, when I was sixteen, along with what now seems to be half the people I knew at the time. We were all going to be "writers," whatever we meant by that.

I can't speak for my friends, but in my case, at least, being a writer meant living a certain kind of life. The setting would be Paris, *la rive gauche*: a sidewalk café. A man (with a beard, a beret dropping over his right eye, a turtleneck sweater, sandals, a pipe) is seated at a round table, a half-empty glass of red wine before him. There are other people around the table, but they are a little dim. And there is talk. Jung. Kafka. Anarchism. The decline of the West. But mostly there is that man. Me. Someday.

I didn't need anyone to tell me that the road from a dusty farming town in the Central Valley of California to that Paris café would be a long and difficult one. In fact, it was supposed to be long and difficult. "You must suffer, suffer"—so said a cartoon character of my youth to a would-be artist. And I had a real-life example of such suffering. When I was 10, my cousin brought her new husband, George, to town. George had actually been to Paris, and he was going to write a novel before returning there. Later, I heard my aunt tell my mother that she had read the manuscript of his novel. According to her, it was "filthy," and what was more, she whispered, she was sure George "drank." In any case, his novel remained unpublished and George never made it back to Paris. At some level I realized that his sad story augured ill for my own dreams of living the life of a writer in a 1950s version of Paris in the '20s.

Nevertheless, in 1956, after my junior year at Berkeley, I decided that if I was ever to become a writer, I'd better try to write. I spent five months working at various jobs, and when I had saved $500 I moved into a one-room apartment in San Francisco. By then the "renaissance" there was in full flower, and the city seemed to me a reasonable facsimile of Paris. In North Beach there were real cafés, where real poets—Kenneth Rexroth, Robert Duncan, Lawrence Ferlinghetti (who actually wore a beret)—sat around and talked. If location had anything to do with becoming a writer, San Francisco seemed the right place to be.

For three months, until my money ran out, I spent my evenings in North Beach and my days at the oilcloth-covered kitchen table in my apartment, writing. Or at least that's what I told myself I was doing. In fact, in those three months I managed to write only about three pages of what I called a novel. It was about a young man living alone in a San Francisco apartment, who looked into the sky one day, saw it split open, and went mad. I fussed for the first week or two over those pages, making sure that every word was perfect. But I had never worked out a plot, and once the young man went mad, I didn't know what else to do with him.

I stopped writing, and devoted my days to reading—all of Dreiser, among other things. What I remember best about that time is not the few paragraphs I wrote, but the wonder I felt as I read the yellowing pages of my second-hand copy of *The Genius*.

In January I went back to Berkeley, and that spring, at the suggestion of one of my teachers, applied to graduate school. Over the next few years, the sidewalk café began to seem no more than an adolescent fantasy, and, before I knew it, I had become not a writer in Paris, but a teacher entangled in committee meetings and bureaucratic infighting.

What brought all this back to me was a conversation I had earlier this year with a one-time colleague of mine, the author of a respectable university-press book on Sir Thomas Browne and, in the days when we taught together, a tenured associate professor and a popular teacher of Shakespeare. A few years ago, at forty-four, he suddenly resigned his teaching position and moved to Boston, where, I heard later, he was working a couple of days a week as a waiter and spending the rest of his time writing. When I went to Boston last winter I looked him up.

We talked about his novel and my work. Then the conversation turned to our respective children, all of whom, we realized, had not only decided to become artists of one sort or another but, unlike us at their age, were actually doing so. I thought about the Paris café, and then I asked him what he had wanted to do with his life when he was twenty.

"Actually," he said, "I wanted to live the way I'm living now—working at a nothing job that doesn't take anything out of me, and writing."

That was a pretty fair description of my own dream when I moved to that apartment in San Francisco. What had happened to it? I think the main reason that I never realized the dream was my mistaken notion of what it means to be a writer, which I had picked up partly from media images of Hemingway and Fitzgerald, Sartre and Camus, and partly from my teachers. Those influences had suggested that writing was something geniuses were somehow able to do without thinking about it; ordinary people dabbled at their peril. That writing is also a craft that can be learned, that a young person might decide to write and then systematically learn how to do so, was never so much as hinted at by anyone I knew. So, when the words for my novel did not automatically come pouring out of me, I had concluded that I must not be a writer.

In fact, I have over the years written enough poetry to make a good-sized book, and enough prose — if it were all gathered together — to make two or three. Yet I feel uncomfortable saying I'm a writer who teaches, preferring instead to see myself as a teacher who writes. Nevertheless, writing is clearly a major part of my life. Yes, I do feel some envy of my friend in Boston, who is at last doing what he dreamed of when he was twenty. And no, I've never written that novel, because I still don't know how to go about it. If most of what I write is about other people's writing, that's all right, because through it I've found a way to share with others the wonder I felt thirty years ago as I read Dreiser.

Since then, I have gradually come to see that writing takes manifold forms, that the conception of writing as a hermetic mystery, which I picked up from my reading and my teachers in the 1950s, is not only wrong, but pernicious. It dishonors the writing that nongeniuses do and denies the hard work at the craft that is essential to all writing, even the writing of "geniuses." It caused my cousin's husband to decide that if he couldn't be a writer, he didn't want to be anything, and I think it caused me to waste several years chasing illusions.

The myth that real writing is the effortless outpouring of geniuses did not die in the 1950s. There is abundant evidence that it still persists — at least among my students, most of whom also dream that someone, someday, will find a spark of "genius" in what they write. As a teacher who writes (or a writer who teaches), I am becoming more and more convinced that it's my job to nurture the writer in every student, while at the same time making it clear that writing is a craft, which can be learned by anyone willing to work at it.

✳ bedfordstmartins.com/academicwriter

To read an essay that Burton Hatlen wrote after reflecting further on technology and how it has affected his writing in the years since he wrote the essay above, click on **Chapter 2** *and then* **Readings.**

||||||||||||||||||||||||||||||||||||||||||||||||||||||||||||||||||||||||||||||||||||||

FOR EXPLORATION

After reading Gates's and Hatlen's essays, reflect on your own assumptions about writing and your experiences as a writer. Set aside at least half an hour, and respond in writing to five or six of the following questions. Skim the list to choose the questions that seem most relevant. As you do so, be sure to reflect on both your academic and your personal writing and reading experiences.

1. What are your earliest memories of learning to write? Of learning to read?

2. How were reading and writing viewed by your family and friends when you were growing up?

3. What role did reading play in your development as a writer? What kinds of texts were you drawn to—traditional print texts or visual texts, such as comics and graphic novels, or a mix?

4. Can you recall particular experiences in school or on the job that influenced your current attitude toward writing?

5. If you were to describe your history as a writer, what stages or periods in your development would you identify? Write a sentence or two briefly characterizing each stage or period.

6. What images come to mind when you hear the term *writer*?

7. What images come to mind when you think of *yourself* as a writer? Try drawing up a list of metaphors, such as "As a writer, I'm a turtle—slow and steady" or "As a writer, I'm a racehorse—fast out of the gate but never sure if I've got the stamina to finish." Write two or three sentences that use images or metaphors to characterize your sense of yourself as a writer.

8. What kinds of writing have you come to enjoy? To dislike? What kinds of writing do you do outside of school? A personal journal? Blog? Podcast? Poetry? Hand-lettered, printed, or online zine? Video? School newspaper or yearbook? Something else?

9. What role have multimedia texts (such as Web sites) played in your reading and writing experiences? What role do images and graphics play in your writing—both in and out of school?

10. What do you enjoy most about the process of writing? What do you enjoy least?

11. What goals would you like to set for yourself as a writer?

FOR EXPLORATION

Using the notes, responses, and reflections generated by the previous Exploration, write a letter to your classmates and teacher in which you describe who you are as a writer today—and how you got to be that way.

Alternatively, create a text that uses words, images, and (if you like) graphics to describe who you are as a writer today. You could hand-draw your text or create it on the computer; you could also make a collage.

For her response to this assignment, student Mirlandra Ebert created a collage, which is shown on p. 28. (To read Mirlandra's analysis of her rhetorical situation, turn to p. 47.)

(continued)

Mirlandra Ebert's Collage, "Who I Am as a Writer"

FOR COLLABORATION

Bring enough copies of the letter or visual text you created in response to the previous Exploration to share with members of your group. After you have all read one another's texts, work together to answer the following questions.

Choose one person to record the group's answers so that you can share the results of your discussion with the rest of the class.

1. To what extent are your attitudes toward writing and experiences as writers similar? List three to five statements with which all group members can agree.

2. What factors account for the differences in your attitudes toward writing and experiences as writers? List two or three factors that you agree account for these differences.

3. What common goals can you set for yourselves as writers? List at least three goals you can agree on.

||||||||||||||||||||||||||||||||||||||||||||||||||||||||||||||||||||||||||||||||||||||

Managing the Writing Process

Writing is not a magical process. Rather, it is a craft that can indeed be learned. But how do writers actually manage the writing process? Notice how differently the following students say that they proceed.

> My writing starts with contemplation. I let the topic I have chosen sink into my mind for a while. During this time my mind is a swirl of images, words, and ideas. Sometimes I draw clusters or diagrams that show how my ideas relate; sometimes I make lists. Whatever works works. But this period of letting my ideas develop is essential to my writing. Gradually my ideas take shape—and at a certain point I just know whether I have the right topic or approach or not. If I think I don't, I force myself to start over. If I do, then I make a plan for my essay. I can't really write without at least a skeleton plan that I can refer to: it stresses me out not to know where I'm headed. Before I get very far into my draft I try to stop and ask myself whether I should write something that is straight text—a regular academic essay—or whether this is a project that needs visuals or graphics. By the time I'm done with my plan, I usually have a pretty clear idea of where I'm going. Next I write a draft, possibly several drafts, before I do a final revision.
>
> —SARA STEINMAN

Maybe it's just my personality, but when I get an assignment I have to leap right into it. It's hard to describe what I write at the beginning. It's part brainstorming, part planning, part drafting, part letting off steam. I just have to write to see what I think! I make notes to myself. What's the best evidence for this argument? Would a graph strengthen my point? What do I really think about this topic? I do most of this early writing by hand because I need to be able to use arrows to connect ideas, circle important points, draw pictures. At this point, no one but me could understand what I've written. I take a break if I can, and then I sit down and reread everything I've written (it can be a lot). That's when I move to the computer. Even at this point I still basically write without doing a lot of conscious planning—I'm going on intuition. The time comes when I've got to change gears and become my own harshest critic. That's when I do a kind of planning in reverse. I might outline my draft, for instance, and see if the outline makes sense. It takes a lot of time and work for me to get to the point where my ideas have really jelled, and even then I've often got several drafts ahead of me.

—Eduardo Alvarez

As a writer, I am first a thinker and then a doer. I've always had to think my ideas out in detail before I begin drafting. Even though for me this is essentially a mental process, it still involves words and images. I can't really describe it—I just keep thinking things through. It's always felt like a waste of time to me to sit down to write without having a clear idea of what I want to say. Since I have two children, I also don't have a lot of time to focus solely on my writing, so I try out different ideas while folding laundry, driving the kids to daycare, after they're in bed. I'm a new media major, so part of my mental planning always involves thinking about media. If the assignment specifies the medium, then I always think how to make the best possible use of it. If it doesn't, then I run through all my options. Eventually I have a pretty clear sense of what I want to say and what medium will best convey it. Sometimes I make a plan before I get to work, especially if it's a long or complicated project. But sometimes I just begin writing. With some projects, my first draft is strong enough that I just have to edit it. Of course, that's not always the case.

—Wei Liao

On the surface, these students' writing processes seem to have little in common. Actually, however, all involve the same three activities: planning, drafting, and revising. These activities don't necessarily occur in any set order. Wei Liao plans in her head and postpones making a written plan until after she has generated a rough draft, whereas Sara Steinman plans extensively before she writes her first word. To be successful, however, all these writers must sooner or later think rhetorically and make choices about their own situation as writers, their readers, their text, and medium. Then they must try out these choices in their heads, on paper, or at the computer; evaluate the effects of these choices; and make appropriate changes in their drafts. Rather than being a magical or mysterious activity, then, writing is a process of planning, drafting, and revising.

thinking
rhetorically

IDENTIFYING COMPOSING STYLES

When designers and writers take their own composing processes seriously, they attempt to build on their strengths and recognize their limitations. They understand that they must vary their approach to writing depending on the task or situation. A student who prefers to spend a lot of time developing written or mental plans for an essay simply doesn't have that luxury when writing an in-class essay exam. For this reason, it's more accurate to refer to *writing processes* rather than *the writing process*. As a writer and designer, you must be pragmatic: You decide how to approach a project based on such factors as the nature and importance of the task, the schedule, the nature and demands of the medium, the experience you have with a particular kind of writing, and so on. Most experienced writers and designers do, however, have a preferred way of managing the composing process.

Heavy Planners.   Like Wei Liao, heavy planners generally plan their writing so carefully in their heads that their first drafts are often more like other writers' second or third drafts. As a consequence, they revise less intensively and less frequently than other students. Many of these students have disciplined themselves so that they can think about their writing in all sorts of places—on the subway, at work, in the garden pulling weeds, or in the car driving to and from school.

Some heavy planners write in this way because they prefer to; others develop this strategy out of necessity. Wei Liao, for instance, says that she simply has to do a great deal of her writing in her head because she's a mother as well as a student, and at home she often has to steal spare moments to work on her writing. As a result, she's learned to use every opportunity to think about her writing while she drives, cooks, or relaxes with her family.

Heavy Revisers.   Like Eduardo Alvarez, heavy revisers use the act of writing itself to find out what they want to say. When faced with a writing task, they prefer to sit down at a desk or computer and just begin writing.

Heavy revisers often state that writing their ideas out in a sustained spurt of activity reassures them that they have something to say and helps them avoid frustration. These students may not seem to plan because they begin drafting so early. Actually, however, their planning occurs as they draft and especially as they revise. Heavy revisers spend a great deal of time revising their initial drafts. To do so effectively, they must be able to read their work critically and, often, discard substantial portions of first drafts.

As you've probably realized, in both of these styles of composing, one of the components of the writing process is apparently abbreviated. Heavy planners don't seem to revise as extensively as other writers. Actually, however, they plan (and, in effect, revise) so thoroughly early in the process that they often don't need to revise as intensively later. Similarly, heavy revisers may not seem to plan; in fact, though, once they write their rough drafts, they plan and revise simultaneously and, often, extensively.

Sequential Composers.   A third general style of composing is exemplified by Sara Steinman. These writers might best be called sequential composers because they devote roughly equivalent amounts of time to planning, drafting, and revising. Rather than trying out their ideas and planning their writing mentally, as heavy planners do, sequential composers typically rely on written notes and plans to give shape and force to their ideas. And unlike heavy revisers, sequential composers need to have greater control over form and subject matter as they draft.

Sequential composers' habit of allotting time for planning, drafting, and revising helps them deal with the inevitable anxieties of writing. Like heavy revisers, sequential composers need the reassurance of seeing their ideas written down: Generating a volume of notes and plans gives them the confidence to begin drafting. Sequential composers may not revise as extensively as heavy revisers, for they generally draft more slowly, reviewing their writing as they proceed. But revision is nevertheless an important part of their composing process. Like most writers, sequential composers need a break from drafting to be able to critique their own words and ideas.

Each of these composing styles has advantages and disadvantages. Heavy planners can be efficient writers, spending less time drafting and revising than other writers, but they must have great mental discipline. An unexpected interruption when they're working out their ideas — a child in tears, a phone call — can cause even the most disciplined thinker to have a momentary lapse. Because so much of their work is done in their heads, heavy planners are less likely to benefit from the fruitful explorations and revisions that occur when writers review notes and plans or reread their own texts. And because heavy planners put off drafting until relatively late in the composing process, they can encounter substantial difficulties if the sentences and paragraphs that had seemed so clearly developed in their minds don't look as coherent and polished on paper.

Heavy revisers experience different advantages and disadvantages. Because they write quickly and voluminously, heavy revisers aren't in danger of losing valuable ideas. Similarly, their frequent rereading of drafts helps them remain open to new options that can improve their writing. However, heavy revisers must learn how to deal with emotional highs and lows that occur as they discover what they want to say through the process of writing itself. They must be able to critique their own writing ruthlessly, discarding large portions of text or perhaps even starting over. And because they revise so extensively, heavy revisers must leave adequate time for revision or the quality of their work can suffer.

What about sequential composers? Because they spend time planning, drafting, and revising—and do so primarily in writing—they have more external control over the writing process than heavy planners and revisers have. Sequential composers are also unlikely to fool themselves into thinking that a quickly generated collection of ideas is an adequate rough draft or that a plan brainstormed while taking the subway is adequate preparation for writing. Sequential composers can, however, develop inefficiently rigid habits—habits that reflect their need to have external control over their writing process. They may, for instance, waste valuable time developing detailed written plans when they're actually ready to begin drafting.

Good writers are aware of their preferred composing style—and of its potential advantages and disadvantages. They take responsibility for decisions about how to manage their composing process, recognizing the difference, for instance, between the necessary incubation of ideas and procrastination. Good writers are also flexible; depending on the task or situation, they can modify their preferred approach. A person who generally is a heavy reviser when writing academic essays, for instance, might write routine business memos in a single sitting because that's the most efficient way to get the job done. Similarly, heavy planners who prefer to do much of the work of writing mentally must employ different strategies when writing collaboratively with others or when engaged in research-based writing.

Procrastination.   There is one other common way of managing the writing process, though it might best be described as management by avoidance—procrastination. All writers occasionally procrastinate, but if you habitually put off writing a first draft until you have time only for a final draft (and this at 3 A.M. on the day your essay is due), your chances of success are minimal. Though you may have invented good reasons for putting off writing ("I write better under pressure"; "I can't write until I have all my easier assignments done first"), procrastination makes it difficult for you to manage the writing process in an efficient and effective manner.

Is procrastination always harmful? Might it not sometimes be a period of necessary incubation, of unconscious but still productive planning? Here's what Holly Hardin—a thoughtful student writer—discovered about her tendency to procrastinate:

> For me, sometimes procrastination isn't really procrastination (or so I tell myself). Sometimes what I label procrastination is really planning. The trouble is that I don't always know when it's one or the other.
>
> How do I procrastinate? Let me count the ways. I procrastinate by doing good works (helping overtime at my job, cleaning house, aiding and abetting a variety of causes). I procrastinate by absorbing myself in a purely selfish activity (reading paperbacks, watching TV, going to movies). I procrastinate

by visiting with friends, talking on the telephone, prolonging chance encounters. I procrastinate by eating and drinking (ice cream, coffee, cookies—all detrimental). Finally, I procrastinate by convincing myself that this time of day is not when I write well. I'd be much better off, I usually conclude, taking a nap. So I do.

Part of my difficulty is that I can see a certain validity in most of my reasons for procrastinating. There are some times of day when my thoughts flow better. I have forced myself to write papers in the past when I just didn't feel ready. Not only were the papers difficult to write, they were poorly written, inarticulate papers. Even after several rewrites, they were merely marginal. I would much rather write when I am at my mental best.

I need to balance writing with other activities. The trouble is—just how to achieve the perfect balance!

Holly's realistic appraisal of the role that procrastination plays in her writing process should help her distinguish between useful incubation and unhelpful procrastination. Unlike students who tell themselves that they should never procrastinate—and then do so anyway, feeling guilty every moment—Holly knows that she has to consider a variety of factors before she decides to invite a friend to tea, bake a batch of chocolate chip cookies, or take a much-needed nap.

NOTE FOR MULTILINGUAL WRITERS

If your first or home language is not English, you may be familiar with different approaches to the composing process of planning, drafting, and revising. Educational systems throughout the world have different approaches to writing and to the teaching of writing. In thinking about your writing process as a student in college, reflect on how your previous experiences as a writer enhance or interfere with your efforts to compose in standard written English. (Different approaches to revision may be especially relevant.) You may want to discuss the results of your reflection with your teacher or your tutor in the writing center.

ANALYZING YOUR COMPOSING PROCESS

The poet William Stafford once commented that "a writer is not so much someone who has something to say as he is someone who has found a process that will bring about new things he would not have thought if he had not started to say them." Stafford's remarks emphasize the importance of developing a workable writing process—a repertoire of strategies that you can draw on in a variety of situations.

Questions for Analyzing Your Composing Process

thinking rhetorically

You can use the following questions to analyze your composing process. Read these questions, and consider how you would answer them. Your teacher may ask you to respond to some or all of these questions in writing.

1. What is your general attitude toward writing? How do you think this attitude affects your writing?

2. Which of the composing styles described in this chapter matches the way you compose? If none seems to fit you, how do you compose?

3. How do you know when you are ready to begin writing? Do you have a "start-up" method or ritual?

4. How long do you typically work on your writing at any one time? Are you more likely to write an essay in a single sitting, or do you prefer to work over a number of days (or weeks)?

5. Do you have writing habits and rituals? What are they? Which ones are productive and supportive? Which ones interfere with your writing process?

6. How often do you import visuals and graphics into texts you are composing? How have you used Web and image-editing programs such as Adobe Photoshop? Do you enjoy doing this? Find it a challenge? Take it for granted?

7. What planning and revising strategies do you use? How do you know when you have spent enough time planning and revising?

8. If your first or home language is not English, how does knowing two or more languages influence your writing process? What language do you typically think in? In what language do you freewrite, brainstorm, or make notes?

9. What role do exchanges with others (conversations, responses from peers or tutors) play in your writing?

10. How do you procrastinate? (Be honest! All writers procrastinate occasionally.)

11. Thinking in general about the writing you do, what do you find most rewarding and satisfying about writing? Most difficult and frustrating? Why?

Writing is a *process,* and stopping to think about your own composing process can prove illuminating. One of my students, for example, formulated an analogy that helped us all think fruitfully about how the writing process works. "Writing," he said, "is actually a lot like sports." Writing—like sports? Let's see what this comparison reveals about the writing process.

| | | | | | | | | | | | | | | | | | | | | | | | | | | | | | | | | | | | | | | | | | | | | | | | | | | | | | | | | | | | | | | | | | | | | | | | | | | | | | | | | | | | | | | | | | |

FOR COLLABORATION

Meet with classmates to discuss your responses to the composing process questions. Begin by having each person state two important things he or she learned as a result of completing the analysis. (Appoint a recorder to write down each person's statements.) Once all members of your group have spoken, ask the recorder to read their statements aloud. Were any statements repeated by more than one member of the group? Working as a group, formulate two conclusions about the writing process that you would like to share with the class. (Avoid vague and general assertions, such as "Writing is difficult.") Be prepared to discuss your conclusions with your classmates.

| | | | | | | | | | | | | | | | | | | | | | | | | | | | | | | | | | | | | | | | | | | | | | | | | | | | | | | | | | | | | | | | | | | | | | | | | | | | | | | | | | | | | | | | | | |

Writing and sports are both performance skills. You may know who won every Wimbledon since 1980, but if you don't actually play tennis, you're not a tennis player — just somebody who knows a lot about tennis. Similarly, you can know a lot about writing, but to demonstrate (and improve) your skills, you must *write*.

Writing and sports both require individuals to master complex skills and to perform these skills in an almost infinite number of situations. Athletes must learn specific skills, plays, or maneuvers, but they can never execute them routinely or thoughtlessly. Writers must be similarly resourceful and flexible. You can learn the principles of effective essay organization, for instance, and you may write a number of essays that are well organized. Nevertheless, each time you sit down to write a new essay, you have to consider your options and make new choices. This is a primary reason that smart writers don't rely on formulas or rules but instead use rhetorical sensitivity to analyze and respond to each situation.

Experienced athletes and writers know that a positive attitude is essential. Some athletes psych themselves up before a game or competition, often using music, meditation, or other personal routines. But any serious athlete knows that's only part of what having a positive attitude means. It also means running five miles when you're already tired at three, or doing twelve repetitions during weight training when you're exhausted and no one else would know if you did only eight. A positive attitude is equally important in writing. If you approach a writing task with a negative attitude ("I never was good at writing"), you create obstacles for yourself. Having a positive, open attitude is essential in tennis, skiing — and writing.

To maintain a high level of skill, both athletes and writers need frequent practice and effective coaching. "In sports," a coach once said, "you're either getting better or getting worse." Without practice — which for a writer means both reading and writing — your writing skills will slip (as will your confidence). Likewise, coaching is essential in writing because it's hard to distance yourself from your own work. Coaches — your writing instructor, a tutor (or writing assistant) at a writing center, or a fellow student — can help you gain a fresh perspective on your writing and make useful suggestions about revision as well.

Experienced athletes and writers continually set new goals for themselves. Athletes who believe that they are either getting better or getting worse continually set new challenges for themselves and analyze their performance. They know that coaches can help but that *they* are ultimately the ones performing. Experienced writers know this too, so they look for opportunities to practice their writing. And they don't measure their success simply by a grade. They see their writing always as work in progress.

Joining a Community of Writers

For many people, one big difference between writing and sports is that athletes often belong to teams. Writers, they think, work in lonely isolation. But does writing actually require isolation and loneliness? If you take a careful look at the day-to-day writing that people do, you quickly recognize that this is hardly the case. Many in business, industry, and the professions work as part of one or more teams. In many cases, these individuals' ability to work effectively with others is key to a successful career.

Even when writers do a good deal of their composing alone, they often find it helpful to talk with others before and while writing. A group of neighbors writing a petition to their city council requesting that a traffic bump be installed on their street to reduce speeding might well ask one person to compose the petition. In order to do a good job, the writer would talk extensively with her neighbors to generate the strongest ideas possible. She would also present drafts of the petition for review and approval.

Online technologies and the Web have increased, not diminished, the opportunity for writers to work collaboratively. Using online spaces, from course Web sites to public writing communities such as Writerly.com ("for writers and readers of all interests and skill levels"), writers everywhere are sharing their writing and getting responses to works in progress.

FINDING A COMMUNITY

The romanticized image of the writer struggling alone until inspiration strikes is both inaccurate and unhelpful. Most writers alternate between periods of independent activity, composing alone at a computer or desk, and periods of social interactions — meeting with friends, colleagues, or team members for information, advice, or responses to drafts. They may also correspond with others in their field, or they may get in touch with people doing similar work through reading, research, or online technologies.

Finally, people who take their writing seriously are just like other people who share an interest. They like to develop real or virtual social relationships with others who feel as they do. These relationships will help them learn new ideas, improve their skills, share their interest and enthusiasm, and develop a community of writers. Sometimes these relationships are formal and relatively permanent. Many poets and fiction writers, for instance, meet regularly to discuss work in progress. Perhaps more commonly, writers' networks are informal and shifting, though no less vital. A new manager in a corporation, for instance, may find one or two people with sound judgment and good writing skills to review important letters and reports. Similarly, students working on a major project for a class may meet informally but regularly to compare notes and provide mutual support.

Unfortunately, college life does not generally encourage the development of informal networks like these, especially among undergraduates. Students juggling coursework, jobs, families, and other activities can find it difficult to get together or to take the time to read and respond to one another's writing. Luckily, many colleges and universities have established writing centers, where you can go to talk with others about your writing. If your campus has a writing center, take advantage of the opportunity to get an informed response to your work.

| | | | | | | | | | | | | | | | | | | | | | | | | | | | | | | | | | | | | | | | | | | | | | | | | | | | | | | | | | | | | | | | | | | | | | | | | | | | | | | | | | | | | | | | | | | | | | |

FOR EXPLORATION

If your campus has a writing center, make an appointment to interview a tutor (sometimes also called a writing assistant or peer consultant) about the services the center provides. You may also want to ask the tutor about his or her own experiences as a writer. Your instructor may ask you to present the results of your interview orally or to write a summary of your discussion.

| | | | | | | | | | | | | | | | | | | | | | | | | | | | | | | | | | | | | | | | | | | | | | | | | | | | | | | | | | | | | | | | | | | | | | | | | | | | | | | | | | | | | | | | | | | | | | |

WORKING COLLABORATIVELY WITH OTHERS

Whether or not you have access to a writing center, you can still participate in an informal network with others who are working to improve their writing skills. Because you're in the same class and share the same assignments and concerns, you and your classmates constitute a natural community of writers. In order to work effectively, however, you and your peers need to develop or strengthen the skills that will contribute to effective group work.

As you do so, remember that people have different styles of learning and interacting. Some of these differences represent individual preferences:

Some students work out their ideas as they talk, for instance, while others prefer to think through their ideas before speaking. Other differences are primarily cultural and thus reflect deeply embedded social practices and preferences. Effective groups value diversity and find ways to ensure that *all* members can comfortably participate in and benefit from group activities.

Effective groups are pragmatic and task-oriented; they balance a commitment to getting the job done with patience and flexibility. Effective groups also take care to articulate group goals and monitor group processes. Sometimes this monitoring is intuitive and informal. But sometimes a more formal process is helpful. If you're part of a group that meets regularly, you might begin meetings by having each person state one way in which the group is working well and one way in which it could be improved. The time spent discussing these comments and suggestions will ensure that your group is working effectively. If problems in the group process, such as a dominating or nonparticipating member, do occur, deal immediately with this difficulty. It's not always easy to discuss problems such as these openly, but doing so is essential to effective group work.

Group activities such as peer response and collaborative trouble-shooting can help improve your writing ability and prepare you for on-the-job teamwork. Problems may arise, but they can be addressed if all participate fully in group activities and respond to difficulties when they occur. Groups are, after all, a bit like friendships or marriages. They develop and change; they require care and attention. If you're committed to keeping the group going, alert to signs of potential trouble, and willing to talk problems out, you can all benefit from group work.

Guidelines for Group Work

These suggestions apply whether you work with the same group of students all term or participate in a variety of groups. (For suggestions on how to benefit from peer response to your writing, see "Benefiting from Responses to Work in Progress," pp. 286–89.)

■ *Take time at the start to review your assignment and to agree on relevant goals and procedures.* For brief collaborative activities, you may need to spend only a few minutes reviewing your teacher's instructions and establishing ground rules. For more extended projects — particularly those that involve group meetings outside of class — plan to spend the first ten or fifteen minutes reviewing your assignment and setting goals for your meeting.

(continued)

(continued)

- *Assign roles, but be flexible.* Sometimes you may function as your group's leader, either informally or formally. At other times, you may be called on to help the group reach consensus or keep on task. Effective group members are willing to assume multiple roles as needed.

- *Encourage productive conflict.* The diverse perspectives and strategies that people bring to a problem or task are one of the main reasons why group activities are so productive. Capitalize on these differences. Encourage the discussion of new ideas. Consider alternative approaches to your subject. Don't be afraid to disagree; doing so may enable your group to find a more creative solution to a problem, to discover a new and stimulating response to a question. Just be sure that the discussion remains friendly and focused on the task at hand.

FOR COLLABORATION

Meet with your group (created by your instructor or formed on your own) to discuss how you can most effectively work as a team. Begin by exchanging names, phone numbers, and email addresses; take time just to get to know each other. You might also see if your group can formulate some friendly rules to guide group activities. (You might all agree, for instance, to notify at least one member, but preferably all members, if you can't make a meeting.) Be sure to write these rules down and consult them as you work together. Try to anticipate problems, such as coordinating schedules, and discuss how to resolve them.

FOR THOUGHT, DISCUSSION, AND WRITING

1. Now that you have read this chapter, set some goals for yourself as a writer. Make a list of several goals you'd like to accomplish in your composition class this term. What would you most like to learn or improve? What would you like to change about your writing process? Then write a paragraph or more discussing how you plan to achieve these goals.

2. You can learn a great deal about your own composing process by observing yourself as you write. To do so, follow these steps:

   Choose an upcoming writing project to study. Before beginning this project, reflect on its demands. How much time do you expect to spend working on this project, and how do you anticipate allocating your time? What challenges does this project hold for you? What strengths and resources do you bring to this project? As you work on the project, keep track of how you spend your time. Include a record in this log of when you started and ended each work session, as well as a description of your activities and a paragraph commenting on your process. What went well? What surprised you? What gave you problems? What might you do differently next time?

After you have completed the project, draw on your prewriting analysis and process log to write a case study of this project. As you do so, consider questions such as these: To what extent was your prewriting analysis of your project accurate? How did you actually allocate your time when working on this project? What strategies did you rely on most heavily? What went well with your writing? What was difficult? Conclude by reflecting about what you have learned from this case study about yourself as a writer.

3. All writers procrastinate occasionally—some just procrastinate more effectively than others. After brainstorming or freewriting about your favorite ways of procrastinating, write a humorous or serious essay on procrastination.

4. The Exploration activities on pp. 26 and 27 encouraged you to reflect on your assumptions about writing and your experiences as a writer. Drawing on these activities and on the rest of the chapter, write an essay in which you reflect on this subject. You may choose to write about pivotal incidents in your experiences as a writer, using particular occasions to support the general statements you make about your experiences.

| | | | | | | | | | | | | | | | | | | | | | | | | | | | | | | | | | | | | | | | | | | | | | | | | | | | | | | | | | | | | | | | | | | | | | | | | | | | | | | | | | | | | | | | | | | | | | | | | | |

Analyzing Rhetorical Situations

Whenever you write—whether you're word processing an essay or designing a brochure for a student organization—you are writing in the context of a specific situation with its own unique demands and opportunities. A management trainee writing a memo to her supervisor faces different challenges than an investigative journalist working on a story for the *New York Times* or a student creating a poster for an in-class presentation. Successful writers know that they must consider the situations in which they write; they can't rely on formulas or blind luck when they compose. They know they need to rely on their rhetorical sensitivity—their understanding of the relationships among writer, reader, text, and medium—to help them make decisions as they write and revise.

In this chapter of *The Academic Writer,* you will learn how to ask yourself questions about your rhetorical situation—questions that will enable you to determine the most fruitful way of approaching your topic and of responding to the needs and expectations of your readers. You will also learn how to read the forms and strategies of writing that characterize different communities of language users. This kind of rhetorically sensitive reading is particularly helpful when you are learning new forms of writing, as happens when students enter college or begin a new job.

Learning to Analyze Your Rhetorical Situation

thinking rhetorically

Rhetoric involves four key elements: writer, reader, text, and medium. When you think about these elements, posing questions about the options available to you as a writer, you are analyzing your rhetorical situation. In your daily life, you regularly analyze your rhetorical situation when you communicate with others—though you most often do this unconsciously and intuitively. Imagine, for instance, that you've been meaning to write to a close friend. Now is the time, but should you email, instant message, send a handwritten letter, or contact him some other way? The answer depends on your situa-

NOTE FOR MULTILINGUAL WRITERS

This chapter's approach to rhetoric and rhetorical sensitivity is grounded in the Western rhetorical tradition. Other traditions hold different values and assumptions about communication. For example, if part of your education took place outside of North America, you may have learned an approach to communication that values maintaining communal harmony as much as (or more than) individual self-expression, which is highly valued in Western rhetoric. The approach you learned may also reflect different stylistic preferences. For some writers from other communities, the English that is written in school, for business, and elsewhere in North America seems abrupt and even rude. As a writer learning to communicate in different languages and communities, you need to understand the assumptions held by writers who are grounded in the Western rhetorical tradition—but you do not need to abandon your own culture's values. Your writing (and your thinking) will be enriched when you learn how to draw on all the rhetorical sensitivity that you have gained as a speaker, listener, writer, and reader, including your home experiences.

tion. If you're writing just to let your friend know that you're thinking of him, you might choose instant message or email because their ease and informality suit this purpose well. If your friend maintains a personal blog, you might visit it, read some posts to see what he's been up to, and then leave a greeting. But suppose you're writing because you've just learned of a death in your friend's family. The seriousness of this situation and the more personal nature of a handwritten note might well prompt a letter.

As simple as it might seem, the question of whether to email, post to a blog, or send a handwritten letter is a rhetorical question, one that calls on you to consider all the elements of rhetoric. As a writer you have choices; the more fully you understand your situation, the better choices you can make. Even though people conventionally send handwritten letters of condolence, for instance, your relationship with your friend might in fact make you decide to email him. This would be particularly likely if you are in the habit of emailing each other every few days, even about personal matters.

USING YOUR RHETORICAL ANALYSIS TO GUIDE YOUR WRITING

Effective writers draw on their commonsense rhetorical sensitivity to determine the most effective ways to communicate with readers. The student deciding whether to email or to write a letter didn't consciously run through a mental checklist but rather drew on his intuitive understanding of his situation. When you face the challenge of new and more difficult kinds of writing, however, as you do in college, it helps to analyze your rhetorical situation consciously.

| | | | | | | | | | | | | | | | | | | | | | | | | | | | | | | | | | | | | | | | | | | | | | | | | | | | | | | | | | | | | | | | | | | | | | | | | | | | | | | | | | | | | |

FOR EXPLORATION

Imagine that you need to compose the following texts:

> An application for an internship in your major

> A flyer for a march that you and other students are organizing to protest an increase in student tuition

> A posting to your class's online discussion board that explains your reaction to a film that you viewed in class

> A substantial research-based essay for a class you are taking

Keeping the elements of rhetoric in mind, spend a few minutes thinking about how you would approach these different writing situations. Write a brief description of each situation, responding to the following questions:

1. What is your role as writer? Your purpose for writing?

2. What image of yourself do you wish to present, and how will you vary your language accordingly?

3. How do the readers of this text influence the form and content of your writing?

4. How does the medium you will use both constrain and enable your communication?

5. What role, if any, should images, graphics, and multimedia play in your text?

| | | | | | | | | | | | | | | | | | | | | | | | | | | | | | | | | | | | | | | | | | | | | | | | | | | | | | | | | | | | | | | | | | | | | | | | | | | | | | | | | | | | | |

thinking rhetorically

Questions for Analyzing Your Rhetorical Situation

Early in any writing project, you can lay a solid foundation by asking yourself the following questions.

Writer

- Why are you writing?
- What do you hope your writing will accomplish? Do you want to convey information? Change the reader's mind? Entertain the reader? Move the reader to action?

(continued)

(continued)

- How might your goals in this writing situation influence the eventual form, content, and medium of your text?
- What role does this rhetorical situation invite you, the writer, to play? Is your role relatively fixed (as in an essay exam)? Or is it flexible?
- What image of yourself do you want to convey to your readers? What voice do you want readers to hear when they read your writing? That of a serious student? A concerned citizen? How will you use the resources of language to achieve this effect?

Reader

- Who is your intended audience? Do you picture a specific audience (subscribers to a special-interest magazine, for instance)? Or a general audience with a wide range of interests? Or do you have a specific reader in mind, such as your teacher?
- What role do you want readers to adopt as they read your writing? What kinds of cues will you use to signal this role to readers?
- If you are writing to a specific audience, do you need to consider demographic characteristics—such as age, gender, religion, income, occupation, education, or political preference?
- How will your writing appeal to your readers' interests, values, and beliefs? Do you expect your readers to be interested in the topic, or do you need to create and maintain their interest?
- How might your readers' needs and expectations influence the form, content, and style of your writing?

Text

- If you are responding to an assignment, does the assignment specify or restrict the form and content of your text? How much freedom do you have?
- Consider the genre your rhetorical situation requires. Are style and other conventions rigidly defined (as in lab reports)? Or are they flexible?
- Does the nature of your subject implicitly or explicitly require that you provide certain kinds of evidence or explore certain issues?
- Could you benefit by looking at examples of the kind of writing that your situation requires, including models of document design?

(continued)

(continued)

Medium

- If you are writing in response to an assignment, to what degree does the assignment specify or restrict the medium you can use?

- Does the kind of text you are composing suggest that some media might be more appropriate and effective than others?

- What expectations might your audience have in terms of medium? Might they be more comfortable with some media than with others? Might some media be more accessible to your audience than others?

- Do you face practical constraints—such as time, expertise, and expense—when determining which medium to use?

The process of analyzing your rhetorical situation challenges you to look both within and without. Your intended meaning—what you want to communicate—is certainly important, as is your purpose for writing. But unless you're writing solely for yourself in a journal or notebook, you can't ignore your readers or your situation. You also need to consider which medium will best convey your ideas. Both at school and on the job, sometimes your medium will be predetermined; at other times, however, you will have options. Analyzing your rhetorical situation helps you to respond creatively as a writer and yet keeps you aware of limits on your freedom.

SETTING PRELIMINARY GOALS

Before beginning a major writing project, you may find it helpful to write a brief analysis of your rhetorical situation, or you may simply review these questions mentally. Doing so can help you determine your preliminary intentions or goals as a writer. (Your intentions will often shift as you write. That's fine. As you write, you'll naturally revise your understanding of your rhetorical situation.) Despite its tentativeness, however, your analysis of your situation will give you a sense of direction and purpose.

In Chapter 2, you read Mirlandra Ebert's response to the Exploration activity on p. 27. Rather than writing a letter about her experience as a writer, Mirlandra created a visually rich text. This text, a collage, appears on p. 28. Here is the analysis of her rhetorical situation that Mirlandra composed before creating her text.

thinking rhetorically

Writer: The poster I will create is about who I am as a writer. There are many experiences that have shaped me and that will continue to shape me, but I don't have to cover all of them. I just need to decide which are the most important and focus on them. I need content that's understandable, but I don't just want to say "I am _____." I don't think I know what goes in the blank. As a person, sometimes I feel like I reinvent myself every day, almost as if I see myself from a different angle and then I interpret myself differently. I feel the same way as a writer. This poster assignment is an opportunity to reflect that aspect of my life. The most important role I see for myself as a writer here is to have a voice in this piece. It should be a contradictory, busy, and chaotic voice (busy in the sense of visually rich and active), but still convey strength and fluidity.

Reader: My intended audience is my professor and my classmates. I want to create a text that everybody in my class can connect with in some way. Most of our class is just out of high school, but there are also nontraditional students who may engage differently with my work. I also need to be aware of gender issues. I need to think about how some aspects of my project, such as the flowered background, will come across. Although my audience is diverse, I think I can hold their interest because there will be so much going on in my poster.

Text: In terms of my text, I have a lot of freedom in this assignment as long as I stay focused on the main topic. The only conventions I need to address are issues of size and readability. I want to be careful to reflect my busy and varied "writing self" but in a way that's not too cluttered to make sense. I don't have to be logical, as I have to be in an essay, so I've got lots of flexibility here. I know I want to express what I've learned from teachers and then engage many smaller ideas about who I am as a writer that have to do with other parts of my life. Before I started on this project, I looked at other posters that students had created. This was helpful, but I want to express my own ideas in my own way. Many examples I looked at used only words and images. I want to move beyond that and include physical objects that represent me.

Medium: In terms of medium, I'm working with the advantages and limitations of posterboard and collage. If I can attach something to posterboard, then it's OK. My audience may expect a basic 2-D poster with pictures and graphics, but I don't think it will create confusion or discomfort if I include other objects. So far I intend to attach a pen I like to write notes with, sticky notes of all sizes, some push pins, my favorite outlining paper, and a hair tie because I'm always messing with my hair when I write. I think these personal objects will make for a more interesting medium.

thinking
rhetorically
Here is another student's analysis of her rhetorical situation. The student is Annette Chambers, and her rhetorical analysis is followed by her essay (p. 49). Annette analyzed her rhetorical situation by using the questions provided on pp. 44–46. She begins with some general reflections on her situation as a writer.

> I am writing an essay about my hobby, fantasy role-playing: what it is, why I like it, how it works, how people respond when I tell them about it — and why their responses bother me. I hope that those reading my essay will be entertained by and interested in my topic. But mainly I want them to understand that people who game are not all wild-eyed, psychologically damaged social misfits. I've been really frustrated with the way people respond when they learn that I participate in fantasy role-playing games. Most people make it clear that they think gaming is weird at best; some have gone so far as to ask me if I didn't fear for my soul since I "play" with "demons." My writing goals require both information and sensitivity to my audience. I need to provide enough information about gaming so people will understand what it is (and, just as important, what it is not) — but not so much that they get bogged down in unnecessary details. I also need to respond to the concerns people have about gaming. I want to show that the stereotypes about fantasy role-playing are just that: stereotypes. But I've got to be careful not to seem angry or defensive. I'm hoping that humor will help here.
>
> I'm writing this essay for an assignment in my composition class. The assignment is pretty general; it asks us to write an informative essay on a subject that we care about. So I have a fair amount of flexibility. I hope that a wide range of people might find my essay interesting and informative. I'm directing this toward a general audience, even though my teacher will be my immediate reader. Though I'm writing this essay for a class, I might submit it for publication to the student or local newspaper or to some magazines that publish brief, general-interest essays, such as airline magazines.
>
> **Writer:** I've already explained why I'm writing and what I hope this essay will accomplish. Given my goals, I want to present myself as open, conversational, pleasant, and not at all defensive about my hobby. I want readers to see me as a bright, articulate person who likes to make believe but is firmly aware of the difference between reality and fantasy. This is really important to my credibility, since my major goal is to convince readers that game-players are normal people just like them.

Reader: I assume that most readers (especially my teacher!) will have little direct experience with fantasy role-playing, which they probably associate in a vague way with games like Dungeons and Dragons™. Since some readers will believe the misconceptions about gaming I talk about, I need to be careful not to alienate them by portraying their concerns as stupid or silly. I hope to appeal to my readers by writing a vivid introduction that will draw readers in, and by using lively examples — and humor — to keep them interested. I hope that my use of humor and my general informality will tell readers that they should just sit back and enjoy the essay.

Text: Because my assignment is open-ended, I have quite a lot of freedom as a writer. But that doesn't mean that anything goes. Since I'm hoping to appeal to a broad range of readers, I need to make my essay interesting. I've read other personal essays, and we've talked about them in class, so I know that writers need to draw readers in. I can't assume that readers will care about my subject; I have to make them care. And I have to provide the kinds of details that will keep them interested as they read.

Medium: I was tempted to illustrate my essay with drawings of some of the figures I play, but since this is an academic essay — and since the drawings wouldn't really add to the content — I finally decided to follow traditional essay format.

Here is Annette's essay about fantasy role-playing. As you read it, keep her analysis of her rhetorical situation clearly in mind. In what ways did her analysis inform the essay that she wrote?

"So, What Are You Doing This Weekend?"

ANNETTE CHAMBERS

It's 2:45 in the morning, and I've just spent two and a half hours logged into email pretending to be an elfish woman on another planet. My name is Miri Ravan, and I'm something over 2,000 years old, though (as is the way of elves) I don't look much over thirty. At the moment, I'm having an uncomfortable discussion with my lover's daughter, D'versey, about relationships, which is hard because she's half succubus, spent her early life in Hell, and has a unique view of life. For example, she finds it odd that I don't casually become involved with anyone I find attractive, and has recently asked me to explain "just what is the difference between acquaintances and friends." Or it's Saturday night, around 10:00, and I've been sitting in a stuffy little living room with five friends for about eight hours. This is how we've spent most Saturdays for almost ten years. I am Annabelle Jordan, a thirty-ish veterinarian with a photographic memory and a knack for "reading" people. I love dogs, hate rap, live in the suburbs of Tacoma, and just happen to hang out with a pack of vampires. Or I might be Maire Clare, an Irish woman living in twelfth-century London, who just happens to be a vampire. Or Silver, a former "personnel reclamation specialist" (read "kidnapper and sometimes assassin") who now runs the shadows of the mean streets of twenty-first-century Seattle.

I suppose I shouldn't be surprised that people look at me funny when I tell them about fantasy role-playing. After we get past the "you mean like Dungeons and Dragons™?" stage, their expressions usually range from curious, to wary, to alarmed. There is, I suppose, something odd, something not quite normal, about pretending to be somebody else for hours at a time, especially when that somebody may not even be human. But then, I've never really understood the attraction of staring at a television screen while grown men chase variously shaped balls around a field or court.

Anyway, gaming is fun—as relaxing to me as watching sports is to others.

Of course, there are other ways to relax that don't make people question your sanity or soul. Rock climbing, for instance. Though rock climbing seems pretty crazy to me, nobody stereotypes climbers as socially inept, psychologically warped, or morally questionable. No one suggests that climbing be banned as harmful to children. And nobody asks climbers if they don't worry about getting "too wrapped up in rock climbing" or wonders, in tones of sincere interest and concern, whether their hobby is "demonic." These are questions I've encountered more than once, and I always find myself pausing while I attempt to frame a reply.

However long the pause, the answer is always "Well, no." I don't worry about getting too involved. I don't spend my days fretting that I identify too strongly with Miri, or that Annabelle is becoming too great an influence on my thinking, or that if I'm not careful I might flip out and start randomly slaughtering innocent bystanders in the mistaken belief that they're monsters. As far as I can tell, no one who knows me well worries about these things either.

Is it possible to get too wrapped up? Yes, certainly; it's possible to take anything too far. It's also possible to fall off a mountain while you're climbing it, but that doesn't mean that all climbers have a death wish. I've been gaming for ten years or so and have encountered exactly one person who I thought allowed himself to get too caught up in the game. But he was like that about other things too. His obsessiveness colored his whole life, not just his role-playing. In some ways the game seemed to serve as a safety valve for him, a way of venting hostility he might otherwise have directed at real people instead of imaginary monsters.

Which brings me to demons. Yes, they do turn up in some of the games I play. So do elves and giants and centaurs and a whole host of other creatures. And, yes, they're powerful and evil and extremely dangerous.

Since my group usually plays characters who at least try to be good, demons are popular enemies. But, no, role-playing isn't about summoning, communing with, speaking to, or even believing in demons. Mostly it's a way of being, for a few hours, someone you're not likely to get to be in real life — perhaps even someone you wouldn't want to be. It's a chance for you and some friends to make up imaginary people and see if you can make them work together toward a common goal.

In case you're unfamiliar with fantasy role-playing, here's how it works. Everyone in the group — usually between three and eight players — has a character, and each character has a defined set of physical abilities and physical and mental characteristics, as well as a background including personality, goals, physical abilities and so forth. There's also a game master (GM) or storyteller who more or less (in my group it's mostly less) controls what's happening by setting up the scenarios to which the player characters respond. The goal is to get as deeply into character as possible, to speak, act, and react as though you are the person you're pretending to be, though the acting is usually limited to gestures and tones of voice.

If I want Annabelle to climb a fifteen-foot rock wall, something she's unlikely to be good at, given the background I've invented and skills I've chosen for her, I don't get up and start scaling the sofa. Instead, I tell the GM what I plan for her to do. Based on a combination of factors including her assigned strength and dexterity, the condition of the wall, and luck, the GM decides whether she manages to scramble over with a few seconds to spare, escapes because one of her companions distracts the werewolves, or falls to her doom.

Now, I don't believe in werewolves any more than I believe in demons, but part of the fun is that Annabelle does. Gaming is a chance to pretend, to play make believe, the way we all do as children. Perhaps it's this similarity to childhood games that makes people uncomfortable. After all, aren't we grown-ups now? Shouldn't we concern ourselves with grown-up things like work and money and having our own children? Well, maybe.

But on the other hand, is getting together to play Dragonquest™ or Vampire: The Masquerade™ really so much weirder than getting together to watch football or play poker? Besides, it's cheap therapy. Everyone in my group has at one time or another arrived looking exhausted, defeated, or just plain irritated, and growled humorously, "I want to kill something." The rest of us sympathize, and then we let him kill something! This may not bring the long-term benefits of therapy, but role-playing is easy and inexpensive, and however much bloodshed our characters may be responsible for, none of us seems to have any trouble maintaining the fantasy-reality distinction.

And yes, we do work, and go to school, and have, for the want of a better phrase, "real lives." Most of us have or are working toward college degrees. All of us have or are looking for jobs. Some of us are engaged or living together with another person. We pay our taxes and brush our teeth and can, with allowances for differing personalities and degrees of sociability, hold down our end of a "normal" conversation. Perhaps the real difference between us and rock climbers is that we spend our Saturdays with our feet planted firmly on the ground.

||||||||||||||||||||||||||||||||||||||||||||||||||||||||||||||||||||||||||||||||||

FOR EXPLORATION

To what extent does Annette Chambers's essay achieve the goals she established for herself in her analysis of her rhetorical situation? Reread Annette's analysis and essay. Keeping her analysis in mind, list three or four reasons that you believe Annette does or does not achieve her goals, and then find at least one passage in the essay that illustrates each of these statements. Finally, identify at least one way that Annette might strengthen her essay were she to revise.

||||||||||||||||||||||||||||||||||||||||||||||||||||||||||||||||||||||||||||||||||

Thinking about Readers

If you look again at Annette Chambers's analysis of her rhetorical situation (pp. 48–49), you'll notice that concerns about her readers influence all aspects of her planning. Annette knows that if she wants to challenge readers' stereotypes about fantasy role-playing, it would hardly make sense to write an angry essay chastising readers for their misconceptions. Her situation invites a light, entertaining, informative approach, one that encourages dialogue and identification. Annette understands as well that the persona she projects will help determine how readers respond to her ideas. Consequently, she presents herself as open, pleasant, and friendly (note the role that humor plays in her essay, for instance)—and she invites readers to assume a similar stance. In so doing, she establishes common ground with readers and encourages them to be as open-minded about her hobby as she is about such hobbies as spectator sports and rock climbing.

Annette recognizes that she must do more than establish common ground and project an inviting, friendly image of herself. She must also respond to readers' misconceptions and provide information about fantasy role-playing. If she gives too many details, readers may get bogged down; too few, and they will fail to understand how "normal" people could be drawn to her hobby. Annette also understands that she's writing for two potential audiences: for her teacher, who will actually read her essay, and for a more general audience. Negotiating this double audience could be tricky, but Annette draws on her understanding of the personal essay to make decisions as she writes. For Annette, the personal essay (an essay grounded in the writer's personal experience) is not an arbitrary form but a means of establishing a particular kind of relationship with readers, one that's conversational and informal. Annette understands that in evaluating her essay her teacher will consider the extent to which it is interesting and well organized, anticipates the needs and interests of a general audience, and comments in significant ways on its topic.

In a different situation — an in-class essay exam, for instance — Annette would adjust her understanding of her reader accordingly. Teachers assign essay exams to determine what students have learned about a subject and how effectively they can express this understanding to others. Given this expectation, a dramatic, attention-getting introduction might irritate, not entertain, her reader. A concise introductory paragraph, one that specifies the writer's main point and indicates how the writer will support this point, would be more appropriate.

Here, for instance, is the introduction to an essay written by Elizabeth Ridlington. Elizabeth wrote this essay for an exam in her introductory political science class. The title of Elizabeth's essay is "Political and Economic Power."

> Since the French Revolution, France has believed the state should be composed of citizens who voluntarily joined the nation because of their belief in certain ideals. The United States similarly believes that all citizens should agree with the principles formed at the time of the Revolutionary War and laid out in the Constitution. Despite this, neither country extends citizenship to everyone who agrees with these ideals and principles. Thus, other factors must influence these nations' understanding of — and laws regarding — citizenship. In this essay I argue that economic and political considerations have been more important in forming either country's understanding of citizenship than have been its founding ideals. Evidence of this can be found in the evolution of the understanding of citizenship, in the forces that initially pulled each nation into a single political unit, and in the outcome of specific crises.

In writing this introduction, Elizabeth understood that in this rhetorical situation her reader, her political science teacher, is interested primarily in her understanding of the topic. Whereas Annette's introduction works hard to interest readers and to engage them with her topic, Elizabeth's introduction

thinking
rhetorically

focuses on establishing a clear position on her topic and on identifying the most important arguments she will use to support this position. Her introduction thus serves dual purposes: It clearly articulates her position, and it reassures her professor that the essay will be clearly organized and well supported.

||||||||||||||||||||||||||||||||||||||||||||||||||||||||||||||||||||||||||||||||||||||||||||||

FOR EXPLORATION

Introductions often signal the relationship the writer intends to establish with readers. The following excerpts introduce two different discussions of stress, both intended for a general audience. As you read these excerpts, think about the differing roles that they invite readers to assume.

> Sally Swanson, a thirty-eight-year-old mother of four, works as a bank teller in Des Moines, Iowa. Like many women, she feels the pressure of running a home, raising children, managing a job, and carving out leisure time for herself. "I did fine until we got a new supervisor last year," she says with an exhausted sigh. "Within two months I had started to burn out." Sally takes antacid pills several times a day. She worries that she may have an ulcer. "I feel as if he's looking over my shoulder all the time," she says. "He never has a good word to say to anyone. Sometimes the tension at the bank is so thick you could cut it with a knife."
>
> — FROM *THE WORK/STRESS CONNECTION: HOW TO COPE WITH JOB BURNOUT*

> Particular kinds of work seem to cause special stress, and the effects on health are manifested in an all-too-common pattern: fatigue, insomnia, eating disorders, nervousness, feelings of unhappiness, abuse of alcohol or drugs. Stress is often related to the nature of the job or imposed irregularities. Rotating shift work, in which hours are erratic or inconsistent with the normal sleep cycle, produces both physical and mental stress by constantly upsetting circadian rhythms that control specific hormonal and other responses. Jobs that involve little variation but require constant close attention, for example, assembly-line work or jobs requiring repetitive tasks with dangerous equipment, seem to be particularly stressful. In one study in a sawmill, people who ran the equipment had much higher levels of stress-related hormones than workers who did not come in contact with machinery, even though their jobs also may have been boring and repetitive.
>
> — FROM *THE COLUMBIA UNIVERSITY COLLEGE OF PHYSICIANS AND SURGEONS COMPLETE HOME MEDICAL GUIDE*

Write a brief description of the writer-reader relationship established in each of these introductions. What signals or cues do the authors provide to enable readers to adopt an appropriate role? Cite at least three examples of these signals or cues.

||||||||||||||||||||||||||||||||||||||||||||||||||||||||||||||||||||||||||||||||||||||||||||||

As a writer, your relationship with readers is always shifting and complex; it varies with the rhetorical situation. When you consider your readers' expectations and interests, you think strategically and thus build on the rhetorical sensitivity you have already developed as a speaker, listener, reader, and writer.

Using Aristotle's Three Appeals

Analyzing your rhetorical situation can provide information that will enable you to make crucial strategic, structural, and stylistic decisions about your writing. In considering how to use this information, you may find it helpful to employ what Aristotle (384–322 B.C.E.) characterized as the three appeals. According to Aristotle, when speakers and writers communicate with others, they draw on these three general appeals:

Logos, the appeal to reason

Pathos, the appeal to emotion, values, and beliefs

Ethos, the appeal to the credibility of the speaker or writer

As a writer, you appeal to *logos* when you focus on the logical presentation of your subject by providing evidence and examples in support of your ideas. You appeal to *pathos* when you use the resources of language to engage your readers emotionally with your subject or appeal to their values, beliefs, or needs. And you appeal to *ethos* when you create an image of yourself, a persona, that encourages readers to accept or act on your ideas.

These appeals correspond to three of the four basic elements of rhetoric (writer, reader, and text). In appealing to *ethos*, you focus on the writer's character as implied in the text; in appealing to *pathos*, on the interaction of writer and reader; and in appealing to *logos*, on the logical statements about the subject made in your particular text. In some instances, you may rely predominantly on one of these appeals. A student writing a technical report, for instance, will typically emphasize scientific or technical evidence (*logos*), not emotional or personal appeals. More often, however, you'll draw on all three appeals in order to create a fully persuasive document. A journalist writing a column on child abuse might open with several examples designed to gain her readers' attention and to convince them of the importance of this issue (*pathos*). Although she may rely primarily on information about the negative consequences of child abuse (*logos*), she will undoubtedly also endeavor to create an image of herself as a caring, serious person (*ethos*), one whose analysis of a subject like child abuse should be trusted.

This journalist might also use images to help convey her point. One or more photographs of physically abused children would certainly appeal to

thinking rhetorically

pathos. To call attention to the large number of children who are physically abused, she might present important statistics in a chart or graph. She might also include photographs of well-known advocates for child protection to represent the trustworthiness of her report's insights. In so doing, the journalist is combining words, images, and graphics to maximum effect.

In the following example, Brandon Barrett, a chemistry major at Oregon State University, uses Aristotle's three appeals to determine how best to approach an essay assignment for a first-year writing class that asks him to explain what his major is and why he chose it.

In presenting her assignment, Barrett's teacher informed students that their two- to three-page essays should include "information about your major that is new to your readers; in other words, it should not simply repeat the OSU catalog. Rather, it should be your unique perspective, written in clear, descriptive language." The teacher concluded with this advice: "Have fun with this assignment. Consider your audience (it should be this class unless you specify a different audience). And remember Aristotle's three appeals. How will your essay employ the appeals of *logos, pathos,* and *ethos*? As you write, keep these two questions in mind: What is your purpose? What do you hope to achieve with your audience?" Brandon's essay is preceded by his analysis of his rhetorical situation and of his essay's appeals to *logos, pathos,* and *ethos.*

thinking rhetorically

Analysis of Rhetorical Situation

I'm writing this essay to explain how I made the most important decision in my life to date: what to major in while in college. I want to explain this not only to my audience but to myself as well, for bold decisions frequently need to be revisited in light of new evidence. There are those for whom the choice of major isn't much of a choice at all. For them, it's a vocation, in the strict Webster's definition of the word: a summons, a calling.

I'm not one of those people, and for me the decision was fraught with anxiety. Do I still believe that I made the right choice? Yes, I do, and I want my essay not only to reflect how serious I feel this issue to be but also to convey the confidence that I finally achieved.

Writer: I'm writing this as a student in a first-year writing class, so while the assignment gives me a lot of flexibility and room for creativity, I need to remember that finally this is an academic essay.

Reader: My primary reader is my teacher in the sense that she's the one who will grade my essay, but she has specified that I should consider the other students in the class as my audience. This tells me that I need to find ways to make the essay interesting to them and to find common ground with them.

Text: This assignment calls for me to write an academic essay. This assignment is different, though, from writing an essay in my history class or a lab report in my chemistry class. Since this is based on my personal experience, I have more freedom than I would in these other classes. One of the most challenging aspects of this essay is its limited page length. It would actually be easier to write a longer essay on why I chose chemistry as my major.

Medium: Our assignment is to write an academic essay. While I could potentially import graphics into my text, I should only do so if it will enrich the content of the essay.

After analyzing his rhetorical situation, Brandon decided to use Aristotle's three appeals to continue and extend his analysis.

Logos: This essay is about my own opinions and experiences and therefore contains no statistics and hard facts. What it should contain, though, are legitimate reasons for choosing the major I did. If I seem insincere or uncertain, then my audience may question the honesty of my essay. My choice should be shown as following a set of believable driving forces.

Pathos: Since my audience is composed of college students, I'll want to appeal to their own experiences regarding their choice of major and the sometimes conflicting emotions that accompany such a decision. Specifically, I want to focus on the confidence and relief that come when you've firmly made up your mind. My audience will be able to relate to these feelings, and it will make the essay more relevant and real to them.

Ethos: The inherent danger in writing an essay about my desire to be a chemistry major is that I may be instantly labeled as boring or snooty. I want to dispel this image as quickly as possible, and humor is always a good way to counter such stereotypes. On the other hand, this is a serious subject, and the infusion of too much humor will portray me as somebody who hasn't given this too much thought. I want to strike a balance between being earnest and being human.

The All-Purpose Answer

BRANDON BARRETT

When I was a small child, I would ask my parents, as children are apt to do, questions concerning the important things in my life. "Why is the sky blue?" "Why do my Cocoa Puffs turn the milk in my cereal bowl brown?" If I asked my father questions such as these, he always provided detailed technical answers that left me solemnly nodding my head in complete confusion. But if I asked my mother, she would simply shrug her shoulders and reply, "Something to do with chemistry, I guess." Needless to say, I grew up with a healthy respect for the apparently boundless powers of chemistry. Its responsibilities seemed staggeringly wide-ranging, and I figured that if there was a God he was probably not an omnipotent deity but actually the Original Chemist.

In my early years, I regarded chemistry as nothing less than magic at work. So what is chemistry, if not magic — or a parent's response to a curious child's persistent questions? Chemistry is the study of the elements, how those elements combine, how they interact with one another, and how all this affects Joe Average down the street. Chemists, then, study not magic but microscopic bits of matter all busily doing their thing.

When all those bits of matter can be coerced into doing something that humans find useful or interesting — like giving off massive quantities of energy, providing lighting for our homes, or making Uncle Henry smell a little better — then the chemists who produced the desired effect can pat themselves on the back and maybe even feel just a little bit like God.

Chemists solve problems, whether the problem is a need for a new medicine or a stronger plastic bowl to pour our Wheaties into. They develop new materials and study existing ones through a variety of techniques that have been refined over the decades. Chemists also struggle to keep the powers of chemistry in check by finding ways to reduce pollution that can be a by-product of chemical processes, to curb the dangers of nuclear waste, and to recycle used materials.

Chemistry is a dynamic field, constantly experiencing new discoveries and applications — heady stuff, to be sure, but heady stuff with a purpose.

Chemistry isn't a static, sleepy field of dusty textbooks, nor does it — forgive me, geologists — revolve around issues of questionable importance, such as deviations in the slope of rock strata. Those who know little about chemistry sometimes view it as dull, but I am proud to say that I plan to earn my B.S. in chemistry. And from there, who knows? That's part of the beauty of chemistry. After graduating from college, I could do any number of things, from research to medical school. The study of chemistry is useful in its own right, but it is also great preparation for advanced study in other fields since it encourages the development of logical thought and reasoning. In one sense, logical thought (not to mention research and medical school) may seem a giant step away from a child's idle questions. But as chemistry demonstrates, perhaps those questions weren't so childish after all.

|||||||||||||||||||||||||||||||||||||||||||||||||||||||||||||||||||||||||||||||||||||||

FOR EXPLORATION

In what ways does Brandon Barrett's essay draw on Aristotle's three appeals? Write one or two paragraphs responding to this question. Be sure to include at least two or three examples in your analysis.

|||||||||||||||||||||||||||||||||||||||||||||||||||||||||||||||||||||||||||||||||||||||

Analyzing Textual Conventions

When you analyze your rhetorical situation, you ask commonsense questions about your writing purpose and situation. As you do so, you draw on your previous experiences as a writer, reader, speaker, and listener. No one had to teach you, for instance, that a letter applying for a job should be written differently than an instant message asking a friend to drop by for pizza. Your social and cultural understanding of job-hunting would automatically cause you to write a formal letter. You make similar judgments as a reader. When you glance through your mail, tossing aside ads while eagerly searching for a letter about a financial aid package, your actions are the result of a rhetorical judgment you're making about the nature and value of these texts.

thinking rhetorically

Whether you are reading or writing, you draw on your previous experiences to make judgments about a text's purpose, subject matter, and form. For familiar kinds of texts, these judgments occur almost automatically. In less familiar situations, you may have to work to understand the form and purpose of a text. I recently received a letter from a former student, Monica Molina, who now works at a community health center, where one of her responsibilities is to write grant proposals. In her letter, she commented:

> It took quite a while before I could feel comfortable even thinking about trying to write my first grant proposal. Most of the ones at our center run 50 to 100 pages and seem so intimidating—full of strange subheadings, technical language, complicated explanations. I had to force myself to calm down and get into them. First I read some recent proposals, trying to figure out how they worked. Luckily, my boss is friendly and supportive, so she sat down with me and talked about her experiences writing proposals. We looked at some proposals together, and she told me about how proposals are reviewed by agencies. Now we're working together on my first proposal. I'm still nervous, but I'm beginning to feel more comfortable.

Students entering a new discipline may be puzzled by unfamiliar language or writing styles. And like Monica, those entering new professions often must learn new forms of writing.

Writers who wish to participate in a new community must strive to understand its reading and writing practices—to learn how to enter its conversation, as the rhetorician Kenneth Burke might say. After all, the forms of writing that characterize different communities reflect important shared assumptions and practices. These shared assumptions and practices—sometimes referred to as textual conventions—represent agreements between writers and readers about how to construct and interpret texts. As such, they are an important component of any rhetorical situation.

The term *textual convention* may be new to you, but you can understand it easily if you think about other uses of the word *convention*. For example, social conventions are implicit agreements among the members of a community or culture about how to act in particular situations. At one time in the United States, for example, it was acceptable for persons who chewed tobacco to spit tobacco juice into spittoons in restaurants and hotel lobbies. This particular social convention has changed over time and is no longer acceptable.

thinking
rhetorically

If social conventions represent agreements among individuals about how to act, textual conventions represent similar agreements about how to write and read texts. Just as we often take our own social conventions for granted, so too do we take for granted those textual conventions most familiar to us as readers and writers. When we begin an email or letter to our parents by writing "Dear Mom and Dad," for instance, we don't stop to wonder if this greeting is appropriate; we know from our experience as writers and readers that it is. Email is so informal that some writers don't even use this salutation but jump right into their message. If they're rhetorically savvy, those composing emails will recognize that when they're writing a work- or school-related email to a superior or teacher, they should include both a salutation and a clear statement of their subject.

Textual conventions are dynamic, changing over time as the assumptions, values, and practices of writers and readers change. Consider some of the textual conventions of email and other online writing. Emoticons, for instance—symbols such as :-) to indicate happiness, :-(to indicate sadness, or :-O to indicate shock or surprise—were developed by online writers to express the kind of emotion often conveyed in face-to-face communication by voice, gesture, and facial expression. Not all who use email use emoticons, and those who do use them know they're more appropriate in some situations than others. But as a textual convention, emoticons clearly respond to the needs of online writers and readers.

SEEING TEXTUAL CONVENTIONS IN USE

Whether you are entering a community of online writers or a new academic or professional community, analyzing your rhetorical situation will enable you to communicate effectively. Because textual conventions play such a critical role in communication between writers and readers, they are an important component of the rhetorical situation. When you think about the kind of writing that you are being asked to do, you are thinking in part about the textual conventions that may limit your options as a writer in a specific situation. Textual conventions bring constraints, but they also increase the likelihood that readers will respond appropriately to your ideas.

The relationship between textual conventions and medium can be critical. Students organizing a protest against increased tuition would hardly write a long analytical essay on this topic. Their goal is to encourage as many students as possible to participate in the protest, so they would be more likely to create an attention-getting flyer that they could inexpensively and quickly create and distribute. After the protest march, they might draft a letter to the editor to summarize the speakers' most important points. They might also set up a blog to post announcements and to encourage student participation.

Some textual conventions are specific. Personal letters typically begin with a greeting and end with a signature. Lab reports usually include the following elements: title page, abstract, introduction, experimental design and methods, results, discussion, and references. Someone writing a lab report can deviate from these textual conventions, but doing so runs the risk of confusing or irritating readers. The medium you choose to compose in can also influence textual conventions. When you communicate through email, you are presented with a predetermined form, with headings that say "To," "Cc," "Bcc," and "Subject."

Other textual conventions are much more general. Consider, for instance, the conventions of an academic essay.

Characteristics of an Effective Academic Essay

- An effective essay is well organized and well developed. It establishes its subject or main idea in the introduction, develops that idea in a coherent manner in the body, and summarizes or completes the discussion in the conclusion.

- An effective essay is logical. It supports its main points with well-chosen evidence, illustrations, and details.

- An effective essay is clear and readable. It uses words, sentences, and paragraphs that are carefully crafted, appropriate for the writer's purpose and subject, and free of errors of usage, grammar, and punctuation.

These statements summarize some of the most general conventions that govern academic essays. Because these statements apply to so many different kinds of writing, you may not know just what they mean in specific situations and in your own writing.

To see how textual conventions operate, let's consider just one of the conventions of an effective essay: It uses an introduction to establish its subject or main idea. This convention is learned early, for many young children introduce stories with the words *Once upon a time.* Most writers and readers understand why an essay needs an introduction. No one likes to be thrown into the middle of a discussion without any idea of the subject. Still, writers aren't always certain about what constitutes the best introduction for a specific essay.

COMPARING AND CONTRASTING TEXTUAL CONVENTIONS

Let's look at three articles by linguist Deborah Tannen to see how one writer tackles the problem of creating an effective and appropriate introduction. Each article is based on Tannen's research into the limitations of what she describes as America's "argument culture," a subject she investigated in her book *The Argument Culture: Stopping America's War of Words.* Tannen is not only a prolific and best-selling writer — she has published 21 books and over 100 articles — but she writes for unusually diverse audiences. If you visit her homepage at <www.georgetown.edu/faculty/tannend/>, you'll notice the following categories for her publications: books, academic publications, general audience publications, and creative writing (poetry, short stories, essays, and plays).

The first article excerpted here — "For Argument's Sake: Why Do We Feel Compelled to Fight about Everything?" (pp. 63–64) — appeared in the Sunday edition of the *Washington Post,* a major newspaper with a large national distribution. The second article — "Agonism in the Academy: Surviving Higher Learning's Argument Culture" (pp. 65–66) — appeared in the *Chronicle of Higher Education.* This weekly newspaper is read by faculty, staff, and administrators in community colleges, four-year colleges, and universities. The final section of each issue of the *Chronicle* concludes with a one-page opinion column. Tannen's article appeared as such a column. The final article excerpted here — "Agonism in Academic Discourse" (pp. 67–68) — was published in the *Journal of Pragmatics,* a British scholarly publication for people who are interested in such topics as pragmatics (the study of language as it is used in a social context), semantics, language acquisition, and so on. Those who read this journal work in academic disciplines such as linguistics, sociology, psychology, anthropology, and philosophy. (Note that the article follows the British style of punctuation.)

For Argument's Sake

Why Do We Feel Compelled to Fight About Everything?

By Deborah Tannen

I was waiting to go on a television talk show a few years ago for a discussion about how men and women communicate, when a man walked in wearing a shirt and tie and a floor-length skirt, the top of which was brushed by his waist-length red hair. He politely introduced himself and told me that he'd read and liked my book *You Just Don't Understand,* which had just been published. Then he added, "When I get out there, I'm going to attack you. But don't take it personally. That's why they invite me on, so that's what I'm going to do."

We went on the set and the show began. I had hardly managed to finish a sentence or two before the man threw his arms out in gestures of anger, and began shrieking — briefly hurling accusations at me, and then railing at length against women. The strangest thing about his hysterical outburst was how the studio audience reacted: They turned vicious — not attacking me (I hadn't said anything substantive yet) or him (who wants to tangle with someone who screams at you?) but the other guests: women who had come to talk about problems they had communicating with their spouses.

My antagonist was nothing more than a dependable provocateur, brought on to ensure a lively

show. The incident has stayed with me not because it was typical of the talk shows I have appeared on — it wasn't, I'm happy to say — but because it exemplifies the ritual nature of much of the opposition that pervades our public dialogue.

Everywhere we turn, there is evidence that, in public discourse, we prize contentiousness and aggression more than cooperation and conciliation. Headlines blare about the Starr Wars, the Mommy Wars, the Baby Wars, the Mammography Wars; everything is posed in terms of battles and duels, winners and losers, conflicts and disputes. Biographies have metamorphosed into demonographies whose authors don't just portray their subjects warts and all, but set out to dig up as much dirt as possible, as if the story of a person's life is contained in the warts, only the warts, and nothing but the warts.

It's all part of what I call the argument culture, which rests on the assumption that opposition is the best way to get anything done: The best way to discuss an idea is to set up a debate. The best way to cover news is to find people who express the most extreme views and present them as "both sides." The best way to begin an essay is to attack someone. The best way to show you're really thoughtful is to criticize. The best way to settle disputes is to litigate them.

It is the automatic nature of this response that I am calling into question. This is not to say that passionate opposition and strong verbal attacks are never appropriate. In the words of the Yugoslavian-born poet Charles Simic, "There are moments in life when true invective is called for, when it becomes an absolute necessity, out of a deep sense of justice, to denounce, mock, vituperate, lash out, in the strongest possible language." What I'm questioning is the ubiquity, the knee-jerk nature of approaching almost any issue, problem or public person in an adversarial way.

Smashing heads does not open minds. In this as in so many things, results are also causes, looping back and entrapping us. The pervasiveness of warlike formats and language grows out of, but also gives rise to, an ethic of aggression: We come to value aggressive tactics for their own sake — for the sake of argument. Compromise becomes a dirty word, and we often feel guilty if we are conciliatory rather than confrontational — even if we achieve the result we're seeking.

Here's one example. A woman called another talk show on which I was a guest. She told the following story: "I was in a place where a man was smoking, and there was a no-smoking sign. Instead of saying 'You aren't allowed to smoke in here. Put that out!' I said, 'I'm awfully sorry, but I have asthma, so your smoking makes it hard for me to breathe. Would you mind terribly not smoking?' When I said this, the man was extremely polite and solicitous, and he put his cigarette out, and I said, 'Oh, thank you, thank you!' as if he'd done a wonderful thing for me. Why did I do that?"

I think this woman expected me — the communications expert — to say she needs assertiveness training to confront smokers in a more aggressive manner. Instead, I told her that her approach was just fine. If she had tried to alter his behavior by reminding him of the rules, he might well have rebelled: "Who made you the enforcer? Mind your own business!" She had given the smoker a face-saving way of doing what she wanted, one that allowed him to feel chivalrous rather than chastised. This was kinder to him, but it was also kinder to herself, since it was more likely to lead to the result she desired.

Another caller disagreed with me, saying the first caller's style was "self-abasing." I persisted: There was nothing necessarily destructive about the way the woman handled the smoker. The mistake the second caller was making — a mistake many of us make — was to confuse ritual self-effacement with the literal kind. All human relations require us to find ways to get what we want from others without seeming to dominate them.

The opinions expressed by the two callers encapsulate the ethic of aggression that has us by our throats, particularly in public arenas such as politics and law.

Issues are routinely approached by having two sides stake out opposing positions and do battle. This sometimes drives people to take positions that are more adversarial than they feel — and can get in the way of reaching a possible resolution. I have experienced this firsthand.

For my book about the workplace, "Talking from 9 to 5," I spent time in companies, shadowing people, interviewing them and having individuals tape conversations when I wasn't there. Most companies were happy to proceed on a verbal agreement setting forth certain ground rules: Individuals would control the taping, identifying names would be changed, I would show them what I wrote about their company and change or delete anything they did not approve. I also signed confidentiality agreements promising not to reveal anything I learned about the company's business.

Some companies, however, referred the matter to their attorneys so a contract could be written. In no case where attorneys became involved — mine as well as theirs — could we reach an agreement on working together.

Negotiations with one company stand out. Having agreed on the procedures and safeguards, we expected to have a contract signed in a matter of weeks. But six months later, after thousands of dollars in legal fees and untold hours of everyone's time, the negotiations reached a dead end. The company's lawyer was demanding veto power over my entire book; it meant the company could (if it chose) prevent me from publishing the book even if I used no more than a handful of examples from this

Agonism in the Academy: Surviving Higher Learning's Argument Culture

By Deborah Tannen

A READING GROUP that I belong to, composed of professors, recently discussed a memoir by an academic. I came to the group's meeting full of anticipation, eager to examine the insights I'd gained from the book and to be enlightened by those that had intrigued my fellow group members. As the meeting began, one member announced that she hadn't read the book; four, including me, said they'd read and enjoyed it; and one said she hadn't liked it because she does not like academic memoirs. She energetically criticized the book. "It's written in two voices," she said, "and the voices don't interrogate each other."

Quickly, two other members joined her critique, their point of view becoming a chorus. They sounded smarter, seeing faults that the rest of us had missed, making us look naive. We credulous three tried in vain to get the group talking about what we had found interesting or important in the book, but our suggestions were dull compared to the game of critique.

I left the meeting disappointed because I had learned nothing new about the book or its subject. All I had learned about was the acumen of the critics. I was especially struck by the fact that one of the most talkative and influential critics was the member who had not read the book. Her unfamiliarity with the work had not hindered her, because the critics had focused more on what they saw as faults of the genre than on faults of the particular book.

The turn that the discussion had taken reminded me of the subject of my most recent book, *The*

Argument Culture. The phenomenon I'd observed at the book-group meeting was an example of what the cultural linguist Walter Ong calls "agonism," which he defines in *Fighting for Life* as "programmed contentiousness" or "ceremonial combat." Agonism does not refer to disagreement, conflict, or vigorous dispute. It refers to retualized opposition — for instance, a debate in which the contestants are assigned opposing positions and one party wins, rather than an argument that arises naturally when two parties disagree.

In *The Argument Culture,* I explored the role and effects of agonism in three domains of public discourse: journalism, politics, and the law. But the domain in which I first identified the phenomenon and began thinking about it is the academic world. I remain convinced that agonism is endemic in academe — and bad for it.

The way we train our students, conduct our classes and our research, and exchange ideas at meetings and in print are all driven by our ideological assumption that intellectual inquiry is a metaphorical battle. Following from that is a second assumption, that the best way to demonstrate intellectual prowess is to criticize, find fault, and attack.

Many aspects of our academic lives can be described as agonistic. For example, in our scholarly papers, most of us follow a conventional framework that requires us to position our work in opposition to someone else's, which we prove wrong. The framework tempts — almost requires — us to oversimplify or even misrepresent others' positions; cite the weakest example to make a generally resonable work appear less so; and ignore facts that supports others' views, citing only evidence that supports our own positions.

The way we train our students frequently reflects the battle metaphor as well. We assign scholarly work for them to read, then invite them to tear it apart. That is helpful to an extent, but it often means that they don't learn to do the harder work of integrating ideas, or of considering the work's historical and disciplinary context. Moreover,

it fosters in students a stance of arrogance and narrow-mindedness, qualities that do not serve the fundamental goals of education.

In the classroom, if students are engaged in heated debate, we believe that education is taking place. But in a 1993 article in *The History Teacher,* Patricia Rosof, who teaches at Hunter College High School in New York City, advises us to look more closely at what's really happening. If we do, she says, we will probably find that only a few students are participating; some other students may be paying attention, but many may be turned off. Furthermore, the students who are arguing generally simplify the points they are making or disputing. To win the argument, they ignore complexity and nuance. The refuse to concede a point raised by their opponents, even if they can see that it is valid, because such a concession would weaken their position. Nobody tries to synthesize the various views, because that would look indecisive, or weak.

If the class engages in discussion rather than debate — adding such intellectual activities as exploring ideas, uncovering nuances, comparing and contrasting different interpretations of a work — more students take part, and more of them gain a deeper, and more accurate, understanding of the material. Most important, the students learn a stance of respect and open-minded inquiry.

Academic rewards — good grades and good jobs — typically go to students and scholars who learn to tear down others' work, not to those who learn to build on the work of their colleagues. In *The Argument Culture,* I cited a study in which communications researchers Karen Tracy and Sheryl Baratz ex-

amined weekly colloquia attended by faculty members and graduate students at a large university. As the authors reported in a 1993 article in *Communication Monographs,* although most people said the purpose of the colloquia was to "trade ideas" and "learn things," faculty members in fact were judging the students' competence based on their participation in the colloquia. And the professors didn't admire students who asked "a nice little supportive question," as one put it — they valued "tough and challenging questions."

One problem with the agonistic culture of graduate training is that potential scholars who are not comfortable with that kind of interaction are likely to drop out. As a result, many talented and creative minds are lost to academe. And, with fewer colleagues who prefer different approaches, those who remain are more likely to egg each other on to even grater adversarial heights. Some scholars who do stay in acaceme are reluctant to present their work at conferences or submit it for publication because of their reluctance to take part in adversarial discourse. The cumulative effect is that nearly everyone feels vulnerable and defensive, and thus less willing to suggest new ideas, offer new perspectives, or question received wisdom.

Although scholarly attacks are ritual — prescribed by the conventions of academe — the emotions propelling them can be real. Jane Tompkins, a literary critic who has written about the genre of the western in modern fiction and film, has compared scholarly exchanges to shootouts. In a 1988 article in *The Georgia Review,* she noted that her own career took off when she published an essay that "began with a

Journal of Pragmatics 34 (2002) 1651–1669

journal of
PRAGMATICS

www.elsevier.com/locate/pragma

Agonism in academic discourse[☆]

Deborah Tannen

Linguistics Department, Georgetown University, Box 571051, Washington DC 20057-1051, USA

Abstract

The pervasiveness of agonism, that is, ritualized adversativeness, in contemporary western academic discourse is the source of both obfuscation of knowledge and personal suffering in academia. Framing academic discourse as a metaphorical battle leads to a variety of negative consequences, many of which have ethical as well as personal dimensions. Among these consequences is a widespread assumption that critical dialogue is synonymous with negative critique, at the expense of other types of 'critical thinking'. Another is the requirement that scholars search for weaknesses in others' work at the expense of seeking strengths, understanding the roots of theoretical differences, or integrating disparate but related ideas. Agonism also encourages the conceptualization of complex and subtle work as falling into two simplified warring camps. Finally, it leads to the exclusion or marginalization of those who lack a taste for agonistic interchange. Alternative approaches to intellectual interchange need not entirely replace agonistic ones but should be accommodated alongside them. © 2002 Elsevier Science B.V. All rights reserved.

Keywords: Academic discourse; Agonism; Disagreement; Ritualized opposition; Exclusion

---

☆ Varying versions of this paper were delivered at the Georgetown Linguistics Society 1995, Washington, DC; Georgetown University Round Table on Languages and Linguistics 1999, Washington, D.C.; Pragma99, Tel Aviv, Israel, August 1999; and as the Hayward Keniston Lecture, University of Michigan, October 27, 1999. A briefer account, written for a more general audience, appears as "Agonism in the Academy: Surviving Higher Learning's Argument Culture", The Chronicle of Higher Education March 31, 2000, B7-8. Some sections of the present paper are based on material that appears in my book The Argument Culture; most, however, is new. I would like to thank Elizabeth Eisenstein, Shari Kendall, Joseph P. Newhouse, and Keli Yerian for leading me to sources that I cite here. For thoughtful comments on an earlier draft, I am grateful to A.L. Becker, Paul Friedrich, Susan Gal, Heidi Hamilton, Natalie Schilling-Estes, Ron Scollon, Malcah Yaeger-Dror, and three anonymous reviewers. This contribution is dedicated to the memory of Suzanne Fleischman, whose death which occurred while I was working on the paper cast a shadow of sadness, and whose own work, like her article cited here, made such an enormous contribution to restoring the person of the scholar to scholarship.

E-mail address: tannend@georgetown.edu (D. Tannen).

0378-2166/02/$ - see front matter © 2002 Elsevier Science B.V. All rights reserved.
PII: S0378-2166(02)00079-6

1652   *D. Tannen / Journal of Pragmatics 34 (2002) 1651–1669*

1. Introduction and overview

In doing discourse analysis, we use discourse to do our analysis, yet we seldom examine the discourse we use. There are, of course, important exceptions, such as Tracy (1997) on departmental colloquia, Fleischman (1998) on the erasure of the personal in academic writing, Goffman (1981) on "The Lecture", Herring (1996) on e-mail lists, Chafe and Danielewicz (1987) who include "academic speaking" and "academic writing" in their comparison of spoken and written language, and Swales' (1990) study of academic writing as well as his recent examination of the physical and interactional contexts that give rise to it (1998). Perhaps most closely related to my topic is Hunston (1993), who examines oppositional argumentation in biology, history, and sociolinguistics articles (two each), and concludes that the less empirical disciplines are more 'argumentative'. Here I turn my attention to an aspect of academic discourse that, as far I know, has not previously been examined: what I call "agonism".

Ong (1981: 24), from whom I borrow the term, defines agonism as "programmed contentiousness", "ceremonial combat". I use the term to refer not to conflict, disagreement, or disputes per se, but rather to *ritualized* adversativeness. In academic discourse, this means conventionalized oppositional formats that result from an underlying ideology by which intellectual interchange is conceptualized as a metaphorical battle. In a recent book (Tannen, 1998), I explore the role and effects of agonism in three domains of public discourse: journalism, politics, and law. Here I turn to the discourse domain in which I first identified the phenomenon and began thinking about it: the academy.

My goal is to uncover agonistic elements in academic discourse and to examine their effects on our pursuit of knowledge and on the community of scholars engaged in that pursuit. In arguing that an ideology of agonism provides a usually unquestioned foundation for much of our oral and written interchange, I focus on exposing the destructive aspects of this ideology and its attendant practices. I do not, however, call for an end to agonism – a goal that would be unrealistic even if it were desirable, which I am not sure it is. Rather, I argue for a broadening of our modes of inquiry, so that agonism is, one might say, demoted from its place of ascendancy, and for a re-keying or 'toning down' of the more extreme incarnations of agonism in academic discourse.

In what follows, I begin by sketching my own early interest in agonism in conversational discourse. Then I briefly present some historical background, tracing the seeds of agonism in academic discourse to classical Greek philosophy and the medieval university. Against this backdrop, I move to examining agonistic elements as well as the cultural and ideological assumptions that underlie them in academic discourse: both spoken (at conferences, in classrooms, and in intellectual discussions) and written (in grant proposals, journal articles, books, and reviews of all of these). I demonstrate some unfortunate consequences of the agonistic character of these discourse types, both for the pursuit of knowledge and for the community of scholars and others who hope to gain from our knowledge. I then suggest that the existence and perpetuation of agonistic elements in academic discourse depends on

||||||||||||||||||||||||||||||||||||||||||||||||||||||||||||||||||||||||||||||||||||||

FOR EXPLORATION

Read the introductions to Tannen's three articles (pp. 63–68), and write three paragraphs characterizing their approaches—one paragraph for each article. (Be sure to read the abstract and the footnote on the first page of the article from the *Journal of Pragmatics,* which provide important clues about Tannen's rhetorical situation and the interests and expectations of her scholarly readers.) How would you describe Tannen's tone in each article? What kind of language does she use in each one? What can you learn from your analysis about the differences among these articles?

||||||||||||||||||||||||||||||||||||||||||||||||||||||||||||||||||||||||||||||||||||||

By glancing at the first pages of Tannen's three articles, you'll notice some striking differences among them. The first page of "For Argument's Sake: Why Do We Feel Compelled to Fight about Everything?" (p. 63), has a good deal of white space and large illustrations. These illustrations, along with the title of the article, help draw readers into Tannen's text. After all, the *Washington Post* is a large multi-section newspaper, and the Sunday edition is much larger than the daily edition. If Tannen and her editors hope to capture readers' interest, they must draw their attention in a dramatic way.

The incident that Tannen describes at the start of her article is certainly dramatic. She recalls her encounter with a strangely dressed man with waist-long red hair who, like her, is waiting to appear on a television show. After he praises her book *You Just Don't Understand,* the man announces that "When I get out there, I'm going to attack you. But don't take it personally. That's why they invite me on, so that's what I'm going to do." After describing the rest of this incident and reflecting on her antagonist, Tannen moves to the major assertion of her article: "Everywhere we turn, there is evidence that, in public discourse, we prize contentiousness and aggression more than cooperation and conciliation." The rest of her article provides examples of a widespread argument culture in America and suggests some of that culture's limitations.

The second article, from the *Chronicle of Higher Education* (p. 65), is more visually dense than the first—though it does have some white space and a drawing of stylized boxers at the bottom of the first page. Rather than using an attention-getting title, in this article Tannen uses the scholarly term *agonism* to identify her subject. She does appeal to her readers' interests, however, with her subtitle, "Surviving Higher Learning's Argument Culture." Most readers would be aware that the academy can be a difficult and argumentative place, so they would appreciate knowing how best to survive in such a climate.

In the *Chronicle* article, as in the first article, Tannen begins by recounting an incident that suggests a culture of argument. Since her readers are educators, she focuses on an experience they might share—participating in a reading group whose members find it easier to criticize than praise a book (even when they haven't read it). After reflecting on this incident, she mentions her recently published book *The Argument Culture* and clarifies what she means by agonism. After briefly describing her book, she sets out the thesis of her article: "The way we train our students, conduct our classes and our research, and exchange ideas at meetings and in print are all driven by our ideological assumption that intellectual inquiry is a metaphorical battle. Following from that is a second assumption, that the best way to demonstrate intellectual prowess is to criticize, find fault, and attack." In the remainder of this article, Tannen provides evidence to support her assertions, considers some of the negative consequences of agonism in the academy, and (in a brief closing paragraph) affirms the benefits of changing the culture of the academy. If the latter would happen, Tannen argues, academics "would learn more from each other, be heard more clearly by others, attract more varied talents to the scholarly life, and restore a measure of humanity to ourselves, our endeavor, and the academic world we inhabit."

An important difference between the *Washington Post* article and the *Chronicle of Higher Education* article involves the examples and evidence that Tannen provides. In the *Post* article, Tannen focuses on examples that a broad range of readers can identify with, such as a phone call to a call-in talk show, the adversarial nature of the legal process, and the ritual attacks on politicians that often appear in the popular press. However, in the *Chronicle* article, she provides a limited range of examples that involve academic life. She also supports her position by citing other scholars whose research supports her position. In these and other ways, Tannen adjusts her argument to address her particular rhetorical situation.

Tannen's third article (p. 67) appeared in the *Journal of Pragmatics,* a specialized publication that has the most cramped and least inviting first page. Rather than using an attention-getting title, Tannen simply announces her subject: "Agonism in Academic Discourse." The article begins with a full page of prefatory material: the article title, the author's name and university address, an abstract, keywords, and a lengthy footnote that mentions previous versions of the article and makes extensive acknowledgments of people who assisted Tannen in writing it.

The article itself is divided into sections with numbered headings. The first section, "Introduction and overview," begins with a dense and heavily referenced discussion of the fact that "In doing discourse analysis, we [scholars] use discourse to do our analysis, yet we seldom examine the discourse we use." After acknowledging exceptions to this statement, Tannen stakes out a major claim for her article: "Here I turn my attention to an aspect of academic discourse that, as far [as] I know, has not previously been examined: what I call 'agonism.'" (Because originality is highly prized in the academy, Tannen's claim that her subject "has not previously been examined" is particularly strong.) After providing further information about this term,

Tannen establishes the framework for her article: "My goal is to uncover ago‐nistic elements in academic discourse and to examine their effects on our pursuit of knowledge and on the community of scholars engaged in that pursuit." Unlike the *Post* and *Chronicle* articles, which are relatively brief, Tannen's article in the *Journal of Pragmatics* is eighteen densely argued pages long. In subsequent sections, she covers such topics as the roots of agonism in ancient Greek and medieval church discourse. Clearly, Tannen expects much more of readers of this scholarly article than she does of readers of the previous two articles. She assumes that readers will be familiar with the many references she cites or will at least appreciate their inclusion. She also as‐sumes that readers will have considerable prior knowledge of her topic and will care deeply about it.

Analyzing the first few pages of each article supplies important clues about these three publications and about Tannen's expectations about their readers. In the less specialized publications, Tannen tries hard to interest readers in her subject. The publishers of those periodicals also seem to pay more attention to visual images and design elements like white space. People who read the *Washington Post,* the most general and least specialized of these publications, often don't have a clear purpose when they read. They purchase newspapers to learn about recent news and to keep up with recent intellec‐tual, cultural, economic, and political developments. Even a person who spends a couple of hours reading the Sunday paper might well pass over Tannen's article. Consequently, a writer like Tannen will attempt to gain these readers' attention — and so will the editors who commission illustra‐tions and design the visual look of the text.

Subscribers to the weekly *Chronicle of Higher Education* represent a more specialized — though still diverse — readership. They either work in or are in‐terested in higher education. One reader might be a faculty member in the hu‐manities; such a reader might well be interested in Tannen's essay. But other readers might work in admissions, financial aid, or athletics. For these read‐ers, the term *agonism* might be unfamiliar. Moreover, just as readers skim daily newspapers like the *Washington Post,* so too do many readers skim the *Chronicle.* As a consequence, even though the readership of the *Chronicle* is less diverse than that of the *Post,* Tannen uses a similar introductory strategy for each ar‐ticle: a catchy title or subtitle, and an interesting opening anecdote.

Tannen faces a different rhetorical situation in addressing readers of the scholarly *Journal of Pragmatics.* If readers of the *Post* and the *Chronicle* read — or skim — these publications to keep current, subscribers to the *Jour‐nal of Pragmatics* read this journal to keep up with advances in their field. These readers undoubtedly subscribe to many professional publications. They don't have the time to read every article, so they skim the tables of con‐tents, noting articles that affect their own research or have broad significance for their field. The prefatory material in Tannen's third article matters very much to them; they can review the abstract to determine not only *if* but also *how* they will read the article. Some will read only an article's abstract, others

thinking rhetorically

will skim the major points, and others will read the article with great care, returning to it as they conduct their own research. Readers of the *Journal of Pragmatics* wouldn't want an engaging introduction like the ones Tannen includes in the *Post* and the *Chronicle* articles. Instead, they want a straightforward, concise approach. They value clear, specific headings and scholarly citations over inviting titles, illustrations, and opening anecdotes.

Although these three articles are grounded in the same research project, they differ dramatically in structure, tone, language, and approach to readers. Textual conventions play an important role in these differences. As shared agreements about the construction and interpretation of texts, textual conventions enable readers and writers to communicate successfully in different rhetorical situations.

|||||||||||||||||||||||||||||||||||||||||||||||||||||||||||||||||||||||||||||||||||||||||

FOR EXPLORATION

1. What kinds of examples are used in each excerpt of Tannen's articles? What function do they serve?

2. What relationship is established in each article between the writer and the reader? What cues signal each relationship?

3. How would you characterize the styles of these three excerpts? Point to specific features that characterize each style. What is the effect of these stylistic differences?

4. What assumptions does Tannen make in each article about what readers already know? Point out specific instances that reflect these assumptions.

5. How would you describe the persona, or image of the writer, in each article? What factors contribute to the development and coherence of this persona?

|||||||||||||||||||||||||||||||||||||||||||||||||||||||||||||||||||||||||||||||||||||||||

Understanding the Conventions of Academic Writing

Some textual conventions are easy to identify. After reading just a few lab reports, for example, you recognize that this form of writing adheres to a set format. Other textual conventions are less easy to discern and to understand. When you join a new community of writers and readers, as you do when you enter college, you need to understand the demands of the writing you are expected to complete. Look again, for instance, at the Characteristics of an Effective Academic Essay on p. 61. When you first read these characteristics, they probably made sense to you. Of course, essays should be well organized, well developed, and logical.

When you begin work on an essay for history, sociology, or economics, however, you may find it difficult to determine how to embody these characteristics in your own writing. You might wonder what will make your analysis of the economic impact of divorce on the modern family logical or illogical. What do economists consider to be appropriate evidence, illustrations, and details? And does your economics teacher value the same kind of logic, evidence, and details as your American literature teacher? For more advice about effective writing in a variety of academic disciplines, see Chapter 7.

✳ bedfordstmartins.com/academicwriter
For a collection of dozens of sample student projects written for courses across the disciplines, go to **Re:Writing** *and then click on* **Model Documents Gallery**.

NOTE FOR MULTILINGUAL WRITERS

The conventions of academic writing vary from culture to culture. If you were educated in another country or language, you may have written successful academic texts that followed textual conventions that differ from those you have to follow now. Conventions that can differ in various cultures include the rhetorical strategies that introduce essay topics, the placement of thesis statements, the kinds of information that qualify as objective evidence in argumentation, the use (or absence) of explicit transitions, and the use (or absence) of first-person pronouns.

   Given these and other potential differences, you may find it helpful to compare the conventions of academic writing in North America with those of your home culture.

FOR EXPLORATION

Freewrite for five or ten minutes about your experiences thus far with academic writing. What do you find productive and satisfying about it? What seems difficult and frustrating? Does your ability to respond to the demands of academic writing vary depending on the discipline? Do you find writing essays about literature easier, for instance, than writing lab reports and case studies? What makes some kinds of academic writing harder or easier for you? If you are a multilingual writer, you may also want to consider how your involvement in multiple language communities influences your experiences as an academic writer of English.

USING TEXTUAL CONVENTIONS

You already know enough about rhetoric and the rhetorical situation to real-ize that there can be no one-size-fits-all approach to every academic writing situation.

thinking rhetorically What can you do when you are unfamiliar with the textual conventions of academic writing in general or of a particular discipline? A rhetorical approach suggests that one solution is to read examples of the kind of writing you wish to do. Discussing these models with an insider—your teacher, per-haps, or an advanced student in the field—can help you understand why these conventions work for such readers and writers. Forming a study group or meeting with a tutor can also increase your rhetorical sensitivity to your teachers' expectations and the conventions of academic writing.

Finally, a rhetorical approach to communication encourages you to think strategically about writing—whether personal, professional, or academic—and to respond creatively to the challenges of each situation. As a writer, you have much to consider: your own goals as a writer, the nature of your subject and writing task, the expectations of your readers, the textual conventions your particular situation requires or allows, the medium in which to express your ideas. The rhetorical sensitivity that you have already developed can help you respond appropriately to these and other concerns. But you can also draw on other resources—on textual examples and on discussions with teachers, tutors, and other students. As a writer, you are not alone. By reach-ing out to other writers, in person or by reading their work, you can become a fully participating member of the academic community.

||||||||||||||||||||||||||||||||||||||||||||||||||||||||||||||||||||||||||||||||||||||

FOR EXPLORATION

Interview a teacher in another course you are taking this term, preferably one in which you have done some writing, so that you can learn more about his or her expectations of student writing. You may wish to ask some or all of the following questions:

1. What do you look for when you read students' writing? How would you char-acterize effective student writing in your discipline?

2. In your discipline, what is the difference between an A and a C student essay (or lab report or case study)?

3. What are the major weaknesses or limitations of the writing produced by your students?

4. What advice would you give to students who want to understand how to write more effectively in classes in your field?

5. Do you think your discipline values qualities in student writing not necessarily shared by other fields, or is good writing considered good writing no matter what the discipline?

6. Could you suggest some examples that I could read that would help me understand the conventions of effective writing in your discipline?

7. What are the differences between effective student writing and effective professional writing in your field?

8. What role do you see yourself playing when you read student writing?

9. Is there anything else you can tell me that would help me better understand the kind of student writing valued in your discipline?

After your interview, write a summary of your teacher's responses. Then write at least two paragraphs reflecting on what this interview has taught you about academic writing.

FOR COLLABORATION

Once you have completed the preceding Exploration, meet with a group of classmates. Begin by reading your summaries out loud. Working together (be sure to appoint a recorder), answer these questions:

- Can you find three statements or beliefs shared by all the people interviewed?

- What were some major points of disagreement? Did some faculty members feel, for instance, that good student writing is good student writing no matter what the discipline, while others believed that their discipline values particular qualities in student writing?

- What surprised you in the interviews? Briefly explain why you were surprised.

- What did these interviews help you understand about academic writing? Include at least three statements that reflect your group's discussion of your interviews.

Be prepared to share your findings with the rest of the class.

FOR THOUGHT, DISCUSSION, AND WRITING

1. From a newspaper or a magazine, choose an essay, an editorial, or a column that you think succeeds in its purpose. Now turn back to the Questions for Analyzing Your Rhetorical Situation on pp. 44–46, and answer the questions as if you were the writer of the text you have chosen. To answer the questions, look for evidence of the writer's intentions in the writing

(continued)

itself. (To determine what image or persona the writer wanted to portray, for instance, look at the kind of language the writer uses. Is it formal or conversational? Full of interesting images and vivid details or serious examples and statistics?) Answer each of the questions suggested by the guidelines. Then write a paragraph or more reflecting on what you have learned from this analysis.

2. Annette Chambers and Brandon Barrett did a good job in anticipating their readers' expectations and interests. In writing their essays, they focused not just on content (what they wanted to say) but also on strategy (how they might convey their ideas to their readers). Not all interactions between writer and reader are as successful. You may have read textbooks that seemed more concerned with the subject matter than with readers' needs and expectations. Or you may have received direct mail advertising or other business communications that irritated or offended you. Find an example of writing that in your view fails to anticipate the expectations and needs of the reader, and write one or two paragraphs explaining your reasons. Your teacher may ask you to share your example and written explanation with your classmates.

3. Write an essay that summarizes and reflects on what you have learned about academic writing as a result of completing the Exploration on pp. 74–75 and the group activity on p. 75.

4. Analyze the ways in which the following three print advertisements (pp. 77–79) draw on Aristotle's three appeals: *logos, pathos,* and *ethos.*

||||||||||||||||||||||||||||||||||||||||||||||||||||||||||||||||||||||||||||||||||||||||||||||||

Ad for U.S. Army

Ad for Habitat for Humanity

Public Service Ad for the National Youth Anti-Drug Media Campaign

CHAPTER 4

Analyzing Texts
and Contexts

thinking
rhetorically

A rhetorical approach to writing looks at the various contexts in which you write. Even if you are writing alone at your computer, you are writing in the context of a specific rhetorical situation. By analyzing that situation, you can identify your purpose and goals as a writer, develop an appropriate persona or voice, and create a relationship with readers. You also can understand and implement the appropriate textual conventions for courses across the curriculum.

Gaining an understanding of context is particularly important when you enter a new community of writers and readers. As you enter the academic community, you need to develop an insider's understanding of the conventions that characterize academic writing. Some of these conventions apply across the disciplines; for example, a successful academic essay must reflect an open, unbiased intellectual engagement with the subject—whether that subject is a Renaissance painting or the Central Bank and the monetary system. Moreover, the logic behind these conclusions and the evidence for them must be provided in the writing so that readers can understand (and possibly question) the writer's assumptions and conclusions.

In an important sense, then, college instructors believe that all academic writing involves argument. But the model of argument they have in mind isn't about winning or losing a debate; it involves using evidence and reasoning to discover a version of truth about a particular subject. I use the words *a version* here to emphasize that the truth is always in process in academic writing and is always open to further discussion. A political scientist or economist who makes a convincing argument about federal policy on harvesting timber in national forests knows that others will add to, challenge, or refine that argument. In fact, having others respond to an observation is a sign that the writing has successfully raised questions that others consider important. In this sense, the scholarly work of the academy is like a conversation rather than a debate.

Understanding Your Audience

Because your instructors are the primary readers of your college writing, you need to understand their values and their goals for you and other students. They all share a commitment to the ideal of education as inquiry. Whether they teach in business, liberal arts, agriculture, engineering, or other fields, your instructors want to foster your ability to think, write, and speak well. When they read your papers and exams, they're looking for evidence of both your knowledge of a subject and your ability to think and write clearly and effectively.

But your instructors will not necessarily bring identical expectations to your writing. Methods of inquiry and research questions vary from discipline to discipline, and textual conventions reflect these differences. A lab report for a chemistry class will use different kinds of evidence and organizational patterns than an essay for an American literature class. Stylistic expectations also vary among disciplines. Passive voice (as in *It was discovered . . .*) is more common in the sciences than in the humanities, for instance.

Despite these disciplinary differences, college instructors generally agree that educated, thoughtful, and knowledgeable college graduates share certain characteristics. They believe, for instance, that perhaps the worst intellectual error is oversimplifying. They want their students to go beyond simplistic analysis and arguments to deeper and more complex understandings. Thus a historian might urge students to recognize that more was at stake in the American Civil War than freeing the slaves, and an engineer might encourage students to realize that the most obvious way to resolve a design problem isn't necessarily the best way.

Most college instructors want students to be able to do more than memorize or summarize information. Indeed, they strive to develop students' abilities to analyze, apply, question, and evaluate information. They also want students to consider multiple perspectives, to recognize that nearly every issue has at least two sides. Because most intellectual issues are complex, instructors often teach students to limit the issue, question, or problem under discussion. They also believe that arguments should be supported by substantial and appropriate evidence, not logical fallacies.

Such habits of mind are intrinsically rewarding. The knowledge that you can analyze a complex issue or problem, work through an argument, and develop your own position on a subject brings intellectual satisfaction and confidence. These same habits of thinking also bring extrinsic rewards, for as executives in business and industry emphasize, they are precisely the habits of mind that lead to success in any field. And they also enable you to participate effectively as a citizen of the world.

What do instructors look for in students' writing? Most broadly, they want evidence of learning and a real commitment to and engagement with the subject. Particularly in the humanities, they want to see that you are making connections between the issues discussed in class and your own life and personal values. And they always want adherence to academic standards of clear thinking and effective communication. Specifically, most instructors hope to find the following characteristics in student writing:

- A limited but significant topic

- A meaningful context for discussion of the topic

- A sustained and full development of ideas, given the limitations of the topic, time, and length

- A clear pattern of organization

- Fair and effective use of sources (both print and online)

- Adequate detail and evidence as support for generalizations

- Appropriate, concise language

- Conventional grammar, punctuation, and usage

The following essay, written by Hope Leman for a class on politics and the media, meets these criteria. The essay was a response to the following assignment for a take-home midterm exam:

> Journalists often suggest that they simply mirror reality. Some political scientists argue, however, that rather than mirroring reality journalists make judgments that subtly but significantly shape their resulting news reports. In so doing, scholars argue, journalists function more like flashlights than like mirrors. Write an essay in which you contrast the "mirror" and "flashlight" models of the role of journalists in American society.
>
> Successful essays will not only compare these two models but will also provide examples supporting their claims.

thinking rhetorically

Since Hope was writing a take-home midterm essay, she didn't have time to do a formal written analysis of her rhetorical situation. Still, her essay demonstrates considerable rhetorical sensitivity. Hope understands, for instance, that given her situation she should emphasize content rather than employ a dramatic or highly personal style. Hope's essay is, above all, clearly written. Even though it has moments of quiet humor (as when she comments on funhouses at the end of paragraph 2), the focus is on articulating the reasons why the "flashlight" model of media theory is the most valid and helpful for political scientists. Hope knows that her teacher will be reading a stack of midterms under time pressure, so she makes sure that her own writing is carefully organized and to the point.

The Role of Journalists in American
Society: A Comparison of the "Mirror"
and "Flashlight" Models

HOPE LEMAN

The "mirror" model of media theory holds that through their writing and
news broadcasts journalists are an objective source of information for the
public. This model assumes that journalists are free of bias and can be relied on to provide accurate information about the true state of affairs in
the world. Advocates of the "flashlight" model disagree, believing that a
journalist is like a person in a dark room holding a flashlight. The light
from the flashlight falls briefly on various objects in the room, revealing
part — but not all — of the room at any one time. This model assumes that
journalists cannot possibly provide an objective view of reality but, at
best, can convey only a partial understanding of a situation or event.

In this essay, I will argue that the "flashlight" model provides a more
accurate and complex understanding of the role of journalists in America than the "mirror" model does. This model recognizes, for instance,
that journalists are shaped by their personal backgrounds and experiences and by the pressures, mores, and customs of their profession. It
also recognizes that journalists are under commercial pressure to sell
their stories. Newspapers and commercial networks are run on a for-
profit basis. Thus reporters have to "sell" their stories to readers. The
easiest way to do that is to fit a given news event into a "story" framework.
Human beings generally relate well to easily digestible stories, as opposed to more complex analyses, which require more thought and concentration. Reporters assigned to cover a given situation are likely to ask
"What is the story?" and then to force events into that framework. Reality is seldom as neat as a story, however, with neat compartments of
"Once upon a time . . ." "and then . . ." and "The End." But the story
framework dominates news coverage of events; thus the media cannot
function as a mirror since mirrors reflect rather than distort reality (except in funhouses).

The "mirror" model also fails to acknowledge that journalists make
choices, including decisions about what stories to cover. These choices
can be based on personal preference, but usually they are determined by
editors, who respond to publishers, who, in turn, are eager to sell their
product to the widest possible audiences. Most people prefer not to read
about seemingly insoluble social problems like poverty or homeless-
ness. As a result, journalists often choose not to cover social issues unless they fit a particular "story" format.

In addition to deciding what to cover, journalists must determine
the tone they will take in their reporting. If the "mirror" model of media

theory were accurate, journalists wouldn't make implicit or explicit judgments in their reporting. But they do. They are only human, after all, and they will inevitably be influenced by their admiration or dislike for a person about whom they are writing, or by their belief about the significance of an event.

From start to finish, journalists must make a series of choices. They first make choices about what to cover; then they make choices about whether their tone will be positive or negative, which facts to include or omit, what adjectives to use, and so on. Mirrors do not make choices — but a person holding a flashlight does. The latter can decide where to let the light drop, how long to leave it on that spot, and when to shift the light to something else. Journalists make these kinds of choices every day. Consequently, the "flashlight" model provides the more accurate understanding of the role that journalists play in American society, for the "mirror" model fails to take into account the many factors shaping even the simplest news story.

||||||||||||||||||||||||||||||||||||||||||||||||||||||||||||||||||||||||||||||||||

FOR COLLABORATION

Working with a group of classmates, respond to these questions about Hope Leman's essay. Appoint a recorder to write down the results of your discussion, which your instructor may ask you to present to the class.

1. Hope begins her essay not by attempting to interest readers in her subject but by defining the "mirror" and "flashlight" models of media theory. In a different context, Hope's introduction might seem abrupt. Given that she is responding to a midterm question and is writing under time pressure, why is this an effective way to begin her essay?

2. As Chapter 10 on planning and drafting explains, writers need to have a controlling purpose when they write. Sometimes they signal this purpose by articulating an explicit thesis statement. Sometimes only subtle cues are necessary. In her essay, Hope includes an explicit thesis statement. Identify this statement, and then discuss the reasons that it is necessary in her particular situation.

3. Academic writing is sometimes viewed as dull and lifeless — as, well, academic. Yet even in this essay written under time pressure, Hope's writing is not stuffy, dull, or pompous. Examine her essay to identify passages where a personal voice contributes to the overall effectiveness of her essay. How does Hope blend this personal voice with the objective and distanced approach of her essay?

||||||||||||||||||||||||||||||||||||||||||||||||||||||||||||||||||||||||||||||||||

Understanding How Analysis Works

As a student, you must respond to a wide range of writing assignments. For an American literature class, you may have to analyze the significance of the whiteness of the whale in *Moby Dick*, whereas a business management class may require a collaboratively written case study. You may need to write a lab report for a chemistry class and to critique a reading for sociology. Although these assignments vary considerably, they all draw on two related skills: analysis and argument. The remainder of this chapter will help you strengthen the first of these two important academic skills — analysis.

Analysis involves separating something into parts and determining how these parts function to create the whole. When you analyze, you examine a text, an object, or a body of data to understand how it is structured or organized and to assess its effectiveness or validity. Most academic writing, thinking, and reading involve analysis. Literature students analyze how a play is structured or how a poem achieves its effect; economics students analyze the major causes of inflation; biology students analyze the enzymatic reactions that comprise the Krebs cycle; and art history students analyze how line, color, and texture come together in a painting.

As these examples indicate, analysis is not a single skill but a group of related skills. An art history student might explore how a painting by Michelangelo achieves its effect, for instance, by comparing it with a similar work by Raphael. A biology student might discuss future acid-rain damage to forests in Canada and the United States by first defining acid rain and then using cause-and-effect reasoning to predict worsening conditions. A student in economics might estimate the likelihood of severe inflation in the coming year by categorizing or classifying the major causes of previous inflationary periods and then evaluating the likelihood of such factors influencing the current economic situation.

Different disciplines emphasize different analytic skills (see Chapter 7). But regardless of major, you need to understand and practice these crucial academic skills. You will do so most successfully if you establish a purpose and develop an appropriate framework or method for your analysis.

ESTABLISHING A PURPOSE FOR YOUR ANALYSIS

Your instructors will often ask you to analyze a fairly limited subject, problem, or process: Mrs. Ramsey's role in Virginia Woolf's *To the Lighthouse*, feminists' criticisms of Freud's psychoanalytical theories, Mendel's third law of genetics. Such limited tasks are necessary because of the complexity of the material. But though you are analyzing a limited topic, the purpose of your analysis is broad: to better understand the material. When you analyze a limited topic, you're like a person holding a flashlight in the dark: The beam

thinking
rhetorically

of light that you project is narrow and focused, but it illuminates a much larger area.

Recognizing this larger purpose can help you make important decisions as you plan, draft, and revise. If your instructor has assigned a limited topic, for instance, ask yourself what makes it an especially good means of understanding the issues at hand. If you're free to choose your own topic for analysis, your first questions should involve its significance. How will analyzing this topic improve your understanding of this subject? As you write, ask yourself regularly if your analysis is leading you to understand your topic more deeply. If you can answer yes, you're probably doing a good job of analysis.

Even though the general purpose of your analysis is to understand the larger subject, you still need to establish a more specific purpose. Imagine, for instance, that your Shakespeare instructor has asked you to write an essay on the fool in *King Lear*. You might establish one of several purposes for your analysis:

- To explain how the fool contributes to the development of a major theme in *King Lear*

- To discuss the effectiveness or plausibility of Shakespeare's characterization of the fool

- To define the role the fool plays in the plot

- To agree or disagree with a particular critical perspective on the fool's role and significance

Establishing a specific purpose helps you define how your analysis should proceed. It enables you to determine the important issues to address or the questions to answer.

There are no one-size-fits-all procedures for establishing a purpose for your analysis. Sometimes your purpose will develop naturally as a result of reading, reflection, and discussion with others. In other instances, it may help to draw on the invention strategies described in Chapter 9; these strategies help you explore your subject and discover questions to guide your analysis. You may need to write your way into an understanding of your purpose by composing a rough draft and seeing, in effect, what you think about your topic. Writing and thinking are dynamically interwoven processes.

DEVELOPING AN APPROPRIATE METHOD FOR YOUR ANALYSIS

Once you have a purpose, how do you actually analyze something? The answer depends on the subject, process, or problem being analyzed; it also depends, in academic writing, on the discipline within which the analysis occurs. Students studying *To the Lighthouse* or Mendel's third law may all use such analytic processes as definition, causal analysis, classification, and comparison.

But the exact form of the processes that each student uses — the way each organizes the analysis and the criteria each uses to evaluate it — may differ. Despite their disciplinary differences, all the students must establish some method for analysis if they are to succeed.

There are no hard-and-fast rules for establishing such a method. In general, however, you should consider the methods of inquiry characteristic of the various disciplines. The following questions can help you develop an appropriate method.

If, after considering these questions and reflecting on your experiences in a class, you continue to have difficulty settling on an appropriate method for analysis, meet with your instructor to get help. You might ask him or her to recommend student essays or professional articles that clearly model the analytical methods used in the field.

Questions for Developing an Appropriate Method for Analysis

thinking rhetorically

- How have your instructors approached analysis in class? Do they rely on a systematic procedure, such as case-study or problem-solving methodology, or does their analysis vary, depending on the subject?
- What kinds of evidence and examples do they draw on?
- What kinds of questions do your instructors typically ask in class discussions? Why might people in the discipline view these as important questions?
- What kinds of answers to these questions do your instructors favor? Why might people in this discipline value such responses?

Understanding the Relationship between Analysis and Argument

All academic writing has an argumentative edge, and sometimes that edge is obvious. If a student writes a political science essay arguing that the government should follow a particular environmental policy, that student is explicitly arguing that the government should do something. Essays that discuss whether something should or should not be done are easily recognizable as arguments — probably because they follow the debate format that many associate with argumentation.

But writers can express judgments — can present good reasons for their beliefs and actions — in other ways. A music theory student analyzing the score of a Beethoven sonata may argue that it should be performed in a certain way. To do so, she must convince her reader, in this case her teacher, that she has a sophisticated understanding of the structure of the sonata. (She might do this by arguing that the second movement of the particular sonata is more daring or innovative than music historians have acknowledged.) Analysis will play a particularly central role in this student's writing: By identifying specific features of the score and positing relationships among these features, she will demonstrate her understanding of Beethoven's use of the sonata form.

As this example demonstrates, analysis and argument are interdependent. Argumentation depends on analysis, for through analysis writers clarify the logic of their thinking and provide evidence for their judgments. (The student arguing that the government should follow a particular environmental policy would certainly have to analyze the potential benefits and disadvantages of that policy and demonstrate that it's workable.) Similarly, analysis always carries an implicit argumentative burden. For when you analyze something, you are in effect asserting "This is how I believe X works" or "This is what I believe X means."

Academic analysis and argument call for similar habits of mind. Both encourage writers to suspend personal biases. This is not to say that academic writers are expected to be absolutely objective. Your gut feeling that "workfare" programs may not provide single parents with adequate support for their children may cause you to investigate this topic for a political science or economics class. This gut feeling is a strength, not a weakness, for it enables you to find a topic that interests you. Once you begin to explore your topic, however, you need to engage it dispassionately. You need, in other words, to be open to changing your mind.

If you do change your mind about the consequences of workfare programs, the reading and writing you have done probably have given you a more detailed understanding of the issues at stake in arguments over workfare programs. If your essay about this topic is to be successful, you will describe these issues and analyze their relationships and implications. You will develop logical connections that make your reasoning explicit. In these and other ways, you will demonstrate to readers that you have indeed understood your subject.

The essay by Hope Leman that begins on p. 83 is a good example of academic analysis. In this essay, Hope is not arguing that something should or should not be done. Rather, she is attempting to understand whether the "mirror" or "flashlight" model best describes the role of journalists in American society.

ANALYZING ACADEMIC ARGUMENTS

Analysis plays a key role in all academic writing. It helps readers and writers understand the world we live in and recognize, examine, and formulate arguments about it. Analysis is certainly not limited to written texts. Because we live in a media-saturated culture, we need to be able to analyze texts that depend heavily on images and graphics—whether they are television ads or multimedia presentations on the Web. In colleges and universities in North America, however, the analysis of written texts is often particularly important.

The remainder of this chapter provides strategies that you can use to become a more sophisticated and critical reader of texts. The key academic skill of analysis is central to all courses offered in the sciences, humanities, business, arts, and social sciences. It is also central to your effective participation in civic, cultural, political, and other affairs. Think of the debates that occurred throughout the world before the United States led a coalition of nations to war in Iraq on March 19, 2003. Some of the questions raised about this war were general: Should the U.S.-dominated coalition attack Iraq? More often, however, the questions were limited: Should United Nations approval be required for such an attack? What form should this approval take? Does a preemptive attack on Iraq meet the philosophical and religious criteria for a just war?

Arguments addressing these and related questions appeared in newspapers and magazines, on radio and television talk shows, and on the Internet in the days and months preceding the Iraq War. Writers developed arguments that addressed a number of complex and multilayered issues. Someone arguing that a preemptive attack on Iraq does not meet the criteria for a just war, for instance, would have to examine various definitions of a just war and present arguments grounded in religion and philosophy.

An analysis of these and other subjects will feel less intimidating if you address three basic questions:

- What question is at issue?

- What position does the author take?

- Do the author's reasons justify your acceptance of his or her argument?

||||||||||||||||||||||||||||||||||||||||||||||||||||||||||||||||||||||||||||||||||||||

FOR EXPLORATION

Take a few moments to freewrite about your previous experiences in analyzing academic arguments. Have you been more interested in some kinds of arguments than others? (You might enjoy analyzing political and historical texts, for instance, but find arguments in other areas less interesting.) Do these differences reflect personal preferences, cultural norms, or some other factors? What was your most positive experience with academic analysis, and what factors made it positive? What was your most negative experience, and what factors made it negative? What questions and concerns do you have regarding the analysis of academic arguments? Be prepared to share what you have written with your classmates.

||||||||||||||||||||||||||||||||||||||||||||||||||||||||||||||||||||||||||||||||||||||

By determining the question at issue, you get to the heart of any argument and distinguish major claims from minor elements of support. You can then identify the author's position and evaluate whether he or she has provided good reasons for you to agree with this position.

DETERMINING THE QUESTION AT ISSUE

When you determine the question at issue, you identify the main issue that is at stake in an argument. To argue that a preemptive war on Iraq meets the philosophical and religious criteria for a just war, for instance, you would have to define these criteria. To argue that the United States and its allies should have waited for a United Nations resolution before attacking Iraq, you wouldn't be raising a question of definition but instead would be examining a question of policy.

thinking rhetorically Greek and Roman rhetoricians developed a method for determining the questions at issue in any argument, called stasis theory. Stasis theory encourages readers to identify the major point on which a particular controversy rests. This method presents six basic questions at issue in argumentative writing:[1]

■ *Questions of fact* arise from the reader's need to know "Does this [whatever it is] exist?"

■ *Questions of definition* arise from the reader's need to know "What is it?"

■ *Questions of interpretation* arise from the reader's need to know "What does it signify?"

■ *Questions of value* arise from the reader's need to know "Is it good?"

■ *Questions of consequence* arise from the reader's need to know "Will this cause that to happen?"

■ *Questions of policy* arise from the reader's need to know "What should be done about it?"

As you determine the kinds of issues addressed in a particular argument, you will draw on your rhetorical sensitivity. (For more on developing rhetorical sensitivity, see Chapter 1, p. 15.) You do so naturally in your everyday life. Imagine that a friend has urged you to drive with her to a concert in a city an hour away. You'd like to attend the concert, but it's on a midweek work night. Depending on your situation, the primary question at issue may be one of value. If you value the concert enough, then you can justify the time, expense,

---

1. In this chapter, I employ the categories presented in John Gage, *The Shape of Reason: Argumentative Writing in College*, 3rd ed. (Needham Heights: Allyn and Bacon, 1991), 40.

and late-night bedtime involved in attending the concert. On the other hand, the primary question at issue for you may be one of consequence: This would be the case if you couldn't justify time away from study, work, and family, especially on a weeknight.

Here is an argument by Amitai Etzioni about the advantages and disadvantages of traditional protections of privacy in North America. Etzioni is a professor at George Washington University and former senior adviser to the White House (1979–1980). He has written over a dozen books, including *The Limits of Privacy* (1999), from which this excerpt is taken. As you read his analysis, consider which of the preceding six questions — fact, definition, interpretation, value, consequence, and policy — are most clearly at stake in his argument.

Less Privacy Is Good for Us (and You)

AMITAI ETZIONI

Despite the fact that privacy is not so such as mentioned in the Constitution and that it was only shoehorned in some thirty-four years ago, it is viewed by most Americans as a profound, inalienable right.

The media is loaded with horror stories about the ways privacy is not so much nibbled away as it is stripped away by bosses who read your e-mail, neighbors who listen in on your cell phones, and E-Z passes that allow tollbooth operators to keep track of your movements. A typical headline decries the "End of Privacy" (Richard A. Spinello, in an issue of *America*, a Catholic weekly) or "The Death of Privacy" (Joshua Quittner, in *Time*).

It is time to pay attention to the other half of the equation that defines a good society: concerns for public health and safety that entail some rather justifiable diminution of privacy.

Take the HIV testing of infants. New medical data — for instance, evidence recently published by the prestigious *New England Journal of Medicine* — show that a significant proportion of children born to mothers who have HIV can ward off this horrible disease but only on two conditions: that their mothers not breast-feed them and that they immediately be given AZT. For this to happen, mothers must be informed that they have HIV. An estimated two-thirds of infected mothers are unaware. However, various civil libertarians and some gay activists vehemently oppose such disclosure on the grounds that when infants are tested for HIV, in effect one finds out if the mother is a carrier, and thus her privacy is violated. While New York State in 1996, after a very acrimonious debate, enacted a law that requires infant testing and disclosure of the findings to the mother, most other states have so far avoided dealing with this issue.

Congress passed the buck by asking the Institute of Medicine (IOM) to conduct a study of the matter. The IOM committee, dominated by politically correct people, just reported its recommendations. It suggested that all pregnant women be asked to consent to HIV testing as part of routine prenatal care. There is little wrong with such a recommendation other than it does not deal with many of the mothers who are drug addicts or otherwise live at society's margins. Many of these women do not show up for prenatal care, and they are particularly prone to HIV, according to a study published in the American Health Association's *Journal of School Health*. To save the lives of their children, they must be tested at delivery and treated even if this entails a violation of mothers' privacy.

Recently a suggestion to use driver's licenses to curb illegal immigration has sent the Coalition for Constitutional Liberties, a large group of libertarians, civil libertarians, and privacy advocates, into higher orbit than John Glenn ever traversed. The coalition wrote:

> This plan pushed us to the brink of tyranny, where citizens will not be allowed to travel, open bank accounts, obtain health care, get a job, or purchase firearms without first presenting the proper government papers.
>
> The authorizing section of the law . . . is reminiscent of the totalitarian dictates by Politburo members in the former Soviet Union, not the Congress of the United States of America.

Meanwhile, Wells Fargo is introducing a new device that allows a person to cash checks at its ATM machines because the machines recognize faces. Rapidly coming is a whole new industry of so-called biometrics that uses natural features such as voice, hand design, and eye pattern to recognize a person with the same extremely high reliability provided by the new DNA tests.

It's true that as biometrics catches on, it will practically strip Americans of anonymity, an important part of privacy. In the near future, a person who acquired a poor reputation in one part of the country will find it much more difficult to move to another part, change his name, and gain a whole fresh start. Biometrics see right through such assumed identities. One may hope that future communities will become more tolerant of such people, especially if they openly acknowledge the mistakes of their past and truly seek to lead a more prosocial life. But they will no longer be able to hide their pasts.

Above all, while biometrics clearly undermines privacy, the social benefits it promises are very substantial. Specifically, each year at least half a million criminals become fugitives, avoiding trial, incarceration, or serving their full sentences, often committing additional crimes while on the lam. People who fraudulently file for multiple income tax refunds using fake identities and multiple Social Security numbers cost the nation between $1 billion and $5 billion per year. Numerous divorced parents escape their financial obligations to their children by avoiding detection when they move or change jobs. (The sums owed to children are variously estimated as running between $18 billion to $23 billion a year.) Professional and amateur criminals, employing fraudulent identification documentation to make phony credit card purchases, cost credit card companies and retail businesses an indeterminate number of billions of dollars each year. The United States loses an estimated $18 billion a year to benefit fraud committed by illegal aliens using false IDs. A 1998 General Accounting Office report estimates identity fraud to cost $10 billion annually in entitlement programs alone.

People hired to work in child care centers, kindergartens, and schools cannot be effectively screened to keep out child abusers and sex offenders, largely because when background checks are conducted, convicted criminals escape detection by using false identification and aliases. Biometrics would sharply curtail all these crimes, although far from wipe them out single-handedly.

The courts have recognized that privacy must be weighed against considerations of public interest but have tended to privilege privacy and make claims for public health or safety clear several high hurdles. In recent years these barriers have been somewhat lowered as courts have become more concerned with public safety and health. Given that these often are matters of state law and that neither legislatures nor courts act in unison, the details are complex and far from all pointing in one direction. But, by and large, courts have allowed mandatory drug testing of those who directly have the lives of others in their hands, including pilots, train engineers, drivers of school buses, and air traffic controllers, even though such testing violates their privacy. In case after case, the courts have disregarded objections to such tests by civil libertarians who argue that such tests constitute "suspicionless" searches, grossly violate privacy, and—as the ACLU puts it—"condition Americans to a police state."

All this points to a need to recast privacy in our civic culture, public policies, and legal doctrines. We should cease to treat it as an unmitigated good, a sacred right (the way Warren and Brandeis referred to in their famous article and many since) or one that courts automatically privilege.

Instead, privacy should rely squarely on the Fourth Amendment, the only one that has a balance built right into its text. It recognizes both searches that wantonly violate privacy ("unreasonable" ones) and those that enhance the common good to such an extent that they are justified, even if they intrude into one's privacy. Moreover, it provides a mechanism to sort out which searches are in the public interest and which violate privacy without sufficient cause, by introducing the concept of warrants issued by a "neutral magistrate" presented with "probable cause." Warrants also limit the invasion of privacy "by specification of the person to be seized, the place to be searched, and the evidence to be sought." The Fourth may have become the Constitutional Foundation of privacy a long time ago if it was not for the fact that *Roe v. Wade* is construed as a privacy right, and touching it provokes fierce opposition. The good news, though, is that even the advocates of choice in this area are now looking to base their position on some other legal grounds, especially the Fourteenth Amendment.

We might be ready to treat privacy for what it is: one very important right but not one that trumps most other considerations, especially of public safety and health.

||||||||||||||||||||||||||||||||||||||||||||||||||||||||||||||||||||||||||||||||||||

FOR COLLABORATION

After you have read Etzioni's argument, list the two most significant stasis questions (see p. 90) at stake in his argument. Find at least one passage that you believe relates to each question. Then meet with a group of classmates, and share your responses to this assignment. (Appoint a timekeeper to ensure that all members of your group have a chance to share their responses.) To what extent did you agree or disagree with other group members on the stasis questions at stake in Etzioni's analysis? As a group, choose the two questions that best apply to Etzioni's argument, and agree on two or three reasons why each question is central to his argument. Be prepared to share the results of your discussion with your class.

||||||||||||||||||||||||||||||||||||||||||||||||||||||||||||||||||||||||||||||||||||

IDENTIFYING AN AUTHOR'S POSITION ON A QUESTION

You may find it helpful to identify an author's position in two stages. First, read the text carefully to determine the main question that the author has presented. If you review the first three paragraphs of Etzioni's argument beginning on p. 91, for instance, you'll note that he observes in paragraph 1 that privacy "is viewed by most Americans as a profound, inalienable right" and goes on to argue in paragraph 3 that "It is time to pay attention to the other half of the equation that defines a good society: concerns for public health and safety that entail some rather justifiable diminution of privacy." The remainder of the excerpt clarifies and supports his position on this issue.

After you have identified the author's position, you can read his or her argument critically. Reading critically doesn't mean simply looking for logical flaws, poor evidence, and so on. Rather, critical readers shift stances as they read to develop a complex understanding of the issues at hand. In this

Questions for Critical Reading

thinking rhetorically

- What is the author's purpose or agenda? This may or may not be identical to the position that the author takes in his or her argument.

- How much do you know about the author's assumptions, beliefs, and experiences?

- What are the author's qualifications to discuss the topic?

- What unstated assumptions or underlying values and commitments does the author seem to hold? How might these influence his or her position?

- What does the author want readers to do as a result of reading this text? Assent to the argument? Act on it? Gain a richer understanding of an issue or problem? Does this purpose seem appropriate to the issues involved? How might this purpose influence the form and content of the author's argument?

- What reasons does the author offer in support of his or her ideas? Are they good reasons?

- What kinds of sources does the author rely on? How current and reliable are they? Are any perspectives left out?

- What objections might be raised to this argument?

- Does this argument include images, graphics, or media? How do they appeal to readers or listeners? Does their appeal seem appropriate or questionable?

- How open to persuasion are you with this particular topic? How willing are you to listen to another point of view? If you agree with the author, can you maintain a critical distance so that you can examine the claims and support that the writer provides?

sense, critical readers know how to play what Peter Elbow calls the believing and doubting game.[2] When you play the believing game, you attempt to believe the author's arguments by engaging these arguments sympathetically. You put yourself in the position of the author or of someone who supports the author's position. What interests and experiences might cause the author to take this position? Similarly, when you play the doubting game, you ask what objections someone with different interests and experiences might make. Other ways of doubting an argument include examining the claims and considering the evidence that supports each claim.

---

2. Peter Elbow, *Writing without Teachers* (New York: Oxford UP, 1973), 147–91.

When you read critically, your goal is not to demolish or disvalue the text you are reading. Rather, you want to increase your understanding of the ideas being expressed. You also want to participate actively in the conversation of which any written text is a part. The questions on p. 95 can help you become a more active and critical reader who reads both with and against the grain of an author's argument.

|||||||||||||||||||||||||||||||||||||||||||||||||||||||||||||||||||||||||||||||||||||||||||

FOR EXPLORATION

Keep in mind the questions presented on p. 95 as you reread the excerpt from Amitai Etzioni's *The Limits of Privacy* (pp. 91–94). After doing so, respond to these questions. What does this guided rereading of Etzioni's text help you to better understand about it?

FOR COLLABORATION

After you have analyzed Etzioni's argument, meet with a group of classmates to share the results of your analysis. Appoint a timekeeper so that all group members have an opportunity to share their results. To what extent did other group members agree with your analysis? To what extent did they disagree? What did you learn as a result of this experience? Be prepared to share your responses with the rest of the class.

|||||||||||||||||||||||||||||||||||||||||||||||||||||||||||||||||||||||||||||||||||||||||||

USING ARISTOTLE'S THREE APPEALS

As the Questions for Critical Reading (p. 95) suggest, you may agree with a writer's position on a subject but nevertheless question the support that he or she provides. One of the hallmarks of a critical reader, in fact, is the ability to maintain a critical distance from an argument, even when you have strong feelings for or against the author's position.

thinking rhetorically

Two analytical frameworks—one ancient and one contemporary—can help you to evaluate the strengths and limitations of academic arguments. (The first of these systems, Aristotle's three appeals, is introduced in Chapter 3, p. 55.) In his *Rhetoric*, Aristotle determined that speakers and writers draw on three general appeals when they attempt to persuade others:

■ *Logos*, the appeal to reason

■ *Pathos*, the appeal to emotion, values, and beliefs

■ *Ethos*, the appeal to the credibility of the speaker or writer

One way to analyze an argument is to determine which type of appeal the author draws on most heavily and his or her effectiveness in using it. When you consider appeals to *logos*, ask yourself if the argument is internally consistent and logical. Also ask if the author has articulated clear and reasonable major claims and supported them with appropriate evidence. Appeals to *pathos* raise different issues: Here you identify the strategies that the author has employed to appeal to readers' values and interests. Finally, appeals to *ethos* encourage you to consider the author's credibility and trustworthiness as demonstrated in his or her argument.

Appeals to *logos* — appeals that involve factual information and evidence — are often considered especially trustworthy by North American readers, particularly in the academy. Logical appeals include facts; firsthand evidence drawn from observations, interviews, surveys and questionnaires, experiments, and personal experience; and secondhand evidence drawn from authorities, the testimony of others, statistics, and other print and online sources. Critical readers do not automatically assume that support drawn from logical appeals is valid. After all, not all sources are equally valid, and facts can be out of date or taken out of context. (For a discussion of how to evaluate print and online sources, see pp. 157–59.)

Critical readers look at all three of Aristotle's appeals in context. Appeals to *pathos* — to readers' emotions, values, and beliefs — can certainly be manipulative and inappropriate. We've all seen ads that seem to promise one thing (youth, beauty, fitness) to sell another. Nevertheless, emotional appeals play key roles in many kinds of arguments, including academic arguments. A student writing about humanitarian issues growing out of the Iraq War might begin her essay by describing the loss of life, order, and basic material necessities that resulted from the war. In so doing, she would be appealing to readers' emotions and emphasizing the importance of her topic. The same is true for appeals to *ethos*. While we might be skeptical when we see an ad where a movie star or sports hero praises a product, this doesn't mean that all appeals to *ethos* are suspect.

In this regard, let's return to the excerpt from Etzioni's *The Limits of Privacy* (pp. 91–94). The biographical information that accompanies this excerpt provides useful information about Etzioni's experience and qualifications; this information can help readers determine whether Etzioni is an authority on issues of privacy. Critical readers will keep this knowledge in mind as they read his argument, but they'll also consider the credibility with which he makes his case. Does he use examples that are fair and reasonable? Does he develop a balanced, thoughtful argument? Does he seem to have society's best interest at heart, or is he pushing an agenda of his own personal assumptions and beliefs? By asking questions such as these, readers can determine whether they should trust Etzioni's credibility as a thinker and writer. Critical readers respect relevant experiences and qualifications that authors bring to various issues, but they focus primarily on what the author does and says in the text that they are currently reading. In this regard, a thoughtful commentary by an average American in a newspaper may be more credible than a guest editorial by a noted expert.

||||||||||||||||||||||||||||||||||||||||||||||||||||||||||||||||||||||||||||||||||||||||||||||

FOR EXPLORATION

Drawing on your understanding of Aristotle's three appeals, as explained in this chapter, analyze the excerpt from Etzioni's *The Limits of Privacy* (pp. 91–94). What appeals does he draw on most heavily? How effective is he in using these appeals? (Be sure to comment on each of the three appeals.)

FOR COLLABORATION

Meet with a group of classmates to share your responses to the previous Exploration. Appoint both a timekeeper and a recorder to summarize your group's responses. Begin by addressing this question: To what extent did members of your group agree about Etzioni's effectiveness in his use of Aristotle's three appeals? After responding, develop a group position on Etzioni's use of Aristotle's three appeals. To do so, first agree on a statement that conveys your group's sense of how Etzioni employed each appeal. Then find one or two examples from his text that support your analysis. Be prepared to share the results of your discussion with the class.

||||||||||||||||||||||||||||||||||||||||||||||||||||||||||||||||||||||||||||||||||||||||||||||

USING TOULMIN'S FRAMEWORK

Aristotle's three appeals constitute one framework for analyzing academic arguments. Such a framework encourages you to step back from your commonsense understandings of—and immediate responses to—an argument. It enables you to gain critical distance on your reading. A second framework that serves this purpose was developed by the British philosopher Stephen Toulmin; it is sometimes referred to simply as Toulmin argument or the Toulmin system. According to Toulmin, most arguments contain common features:

▪ *Claims* are statements of fact, opinion, or belief that provide the fundamental structure for arguments.

▪ *Qualifiers* are one or more statements that limit or clarify the claim in some way.

▪ *Warrants* are links from the claim to reasons and evidence. Warrants often take the form of assumptions and beliefs that may or may not be explicitly stated.

▪ *Reasons* are smaller assertions that support claims. They often begin with the word *because*.

▪ *Evidence* includes examples, facts, statistics, statements by authorities, and personal experience used to back up reasons (and sometimes warrants).

Toulmin's framework encourages readers to consider every chain in an argument's development — including those aspects of the argument, such as warrants, that at times are left unstated. Sometimes a warrant is so self-evident that writers don't state it explicitly. Few readers would object to the assertion that "Sylvia should make an excellent lawyer because she excelled in her classes in law school and in her early years of legal practice," even though the warrant for this claim ("Excelling in law school and in the early years of legal practice are good predictors of a person's success after law school") is missing. On other occasions, the absence of a warrant is a major flaw in the development of an argument. Many arguments about controversial subjects such as abortion and the environment flounder because the writers assume warrants (such as the warrant that endangered species should be protected despite financial considerations like real estate development and oil exploration) that others don't share.

With Toulmin's system in mind, consider Etzioni's discussion of HIV testing of infants. This discussion appears in paragraphs 4 and 5 of his excerpt (pp. 91–92). Etzioni's major claim is clear. In the last sentence of paragraph 5, he argues that "To save the lives of . . . children . . . [of women who have HIV, these children] must be tested at delivery and treated even if this entails a violation of mothers' privacy." Note that Etzioni's claim is qualified by his recognition that violating the mother's privacy is a serious matter. To meet his burden of proof, Etzioni must demonstrate that the benefits of testing infants for HIV outweigh the costs to new mothers, whose privacy rights will be violated.

Etzioni provides several reasons in support of his argument. He points out, for instance, that recent research by the *New England Journal of Medicine* shows that infants born with HIV can ward off the disease if they are tested at birth and treated immediately. As evidence of the need for such testing, he adds that "An estimated two-thirds of infected mothers are unaware" that they have HIV. Etzioni undertakes a second and related line of reasoning when he argues that efforts to address this problem without requiring the mandatory testing of all newborn infants have failed.

Etzioni's argument about HIV testing can be analyzed as follows:

Claim: Testing newborn infants for HIV should be mandatory.

Qualifier: Mandatory testing should occur even though this represents a violation of mothers' privacy.

Warrant: Concerns for the health of newborn infants should take precedence over the need to maintain the privacy of their mothers.

Reasons: (1) With testing and treatment, the lives of most infants who are born with HIV could be saved. (2) High-risk mothers who are particularly at risk of having infants with HIV are least likely to be aware that they have the disease and least likely to agree to voluntary testing. (3) Efforts to increase the number of infants who are tested for HIV without requiring mandatory testing have failed.

Evidence: (1) Authoritative medical data emphasize the benefits that can be gained by testing and treatment. (2) Data from such sources as the *Journal of School Health* confirm that high-risk mothers are particularly prone to HIV. (3) Unnamed sources estimate that two-thirds of infected mothers are unaware they have HIV.

This analysis outlines the basic structure of Etzioni's argument, but it still leaves room for readers to disagree about whether testing should be mandatory. Those who hold strong civil libertarian views may disagree with Etzioni's warrant, while others may question the reliability of the estimate that "two-thirds of infected mothers are unaware" that they have HIV. Etzioni's failure to provide evidence for this estimate — when he does provide evidence for other reasons that support his claim — might reasonably make some readers skeptical. They might argue that the number of women who are unlikely to know they have HIV and unlikely to be tested is much smaller than Etzioni suggests, and that given this fact the need to protect mothers' privacy should take precedence.

Finally, some readers might point out that Etzioni doesn't specify who should require mandatory testing (the federal government? the states?) or how it might best be carried out. Since Etzioni's discussion of mandatory HIV testing is part of a larger argument about privacy, it may be unrealistic to expect him to discuss issues of implementation, but critical readers would nevertheless note that these issues are unaddressed in Etzioni's text.

|||||||||||||||||||||||||||||||||||||||||||||||||||||||||||||||||||||||||||||||||||||

FOR EXPLORATION

Choose another section of Etzioni's argument (pp. 91–94), such as his discussion of biometrics, and analyze it according to Toulmin's system. What does this analysis reveal that you did not notice in earlier readings of the excerpt?

|||||||||||||||||||||||||||||||||||||||||||||||||||||||||||||||||||||||||||||||||||||

Recognizing Fallacies

When you analyze an argument, you should be aware of fallacies that may be at work. Fallacies are faults in an argument's structure that may call into question the argument's evidence or conclusions. Some fallacies are easy to recognize. If someone told you that anyone who votes Republican is an imbecile, you would recognize that this assertion is illogical and unfair. (Such a statement is an example of an *ad hominem* fallacy; see below.) At other times, fallacies can be harder to determine. After all, arguments always occur in some specific rhetorical situation: What looks like a fallacy in one situation may appear quite different in another. Sometimes judgments about a person's character or actions are relevant to an argument, for instance. Just because a writer or speaker grounds part of an argument in such a judgment doesn't mean that he or she is committing an *ad hominem* fallacy. To determine whether an argument is grounded in a fallacy, you need to consider it in the context of its specific rhetorical situation, including the place and time in which the argument was or is being made.

thinking rhetorically

Since the time of Aristotle, rhetoricians have developed diverse ways of naming, describing, and categorizing various fallacies. Often the fallacies are categorized according to Aristotle's three major appeals of argument—ethical appeals (appeals to *ethos*), emotional appeals (appeals to *pathos*), and logical appeals (appeals to *logos*). As you read the following brief descriptions of these fallacies, remember that the point of studying fallacies is not to discredit the ideas of others. Writers who want to develop fair, well-reasoned arguments realize that fallacies tend to shut down, rather than encourage, communication. The following guidelines list some of the most significant fallacies that appear in arguments.

Guidelines for Identifying Fallacies

Ethical Fallacies

Writers who employ ethical fallacies attempt to destroy the credibility of those who disagree with them. Examples of ethical fallacies include the following:

■ An *ad hominem* attack is an unfair attack on a person's character or actions, one that diverts attention from the issue at hand. An example of an ad hominem attack would be the statement that "Any American who opposes the war in Iraq is unpatriotic." A person's position on a war does not necessarily reflect his or her patriotism.

(continued)

(continued)

▨ *Guilt by association* is an effort to damage a person's credibility by associating him or her with an unpopular or discredited activity or person. A student who argues that hip-hop music is bad because some hip-hop musicians such as Bobby Brown have been involved in criminal activities is committing the fallacy of guilt by association. Some—but not all—hip-hop musicians have engaged in criminal activities, but their personal behavior is separate from the music that they create.

Emotional Fallacies

Emotional appeals can play a valid and important role in argumentation, but when these appeals are overblown or unfair, they distract readers from attending to the point that is being argued. Examples of emotional fallacies include the following:

▨ A *bandwagon appeal* argues that readers should support a person, activity, or movement because it is popular. This appeal is particularly common in advertising, where promoters often argue that "X is the best-selling product of its kind."

▨ A *slippery slope* fallacy occurs when writers exaggerate the future consequences of an event or action, usually with an intent to frighten readers into agreeing with their argument. If those who oppose censorship of pornography argue that "Once we start banning one form of literature, censorship will spread, and the next thing you know, we'll be burning books!" they are committing the slippery slope fallacy.

Logical Fallacies

Logical fallacies are arguments in which the claims, warrants, or evidence are invalid, insufficient, or disconnected. Examples of logical fallacies include the following:

▨ *Begging the question* involves stating a claim that depends on circular reasoning for justification. Arguing that "Abortion is murder because it involves the intentional murder of an unborn human being" is tantamount to saying that "Abortion is murder because it is murder." This fallacy often detracts attention from the real issues at hand, for the question of whether a fetus should be considered a human being is complex.

▨ A *hasty generalization* is drawn from insufficient evidence. If someone says, "Last week I attended a poetry reading supported by the National Endowment for the Arts, and many of the speakers used profanity. Maybe the people who want to stop government funding

(continued)

(continued)

for the NEA are right," this would be a hasty generalization. One performance doesn't constitute a large enough sample for such a generalization.

■ A *non sequitur* is an argument that attempts to connect two or more logically unrelated ideas. If someone states that "I hate it when people smoke in restaurants; there ought to be a law against cigarettes," this would represent a non sequitur, for eliminating smoking in restaurants and the negative effects of second hand smoke does not require the elimination of legal tobacco sales.

Putting Theory into Practice: Academic Analysis in Action

Readers engage in academic analysis not to criticize or dissect another's argument but rather to understand that argument as fully as possible. When you analyze an academic argument, you attempt to go beyond your immediate response—which often takes the form of binary-driven observations ("I agree/don't agree, like/don't like, am interested/ not interested in X")—to achieve a fuller, more complex understanding of it. Here is an example of a successful analysis of an academic argument. This essay by Stevon Roberts, a student at Oregon State University, analyzes the excerpt from Etzioni's *The Limits of Privacy* presented earlier in this chapter (pp. 91–94).

The Price of Public Safety

STEVON ROBERTS

As a former senior adviser to the White House and author of *The Limits of Privacy*, Amitai Etzioni is a formidable advocate for revision of one of America's most cherished luxuries: protection of personal privacy. In "Less Privacy Is Good for Us (and You)," an argument excerpted from the above volume, Etzioni urges Americans to look critically at traditional expectations for personal privacy and to be prepared to sacrifice those expectations for increased public health and safety. Although the volume was published before the terrorist attacks on September 11, 2001, and the essay makes no specific references to the tragedy, the events of that day give an increased sense of urgency to Etzioni's message and consequently might make Americans more receptive to protocols that afford protection from public risks in general.

In the interest of public health risks, Etzioni opens his argument with recent HIV testing procedures in hospitals that may infringe on the rights of pregnant women. He then shifts gears and takes a brief look at public outrage from the Coalition for Constitutional Liberties regarding driver's license availability. Next, he gives us a crash course in "biometrics," a controversial new technology that could save billions of dollars lost to fraud every year. Finally, Etzioni addresses our fears (and those of other civil libertarians) that these and other procedures that are designed to increase our public health and safety will not be implemented justly and ethically. Etzioni admits, however, that a growing number of people and interest groups are not convinced that old laws—such as the Fourth Amendment, which protects the United States from becoming a military state—can protect us from new technology. We are left to wonder: is Etzioni justified in making his unconventional claims despite such well-founded opposition?

After some brief media references, Etzioni's first substantial argument involves a real-world privacy dilemma facing pregnant women as well as various health and legal groups. Specifically, he focuses on HIV testing of newborns. This is an excellent place to start because the reactions of these groups help to shed light on our current attitudes toward privacy. Etzioni refers to the *New England Journal of Medicine*, which published evidence suggesting that infants born to HIV-infected women could ward off the disease with early diagnosis and treatment with AZT. In order for the infants to be treated, they must be tested. This becomes a privacy issue because testing infants for HIV also reveals whether "the mother is a carrier, and thus her privacy is violated" (669).

As Etzioni acknowledges, arguments in favor of required HIV testing of infants have met strong—and even vehement—opposition from civil libertarians, as well as from some gay activists. Indeed, the question of whether to test infants for HIV has been so contentious that most states, as well as the federal government, have avoided taking it on. In this regard, Etzioni chastises Congress for "pass[ing] the buck by asking the Institute of Medicine (IOM) to conduct a study of the matter." This effectively illustrates Congress's lack of willingness to become involved. IOM's solution suggests that all pregnant women should consent to HIV testing as part of their routine prenatal care. However, Etzioni feels this would leave out many women who "are drug addicts or otherwise live at society's margins" (669). Such women, he argues, "do not show up for prenatal care, and they are particularly prone to HIV, according to a study published in the American Health Association's *Journal of School Health*" (669). A succinct sentence sums up his solution: "To save the lives of their children, they [infants] must be tested at delivery and treated even if this entails a violation of mothers' privacy" (669).

This is a well-documented and compelling argument. Other parts of Etzioni's text, however, are not so well rounded. Instead of taking seriously the arguments forwarded by civil libertarians and others who raise concerns about privacy, Etzioni focuses on the media, which he believes tell "horror stories" about "The Death of Privacy" (669). When he does address the views of such groups, he represents their concerns by an inflammatory statement from the Coalition for Constitutional Liberties, which accuses those in favor of the plan of pushing the country "to the brink of tyranny" (669).

With this brief (and wholly unsuccessful) transition, Etzioni moves from the Coalition's alarmist complaints to Wells Fargo's introduction of "a new device that allows a person to cash checks at its ATM machines because the machines recognize faces" (670). These machines rely upon a new technology called biometrics, which, Etzioni explains, can use "natural features such as voice, hand design, and eye pattern to recognize a person with the same extremely high reliability provided by the new DNA tests" (670). Etzioni acknowledges that biometrics is a controversial technology, and he concedes that it will "practically strip Americans of anonymity, an important part of privacy" (670). With this new technology, people would find it difficult to change their names, move to another part of the country, and gain a fresh start in life. His solution is a hope that "future communities will become more tolerant of such people, especially if they openly acknowledge the mistakes of their past and truly seek to lead a more prosocial life" (670).

To his credit, Etzioni is quick to follow up the drawbacks of biometrics with compelling statistics about the potential benefits. He says, "Above all, while biometrics clearly undermines privacy, the social benefits it promises are very substantial" (670). He references $1 billion to $5 billion lost annually to tax fraud, $18 billion to $23 billion annually in lost child support, and $18 billion a year lost to fraud committed by illegal aliens with false IDs. In addition to the potential economic benefits, he says sex offenders who use false IDs would be more effectively screened, and would less easily find work at child care centers or schools (670).

Etzioni's presentation of biometrics is, ironically, both calculated and lacking in logistics. His predominantly economic appeal doesn't mention the cost associated with Wells Fargo's new face-recognizing ATM machines. Because he makes no attempt, even hypothetically, to weigh the cost of biometrics implementation against the savings from fraud protection or other liabilities, readers are left to assume that the overall results are beneficial, when that might not, in fact, be the case. For example, although he discusses credit card fraud, there is no mention of Internet credit card fraud. Biometrics countermeasures to combat this threat are likely to manifest as purchasable hardware devices, putting an unfair financial burden on lower-level consumers while taking the liability away from the credit card companies. It seems reasonable that while calculating the potential benefits, Etzioni should also calculate potential losses or system limitations, as he does when admitting that biometrics would not singlehandedly wipe out abusers from child care centers.

Additionally, the author's appeals to pathos are lacking substance. In fact, his only olive branch to the human condition is a concession that biometrics may make it difficult for criminals seeking a new life. His flaky solution to this problem is a touchy-feely dream in which everyone magically becomes more tolerant of criminals that repent and sin no more. Further, he makes no mention at all of persons seeking new lives for reasons other than legal trouble, such as women who have fled abusive husbands.

Etzioni concludes his argument by considering court trends in balancing the need to protect personal privacy with concerns about public health and safety. Although useful, this segment does not appear to lie in a strategic part of his argument. Court cases often set a context for interpretation and might benefit readers more in the beginning of an argument. He observes the courts have tended to "privilege privacy and make claims for public health or safety clear several high hurdles" (670). More recently, however, the courts are lowering these barriers with growing concern for public interest. For example, the courts have mandated drug testing for those who "directly have the lives of others in their hands, including pilots, train engineers, drivers of school buses, and air traffic controllers, even though such testing violates their privacy" (670). Etzioni reports that the ACLU feels these new laws "condition Americans to a police state" (671).

All of this, according to Etzioni, "points to a need to recast privacy in our civic culture, public policies, and legal doctrines. We should cease to treat it as an unmitigated good, a sacred right (the way Warren and Brandeis referred to in their famous article and many [other legal theorists have] since) or one that courts automatically privilege" (671). He feels that we should instead rely on the Fourth Amendment, which has built into its text safeguards that balance privacy and public security. His interpretation of the document's reference to "unreasonable" search protocols recognizes the difference between searches that "wantonly violate privacy," and those that "enhance the common good to such an extent that they are justified, even if they intrude into one's privacy" (671). Additionally, the amendment addresses sufficient cause by introducing warrants "issued by a 'neutral magistrate' presented with 'probable cause'" (671). Etzioni apparently believes interpretation of this document will be uniform from one court to the next. This assumption is problematic at best.

The author leaves us with a new vision of privacy as a "very important right but not one that trumps most other considerations, especially of public safety and health" (671). With this parting thought, the author packages a difficult and complex concept into a pill that is not terribly difficult to swallow. By the same token, however, his oversimplification may leave some readers feeling like something is missing.

Indeed, something is missing—the rest of Etzioni's book, from which this excerpt originates. Readers of this argument can only hope that Etzioni deals carefully and respectfully with the arguments of civil libertarians in other parts of his work, for he certainly does not do so here. His tendency to use only the most inflammatory statements from his opponents suggests he has no interest in fully addressing their respective concerns.

All things considered, Etzioni begins his essay with a clear purpose and a logical, tangible starting point. Through the inclusion of several diverse public-interest groups, health organizations, courts, and governmental bodies, he initially appears to address all aspects of the moral dilemma. This is especially true in the obvious benefit to newborns with HIV that are diagnosed early. But in this excerpt, he distracts readers from the true opposition by focusing primarily on the media, while turning the Coalition for Constitutional Liberties and the ACLU into radical doomsayers that jeopardize public welfare. He marginalizes their concerns, advocates for increased biometrics applications on the chance that billions of dollars might potentially be protected from fraud, and opposes legislation that would protect potential victims because society potentially could be more forgiving. Consequently, his venture into the hypothetical realm leaves opponents (and critical readers) unsatisfied.

WORK CITED

Etzioni, Amitai. "Less Privacy Is Good for Us (and You)." *Current Issues and Enduring Questions*. Ed. Sylvan Barnet and Hugo Bedau. 8th ed. Boston: Bedford, 2008. 668-71.

| | | | | | | | | | | | | | | | | | | | | | | | | | | | | | | | | | | | | | | | | | | | | | | | | | | | | | | | | | | | | | | | | | | | | | | | | | | | | | | | | |

FOR EXPLORATION

Now that you have read Etzioni's argument several times and have also read Stevon Roberts's analysis of it, reread Stevon's essay to determine its strengths and limitations. Identify two or three passages from the essay that struck you as particularly significant and helpful, and write several sentences of explanation for each passage. No essay, however successful, is perfect, so you should also identify one or more ways this essay might be even more successful.

| | | | | | | | | | | | | | | | | | | | | | | | | | | | | | | | | | | | | | | | | | | | | | | | | | | | | | | | | | | | | | | | | | | | | | | | | | | | | | | | | |

||||||||||||||||||||||||||||||||||||||||||||||||||||||||||||||||||||||||||||||||||||||||||

FOR COLLABORATION

Bring your response to the previous Exploration to class to share with a group of peers. Appoint a timekeeper and a recorder. After all group members have shared their responses, answer these questions: (1) To what extent did other members of your group agree in their evaluation of Stevon Roberts's analysis? To what extent did they disagree? (2) Now that you have heard everyone's responses, what two or three passages does your group feel best demonstrate Stevon's analytical skills? (3) How might Stevon's essay be further strengthened? Be prepared to share the results of your discussion with the class.

||||||||||||||||||||||||||||||||||||||||||||||||||||||||||||||||||||||||||||||||||||||||||

Reading Visual Texts

As an academic writer, you will often be asked to analyze traditional print texts. Because of developments in communication technologies that increasingly emphasize the visual, the ability to analyze visual texts is gaining importance in academic writing. The ability to be a critical reader of visual texts is also important in your daily life — at least if you want to be a wise consumer and an engaged citizen.

If you think about the full range of reading that you do, you can easily identify a number of texts, such as magazines, blogs, and Web pages, where visual elements are as important as the words on the page. If you want to be an engaged and critical reader, then, you must develop the ability to read visual texts with the same insight you bring to written texts.

For instance, look at the black-and-white reproductions of two magazine covers on pp. 109 and 110. The first cover is from *Wired*, a nationally distributed, advertisement-filled magazine for those interested in online, wireless, and other newly developed information technologies. The second cover is from *The Co-op Thymes*, the monthly newsletter of the First Alternative Co-op in Corvallis, Oregon.

Each cover provides important cues that attentive readers will notice as they analyze both image and text. Each cover also assumes that whoever looks at the cover will read the images and words presented there in sophisticated ways. The *Wired* cover, for instance, assumes that readers will immediately associate the Disney characters (Goofy, Peter Pan, Donald Duck, and Mickey Mouse) who are raising a flag on a pile of rubble with the famous photo of an American flag being raised on a hill on Iwo Jima, a Japanese island, during World War II. The colors of the magazine's cover are the red, white, and blue of the American flag—blue figures raising a blue flag against a white background with primarily red type—which further reinforces this association. In case you aren't familiar with the original photograph of the flag-raising at

Cover from February 2002 Issue of *Wired* Magazine

Iwo Jima, see the reproduction of it on p. 111. Many people have argued that the February 23, 1945, photograph of five marines and one navy corpsman raising the flag on the top of Mount Suribachi after one of the most brutal battles of World War II is the most memorable photograph of the war. It is

Cover from *The Co-op Thymes*, the Monthly Newsletter of the First Alternative Co-op in Corvallis, Oregon

almost certainly the most reproduced image in the United States from both World War I and World War II. This image—which was photographed by Joe Rosenthal, a photographer covering the Pacific War for the Associated Press—has appeared on a postage stamp and on the cover of countless magazines and newspapers. It also served as the model for the Marine Corps War Memorial in Arlington, Virginia. In October 2006, *Flags of Our Fathers*, a film about the aftermath of the raising of the flag at Iwo Jima for those involved, appeared in theaters across America.

Despite its popularity, this photograph has always been surrounded by controversy. When the photograph was first published, viewers assumed that

Joe Rosenthal's "Flag Raising on Iwo Jima" (February 23, 1945)

it was taken during the original post-battle flag-raising. In fact, the initial flag-raising was interrupted by a brief mortar attack, and Rosenthal photographed a second (somewhat staged) raising of the flag. For many in the United States, however, this photograph serves now—as it did during the war—as an image of American determination and of hope for the future at a time of great uncertainty. In fact, after the attacks on the World Trade Towers and Pentagon on September 11, 2001, many saw a resemblance between the Iwo Jima photograph and a much-reproduced photograph of New York City firemen raising the U.S. flag over the rubble of the Towers.

So why did the editors of *Wired* choose to design a cover that shows Disney characters and alludes to a famous and, for many, beloved photograph? The cover's headline gives an important clue: It informs readers that this issue of *Wired* includes a special report on "Disney, Invader: Inside the Ultimate Culture Machine." Observant readers of the cover will note that the biggest and most emphatic word in the title is *Invader*.

Clearly, this cover draws on international debates about what some have characterized as American cultural imperialism. Protests against this Americanization have taken multiple forms—from demonstrations at meetings of the World Trade Organization to the "slow food" movement in Europe, which is sometimes billed as an effort to resist the "McDonaldsization" of Europe. The article that is featured on the cover of this issue of *Wired*—"The Ever-Expanding, Profit-Maximizing, Cultural-Imperialist, Wonderful World of Disney: The Serious Business of Selling All-American Fun" by Jonathan Weber—considers these issues.

Although both the cover image and the title of the feature article seem to suggest that Disney has been victorious in its effort to expand its domain around the world, the article portrays a complex relationship between corporations that are attempting to export American culture and the people in other countries who may—or may not—be eager to consume this culture. Complex political, economic, cultural, and technological factors are at play in any such effort. In fact, the author of this article argues that companies like Disney are as likely to fail as to succeed in their interactions with other cultures—or to be changed in significant ways by them. Here, for instance, is the concluding paragraph of the article:

> Disney's challenges both at home and abroad illustrate just how hard it is for even the biggest of American brands to keep growing—and give lie to many of the fears people have about cultural imperialism. Unlike other industries—oil, say, or agriculture, or even technology—cultural businesses depend on giving people what they want, as opposed to what they need. It is true that the giant media conglomerates can sometimes suffocate competition and choice. But in television and theme parks in most of the world, there has never been much competition anyway, and in the sale of plush toys it is hardly an issue. For the most part, people will decide what elements of American culture they want. The Disneys of the world are slaves to the tastes of Chen Ping and Wei Qing Hua [a Chinese man and woman who are interviewed as they visit a theme park at the start of the article], not the other way around.

What, then, is the relationship between the bold, provocative cover of *Wired* and the feature article to which it alludes? Clearly, the cover is designed to catch the attention of those glancing at the magazine at a store or newsstand and to raise questions. Why are the Disney characters posed like the soldiers in the Iwo Jima photograph? Who is Disney invading, and why? Publishers hope that a provocative cover will persuade an indecisive consumer to pick up a magazine and head for the checkout stand. Granted, the editors of *Wired* took a risk in parodying a revered photograph. But as readers of *Wired* are aware, this magazine delights in flaunting conventional expectations through cutting-edge design elements, such as unusual colors, fonts, margins, photographs, and images. The designers of this cover clearly believed that readers would view their parody as thought-provoking rather than as disrespectful.

Just as writers of traditional print texts must consider the needs, interests, values, and assumptions of their readers, so too must those composing visual texts. This was true of the cover of *Wired*, and it is equally true of the cover of *The Co-op Thymes*. Unlike *Wired*, which is a nationally distributed, mass-market magazine, the *Thymes* is a locally distributed newspaper for shoppers at the First Alternative Co-op in Corvallis, Oregon. The *Thymes* is mailed to members of the natural foods co-op each month; it's also available for free at checkout stands.

If *Wired* covers are designed to project the magazine's hip, with-it technological focus, the cover of the *Thymes* reflects the focus of both the newspaper and the First Alternative Co-op. According to the Co-op's mission statement, as presented in the first page of the newsletter,

> First Alternative is a community market aspiring to be a model for environmental sustainability through our purchasing and workplace practices. We

- Seek to honor our traditions and build upon our potential.
- Are committed to cultivating tolerance and diversity in our operations.
- Strive for excellence in our products and services. . . .
- Will act ethically and appropriately in our pricing practices.
- Seek to provide a democratic business climate, fostering worker and member participation, according to cooperative principles.

Although the cover of this December issue of the *Thymes* evokes holiday traditions associated with that month, it also reflects the Co-op's mission statement. The illustration that is the primary feature of the cover, for instance, evokes both tradition and change — particularly change in the diversity of those celebrating the holiday together. As the original cover (which is printed in warm colors of blue, green, yellow, and related tones) makes clear, the individuals who have gathered to celebrate the holiday season represent multiple ages and ethnicities. They are definitely celebrating a holiday, as the candles, party hats, wine, and food suggest. The illustrator, Lucinda Kinch, has taken care, however, not to suggest a particular winter holiday, such as Christmas, Hanukkah, or Kwanza. Instead, she evokes the cooperative spirit that the First Alternative Co-op and its newsletter hope to encourage.

Although the cover of *Wired* serves primarily to catch consumers' attention and to provoke thought, the cover of the *Thymes* is designed not to encourage potential sales but to reflect the mission of the Co-op and to provide information about items of interest to readers and customers. Thus the text on the left side of the *Thymes* cover is divided into two sections of white text printed on a blue background: The top section lists the principles that guide the Co-op, while the bottom section lists the articles in this issue. Even though the *Thymes* is a free publication, the editors and designers want to encourage Co-op members and visitors to read the newsletter. Doing so is one way of becoming more involved with the Co-op.

As publications, *Wired* magazine and the *Thymes* differ in significant ways. Their missions are different, as are the images they project and the readership they hope to attract. These differences are evident even in such apparently minor features as the paper they're printed on: *Wired* is printed on expensive glossy paper, and the *Thymes* is printed on inexpensive newsprint. Nevertheless, the covers demonstrate great sensitivity to their readers' needs and expectations and to their larger rhetorical situations. Both covers also assume that readers will bring cultural knowledge and well-developed analytical skills to their reading of these visual texts.

Not all magazine covers invite such in-depth reading, however. Covers of weekly news magazines such as *Time* and *Newsweek* generally present a photograph of a person or of a news event such as a natural disaster. The familiarity of this type of design feature helps reassure readers that they know what to expect in these magazines. If the photograph of a person appears on the cover of *Newsweek*, for instance, readers know that one of the issue's major stories focuses on this person. Such knowledge increases the readability of the cover and of the following story. The cover's implicit message is this: "If a person or event is important in the United States or to Americans, our magazine will feature it."

Why is it important to be able to read visual images and to understand the potentially powerful role that design and visual elements can play in written texts? Perhaps the most important reason has to do with the increasingly pervasive role that images have come to play in modern life. Driving down the street, watching television, skimming a magazine, reading online: In these and other situations, we're continually presented with images and texts, many of which are designed to persuade us to purchase, believe, or do certain things. Often these images can be a source of pleasure and entertainment. But given the persuasive intent of many images, critical readers will develop ways to not just "read" but "read into" these images. The guidelines on p. 115 present questions you can ask to analyze any visual text.

❋ bedfordstmartins.com/academicwriter
For more advice and practice analyzing visual texts, go to **Re:Writing** *and then click on* **Visual Analysis**.

Guidelines for Analyzing Visual Texts

- What is your general impression of the design and presentation of words and images in this text? Is the presentation cluttered or spare? Colorful or subdued? Carefully organized or (apparently) randomly presented? Calm or busy? Traditional, contemporary, or cutting-edge?

- What design elements are important in this text? Does it present a single dominant image? A variety of images? If so, how are the images related? What is your eye drawn to first? Why?

- What is the relationship between image and text? Does one predominate? Is the relationship explicit or implicit? Does the text function primarily to present information or to reinforce or extend—or even to subvert or undermine—the image?

- In what ways does the design appeal to logic and to reason? To emotion? What role (if any) does the credibility of a company or individual play in this text? Does the text assume that readers would recognize a trademark or corporate name, for instance, or a photograph or drawing of a well-known figure?

- Does the text assume prior knowledge about an image (as with the *Wired* cover)? What sort of knowledge? Historical? Artistic? Cultural? Political? What role does this prior knowledge play in helping the visual text achieve its impact? Does it work differently depending on the reader's prior knowledge?

- How would you describe the impact or message of the text? Does it achieve its intended impact? Why?

FOR EXPLORATION

Look at the advertisements on pp. 77–79 at the end of Chapter 3. Choose the ad that most intrigues, moves, or puzzles you, and analyze it according to the Guidelines for Analyzing Visual Texts presented above, writing your responses to each question. Finally, write one or two paragraphs about what you have learned as a result of this analysis.

FOR THOUGHT, DISCUSSION, AND WRITING

1. Interview an instructor who teaches a class you are taking this term or a class in your major area of study. Ask this person to describe his or her understanding of the goals of undergraduate education and the role that your

particular class or field of study plays in achieving these goals. Discuss the special analytic skills required to succeed in this course or field. Ask this person what advice he or she would give to someone, like yourself, who is taking a class in this field or planning to major in it. Be prepared to report the results of this interview to the class. Your instructor may also ask you to write an essay summarizing and commenting on the results of your interview.

2. Find an editorial or opinion column that interests you in a newspaper or general news magazine, such as *Newsweek* or *Time*. Using stasis theory as described on p. 90, determine the most important questions at issue in this editorial or column. Then use the Questions for Critical Reading on p. 95 to analyze the text you have chosen. Write a brief summary of what these activities have helped you to understand about your reading. If your analysis has raised questions for you as a reader, articulate them as well.

Now choose either Aristotle's three appeals (pp. 55–56) or Toulmin's framework for analyzing arguments (pp. 98–99) to further analyze the text you have chosen. After doing so, reread the summary you wrote earlier. What has this additional analysis helped you to better understand about your reading?

Your teacher may ask you to write an essay analyzing the editorial or opinion column you have chosen.

| | | | | | | | | | | | | | | | | | | | | | | | | | | | | | | | | | | | | | | | | | | | | | | | | | | | | | | | | | | | | | | | | | | | | | | | | | | | | | | | | | | | | | | | | | | | |

Making and Supporting Claims

A s Chapter 4 emphasizes, analysis and argument are linked in powerful ways. To write an effective argument, you must analyze both your own ideas and those of others. But academic argument requires more than strong analytical skills. A successful academic argument also requires careful, well-supported reasoning that anticipates your readers' interests and concerns.

Understanding—and Designing— Academic Arguments

The first step in writing a successful academic argument is to understand the ways in which academic arguments are similar to and different from other kinds of arguments. From one perspective, all language use is argumentative. If you say to a friend, "You've just got to hear Coldplay's new CD!" you're making an implicit argument. A sign that calls out "Best Deep-Dish Pizza in Chicago" is also making an argumentative claim. Even prayers can be viewed as arguments. Some prayers represent direct appeals to God; others function as meditations directed toward self-understanding. In either case, those who pray are engaged in an argument for change—either in themselves or in the world around them.

As these examples suggest, arguments serve many purposes beyond confrontation or debate. Sometimes the purpose is to change minds and hearts or to win a decision; this is particularly true in politics, business, and law. But winning isn't always the goal of argument—especially in the academy, where writers focus on contributing to the scholarly conversation in their fields. Given this focus, students who bring a debate model of argumentation to academic writing often encounter problems. Think about the terminology used in debate: Debaters *attack* their *adversaries,* hoping to *demolish* their *opponents'* arguments so that they can *win* the judge's assent and claim *victory* in the contest. In academic arguments, however, the goal is inquiry and not conquest. Your teachers aren't interested in whether you can attack or demolish your opponents. Rather, they value your ability to examine an issue or problem from multiple perspectives. Their commitment isn't to winning but to clear reasoning and substantial evidence.

Not all scholarly arguments are identical, however. Because they reflect the aims and methods of specific disciplines, they can vary in significant ways. Interpretation—whether of literary texts, artwork, or historical data—is central to arguments in the humanities. Scholars in the social sciences often argue about issues of policy; they also undertake studies that attempt to help readers better understand—and respond to—current issues and events. A sociologist might review and evaluate recent research on the effects of children's gender on parents' child-rearing practices and then present conclusions based on her own quantitative or qualitative study. Argument is also central to research in the sciences and applied sciences. Engineers who argue about how best to design and build trusses for a bridge, or chemists who present new information about a particular chemical reaction, are making claims that they must support with evidence and reasons.

Although scholarly arguments reflect disciplinary concerns, all scholars agree that the best arguments (1) explore relevant ideas as fully as possible and from as many perspectives as possible, (2) present their claims logically, and (3) include appropriate support for all significant claims. These preferences distinguish academic arguments from other kinds of arguments. You and your friend might spend an hour on a Saturday night arguing about the merits of Coldplay's new album, but your discussion would undoubtedly be fluid and improvisational, with many digressions. In academic argument, great value is placed on the careful, consistent, and logical exploration of ideas.

In a way, what is true of design is also true of academic arguments. (See the discussion of writing as design in Chapter 1.) Most academic arguments are open-ended and cannot be fully specified. Philosophers have been arguing for centuries, for instance, about whether it is possible to justify warfare, just as historians have argued about the significance and consequences of specific wars. In this sense, academic argument is endless: No important topic or issue is ever resolved once and for all. Similarly, there is no one correct process of composing or designing arguments. Some scholars who study what philosophers term *just war theory* take a historical approach; others emphasize ethical arguments.

As is the case for designers, the process of finding problems is central to writers of academic arguments. A literary scholar who believes that other critics of Toni Morrison's *Beloved* have inadequately recognized the importance of religious imagery in that novel is in effect identifying a new problem. Since literary texts—like other complex data sets—are open to multiple interpretations, this critic's argument will depend in part on subjective value judgments. The same occurs when a historian argues that previous accounts of the fall of Saigon near the end of the Vietnam War overemphasize Western media's role in this event, or when an economist argues that current theories of macroeconomics cannot account for the development of e-commerce on the Internet.

Perhaps most important, like designers, those composing academic arguments are concerned with what might, could, and should be. A biologist proposing a new method for protecting wetlands; a sociologist reporting the results of a new study on children in foster care; a communication scholar analyzing the effect of *The DaVinci Code* on public perceptions about Catholicism; a historian reconsidering previous studies of the spread of the Black Plague in medieval Europe: All are composing writing that matters — that expands the scholarly conversation and makes a difference.

Exploring Aristotle's Three Appeals

Academic writing places a high premium on the quality of ideas, evidence, and organization — on logical appeals, or *logos*. This doesn't mean, however, that as a writer you should avoid emotional appeals (*pathos*) and ethical appeals (*ethos*). All writers — whether they're composing a letter to a friend, an editorial for the student newspaper, or an essay for a history class — need to establish their credibility, and they can accomplish this in many ways. Academic writers generally incorporate ethical appeals by demonstrating knowledge of their subject and of the methodologies that others in their field use to explore it. They reinforce their credibility when they explore their subject evenhandedly and show respect for their readers. Writers demonstrate this respect, for instance, when they anticipate readers' concerns and address possible counterarguments. In so doing, writers seek to establish common ground rather than to win readers over to a particular position. (For more on analyzing rhetorical situations, see Chapter 3.)

thinking rhetorically

Just as all writers appeal to *ethos*, so too do they appeal to *pathos* — to emotions and shared values. Sometimes this type of appeal is obvious, as in requests for charitable contributions that feature heart-wrenching stories and images. Even texts that are relatively objective and that emphasize appeals to *logos*, as much academic writing does, nevertheless draw on and convey emotional appeals. An academic argument that uses formal diction and presents good reasons and evidence is sending readers a message based on *pathos*: "This subject is much too important for me to treat it frivolously. It requires the attention that only reasoned argument can give."

Appeals to *pathos* can also emphasize just how much is at stake in understanding and addressing a problem or event. Scholars writing about the Holocaust, for instance, often use vivid descriptions to encourage readers to connect personally with their text. Moreover, to bring immediacy and impact to an argument, writers often employ figurative language, such as metaphors, similes, and analogies. (For example, some scholars who have written about the massacre that occurred when Nanking, China, fell to the Japanese on

December 13, 1937, refer to this event as the Rape of Nanking.) They also may use images and graphics to highlight and support their point.

Understanding the Role of Values and Beliefs in Argument

As a writer, when you argue you give reasons and evidence for your assertions. A student arguing against a Forest Service plan for a national forest might warn that increased timber harvesting will reduce access to the forest for campers and backpackers or that building more roads will adversely affect wildlife. This writer might also show that the Forest Service has failed to anticipate some problems with the plan and that cost-benefit calculations unfairly reflect logging and economic-development interests. These are all potentially good reasons for questioning the plan. Notice that these reasons necessarily imply certain values or beliefs. The argument against increasing the timber harvest and building more roads, for instance, reflects the belief that preserving wildlife habitats and wilderness lands is more important than the economic development of the resources.

Is this argument flawed because it appeals to values and beliefs? Of course not. When you argue, you can't suppress your own values and beliefs. After all, they provide links between yourself and the world you observe and experience (in Toulmin's terms, these links are warrants). They thus play an important role in any argument. (To review Toulmin's system for analyzing arguments, see p. 98.)

Suppose that you and a friend are getting ready to go out for breakfast. You look out the window and notice some threatening clouds. You say, "Looks like rain. We'd better take umbrellas since we're walking. I hate getting soaked." "Oh, I don't know," your friend replies. "I don't think it looks so bad. It usually rains in the afternoon in summer. I think we should risk it." Brief and informal as this exchange is, it constitutes an argument. Both you and your friend have observed something, analyzed it, and drawn conclusions — conclusions backed by reasons. Although you each cite different reasons, your conclusions reflect your different personal preferences. You're generally cautious, and you don't like getting caught unprepared in a downpour, so you opt for an umbrella. Your friend is more of a risk taker.

If your individual preferences, values, and beliefs shape a situation like this where only getting wet is at stake, imagine how crucial they are in more complicated situations — such as determining whether a controversial proposal is right or wrong, just or unjust, effective or ineffective. Argument necessarily involves values and beliefs, held by both writer and reader, that cannot be denied or excluded — even in academic argument, with its emphasis on evidence and reasoned inquiry. The student arguing against the Forest Service plan can't avoid using values and beliefs as bridges between reasons and conclusions. And not all of these bridges can be explicitly stated; that would lead to an endless chain of reasons. The standards of academic argument require, however, that writers explicitly state and defend the most important values and beliefs undergirding their argument. In this case, then, the student opposing the Forest Service plan should at some point state and support the belief that preserving wildlife habitats and wilderness lands should take priority over economic development.

It's not easy to identify and analyze your own values and beliefs, but doing so is essential in academic argument. Values and beliefs are often held unconsciously, and they function as part of a larger network of assumptions and practices. Your opinions about the best way for the government to respond to unemployed individuals reflect your values and beliefs about family, the proper role of government, the nature of individual responsibility, and the importance of economic security. Thus if a political science instructor asks you to argue for or against programs requiring welfare recipients to work at state-mandated jobs in exchange for economic support, you need to analyze not just these workfare programs but also the role your values and beliefs play in your analysis.

The following guidelines will enable you to respond more effectively to the demands of academic argument.

Guidelines for Analyzing Your Own Values and Beliefs

■ *Use informal invention methods to explore your values and beliefs about a subject.* To discover why you believe what you believe, you need to consider more than rational, logical arguments: You need to tap into your experiences and emotions as well. Freewriting, looping, brainstorming, and clustering are excellent ways to explore the values and beliefs that underlie your stance toward an issue. (To review these strategies, see Chapter 9.)

■ *Avoid writing about certain subjects if you hold such strong views that you will have difficulty viewing it from multiple perspectives.* Freewriting about your feelings on, for example, gun control may help you realize that your convictions about this issue are so deeply rooted in your beliefs, values, and experiences as to be unchangeable. In such a situation, you would do better to choose a different subject.

■ *Pay attention to links between a claim and its support.* In the Toulmin system, these links are called warrants, and they are often unstated and assumed. For example, most arguments in favor of environmental protection are grounded in the warrant that preserving the environment is more important than such other goals as increasing the local, regional, or national economy. (To review the Toulmin system, see p. 98.)

(continued)

(continued)

thinking
rhetorically

■ *Analyze your rhetorical situation to determine which values and beliefs you need to acknowledge and justify in your arguments and which you can assume as warrants.* If you are proposing a course of action to an audience that already broadly agrees with your values and beliefs, you can assume considerable common ground and focus primarily on your proposal. If your audience is mixed or questions your values and beliefs, you may need to acknowledge and justify them. (See pp. 44–46 for questions you can use to analyze your rhetorical situation.)

■ *Imagine a "devil's advocate" who holds different values and beliefs.* Many writers find it helpful to engage in a silent dialogue with one or more "devil's advocates" — imaginary persons whose views differ considerably from their own. If you are arguing that the federal government needs to increase funding for college student loans, you might try a mental or written dialogue with a hard-headed, pragmatic congressperson or corporate executive who resists your argument because of concerns about the national debt. Such challenges might help you recognize that your assumptions about the need for all students to have access to a college education are not universally shared and that other concerns might also be reasonable.

thinking
rhetorically

When you argue, you must consider not only your own values and beliefs but also those of your readers. The student writing about the Forest Service plan would present one argument to a local branch of the Sierra Club (an organization that advocates for protecting the environment) and a very different argument to representatives of the Forest Service. In arguing to the Sierra Club, the student would expect readers to agree with his major warrants and therefore might focus on how the group could best oppose the plan and why members should devote time and energy to this particular project. The argument to the Forest Service would be quite different. Recognizing that members of the Forest Service would know the plan very well, would have spent a great deal of time working on it, and would be strongly committed to it, the student might focus on a limited number of points, especially those that the Forest Service might be willing to modify. The student might also assume a tone that isn't aggressive or strident to avoid alienating his audience. He would articulate his most important warrants and align them whenever possible with the beliefs and values of those who work for the Forest Service.

In academic argument, of course, your reader is generally your instructor. In this rhetorical situation, the most useful approach is to consider values and beliefs that your instructor holds as a member of the academic community. In writing for an economics or a political science instructor, the student arguing against the Forest Service plan should provide logical, accurate, and appropriate evidence. He should avoid strong emotional appeals and harsh expressions of outrage or bitterness, focusing instead on developing a succinct, clearly organized, carefully reasoned essay.

NOTE FOR MULTILINGUAL WRITERS

The standards of academic argument that are discussed in this book reflect the Western rhetorical tradition — a tradition that you are learning if you are new to this country. This tradition encourages writers to clearly articulate and defend their values and beliefs. Non-Western rhetorical traditions, including your own, may be different. Some traditions, for instance, encourage writers to convey their assumptions and values *indirectly*. Try to identify the differences between your home culture and the Western rhetorical tradition in the way writers address their values and beliefs. If you discuss these differences with your teacher and classmates, you will enrich everyone's understanding of the way that rhetorical practices differ in various contexts.

FOR EXPLORATION

Think of an issue that concerns you, such as a campus controversy, a recent decision by your city council, or a broad national movement (e.g., to provide public child-care facilities, house the homeless, or improve public transportation). After reflecting on this issue, use the guidelines presented earlier in this section to analyze your values and beliefs. Then respond to the following questions.

1. Given your values and beliefs, what challenges would writing an academic essay on this subject pose for you?

2. To what extent did your analysis help you understand that others might reasonably hold different views on this subject? Make a list of the possible opposing arguments. Then briefly describe the values and beliefs that underlie these counterarguments. How might you respond to these arguments?

3. Now write the major assertions or arguments that you would use to support your controlling idea, or thesis. Below each assertion, list the values or beliefs that your readers must share with you to accept that assertion.

4. How have the Guidelines on pp. 121–22 and this Exploration helped you understand how to write an effective academic argument? If you were to write an academic argument on this issue, how would you now organize and develop your ideas? What strategies would you use to respond to your readers' values and beliefs?

Appeals to *ethos* and *pathos* play important roles in academic argument. For an academic argument to be effective, however, it must be firmly grounded in *logos*. The remainder of this chapter presents strategies that you can follow to meet the logical and evidentiary demands of academic writing. These strategies will help you to (1) determine whether a claim can be argued, (2) develop a working thesis (an appropriately limited claim), (3) provide good reasons and sound evidence for your argument, (4) acknowledge possible counterarguments, and (5) consider whether visuals would strengthen your argument.

Determining Whether a Claim Can Be Argued

You can't argue by yourself. If you disagree with a decision to increase school activity fees, you may mumble angry words to yourself—but you'd know that you're not arguing. To argue, you must argue with someone. Furthermore, the person must agree with you that an assertion raises an arguable issue. If you like hip-hop music, for example, and your friend, who prefers jazz, refuses to listen to (much less discuss) your favorite CD, you can hardly argue about her preferences. You'll both probably just wonder at the peculiarities of taste.

Similarly, in academic argument you and your reader (most often your instructor) must agree that an issue is worth arguing about if you're to argue successfully. Often this agreement involves sharing a common understanding of a problem, process, or idea. A student who writes an argument on the symbolism of Hester Prynne's scarlet *A* in *The Scarlet Letter,* for example, begins from a premise that she believes the teacher will share—that Hester's *A* has significance for the impact and significance of the novel.

The Guidelines on p. 125 can help you compose an effective and arguable claim.

Developing a Working Thesis

Arguable claims must meet an additional criterion: They must be sufficiently limited so that both writer and reader can determine the major issues at stake and the lines of argument that best address them. In a late-night discussion with friends, you may easily slip from a heated exchange over the causes of the current unrest in world affairs to a friendly debate about whether Taylor Hicks really deserved to win the *American Idol* competition in 2006. In an academic argument, however, you must limit the discussion not just to a single issue but to a single thesis—a claim you will argue for. It's not enough, in other words, to decide that you want to write about nuclear energy or the need to protect the wilderness. Even limiting these subjects—writing about the Three Mile Island

Guidelines for Developing an Arguable Claim

■ *Choose an issue that has no easily identifiable solution and that has something significant at stake.* If you state that identity theft costs consumers huge amounts of time and money, this claim is unarguable because it simply states a fact that can be verified. An arguable claim would present a position (for example, "Financial institutions have a responsibility to tighten their security and safeguard their databases to deter identity fraud").

■ *Choose an issue or problem that readers might have varying perspectives on.* An arguable claim takes a position with which many people could reasonably hold diverse positions.

■ *Attempt to persuade readers to believe or do something.* The purposes and occasions for argument can vary. Some arguments attempt to convince readers that an act or belief is right or wrong, helpful or unhelpful. Other arguments explore deeply complex issues or problems with a goal of understanding, not persuasion.

nuclear reactor or the Forest Service's Land Management Plan for the White Mountain National Forest—wouldn't help much. That's because your thesis must be an assertion—something, in other words, to argue about.

A clear, limited thesis is vital because it indicates (for you and for your reader) what's at stake. For this reason, many instructors and writers suggest that academic arguments should contain an explicit thesis statement—a single declarative sentence that asserts or denies something about the topic. The assertion "The U.S. Forest Service's Land Management Plan for the White Mountain National Forest fails adequately to protect New Hampshire's wilderness areas" is an example of a thesis statement.

Developing a clear, limited thesis statement can help you as a writer stay on track and include evidence or details relevant to the main point rather than extraneous or loosely related information. Readers—especially busy readers like your college instructors—also find thesis statements helpful. A clearly worded thesis statement helps instructors read your writing more efficiently and critically.

Here is the first paragraph of an essay written for a class on Latin American history. The thesis statement is italicized. Notice how it clearly articulates the student's position on the topic, the role of multinational and transnational corporations in Central America.

Over the past fifty years, Latin American countries have worked hard to gain economic strength and well-being. To survive, however, these countries have been forced to rely on multinational and transnational corporations for money, jobs, and technological expertise. *In doing so, they have lost needed economic independence and have left themselves vulnerable to exploitation by foreign financiers.*

A clear thesis statement can help both writer and reader stay on track as they "compose" an essay.

Like many other writers, at times you'll have to think—and write— your way to a thesis. You may know the subject you want to discuss, and you may have a tentative thesis in mind from the start. Sometimes, however, only by actually writing a rough draft—by gathering your ideas and putting your evidence in order—can you determine what thesis you can support. In situations like this, you'll revise your thesis as you write to reflect your increased understanding of your topic and your rhetorical situation.

Providing Good Reasons and Supporting Them with Evidence

To support a claim in a way that readers will find truly persuasive, you'll need to provide good reasons. These reasons should rely on evidence to appeal to credibility, emotion, and logic. Chapter 4 discusses stasis theory, Aristotle's three appeals, and the Toulmin system to analyze and evaluate arguments; you can use these analytical tools to construct and revise your own arguments. Let's say that you've drafted an argument challenging increased standardized testing in the public schools. You're majoring in education, and you have strong feelings about federally mandated assessments, such as the No Child Left Behind legislation. Your draft explores your ideas as freely and fully as possible. Now it's two days later—time to step back and evaluate the draft's effectiveness. So you turn to Aristotle's three appeals.

thinking rhetorically

As you reread your draft with the appeals of *ethos*, *pathos*, and *logos* in mind, you realize that you've gathered a lot of evidence about the limitations of standardized testing—and thus made good use of appeals to *logos*. Your argument is much less successful in employing the appeals of *ethos* and *pathos*, however. Your rereading has helped you realize that the passion you bring to this subject caused you to write in a strident tone, which might make readers distrust your credibility and sense of fairness. You haven't considered the advantages of standardized testing or the reasons that some people find it helpful and even necessary. Critical readers might well suspect that you've stacked the deck against standardized testing.

Clearly, you need to strengthen your argument's appeal to *ethos*. You revise your tone so that it's more evenhanded; more important, you consider multiple points of view by presenting and evaluating possible counterarguments. Perhaps in the process you'll discover some shared values and beliefs that can strengthen your argument. (You could acknowledge your opponents, for instance, for recognizing the importance of education as a national, and not just local, concern.) You'll want to find as many ways as possible to demonstrate that you realize your subject is complex and that reasonable people might have different ideas on the best way to address it.

What about *pathos*? In rereading your essay, you realize that in gathering strong evidence to support your claim, you've failed to give your subject a human face. You've got plenty of statistics and expert testimony but little that demonstrates how standardized testing affects real students and teachers. Based on your own experiences and those of peers, you have good examples of this negative impact, so you write yourself a reminder to include at least one such example in your revised draft. You also look for other ways to remind readers that national debates over standardized assessment aren't about impersonal test scores but about the real-life learning and teaching experiences of students and teachers across America.

As this example suggests, such analytical tools as Aristotle's three appeals, stasis theory, and the Toulmin system can play a key role in the construction of arguments. You may not use these tools to write the first draft of your argument (after all, your inital flow of ideas might be limited if you constantly asked yourself, "Does Toulmin's system call this point a claim, reason, warrant, qualifier, or evidence?"), but once you have a rough draft you can use these tools to test your ideas and identify problems that need to be addressed and areas that need to be strengthened. The student who's arguing that recent increases in standardized testing threaten the quality of students' education, for instance, might find it helpful to identify the most important stasis questions at issue in her argument. Are they questions of fact? Definition? Interpretation? Value? Consequence? Policy?

In addition to using analytical tools, you can ask commonsense questions about the evidence that you include to support your claims.

|||||||||||||||||||||||||||||||||||||||||||||||||||||||||||||||||||||||||||||||||||||||||||||||

FOR EXPLORATION

Think again about the issue you analyzed in response to the Exploration on p. 123. Formulate a tentative, or working, thesis statement that reflects your current position on this issue. Articulate two or three reasons or claims that support your thesis, and then list the major evidence you would use to support these claims. Finally, write a brief statement explaining why this evidence is appropriate, given your thesis statement and the reasons or claims that you have written.

|||||||||||||||||||||||||||||||||||||||||||||||||||||||||||||||||||||||||||||||||||||||||||||||

Questions for Evaluating Evidence

- How representative are my examples? Will readers find these examples relevant to my argument?
- Do I provide enough examples to make my point? Too many?
- Is the significance of my examples clear? Are they clearly related to my key points?
- If I have used statistical evidence, who compiled this evidence? A disinterested source? If not, do I have a good reason for presenting statistics from a source with an established position on my topic? (Such would be the case, for instance, if you cited statistics from MasterCard and Visa in an argument about the need for tighter security to prevent identity fraud.) Are the statistics based on an adequate sample, and have I drawn appropriate inferences from them, given the sample size? Have I considered multiple interpretations of this statistical evidence?
- What authorities, if any, do I draw upon to support my argument? Are these authorities qualified to comment on my topic? Why? Are any of them likely to be biased? Are their comments timely? If they are not—if I am citing an ancient authority on a contemporary topic, for instance—do I have a clear reason for why this authority's comment is relevant? Do I need to share the authorities' credentials with readers, or can I assume that readers already know and respect these sources?

Acknowledging Possible Counterarguments

Since academic argument is modeled on inquiry and dialogue rather than debate, as a writer you must consider multiple sides of an issue. Discussing and responding to counterarguments demonstrate that you've seriously analyzed an issue from a number of perspectives—that you've drawn reasonable conclusions.

There are a number of ways to discover counterarguments. You could dialogue with one or more devil's advocates (see p. 122), or you could discuss your subject with a group of classmates. You might even interview someone who holds a different position. Being aware of your own values and beliefs can also help you identify counterarguments. The student arguing against the Forest Service plan might consider the views of someone with different values, perhaps a person who believes in the importance of economic development, such as the owner of a lumber company. Finally, reading and research (both print and online) can expose you to the ideas and arguments of others.

How you use counterarguments will depend on your subject and rhetorical situation. In some instances, counterarguments can play an important structural role in your essay. After introducing your topic and indicating your thesis, for example, you might present the major counterarguments to your position, refuting each in turn. You might also group the counterarguments, responding to them all at once at an appropriate point.

||||||||||||||||||||||||||||||||||||||||||||||||||||||||||||||||||||||||||||||||||

FOR COLLABORATION

This activity will help you recognize possible counterarguments to the thesis that you have been writing about in this chapter. To prepare, be sure that you have a clear, easy-to-read statement of your working thesis and of the major evidence you would use to support it. Now spend five to ten minutes brainstorming a list of possible counterarguments.

Bring these written materials to your group's meeting. Determine how much time the group can spend per person if each student is to get help. Appoint a timekeeper. Then have each writer read his or her working thesis, evidence, and possible counterarguments, followed by members of the group suggesting additional counterarguments that the writer has not considered. Avoid getting bogged down in specific arguments; instead, focus on generating as many additional counterarguments as possible. Continue this procedure until your group has discussed each student's work.

||||||||||||||||||||||||||||||||||||||||||||||||||||||||||||||||||||||||||||||||||

Using Visuals to Strengthen Your Argument

Images and graphics play an increasingly important role in communication today. Everywhere we turn — when we walk down the street, watch television, or surf the Web — images and graphics compete for our attention (and, often, our money). Think of the power of such logos as Target's red-and-white bull's eye or McDonald's golden arches. Also, most news media use photographs, audio clips, and video clips to heighten the impact of their stories. And thanks to new software technologies, ordinary citizens can create texts that mix words, images, and graphics. Consider, for instance, the personal Web site created by Farhan Ahmed, a student at Lafayette College (see p. 130). As a writer and reader in the twenty-first century, you know that visuals will be important in your professional and personal life. But what role should they play in the academic writing you currently do as a student?

Because academic argument typically emphasizes *logos* over *ethos* and *pathos*, rhetorical common sense suggests that you should use visuals when they strengthen the substance of your argument. Tables, charts, graphs, maps, and photographs can usefully present factual information that appeals to *logos*. In writing about the collapse of the Tacoma Narrows Bridge in Tacoma, Washington, on November 7, 1940, engineering student Brenda

A Student's Personal Web Site

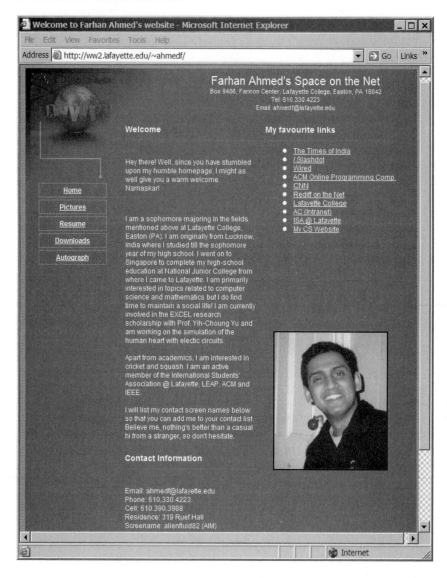

Shonkwiler used a number of images and graphics to good effect. In her essay, Brenda argues that engineers learned a number of key lessons from the bridge's failure, and that engineering students should continue to study this dramatic event. Brenda emphasized that there had been many indications of a potential bridge failure. Indeed, the bridge had such a strong tendency to twist and turn in the wind that it earned the nickname "Galloping Gertie." To help readers visualize this unusual event, Brenda included three still photos of the bridge twisting and, ultimately, collapsing. One of these photos, which shows the center of the bridge undulating moments before the bridge collapsed, is presented on p. 132.

✳ bedfordstmartins.com/academicwriter
  For the complete text of Brenda Shonkwiler's research essay, click on **Student Writing**.

Brenda also included a diagram identifying the major features of a suspension bridge, as well as other charts, graphs, and tables. For example, her table on p. 133 provides basic information about suspension bridge failures throughout the world due to wind. In these and other ways, Brenda strengthened the substance — and visual impact — of her argument. The following guidelines will help you make the most effective use of images and graphics in your academic writing.

Guidelines for Using Visuals in Academic Writing

- *Consider both the conventions of the discipline and your specific assignment.* Disciplinary conventions are part of your rhetorical situation, and they can be especially helpful when you need to determine whether to include images and graphics. The social sciences and sciences have a tradition of using images and graphics to present and organize information; the humanities rely more upon the written word. Consider your teacher's expectations and the constraints of your assignment. Look for examples of similar arguments. When in doubt, consult your teacher.

  thinking rhetorically

- *Use charts, graphs, tables, and illustrations to organize information.* A simple chart or table can present information that would take several paragraphs to describe. These efficient devices free up space for analysis and thus contribute to your argument's effectiveness. (See Chapter 11 for suggestions for creating and using visuals.)

- *Use photographs and illustrations to bring a text to life or to portray experiences that are difficult to imagine.* Most of us can only wonder what a bridge that's twisting and turning violently in the wind would be like, so Brenda Shonkwiler included a photo in her essay that captures this experience. An art history student might include a reproduction of a work she's discussing, while an anthropology student describing her research on life in rural trailer parks might include photos of such parks.

- *Avoid using visuals as decorations.* Academic writing is primarily about substance. Images and graphics can enrich your writing. But substance should always come first; visuals, second.

Student Essay Using Image for Evidence

Fig. 2. <u>Film still of the Tacoma Narrows Bridge twisting</u>, 7 Nov. 1940, Tacoma Narrows Collection. Twisting just before failure.

Suspension bridges, in general, are more flexible than other types of bridges. To decrease the flexibility, suspension bridges are typically stabilized with stiffening trusses. Such stiffening trusses are frameworks consisting of many intercon-nected braces that allow wind to flow through them with relatively little resistance, while diminishing (dampening) vertical and torsional motions. The Tacoma Narrows Bridge had been stiffened with solid girders (horizontal beams) instead of trusses. (See Fig. 4.) Koughan says that the girders "were unusu-ally shallow, only [eight feet] deep, in comparison

Student Essay Using Table for Evidence

expect the bridge to fail catastrophically the way it did. (161)

Actions Taken. According to Koughan, engineers tried several methods to minimize or eliminate the motion of the Tacoma Narrows Bridge, without success. First, they had tie-down cables strung from the plate girders to fifty-ton concrete blocks on the shore, but the cables soon snapped. They then installed inclined cables to attach the main cables to the bridge deck in the middle of the long span, but these cables failed to prevent the bridge from

Table 1
Suspension Bridge Failure Due to Wind

Bridge (location)	Span (ft.)	Failure Date
Dryburgh Abbey (Scotland)	260	1818
Union (England)	449	1821
Nassau (Germany)	245	1834
Brighton Chain Pier (England)	255	1836
Montrose (Scotland)	432	1838
Menai Strait (Wales)	580	1839
Roche-Bernard (France)	641	1852
Wheeling (United States)	1,010	1854
Niagara-Lewiston (USA--Canada)	1,041	1864
Niagara-Clifton (USA--Canada)	1,260	1889
Tacoma Narrows Bridge	2,800	1940

Source: Petroski 160.

Putting Theory into Practice: Academic Argument in Action

One of the major themes of this textbook is that written communication is situated within a particular context. Therefore there is no one-size-fits-all form of argument—or of any other kind of writing. Instead, just as designers must respond to the specifics of their situation, so too must writers respond to the specifics of their rhetorical situation. (To review the concept of the rhetorical situation, see Chapter 3.)

thinking rhetorically

Below is another example of an academic argument. This essay was written by Stevon Roberts, whose analysis of the excerpt from Amitai Etzioni's *The Limits of Privacy* appears in Chapter 4 (pp. 103–107). After analyzing Etzioni's argument, Steve wanted to explore his own views on privacy issues, particularly on the Internet and Web.

He wrote the essay for his first-year writing class. Here is how Steve analyzed his rhetorical situation:

> I am writing an argumentative essay for my composition class. I want to convince my readers—my instructors and my classmates—that they should take steps to improve the security of their identity and privacy online. Most of my readers are aware that this is an issue they should care about. They've heard about identity theft and know what a huge problem it can be. They just think it won't happen to them. In my essay I have to provide solid evidence that we can't count on others, like state and federal agencies, to protect us. I also need to persuade readers that even if they aren't techno geeks (like me!) they can take some basic steps that will protect them.
>
> In terms of Aristotle's appeals, *logos* is very important to my argument, but so are *ethos* and *pathos*. As I said, many people prefer to think that identity theft and other online invasions of privacy won't happen to them. I need an introduction that will capture their attention, and I also need to project a nonthreatening, reliable image.

Here is Steve's essay.

My Identity Crisis—and Yours

STEVON ROBERTS

My name is Steve. It is also Clint Eastwood, Harrison Ford, and George W. Bush. I have been known as One-two-three, Four-five-six, and Seven-eight-five-eight-three-one (I can't tell you the rest because that's private). I have lived in Springfield, Eugene, and Corvallis, Oregon—and in Singapore and the District of Columbia at 1600 Pennsylvania Avenue. Some-times I make less than $20,000 a year, and sometimes my salary would make Bill Gates turn green with envy. Do I suffer from multiple personality disorder? No. But I have learned the hard way about the need to protect my privacy online. As a result, I now intentionally provide false information for businesses requesting my name, address, Social Security number, an-nual salary, marital status, music tastes, and weekend hobbies.

Am I paranoid? Maybe. But I have learned how to avoid having a telephone that rings off the hook with telemarketers peddling long-distance telephone or cable services and how to maintain multiple email accounts with various pseudonyms to keep marketers from bombing my primary inbox with mass mailings for loan refinancings and Viagra. You might be thinking that avoiding nuisances like these is simply not worth the hassle of managing multiple email accounts, logins, passwords, and so on. I encourage you to reconsider. There is a growing security risk as-sociated with the mass distribution of information over computer net-works. People who freely give out their names, numbers, or addresses are not just vulnerable to mass soliciting: they are targets for hackers and identity thieves.

Like me, your initial reaction to statements like these might be, "That would never happen to me. The chances of getting my computer hacked or having my identity stolen are minuscule." Besides, aren't there state and federal agencies as well as Internet service providers charged with protecting citizens from these crimes? What about all those businesses implementing increased security and privacy policies on their Web sites? These kinds of "protections" lulled me into a false sense of security. Then, a few years ago, "more than five million Visa and MasterCard accounts throughout the nation were accessed . . . after the system at a third-party processor was hacked" ("Millions of Visa, MasterCard Numbers Exposed"). One of those accounts was mine. This experience convinced me that there are some businesses I couldn't trust to protect my privacy and identity. I had to take a more active role in pro-tecting myself, and I hope I can convince you to do the same.

Such an effort may sound daunting and unnecessary, given the num-ber of institutions and legislative bodies trying to protect us. It's impor-tant to recognize, however, that the laissez-faire nature of the Internet — one of its great strengths — is also a limitation where privacy is con-cerned. The speed with which technologies develop comes at a great cost: those who we have traditionally relied on to protect us cannot anticipate emergent problems, so they are always one step behind. As a result, at-tention to our personal privacy often yields to more immediate prob-lems, such as hacking and virus control. Given this situation, citizens need to develop habits and strategies that minimize the exposure of per-sonal information.

Chances are good that you have already had at least some exposure to this topic. Awareness of the danger is an important first step to take. But how willing are you to act on this awareness? How many take the time to learn who's collecting information and what they're collecting it for? One of the fastest-growing channels for private information exchange has silently exploited an estimated ninety percent of all computers connected to the Internet. Appropriately, it's called "spyware." ZDNet's Robert Vamosi describes spyware (also known as adware) as a "hidden software program that transmits user information via the Internet to advertisers in exchange for free downloaded software." Let's say that you want to install a program—maybe a download manager. To do so, you register the software with your name, address, phone number, email, and various other kinds of information. What the software distributors don't always tell you during installation (or more often don't tell you in LARGE ENOUGH PRINT) is that while you're being a good citizen of the Internet and registering your download manager, a hidden program may be simultaneously installed that transmits this personal information to advertisers who can target you for advertisements (Vamosi).

This may not sound particularly problematic, but spyware can transmit personal information not only to advertisers (which is bad enough) but also to those who would use this information for illegal purposes. Think about it: every time private information is transmitted, the chance for unauthorized interception by hackers increases. Collection, pooling, and distribution of this data increase the number of repositories waiting to be hit by the next hacker or identity thief. Because many legitimate software programs are packaged together with spyware and installed by unwary users, Internet service providers and policymakers cannot police their installation and usage. Spyware has already infested a wide variety of programs, including password managers, download managers, messaging programs, screensavers, and peer-to-peer file sharing programs.

In addition to being a courier for spyware, peer-to-peer (also known as "P2P") software has other inherent risks. This software allows users to share selected contents of their hard drives (such as music and movies) over a network supported by other users, or "peers." In the wake of Napster's collapse, people have indiscriminately flocked to these alternative networks for music and video—perhaps without understanding that they are not as secure as Napster was. P2P networks are not organized around a central, regulated network, so there are no built-in safeguards against hackers. P2P software may give your Internet provider address (sort of like a long telephone number for your computer) to malicious users. P2P programs can also be reverse engineered—that is, "hackers [have] the ability to change the software code so that it can be used for other purposes" (Kabay). The software may be used, for example, to gain unauthorized access to your computer and plant viruses or steal sensitive information like private files and bank account numbers.

If you work online, you're undoubtedly familiar with the irritating bulk email that we refer to as spam, but you may not be familiar with its potential threats to privacy. Recent software innovations combined with lax attitudes toward protecting email addresses have led to an epidemic of spam for inboxes around the country. America Online (AOL) alone "blocks 780 million pieces of junk e-mail daily, or 100 million more e-mails than it delivers" (Vise). Spam wastes time. It monopolizes bandwidth and computer processing power, costing corporations billions of dollars a year. And now, it poses a security risk. According to InfoWorld's Heather Harreld, "Marketing companies have begun to embed invisible HTML [hypertext markup language] 'bugs' or 'beacons' in their e-mail. Because these tiny one-pixel images must be retrieved from the sender's server when the message is opened, they can tell the sender when and how often a recipient looks at a message." As Harreld points out, HTML code embedded in the message can "allow the sender to gather information like the recipient's IP address, the type of browser they use, and the Web sites they visit." Sharon Ward, director of enterprise business applications at Hurwitz Group, in Framingham, Massachusetts, believes "It's just a matter of time [before] someone [can] figure out how to use these things against people or corporations." Ward speculates that this latest marketing development might be a hacker's newest tool — a "tricky little Trojan Horse for getting viruses into unsuspecting people's e-mail" (Harreld).

With businesses and identity thieves becoming increasingly aggressive in trying to steal private information, you need to take preventative measures to avoid becoming a victim of identity theft or fraud. Install a firewall on your home computer. (Your school and your office probably already have firewalls.) Firewalls are user-configurable gateways that are designed to block information from going into or out of a computer on certain ports or from certain software. It is also important to spend more time choosing the software you run on your computer in the first place — all of it. By reading software reviews (which are abundant online), you may be able to keep your machine from getting spyware, which is often much easier than getting rid of it (although you can look into antispyware software now available). If you are averse to reading reviews for yourself, ask your favorite computer guru what software you should (or shouldn't) be running.

How much money you invest will probably depend on how you use your computer, but any firewall or antispyware program is better than none at all. Time spent installing and updating the software is well spent when you compare it with the processing time and Internet bandwidth that spyware can leech away from your computer. More important, it is far less time than you will spend on hold with your bank's customer service center and with credit bureaus if your credit card is illegally used. This is a high price to pay compared to the simple tasks one can take to reduce exposure of personal data. Some Internet service providers will even assist you with the installation of this software since it helps maintain their network security as well as yours. Although you are ultimately responsible for protecting your own personal information, it's nice to have allies who are willing to help.

Yahoo, one email provider, has been especially proactive in promoting public awareness and participation with a contest for people who report unsolicited email. It uses the information that you send to help protect against further spamming for you as well as others. This is a great alternative to blocking spam or sending a "do not send me any more mail" request, which (contrary to popular belief) only affirms the presence of a valid email account and makes you a likely candidate for continued spamming. But better than this is not giving out your email address (or any personal information) if you don't absolutely have to. When you fill out applications or registration forms, fill in only the required fields, and read privacy policies with careful attention to where your information may be sent. Be sure to deselect any checkboxes for newsletters, agreements to make your information available to others, and so forth. It may also be in your interest to give businesses whose privacy policies you aren't satisfied with an alternative email address that doesn't include your real name. This will help to reduce pooling and distribution of your information, and it is time well spent when you compare it to the time spent wading through pages and pages of spam sent to your primary business or personal email accounts (is there an echo in here?).

These steps are relatively easy to take, and they can dramatically improve the security of your identity and privacy online. I would caution you, however, not simply to follow my advice and then forget all about it. It will always be tempting to let others work to maintain your privacy and identity. Recent history has demonstrated, however, that the rapid evolution of online technologies has presented new challenges as well as new opportunities, and those who use the Web must remain vigilant and evolve to meet those challenges or face ever-increasing threats to security. My solutions have evolved to include juggling multiple email accounts and offering intentionally false data to confuse information archives, but your solution may not need to be so complex. Perhaps you'll start with two email addresses — one you give to businesses and one you give only to your close friends or office. By taking responsibility with these steps and being on the lookout for new habits and strategies to improve your privacy and security, you can help thwart this crisis concerning peoples' identities.

WORKS CITED

Harreld, Heather. "Embedded HTML 'Bugs' Pose Potential Security Risk." *InfoWorld* 5 Dec. 2000. 8 Oct. 2003 <http://www.infoworld.com/articles/hn/xml/00/12/05/001205hnwebbug.html>.

Kabay, M. E. "Peer-to-Peer Software and Security." *Network World* 28 Aug. 2000. 12 Oct. 2003 <http://www.networkworld.com/newsletters/sec/2000/0828sec1.html?nf>.

"Millions of Visa, MasterCard Numbers Exposed." *ZDNet* 18 Feb. 2003. 8 Oct. 2003 <http://news.zdnet.com/2100-1009_22-984842.html>.

Vamosi, Robert. "What Is Spyware?" *ZDNet* 28 June 2001. 12 Oct. 2003 <http://www.zdnet.com/products/stories/reviews/0,4161,2612053,00.html>.

Vise, David A. "AOL Joins Microsoft in a Reply to Spam." *Washington Post* 21 Feb. 2003: EOI. *Washingtonpost.com*. 11 Oct. 2003 <http://pqasb.pqarchiver.com/washingtonpost/search.html>.

FOR EXPLORATION

Reread Stevon's essay, annotating as you read. Can you identify a thesis? What major claims support this thesis? And what reasons and evidence support the claims? Finally, evaluate the overall effectiveness of Stevon's argument. What are its strengths? What weaknesses, if any, can you identify? How effectively does Stevon's essay respond to his analysis of his rhetorical situation?

FOR COLLABORATION

Meet with a group of peers to discuss your responses to the preceding exploration. Appoint a timekeeper. After all have had an opportunity to share their ideas, answer these questions: To what extent did you agree in your assessment of Stevon's essay? To what extent did you disagree? What did evaluating his essay help you better understand about the demands of academic argument? Be prepared to share your ideas with your classmates.

When you enter a college or university, you join an academic community with unique values, beliefs, and methods of inquiry. Yet few members of that community will discuss these directly with you. Instead, your instructors leave it to you to understand the academic rhetorical situation and to master the skills necessary to succeed in their courses. You don't have to face this challenge alone, however. Your composition instructor and your classmates, acting as both coaches and supporters, can help you develop the critical thinking, reading, and writing skills necessary for success in school. What is at stake in your composition course, then, is not just earning a passing grade or fulfilling a requirement, but becoming a fully participating and successful member of the academic community.

| | | | | | | | | | | | | | | | | | | | | | | | | | | | | | | | | | | | | | | | | | | | | | | | | | | | | | | | | | | | | | | | | | | | | | | | | | | | | | | | | | | | | | | | | | | | |

FOR THOUGHT, DISCUSSION, AND WRITING

1. This chapter has presented activities designed to improve your understanding of academic argument. The Exploration on p. 123, for instance, asks you to identify the values and beliefs that have led you to hold strong views on an issue. The one on p. 127 asks you to formulate a working thesis and to list the major evidence you would use to support it. Finally, the group activity on p. 129 encourages you to acknowledge possible counterarguments to your thesis. Drawing on these activities, write an essay directed to an academic reader on the topic you have explored, revising your working thesis if necessary.

2. This chapter focuses on argumentative strategies that apply across the academic curriculum. While scholars in all disciplines would probably agree with this discussion, they might add that arguments in their own disciplines have unique features. Interview a teacher whose course you are currently taking in one of the following areas: the humanities, the social sciences, the natural and applied sciences, or business. Ask this teacher what characteristics he or she looks for in a successful academic argument in this discipline. Also ask what kinds of visuals are appropriate. Then write a brief summary describing what the interview helped you to understand about argument in this discipline.

3. Newspaper editorials and opinion columns represent one common form of argument. If your college or university publishes a newspaper, read several issues in sequence, paying particular attention to the editorials and opinion columns. (If your school doesn't publish a newspaper, choose a local newspaper instead.) Choose one editorial or opinion column that you believe represents a successful argument; choose another that strikes you as suspect. Bring these texts to class, and be prepared to share your evaluations of them with your classmates.

| | | | | | | | | | | | | | | | | | | | | | | | | | | | | | | | | | | | | | | | | | | | | | | | | | | | | | | | | | | | | | | | | | | | | | | | | | | | | | | | | | | | | | | | | | | | |

Doing Research: Joining the Scholarly Conversation

When you hear the word *research*, you probably think of looking for articles and books in the library or of surfing the Web to fulfill a class assignment. But research is actually a much more common activity in your life. You're conducting research, for instance, if you consult a current issue of *Consumer Reports* before purchasing a DVD player, watch a TV show about dog training to help you discipline your puppy, or use a travel-planning Web site such as hotels.com to plan a vacation. Indeed, research is rooted in curiosity. We all conduct research to find information, make decisions, and better understand our world.

When doing academic research, you may need to learn certain techniques, such as how to use library databases or evaluate Web sources, but it's your curiosity that will drive you to ask questions, consider other people's views, and perhaps even revise your original assumptions about a topic. The strategies in this chapter will help you in this process—whether you're spending an hour online to gather information to enrich an essay or undertaking a more substantial research project. In either case, you need to think about your project with specific questions in mind: What do I as the writer need to know? Where can I find the most appropriate sources? What will my audience want to learn? By asking these and other questions, you can join the scholarly conversation on your topic.

||||||||||||||||||||||||||||||||||||||||||||||||||||||||||||||||||||||||||||||||||||

FOR EXPLORATION

Think back to some academic research you've done in the past. First identify a positive research experience, and write several paragraphs about it. What made this research satisfying and productive? Now write a few paragraphs about a research experience that was frustrating, unproductive, or in other ways difficult. What have you learned by thinking and writing about these two experiences? Jot down a few pointers you should follow to improve your future research efforts.

||||||||||||||||||||||||||||||||||||||||||||||||||||||||||||||||||||||||||||||||||||

Getting Started on a Research Project

Research is a goal-driven activity. In some cases, your goal may be simply to clarify or supplement information you already have. Suppose, for instance, that you're writing an essay for your composition class about your grandfather's military experiences during the Vietnam War. Although your essay would focus primarily on his stories, you might want to put his account in historical and political context, which would require you to consult a few sources. This is very different from a formal research paper about the Vietnam War for an American history course, which might focus on one of the following issues: Should the United States have become involved in the Vietnam War at all? Was the U.S. decision to use Agent Orange to defoliate trees in Vietnam an ethical one? How effective was the military draft during the Vietnam War? Topics like these could be addressed only in a paper of considerable length and would require extensive research.

Regardless of your research project, you need to know how to locate, evaluate, use, and document sources. For more formal papers, you'll need to keep track of a wide variety of sources: You might consult twenty or thirty print and online sources and perhaps also engage in field research (such as interviewing). As you begin your research, then, think about the scope and nature of your project.

Developing an Appropriate Search Strategy

Whether you're doing a small amount of research or a substantial project, you need to develop an appropriate search strategy, one that will enable you to gather information in a timely fashion. Your work will be more efficient if you turn your narrowed topic into a goal-driven research question. A *research question* asks, in a fairly specific way, what you want your research to answer. It helps you focus on the kinds of sources that will be most helpful—and avoid sources that contain extraneous information. Suppose, for example, that you're writing a research paper for a health course, and your topic is "the media's coverage of AIDS." An appropriate research question might be "How do today's media cover survivors of AIDS, and how has that coverage changed since the 1980s?" On the other hand, if your topic is "AIDS services in your community," you might phrase your research question this way: "Does our community offer adequate services for survivors of AIDS—for those recently diagnosed as well as long-term survivors?"

In addition to having a specific research question, it's also essential to become familiar with your library's resources. Many campus libraries offer tours, workshops, and online tutorials to familiarize users with print and electronic resources. (You may also want to consult the research chapters of

Questions to Help You Start Your Research

▪ Do you have a clear sense of your assignment? Do you need to explain something, compare one idea to another, or argue a particular point of view? When is the final project due? Will you need to turn in any-thing—such as a first draft—before that date?

▪ Who is your audience? Will your readers already know something about the topic, or will you need to provide background information and define some terms?

▪ What role will research play in this writing project? Will your research provide only supplementary details and examples? Or will you investigate a subject thoroughly and present the results to readers?

▪ What knowledge do you already have on the topic? Do you need to do general reading, Web surfing, and talking with others to narrow the topic? Or do you have a specific research question in mind and feel that you're ready to get started?

▪ Does the topic require particular research strategies or sources? Many health topics, for example, call for up-to-date sources. For an essay on the evolution of rock 'n' roll, though, you would need to consult historical material and listen to some early recordings.

▪ Given the due date for your final project, how should you allocate your time? In a paper on corporate fraud for a business course, for instance, you might want to interview the CEO of a local company. You would thus need to build in the time for this activity—along with time for print and online research.

such writing handbooks as *The St. Martin's Handbook*.) Be sure, as well, to talk to a reference librarian. When you pose specific questions, reference librarians can often direct you to just the right sources or databases, saving you lots of time in the long run. Thus instead of saying "I'm looking for information on dolphins," it would be far better to say "I'm looking for recent research that compares the language of dolphins to that of humans."

Remember, too, that your instructor, teachers in other disciplines, and persons working in business and your community may be potential resources. A linguistics specialist or marine biologist on your campus, for example, might be worth interviewing if you were researching the language of dolphins.

It's also important to understand some basic research concepts and to keep track of your sources—and deadlines—from the very beginning. The following sections provide an overview of key topics: kinds of sources, working bibliographies and research logs, and time management.

KINDS OF SOURCES: PRIMARY OR SECONDARY, OLDER OR NEWER, SCHOLARLY OR POPULAR

Primary sources contain original information; they include historical documents, diaries, photographs or artwork, novels, data from experiments, and many other kinds of firsthand accounts. Your own field research, such as a survey of your classmates' opinions, is also a primary source. *Secondary sources,* on the other hand, are written *about* primary sources; they include encyclopedia articles, biographies, and analyses or descriptions of the work of others. Suppose, for instance, that you were researching the causes of the French Revolution for a European history paper. If you read the letters of Louis XIV, they would be primary sources, but if you also investigate what historians have said about the letters, their analyses would be secondary sources. For most research projects, you'll want to use both primary and secondary sources.

The purpose of your research will sometimes affect whether a source is primary or secondary. For example, an article by film director Steven Soderbergh offering an interpretation of the classic movie *Catch-22* would be a secondary source in an essay about that movie. If you're writing an essay about Soderbergh himself, then the article would be a primary source.

Another aspect of sources—related to your purpose in writing—is whether newer or older sources are more appropriate. Suppose that for an introductory psychology paper you were analyzing the theories of Sigmund Freud in light of the Victorian era in which he lived. For this kind of research, you would probably rely heavily on older, historical sources. But if you were studying contemporary neo-Freudians and how they view Freud's ideas today, you would need to consult fairly current information. Research essays that involve new developments in health, science, or technology also require up-to-date sources.

Another important distinction is that between scholarly and popular sources. An article in Wikipedia, a blog entry, a newspaper, a popular magazine such as *Newsweek,* or a news source online such as *Slate*—all may help you gain an overview of a topic. But for most academic research projects, you'll also want to consult the work of experts in scholarly publications. Scholarly periodicals, like the *American Journal of Sociology*, often have the word *Journal* in the title, contain few or no commercial ads, and can be accessed through library databases. If you look at the Works Cited list for "Sweatshop U.S.A.," you'll see that Alletta Brenner consulted a number of scholarly books and journals (pp. 180–81).

STARTING A WORKING BIBLIOGRAPHY AND A RESEARCH LOG

Regardless of the kinds of sources you use, it's essential to keep track of them from the outset. The best way to do so is by starting a *working bibliography*—a list of information (author, title, pages, publisher, publication date, type of reference, etc.) about each source you consult. When you ultimately write and revise your paper, you'll need to provide a complete bibliographic entry for each source you've used. This task will be much easier if you jot down the source information as you go along. (Nothing is more frustrating than searching for the correct publisher or page reference—through a floor littered with books and photocopies of articles and Web pages—at 3 A.M. when your paper is due later that morning.)

In the past, most writers kept entries for their working bibliography on three-inch by five-inch cards. Although some writers still use such cards because they like the ease of shuffling them around—by topic or by alphabetical order—many writers now use computer programs to organize their sources. Whichever method you use, be sure to follow the documentation style your instructor requires. The Writers' References section of this book (see pp. 307–64) provides essential information for Modern Language Association (MLA) and American Psychological Association (APA) styles.

✳ bedfordstmartins.com/academicwriter
For more help documenting sources using MLA, APA, Chicago, or CSE styles, go to **Re:Writing** *and click on* **The Bedford Bibliographer**.

Many writers also use a *research log*—a way to track what they've done and jot down reminders. You might, for instance, purchase a pocket-sized notebook for recording to-do lists, keywords you used in successful searches, new ideas to pursue, names of people you should talk to, and so on. Or you may want to set up a computer folder (or subfolders) to keep track of this kind of information. No matter how you keep the research log, the point is to bring order to the research process.

MANAGING YOUR TIME

Poor time management can torpedo an otherwise feasible research project. I don't say this to discourage you but to remind you that some factors are beyond your control or require careful planning. Consider issues of access. If your project requires older sources, such as newspapers from the 1940s, do you have enough time to obtain microfiched copies and work your way through them? Does your college library have the microfiched copies you need? If not, you'll want to find out about interlibrary loan policies and request the items you need at the earliest possible moment. Depending on the college, interlibrary loans may move quickly or slowly.

Whether or not to do field research is another issue that involves time management. For a cultural anthropology course, suppose you were examining the increasing popularity of body piercing in contemporary American culture. As part of your research, you decide it would be interesting to get

Guidelines for Managing a Research Project

▪ *Check the basics.* Make sure you have a solid understanding of the assignment, your audience, and the deadlines you need to meet.

▪ *Narrow the topic.* Do some preliminary research, if necessary, to make your topic more specific.

▪ *Develop a preliminary search strategy.* Decide which kinds of sources are likely to be the most helpful and whether time constraints might be a problem with any of them.

▪ *Establish a timetable for the project, and review it often.* List the activities you need to complete, along with tentative due dates. Schedules may vary quite a bit from one research project to another. Here is a timetable one student developed:

Activity	Complete by
▪ Write a research question that is based on narrowed topic.	_____
▪ Conduct print and online research, narrowing topic further if necessary.	_____
▪ Start a working bibliography and research log.	_____
▪ Write a preliminary thesis.	_____
▪ Develop a rough outline for the project.	_____
▪ Collect or draft visuals.	_____
▪ Read and evaluate additional sources.	_____
▪ Draft the essay, including all visuals. Rough draft due.	_____
▪ Get responses to the draft from classmates and instructor.	_____
▪ Revise the draft; prepare a list of works cited or bibliography.	_____
▪ Edit the final draft.	_____
▪ Proofread final draft. Final draft due.	_____

If you check your list and completion dates often, you'll know when to build in more—or less—time for an activity and still meet the final deadline.

your classmates' opinions on body piercing. Conducting an adequate survey, however, will take too much time since you have only two weeks to complete the assignment. Instead, you decide to interview a few students informally, which could still enliven your paper with some firsthand perspectives.

Even in less complex situations, when you're relying solely on library and Internet sources, the demands on your time may seem overwhelming. Library books, photocopies of articles, printouts of Web sites, and your own notes can quickly accumulate into a confusing mass of material. To avoid such pitfalls, be sure to manage your time efficiently and put your organizational skills to work. The Guidelines for Managing a Research Project that appear on p. 146 can help you stay organized.

NOTE FOR MULTILINGUAL WRITERS

If much of your research experience has been in a language other than English, when you start a research project in English you may want to work closely with general reference librarians and other librarians who specialize in your subject area. (Most university libraries have staff who specialize in areas such as the humanities, social sciences, biological sciences, or education.) If possible, meet weekly with a tutor in your writing center as well. At these meetings, you can review your ongoing work as well as your research timetable.

Library Research

Conducting research online is convenient and saves time. But your college library has resources — from reference librarians to catalogs and databases — that offer the ideal place to start.

Searching Catalogs and Databases

It's well worth getting to know your college library's Web site for useful information about its collections, hours, and so on. There are many types of information available; the most useful may be access to the online catalog and an array of databases. Many of these databases connect to indexes of periodicals, news stories and legal information, and bibliographies, and some provide downloadable copies of complete articles or other works.

Specialized indexes and databases are available for many disciplines, and it may help to talk with a reference librarian to determine which database or index is appropriate to your subject. Choosing the appropriate database or index requires you to start with a broad subject area and then to focus your search. Many libraries list databases by category; try browsing a broad subject area first, gradually narrowing it to the appropriate databases or indexes. Some libraries also offer a metasearch tool to search several databases at once.

Searching the catalog and databases effectively requires carefully chosen subject words, keywords, and other advanced search options.

EFFECTIVE KEYWORD AND SUBJECT-WORD SEARCHES

Before buying your first digital camera, did you search Google or a shopping search tool by typing in the words *digital camera*? Did you come up with thousands of hits or results? Chances are you then tried to narrow your keyword search so that you didn't have to plow through so much unrelated information.

This is the same kind of problem you need to solve when doing a keyword search for a research project—whether on a database, in a catalog in the library, or on the Web. For a research essay about the causes of human trafficking, if you typed in "human trafficking" on Google you would come up with about two million hits. Even if you then searched within these results and typed in "garment manufacturing" to focus your search on a particular industry, your search would still be too broad; the narrowed search would yield over seventy thousand hits. This is still an unwieldy number, so you might need to narrow your search even further. As this example shows, keyword searches offer numerous possibilities, but you need to think about the best words or phrases to use.

Google Advanced Search

When doing keyword searches, be sure to take advantage of advanced searching options, which are often on a separate page (for an example, see p. 148). Some catalogs, databases, and search tools let you use the Boolean operators AND, OR, or NOT, or parenthetical expressions, to make your search more specific. You can also use such symbols as + and - and quotation marks to conduct more focused searches. Nowadays, many of these options are already built in to advanced searches on library or Web databases and sites. The search tool at Google, however, may not use the same terms or symbols as another search tool or a library database, so it's a good idea to seek out search "rules" as you refine your search.

When working with library databases or catalogs, you can also search by using subject headings, which categorize sources according to subject matter. Most college libraries follow the classification system of the *Library of Congress Subject Headings* (LCSH). So when doing a subject-word search, it can be helpful to browse the library site for the precise words or phrases specified by the LCSH. Also, many library catalogs indicate the official subject heading that corresponds to the subject you've chosen, as in the search for information on "trafficking people" shown here. This library's catalog suggests using the LCSH subject heading "human trafficking" instead.

**Subject Word Search Results Showing
Suggestion for Official Subject Heading**

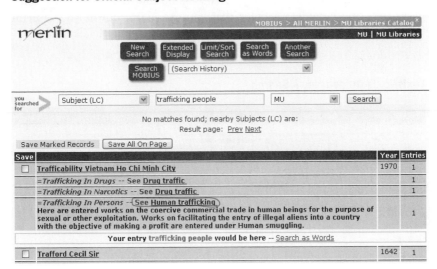

REFERENCE WORKS

Using your library's collections of reference works is a good first start for many research projects. Encyclopedias, bibliographies, disciplinary guides, and other specialized reference works such as biographical resources, al-manacs, yearbooks, and atlases are particularly helpful for getting an overview of a topic. But working with these resources (some are online, some are only in print), you can quickly find ways to narrow your topic and identify keywords for further research.

BOOKS

The library catalog provides directions for locating books, including basic information on the author, title, and subject, as well as publication informa-tion and where a book is shelved. You can note whether an item is checked out, when it's due back, and whether you'll need to leave time for an interli-brary loan. Many library catalog sites allow you to save information about books while you continue searching. Books on related topics are shelved to-gether in the stacks, so take the time to browse nearby shelves for other works relevant to your topic.

PERIODICALS

The library catalog lists the titles for all the periodicals in the library. To find a particular article or issue, you'll need to search an index. Whether in print or in a database, an index provides information about articles from newspa-pers, magazines, and scholarly journals. Some indexes are full-text data-bases, offering complete articles that you can skim, download, or print. Others include only abstracts that give an overview of an article's contents.

LexisNexis Guided News Search

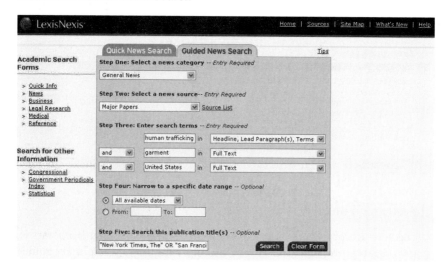

LexisNexis Guided News Search Results

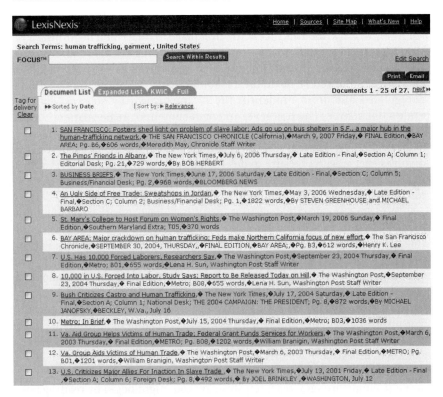

Indexes of periodicals can be general—including material mainly from general-interest publications—or specialized. General indexes, including LexisNexis, InfoTrac, and FirstSearch, are useful for accessing an enormous number of newspaper, magazine, and scholarly articles. Using LexisNexis, for example, you could search for articles with "human trafficking" as a key term, with the additional terms "garment" and "United States" in the text of the article (see p. 150). Using the site's advanced search options, you could further limit the search to three major newspapers; the results list includes twenty-seven articles that can manageably be skimmed for appropriate sources (see above).

SPECIAL COLLECTIONS

Many libraries house invaluable collections or archives of documents and other media that contain a wealth of primary sources—from memoirs to letters to posters to government documents—that are accessible for student research projects. When you use such primary sources you can gain a deeper understanding of a historical event or period.

Internet Research

For many writers, the Internet is the first place to turn when beginning a research project. After all, many resources — including reliable sources available via your school's library and other trustworthy sites — are accessible on the Internet. But you've no doubt also found that some online information is unregulated and from unidentifiable or untrustworthy sources. Further, while some sources (such as government documents) are permanently available, for many other sites a page you find Monday afternoon may be substantially revised by Tuesday morning — or deleted entirely. Online research requires special care; be sure to download, save, or print materials you may want to use, along with all bibliographical information, including the date you accessed them.

To make appropriate decisions about how best to research your topic, you need to understand the strengths and limitations of the resources available — and this is especially true when conducting research online. Participating in a discussion forum on your topic can provide a stimulating array of contemporary views; a carefully worded query to such lists or groups may identify additional resources. But to gain an adequate historical perspective on legislation governing water quality, for example, you would also need to consult scholarly books and articles as well as government documents. In addition, you might want to interview several scientists and legislators who are experts in this area.

Particularly in substantial research projects, you may find it helpful to develop a multipronged research strategy. You might begin by reading postings to a newsgroup or discussion forum, consulting your library's catalog, and surfing the Web for relevant sites. But you would also want to consult more specialized sources, such as databases or primary documents.

WEB BROWSERS

Web browsers such as Internet Explorer, Mozilla Firefox, or Safari for the Mac allow you to access dramatically large amounts of information. If you're writing an essay on the French artist Paul Cézanne for an art history class, for instance, you can use a search tool such as Google to locate the Web site of the Louvre in Paris. With just a few more clicks you can download reproductions of some of Cézanne's best-known paintings, as well as commentaries by art historians. Later, you can use the information saved in your browser's *history* function to retrace your steps and locate sources you need more information from. Bookmarking (or saving as a *favorite*) lets you save addresses for pages you'll want to visit again later. You may also want to take advantage of online bookmarking tools such as Del.icio.us and Diigo, which allow you to store and organize bookmarks using keywords or "tags." Useful for storing bookmarks when you're working away from home, these tools also allow you to share bookmarks with others.

INTERNET SEARCHES

There are many options for searching the Internet for sources; note that not all search tools work in the same way, so not all return the same kinds of results. The two primary ways to search using popular search sites (Google, Yahoo!, Lycos, and others) are with subject categories and with keyword searches. Many search sites offer subject directories that let you look deeper through general categories until you reach more specific ones. It can be useful, early on in your research, to try a keyword search within subject directories. The results can include subject headings that are more focused and shorter lists of related topics and sources.

To use keywords in the search engine at Google, choose your terms with care. (See p. 148 for more on keyword searches.) You may need to use multiple keywords within the engine's advanced search options, which vary. In addition to refining a search using Boolean operators along with keywords, you may want to set other preferences, to limit the results to sources written in English, or to sources published only in a certain time period.

Note that some search sites offer a choice of search engines, giving different results. And metasearch tools such as Ixquick, WebCrawler, and Dogpile allow you to work with multiple search engines simultaneously and then compile results for you.

AUTHORITATIVE SOURCES: ARCHIVES, GOVERNMENT SITES, AND NEWS SITES

The Web offers many excellent sources of reliable information, from scholarly online archives to exhaustive collections of federal, state, and local government documents. Government sites, from the Census Bureau to the Library of Congress, offer large collections of data and articles that contain legal and statistical information, as well as official reports and news releases.

Online scholarly archives or museum or library sites offer valuable collections of print and other media and primary source materials, from literary texts to photographs and artwork to historical speeches and other audio and video recordings. You can download for free many of the historical and literary primary (and secondary) sources available from these scholarly or professionally edited archives and virtual libraries.

For research on current topics, news sites — including online versions of reliable newspapers such as the *New York Times, Washington Post*, and *Los Angeles Times* — can be useful. Other news and general interest magazines, such as *Newsweek, U.S. News and World Report, Scientific American*, and *The New*

Yorker, can be accessed online for all or part of their content. Television news organizations and search sites such as Google and Yahoo! also offer online updates of current news stories. And online general interest magazines such as *Slate* and *Salon* provide current and archived content for free. These services can be reliable starting points for online research, especially for current issues. Blogs, personal Web pages, and other less mainstream news sources may also hold useful information, but you should evaluate them with care. As with any private organization or publisher online, be sure to evaluate blog postings for the author's credibility. You might ask, for example, whether the blog is published by a reliable source (such as a major news organization) or whether the author is well known in the field. You can also learn a lot about a blog by checking its links, its "About" page, and who links *to* the blog (using Technorati, for example).

✳ bedfordstmartins.com/academicwriter
For additional advice on searching the Web for appropriate sources, go to **Re:Writing** *and click on* **The Bedford Research Room**.

DISCUSSION FORUMS

A variety of resources are available in the form of experts and subscribers to online discussion forums. By searching a discussion list's online archive or by participating in a discussion, you can gather information from experts or others with an interest in your topic. Take care, however, to evaluate the credibility of people writing in discussion forums, even those that are scholarly; everyone involved may not be an expert or without bias. To locate a discussion list on your topic, try searching Google Groups' topics, or other sites such as Tile.net or CataList.

Conducting Field Research

In addition to using print and online resources, you might want to interview an expert on your topic, obtain opinions via a questionnaire, or observe something firsthand. These kinds of activities are known as *field research* because they take you out of the library or computer lab and put you directly in the field. Many students find that field research helps them build enthusiasm for their subject because they're creating information that no one before has compiled in quite the same way.

If you were writing an essay about sexual harassment on college campuses, for instance, you would probably do some library research to gain historical perspective and learn about incidents on campuses other than your own. But you might also decide to interview a faculty member involved in enforcing your own school's sexual harassment policy — and an individual who has publicly opposed that policy. Or you might distribute a questionnaire to measure other students' opinions (asking, for instance, how they define sexual harassment; how prevalent they think it is at your school; what, if any, policies they'd like to see enforced). You could also spend time observing the behavior of male and female students in a social setting. Although you wouldn't likely use all these field research techniques in one project, each can bring a special perspective to some topics.

INTERVIEWS

Interviews often provide information that's unavailable through other kinds of research. For a psychology paper about child abuse, for example, you might interview a local caseworker who works with abused children. For a political science paper on the Iraq War, you might consult a veteran of the war. Keep in mind that a good interviewer is first of all a good listener — someone who is able to draw out the person being interviewed. Since interviews are more formal than most conversations, be sure to prepare carefully for them.

Guidelines for Conducting Interviews

- *Request an interview in advance.* Explain why you want the interview, how long it will take, and what you hope to accomplish. On the day of the interview, show up on time.
- *Bring a list of written questions, but be flexible.* If the interviewee focuses on one question or moves to a related issue, just accept this change in plans and return to your own questions when appropriate. If the interviewee doesn't want to answer a direct question, try asking about the subject in a less direct fashion.
- *If you wish to tape-record the interview, remember to ask permission first.*
- *Take notes during the interview, even if you use a tape recorder.* Your notes will refresh your memory later on, when you don't have time to review the entire tape; they can also help you identify the most important points of the discussion.

QUESTIONNAIRES

Questionnaires can provide information about the attitudes and experiences of a large number of people. You might, for instance, survey your fellow students about their views on college sports or your school's policy on hate speech. Some disciplines, such as sociology and political science, use questionnaire and polling data extensively—as scientific measurements of the general population's views. In introductory classes, though, students generally use questionnaires to get a rough idea of broad trends or differing perspectives on a topic.

Guidelines for Designing and Using Questionnaires

■ *Determine the purpose of the questionnaire.* How will the results tie in to the rest of your research project? Be sure to explain your purpose briefly at the top of the questionnaire.

■ *Decide who will receive the questionnaire.* For an Introduction to Business paper, you might want to survey an entire small company of fifteen people. But for large groups, a representative sample works well. To survey all the business majors at your school, for instance, you might get a list from the business school and send a questionnaire to every fifth name.

■ *Decide how you will distribute the questionnaire and obtain responses.* Will you email it, send it by regular mail, or hand it out in person? Make sure the questionnaire states clearly *how* respondents should return it: Via your email address? By using the postage-paid reply envelope you've enclosed? Some other way?

■ *Consider whether you need any "personal characteristics" questions*—such as gender, income, marital status, age, or education—in addition to those about your primary subject. If, for a sociology paper, you were gathering opinions about the homeless in your community, the respondents' income levels may be relevant. In other cases, you may want to compare the answers given by men and women of various ages.

■ *Write questions that are clear and to the point.* It's usually best to use yes-or-no or multiple-choice questions, or those that involve ranking on a scale from 1 to 5 (say, from most to least effective). Remember that if a questionnaire is too long or complicated, few people will fill it out.

■ *Show a draft of your questionnaire to some friends before copying and distributing it.* Seek feedback on the clarity, fairness, and user friendliness of your questions.

■ *Give respondents a deadline for returning the questionnaire.*

■ *Analyze the questionnaire results carefully,* looking for trends, major points of agreement and disagreement, and so forth. Try to summarize what you have learned before incorporating the results into your paper.

OBSERVATION

Sociologists and anthropologists have rich traditions in firsthand observation. They often do research as participant-observers, living in and moving among various communities to observe social customs and patterns of behavior. Scholars using this approach have gathered data on many kinds of groups, from day-care centers to crack houses to corporate boardrooms.

Although you won't be doing such full-scale research, you can still generate stimulating material by closely observing various activities or groups. If you're writing a paper on the effectiveness of your local city council, you might attend several meetings and take the role of participant-observer during question-and-answer sessions. Also think about groups you already belong to. If you're writing about gender differences and work as a restaurant waitperson, you might study the tipping practices of men and women. As with other forms of field research, observation can bring interesting new perspectives to a subject.

Evaluating Sources

You already have considerable experience in evaluating sources: You instinctively draw on this experience when you choose a well-established Web site over an unfamiliar one, or an article by an expert instead of a brief essay in a popular magazine. But to fully evaluate sources, you need to consider other issues as well.

✳ bedfordstmartins.com/academicwriter
   For additional advice on evaluating sources, go to **Re:Writing** *and click on* **The Bedford Research Room**.

Questions for Evaluating Sources

▪ *Is the source useful to you and appropriate for your audience?* Is the source directly related to your narrowed topic and research question? Does it contain specific information—or does it merely talk about your subject in a general way? Is it appropriate for your audience—or is the information too easy or too difficult?

▪ *Who is the author?* Is he or she a recognized expert on the topic? Have other sources referred favorably to this author's work?

(continued)

(continued)

■ *Who is the publisher or sponsor?* What do the means of publication tell you about the source? Is a Web site, for instance, sponsored by an established government organization such as the National Cancer Institute, by a company that's trying to sell a new chemotherapy drug, or by an individual who has survived cancer? Is the publisher of a particular book one that you know or can easily find out about? Is an article from a reputable journal or newspaper?

■ *What is the source's purpose?* Is the source trying to persuade you to do something or think in a certain way? If so, does the source include factual information to back up its opinions? The Web sites about cancer mentioned previously, for example, might all contain useful information, but the latter two would likely have an obvious slant.

■ *Can you tell if the source is accurate and up-to-date?* Is it cited in other works you're evaluating? Does the author use footnotes and other references, indicating that his or her conclusions are research-based? What does your own knowledge of the topic tell you about the source's accuracy? If you're writing about a recent topic, such as a scientific discovery, is the source current enough? If you're looking at information on a Web site, when was the material last updated?

CHECKING ONLINE SOURCES CAREFULLY

While most television viewers can easily distinguish an infomercial from a serious scientific documentary, such distinctions can be murky on the Web. Some Web sites, such as that of the Library of Congress, are clearly authoritative, but others are much harder to evaluate. As you navigate online sources, pay special attention to issues such as sponsorship, timeliness, and purpose.

Guidelines for Evaluating Online Sources

■ *Check the credibility of the sponsor.* Try to determine (usually from the homepage) the organization or person who takes responsibility for the authority and accuracy of the site's information. Are the sponsor's qualifications indicated? Is it easy to contact this organization or person? Are phone number, mailing address, and email address provided? If the answer is "no," you might be wise to consider other sources.

■ *Look at the URL.* The ending of a URL generally tells what kind of group sponsors the site. A university site, for instance, normally ends in .edu (for *educational*). Also look for *commercial* (.com), *governmental* (.gov), *network* (.net), and *nonprofit* (.org).

■ *Check the credibility of the author.* If material within a site has an individual author, is the author's name clearly indicated? Are the author's qualifications provided, and can you verify them? For example, is there information about the author's expertise, a list of his or her professional memberships, or a link to the author's own site?

■ *Evaluate the writing and design of the site.* A Web site may have a credible sponsor, but if the writing is poor or the site is disorganized, its information may not be very useful. Is the site free of grammatical and spelling errors? Are sources included for outside information (such as graphs or photographs)? Do the links work?

■ *Determine the site's audience and purpose.* Although no Web site can be completely objective, it's important to think about potential bias—why a particular site was created and who its intended audience is. For example, LibraryofCongress.gov exists to provide educational information to the general public; it isn't selling this information or making a profit from it. A site such as Gerber.com, however, may have a dual purpose and a more targeted audience: to provide health information to parents of young children and to sell Gerber baby food. Depending on your topic, a site with a clear bias may still provide useful information, as long as you're aware of its slant.

■ *Check the timeliness of the information.* Even if an online source deals with a current topic, such as Palestinian-Israeli relations or an upcoming election, you should not assume that the source is up-to-date. What is the publication date? When was the material last updated? Does your topic require information that's more recent? Are the site's links up-to-date?

||||||||||||||||||||||||||||||||||||||||||||||||||||||||||||||||||||||||||||||||||||||||

FOR EXPLORATION

Choose an interesting word or phrase, and use one or more search engines to search for it on the Web. After reviewing the results, choose two sites that interest you. Using the guidelines above, evaluate these sites. Write a paragraph or two for each site summarizing the results of your analysis.

||||||||||||||||||||||||||||||||||||||||||||||||||||||||||||||||||||||||||||||||||||||||

✳ bedfordstmartins.com/academicwriter

For additional advice and a tutorial on evaluating online sources, go to **Re:Writing** *and click on* **Evaluating Online Sources**.

READING MORE CLOSELY AND SYNTHESIZING MATERIAL

Once you find a potentially useful source, study it with care so you can zero in on the specific information you need. Look, for instance, at the different elements in a source, such as an abstract, preface, introduction, and conclusion. Skim subheadings as well. They may direct you to some essential data, to an expert's point of view, or to a useful quotation. Last but not least, be sure to check footnotes and bibliographies, which can often lead you to other good sources — and to new opinions on the topic.

As you dig more deeply into your sources, you may begin to feel as though you're having a conversation with some of the experts. And, indeed, this is the way good research works: You'll agree with some sources, disagree with others, and begin to see trends in the information you gather. In other words, you'll be *synthesizing* information and reaching your own conclusions as you go along. For example, when Alletta Brenner researched human trafficking in American garment manufacturing, she began to see some major factors underlying human trafficking. She thus decided to group her information into three main categories: violations by factory owners, available immigrant labor, and poor enforcement of laws (see paragraph 3 of Alletta's essay on p. 169).

Using Sources: Quoting, Paraphrasing, and Summarizing

When you conduct research, you gather information from a number of sources. In many instances, you also come to know who the experts are on your topic, what issues they think are important, and whether you agree with them. How should you use these various types of information in your research paper?

You have three options for integrating sources into your writing. You can *quote* your source's words exactly. You can *paraphrase* them by explaining their meaning in your own words. Or you can *summarize* the source's information by significantly abbreviating a paragraph, a chapter, or even an entire book.

As you think about these options, keep in mind that many student writers tend to overquote material from their sources. In other words, they quote wording that isn't particularly striking rather than integrating the information by paraphrasing or summarizing. For example, if Report A says, "From the year 1990 up until the present time, we have seen some modest improvement in the rate of adult literacy in the United States," it's probably not necessary to quote this statement. Instead, you could paraphrase it: *According to Report A, the adult literacy rate in the United States has increased somewhat since 1990* (and end with an in-text citation of the source). As you go through your research material, how can you figure out whether it's better to quote a source or relay the information in some other way? The following guidelines will help you answer this question.

Guidelines for Determining When to Quote, Paraphrase, or Summarize

Quote *directly when the exact wording in a source is crucial:*

- When the language is especially powerful and memorable
- When the author is an authority whose expertise buttresses your own position
- When you disagree with the source but want to allow the author to speak in his or her own words

Paraphrase *when you want to convey information in your own words:*

- When the author's own words are not particularly memorable but the details in the source are important
- When you don't want to interrupt your discussion with a direct quotation

Summarize *when you want to present only the main idea of a long passage:*

- When the details of a paragraph, chapter, or entire book are not important
- When comparing two or more lengthy arguments or analyses (as in two books with opposing views)

Whether you quote, paraphrase, or summarize, it's essential to acknowledge sources accurately, both in the text of your paper and in the works cited list (or bibliography). Within the text itself, you'll often want to use a *signal phrase* to introduce a source. Such phrases not only mention the source but also may indicate—with an appropriate verb—your attitude toward it. For instance, the signal phrase *Although Chomsky claims* gives the distinct impression that you disagree with Chomsky. You could, however, create a different impression by saying, at the end of a sentence, *which is confirmed by noted linguist Noam Chomsky.* Or you might introduce this source in a more neutral fashion: *Chomsky believes,* or *As Chomsky points out,* or *Chomsky's research suggests.* Be careful to use appropriate signal phrases and to vary their location; they shouldn't always appear at the beginning of a sentence. Remember as well that the documentation style you're following (MLA, APA, or others) will generally specify what to include in a signal phrase or an in-text citation (see pp. 307–64).

Even when you understand *why* you're quoting, paraphrasing, or summarizing a passage, you may be unsure about *how* to do so. When is a paraphrase just a paraphrase—and not *plagiarism* (the inappropriate use of another person's words and ideas)? Is it permissible to omit or change words in a direct quotation? The following sections will shed some light on these issues.

QUOTING ACCURATELY

When you incorporate a quotation into your writing—for any reason—you must include the exact words from the source. The following original passage is from a classic essay about illiteracy in America. Read the original, and then see how one student used a short quotation from it in her research essay (following MLA style).

Original Passage

> Illiterates cannot travel freely. When they attempt to do so, they encounter risks that few of us can dream of. They cannot read traffic signs and, while they often learn to recognize and to decipher symbols, they cannot manage street names which they haven't seen before. The same is true for bus and subway stops. While ingenuity can sometimes help a man or woman to discern directions from familiar landmarks, buildings, cemeteries, churches, and the like, most illiterates are virtually immobilized. They seldom wander past the streets and neighborhoods they know. Geographical paralysis becomes a bitter metaphor for their entire existence. They are immobilized in almost every sense we can imagine. They can't move up. They can't move out. They cannot see beyond.
>
> —JONATHAN KOZOL, "THE HUMAN COST OF AN ILLITERATE SOCIETY"

Short Quotation

> Kozol points out that people who are illiterate often can't leave their own neighborhoods, which is "a bitter metaphor for their entire existence" (256).

In this example, Kozol is mentioned in a signal phrase, quotation marks surround his exact words, and a page reference appears at the end in a parenthetical citation (before the period, per MLA's style).

Long Quotation

If you want to quote a longer excerpt, set it off in block style with no quotation marks. Introduce the quotation with a sentence or signal phrase, and include a page reference at the end.

Although illiteracy creates serious problems in many aspects of a person's life, its effect on mobility is particularly devastating. Jonathan Kozol puts it this way:

> Illiterates cannot travel freely. When they attempt to do so, they encounter risks that few of us can dream of. They cannot read traffic signs and, while they often learn to recognize and to decipher symbols, they cannot manage street names which they haven't seen before. The same is true for bus and subway stops. While ingenuity can sometimes help a man or woman to discern directions from familiar landmarks, buildings, cemeteries, churches, and the like, most illiterates are virtually immobilized (256).

Square Brackets and Ellipses

Occasionally you may want to change a quotation to make it fit appropriately into your paper—or to eliminate some details in the original. Use square brackets ([ ]) to show changes and ellipses (. . .) to show deletions. Be careful to use both techniques sparingly and not to distort the meaning of the original source. Here's how a student used brackets and ellipses in the previous quotation.

> Although illiteracy creates serious problems in many aspects of a person's life, its effect on mobility is particularly devastating. As Kozol puts it, "Illiterates cannot travel freely. . . . They cannot read traffic signs and . . . cannot manage street names which they haven't seen before. . . . [M]ost illiterates are virtually immobilized" (256).

WRITING A PARAPHRASE

A paraphrase expresses an author's ideas in your own words. To write an acceptable paraphrase, you should use different sentence structures and language than the original, but keep the overall length about the same. Following is an acceptable paraphrase of the original passage on p. 162. Note that it begins by introducing the source and ends with a page reference in a parenthetical citation.

Acceptable Paraphrase

> Jonathan Kozol, an expert on literacy, explains that illiterates are unable to travel on their own outside of their immediate neighborhoods—and that it is hazardous for them to do so. People who can't read can't figure out most signs—for traffic, unfamiliar streets, bus stops, and so on. Occasionally they might be able to determine where they're going by

looking at a part of the landscape that they know, such as a church or building. But most of the time illiterates are unable to move very far from the area where they live. In a way, the inability to travel symbolizes the lives of illiterate people, who are frozen in their economic and social situation and thus lack hope about the future (256).

Unacceptable Paraphrase

An unacceptable paraphrase results from one or more of the following mistakes: using the author's own words (without putting quotation marks around them); following the author's sentence structure — and just substituting synonyms for some of the author's words; putting your own ideas into the paraphrase. Be on the lookout for such errors in your paraphrases so that you don't plagiarize someone's material inadvertently. Remember, too, that it's fine to include a quotation within a paraphrase. The unacceptable paraphrase below is based on Kozol's original passage on p. 162. As you read this paraphrase, try to pinpoint the mistakes in it.

> Jonathan Kozol, an expert on literacy, says that illiterate people cannot travel very easily. When they try to travel, they run into problems that most of us can't imagine. Illiterate people are unable to decipher traffic signs, unfamiliar street signs, and many other kinds of directional aids. Sometimes a familiar landmark or building may help an illiterate person figure out how to go somewhere, but most illiterate people remain immobilized in their own neighborhoods. They are, in a sense, geographically paralyzed. They can't move in any direction — or see the future. Because of these problems, the United States needs to take immediate steps to eliminate illiteracy in this country (256).

This paraphrase contains plagiarized material: Some words or phrases are identical to the original, and some sentence structures follow the original too closely. In addition, the writer has added her own opinion at the end — something Kozol didn't say in the original paragraph.

WRITING A SUMMARY

Unlike a paraphrase, a summary is a brief account of an original piece of writing, such as a paragraph, a chapter, or even an entire book. Always write a summary in your own words, and try to condense the source's most important ideas. Here is a summary of Jonathan Kozol's original paragraph on p. 162.

Summary

> Because illiterates cannot read signs and other directional aids, they cannot travel far from where they live. In much the same sense, they cannot move socially or economically to improve their lives (Kozol 256).

TAKING NOTES

Quotations, paraphrases, and summaries all rely on notes taken while you're doing your research. It's essential, therefore, to take accurate notes and to recheck each one against the original source. For any source that you plan to use, its basic publication information should already be in your working bibliography (see p. 144). On a note, then, include just enough data to identify the source (such as the author and a short title), give a page reference, and indicate what kind of note it is (e.g., *quotation* or *paraphrase*).

Most writers take notes on a computer, but some prefer to use note cards or a notebook. The choice is up to you. For online research, a good approach is simply to download the material you need — along with the pertinent publication data. Once you have a downloaded copy, you can mark it up for your own purposes, and you don't have to worry about introducing an error into your note.

USING VISUALS EFFECTIVELY

When taking notes and collecting source materials, pay close attention to the visuals you plan to use — tables, photographs, figures, maps, and other kinds of illustrations. Keep in mind that visuals should always be used to *support* a point you're making — not just to dress up a paper. Remember, too, that you need to cite sources for visuals, as you do for written materials from others.

Once you've chosen a visual that will enhance your essay, be sure to incorporate it into your written text appropriately. Here are a few tips to follow:

- Refer to the visual in your text, and explain its content if necessary.
- Position the visual close to where you mention it.
- Label the visual and cite its source.

In "Sweatshop U.S.A.," Alletta Brenner includes two photographs, both of which support her argument. Note that she puts the photographs near the text references to them (pp. 169–70) and includes labels and source citations as well, following MLA style. (For more information on using visuals, see Chapter 11.)

Understanding and Avoiding Plagiarism

Plagiarism is, quite simply, the intentional or unintentional use of others' words, ideas, or visuals as if they were your own. Whether you are a student, a scientist, a historian, or a politician, charges of plagiarism can have serious consequences. At some colleges, for example, students who plagiarize fail

Guidelines for Avoiding Plagiarism

- ■ *Develop a working bibliography that is complete and accurate.*
- ■ *Be a careful note taker.* Indicate the type of note (e.g., *paraphrase* or *statistical data*), the source, and page number(s) if available.
- ■ *Use quotation marks around direct quotations.* Follow this practice not only in your research paper but also in your notes.
- ■ *Use ellipses and square brackets* to indicate changes or added words when deleting or changing material in a quotation. (See p. 163.)
- ■ *Write paraphrases and summaries in your own words.* Label them appropriately, and include source information and page numbers. If you include an author's language *within* a paraphrase or summary, put quotation marks around the direct quotation.
- ■ *Include citations for all source material* — written works as well as visuals — both within the text of your paper and in a works cited or reference list.
- ■ *When in doubt, ask your teacher or a tutor in the writing center.* If you don't have time to consult a teacher or a tutor, include a citation.

not only the assignment but also the entire course; at colleges that have honor codes, students may even be expelled for plagiarism.

Some cases of plagiarism are *intentional*: A student submits an essay written by a friend as his own, purchases a research paper from an online company, or copies a passage directly from a source without providing attribution. More often, however, plagiarism is *unintentional* and is the result of either sloppy note taking or lack of knowledge about the conventions of documentation. A number of years ago, for instance, noted historian Doris Kearns Goodwin inadvertently included plagiarized material in one of her books. When the plagiarism was discovered, she apologized and explained that she had made errors while taking notes — and had not rechecked all of her original sources sufficiently. If even experienced writers occasionally make such mistakes, students need to take special care to avoid unintentional plagiarism.

COMMON KNOWLEDGE

Even if you understand what plagiarism is, you may wonder whether you need to give credit to a source for every kind of information. The answer is "no." Information that appears in many sources is known as *common knowledge* and does not require a citation. The capital of Austria, the distance from Chicago to New York, the team that won the World Series in 1990 — all are examples of common knowledge.

Let's look at another instance: It's commonly known that Senator John Kerry was the Democratic candidate for president in 2004 and that he lost the election. Because these facts appear in numerous sources, you wouldn't cite a source for them. However, if you use lesser-known information about Kerry, you would definitely need to cite the source. An analysis by his campaign manager as to why Kerry lost the election would require a citation because it is information few people are aware of and it probably exists in only one or two sources.

NOTE FOR MULTILINGUAL WRITERS

The concept of plagiarism is central to the modern Western intellectual tradition. It rests on the notion of intellectual property — the belief that language can be "owned" by writers who create original ideas. But even many students educated in the West are confused by what constitutes plagiarism, and what seems obvious to some in the West may look quite different to those from other cultures. Indeed, in some countries, students are taught to use the words of others without citing sources. Doing so is considered a sign of respect for one's cultural tradition. Moreover, writers in some countries assume that readers will recognize the words from others that are interwoven with the writers' own words. As a student in a North American college, you need to follow Western documentation and citation practices, which reflect Western ideas about language and ownership.

Using Appropriate Styles of Documentation

You probably are aware that different disciplines use different documentation styles. MLA (Modern Language Association) style and APA (American Psychological Association) style are two of the most frequently required styles for undergraduates. MLA style is typically used in English and other areas of the humanities, whereas APA style is common in the social sciences. These styles specify the information to be included in a reference and the format to be followed. See the Documentation Guidelines at the back of this book for examples and explanations. MLA guidelines begin on p. 307, and APA guidelines begin on p. 342.

Another popular documentation style is *Chicago* style, which is used in some disciplines in the humanities, including history. It's based on the guidelines in *The Chicago Manual of Style*, which is published by the University of Chicago Press. The Council of Science Editors (CSE) also has its own style, one that's commonly used in mathematics and the physical sciences. As you begin your research, it's important to find out which documentation style you should follow. If an instructor doesn't specify MLA, APA, *Chicago*, CSE, or some other style, be sure to ask what style you should use.

Sample Research Essay Using MLA Documentation Style

Here is a research essay by Alletta Brenner, a student at the University of Oregon.

✳ bedfordstmartins.com/academicwriter
   For additional sample research projects using MLA, APA, Chicago, or CSE documentation styles, go to **Re:Writing** *and click on* **Student Writing**.

Brenner 1

Alletta Brenner

Professor Clark

WR 222

11 May 2007

Name, instructor,
course, and date
double-spaced
and aligned at
left margin

Sweatshop U.S.A.: Human Trafficking
in the American Garment-Manufacturing Industry

Title centered

In early 1999, Nguyen Thi Le, a Vietnamese mother of two, signed
a four-year contract to work for a garment factory in American Samoa.
The island is a U.S. territory with a low minimum wage where enterprises
seeking to benefit from cheap labor costs can produce items with a
"Made in U.S.A." label. Dazzled by the opportunity to live in America
and earn American wages, Nguyen eagerly looked forward to her new
job, even though she would have to move an ocean away from her
family and take out high-interest loans to cover the five thousand
dollar fee for airfare and work permits. Despite these hardships, the
job seemed to offer her the chance to earn wages more than twelve

Fig. 1. Two Vietnamese workers after they were beaten at the
Daewoosa factory, American Samoa, 2000. National Labor
Committee.

Brenner 2

times those available at home. If she worked abroad for just a few years, Nguyen believed, she could dramatically improve the quality of her family's life (Gittelsohn 16).

However, upon arrival, Nguyen found a situation radically different from what she had expected. She and the other Daewoosa workers were paid only a fraction of the wages the garment factory had promised. The factory owner deducted high fees — sometimes half their monthly paychecks — for room and board that the contract had indicated would be "free," and when orders were slow, the owner didn't pay them at all. Kept in a guarded compound, Nguyen and her fellow garment sewers had to work sixteen- to eighteen-hour days under deplorable conditions. When they complained, they were often punished with violence, intimidation, and starvation (see figs. 1 and 2). According to the New York Times, when word of these abuses surfaced and the factory finally

Opens with a narrative to engage readers' interest

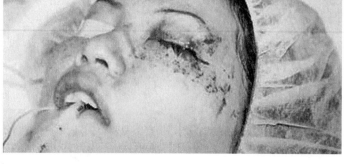

Fig. 2. Daewoosa woman worker who lost her eye after being brutally beaten on November 28, 2000. National Labor Committee.

Brenner 3

shut down in 2001, the women were left out on the streets with no means to return home (Greenhouse). Stuck in Samoa, Nguyen learned that back home, loan sharks were hounding her family to repay the debt she had incurred. Though Nguyen eventually received U.S. government aid, which allowed her to move to the American mainland and acquire a new job, it will take many years for her to recover from the damage to her personal and financial life ("Made in the U.S.A."?).

Human Trafficking: An Overview

Though what happened to Nguyen and the other workers may seem unusual to you, such occurrences are common in the United States today. Every year thousands of persons fall victim to human trafficking: they are transported either against their will or under false pretenses for the purpose of economic or sexual exploitation. In recent years, politicians as well as the media have paid more attention to human trafficking. Movies, newspaper articles, presidential speeches, and United Nations resolutions portray human trafficking as a negative consequence of globalization, capitalism, and immigration. Yet rarely do such accounts analyze the larger questions of how and why human trafficking exists. This essay will address some of these larger questions. In the American garment-manufacturing industry, three forces fuel human trafficking: violations by factory owners, an available immigrant labor force, and poor enforcement of laws. Before analyzing these factors, this discussion will take a closer look at the term human trafficking and the scope of its practice.

The official definition of the term human trafficking evolved in 2001 as a part of a United Nations treaty on transnational crime. The UN's Protocol to Prevent, Suppress and Punish Trafficking in Persons defines human trafficking as the "recruitment, transportation, transfer,

Main topic of human trafficking introduced

States thesis and key questions for essay

Definition and background information provided

harboring or receipt of persons by means of threat or use of force or other means of coercion, abduction, fraud, deception, abuse of power or position of vulnerability . . . for the purpose of exploitation" (Article 3). According to this definition, human trafficking has three components: 1) movement over geographical space, either across or within national borders; 2) the extraction of profits by the exploitation of victims' bodies or skills; and 3) the coercion of victims, which may include a wide range of tactics and forms (Gallagher 986-87).

How, then, does human trafficking work in practice? It can occur both within and across national borders and may involve a single perpetrator or an organized criminal network of recruiters, transporters, sellers, and buyers. The victims of human trafficking usually want to migrate and seek new employment. Van Impe reports that human traffickers typically pose as employers, employment agencies, or smugglers, offering to help victims by assisting them in entering a country or providing a job (114). Once an individual accepts this help, the trafficker may keep up the charade for quite some time, so when victims eventually realize what has happened, they may feel there is no choice but to submit to the trafficker's demands. After individuals have moved and started working, human traffickers use abusive and illegitimate tactics to force victims to work. They may, for example, threaten victims with physical violence, deportation, or debt bondage, wherein traffickers claim that a victim owes them money for transport or other services and then force him or her to work off the debt (U.S., Dept. of State, Trafficking 21).

How widespread is human trafficking in the United States? Both because of its relative wealth, and because it is a destination country for millions of migrant workers every year, the United States is one of the primary destinations for trafficked persons worldwide ("Country

Brenner 5

Report"). The U.S. Department of State estimates that between fourteen and eighteen thousand persons are trafficked in the United States each year (Trafficking 1-4); although the basis for these numbers is unclear, they appear to be consistent with global estimates on human trafficking. Not all victims are foreign-born, but immigrants are particularly vulnerable to such exploitation. In the United States, two thirds of all human-trafficking cases investigated and brought to court since 2001 have involved foreign-born migrant workers, according to a recent report by the U.S. Department of Justice (75-91).

Signal phrase for source at end of sentence, before in-text citation

Human Trafficking in American Garment Manufacturing

Some of the largest human-trafficking cases uncovered to date in the United States have occurred in the garment-manufacturing industry. In addition to the Daewoosa factory in American Samoa, investigators have found large sweatshops utilizing human trafficking in California, New York, and the Northern Mariana Islands. Police discovered one of the worst cases in El Monte, California, in 1995, where they found seventy-two Thai immigrants in an apartment complex surrounded by razor wire and armed guards. Trafficked from Thailand, the men and women had endured eighteen-hour workdays, seven days a week for seven years, sewing clothing for some of the nation's best-known clothing companies. Constantly threatened by violence to themselves and their families at home, the victims were forced to live in the same tiny, filthy apartments in which they worked. Grossly underpaid and forced to buy food and other necessities from their captors at inflated prices, the workers were in constant debt. To make matters worse, when police discovered and raided the compound, they arrested the workers for immigration violations and put them in jail. Only when local leaders and nongovernmental organizations spurred public outrage over the

Brenner 6

case were the workers released on bond and able to begin normal lives
in the America they had once envisioned (Ross 143-47).

First subtopic:
violations by
factory owners

Violations by factory owners are one reason human trafficking such
as that in El Monte occurs. Because most American clothing companies
outsource the production of their garments to factories around the
world, U.S. factories are under constant pressure to lower costs.
Unfortunately, this pressure often translates into poorer wages and
working conditions for those who produce clothing in this country and
illegal activity on the part of their employers (Bonacich and Appelbaum
137). A common violation is the failure of factory owners to pay
workers the legally mandated minimum wage. Unlike most U.S. workers,
garment workers earn a piece-rate wage rather than an hourly wage.
Because the amount of available work and the going rate for items
sewed constantly fluctuates, the amount workers earn often reflects
downward pressure. Employers, however, are supposed to make up the
difference so that workers still make the minimum wage. When
employers fail to do so or attempt to comply with the law by forcing
workers to speed up production, the result is substandard pay. Some
workers in the American garment-manufacturing industry earn less
than four dollars an hour, and those who work from home make even
less, sometimes as little as two dollars per hour.

Studies of garment manufacturers throughout the United States
have found that violations of wage, hours, and safety laws are the rule,
not the exception. For example, one study of textile-manufacturing
operations in the New York City area found that seventy-five percent
of them were operating in the informal sector — not legally licensed or
monitored — with substandard wages and working conditions ("Treated
Like Slaves" 5). A different study described in Behind the Label found
that sixty-one percent of garment manufacturers in Los Angeles were

Brenner 7

violating wage and hours regulations, underpaying their workers by an estimated seventy-three million dollars every year. Yet another study found that in more than half of firms inspected, workers were in danger of serious injury or death as a result of health and safety law violations (Bonacich and Appelbaum 3).

Violations by factory owners, however, are only one part of the picture in the garment industry. Another factor is the availability of an immigrant labor force. Factories that produce clothing in the United States and its territories are heavily dependant upon immigrants to meet their labor needs. For example, Bonacich and Appelbaum report that in Los Angeles, which has the highest concentration of garment manufacturers in the nation, eighty-one percent of workers are Asian and Latino immigrants (171-75). In American territories, immigrant labor is even more prevalent. In Saipan, the U.S. territory with the largest number of garment factories, almost all garment workers are foreign-born. Because the indigenous populations of many territories are so small, most garment manufacturers could not survive without imported labor. For this reason, territories do not operate under the same immigration laws as the American mainland, where relatively few visas are available to low-skilled workers. Consequently, employers in U.S. territories are able to legally recruit and import thousands of employees from Asia and South America (Parks 19-22).

For a number of reasons, the use of a predominantly immigrant workforce makes it easier for unscrupulous manufacturers to coerce and exploit workers. First, immigrant workers facing economic hardships often have no choice but to take risks and accept poor treatment and pay. A book published by Human Rights Watch quotes one Guatemalan woman who stayed with her abusive employers for many years:

Second subtopic: available immigrant labor force

I am the single mother of two daughters. The salary there [in
Guatemala] is not sufficient for their studies, their food, their
clothes. I want them to get ahead in life. . . . Sometimes one
is pressured by the economic situation. It's terrible what one
suffers. . . . Sometimes I ask myself why I put up with so much.
It's for this, for my mother and my daughters. (Pier 9-10)

A second reason is that those who enter the country illegally fear
deportation. Indeed, as Lelio points out, because of their status, illegal
immigrants often work in the informal sector "under the table" in
order to avoid authorities, which makes it much easier for traffickers
to exploit them (68-69). These jobs may be within individual homes,
or at businesses owned by other immigrants within tightly knit ethnic
communities. The strong fear of deportation that permeates many such
communities enables factory owners to effectively enforce a code of
silence on their employees, legal and illegal immigrants alike (Bonacich
and Appelbaum 144-47).

A third reason is that many immigrants lack English language skills
and knowledge of American laws and culture. Thus they find it difficult
to do anything about the situation they're in.

Even though most immigrant workers at garment factories in
American territories are there legally, they are just as vulnerable to
human trafficking. Like immigrant workers in the mainland United
States, they are often under a great deal of pressure to support families
back at home. Because most immigrant workers in the territories take
out high-interest loans simply to get their jobs, they are even more
likely to accept deplorable working conditions than are illegal
immigrants on the mainland. When employers fail to pay their workers
appropriately (or sometimes at all), they can prevent workers from
paying off their debts and thereby keep them as virtual prisoners.

Brenner 9

Indeed, human rights organizations have reported that thousands of garment workers live in severe debt bondage throughout American territories in the Pacific (Clarren 35-36).

The incidence of human trafficking gets further impetus from the "guest workers" immigration laws. Because such workers' visas depend on their employment with a particular firm, leaving the employer with whom they are contracted would break the terms of their visa. Ironically, this places legal guest workers in a more precarious position than those who immigrate illegally, for guest workers who violate the terms of their visas face deportation. Though some workers do leave and turn to prostitution or other forms of black market work to survive, the fear of being sent back home is a constant one. As a result, most stay with their abusive employers, hoping to someday pay off their debts and leave (Clarren 38-41).

A final factor that contributes to human trafficking in the garment industry is that where protective labor laws and standards do exist, their enforcement tends to be lax (Branigin 21-28). Despite the rampant violation of labor and safety laws throughout the industry, most garment manufacturers are able to avoid legal repercussions. Even when human-trafficking cases in the garment industry do occur, they tend to run much longer than other trafficking cases, averaging over six years in duration (U.S., Dept. of State, Matrix 6-9). This occurs for several reasons. First of all, as noted previously, many garment factories operate illegally. Because the Department of Labor only investigates such operations when someone makes an official complaint, traffickers who can control their victims are able to avoid detection. This is generally not a difficult task because victims of trafficking often lack the skills and knowledge required to take such action.

Third subtopic: poor enforcement of laws

Brenner 10

Second, inspectors from the Department of Labor and Occupational Safety and Health Administration rarely visit those factories that do operate legally. Even when workers complain, it can take up to a year for the government to open a case and make inspections. Moreover, when an investigation finally begins, owners often have advance warning, allowing them to conceal violations before the inspectors arrive. Some factory owners under investigation have been known to close up shop and disappear, leaving their employees out on the streets with months of back pay owed to them. These tendencies are especially prevalent in U.S. territories because of the geographic and bureaucratic distance between the islands and the governmental bodies that are supposed to regulate them. With the enforcement of most laws left up to local officials and agencies, many of whom stand to profit from arrangements with factory owners, human traffickers find it easy to avoid government interference. The risk for such activity is thus relatively low (Ross 210-11).

Conclusion

Conclusion
restates the
problem

In 2001, the same year that Nguyen's case hit the American media, President Bush proclaimed that the United States has a special duty to fight against "the trade in human misery" that human trafficking represents today. Since then, the United States has created a wide range of anti-trafficking laws and measures, but little has changed in the lives of human-trafficking victims. Although the owner of the Daewoosa factory was eventually convicted of enslaving more than 250 workers in his factory, other garment manufacturers continue to operate much as they did a decade ago. Some high-profile American clothing companies, such as the Gap, have promised to stop contracting with factories that violate labor laws; however, the essential set-up of the industry remains fully intact. Until these problems are directly addressed, human trafficking will continue to be a blemish on the American dream and, as President Bush recognized in a 2004 speech, "a shame to our country."

Works Cited

Bonacich, Edna, and Richard Appelbaum. <u>Behind the Label: Inequality
in the Los Angeles Apparel Industry</u>. Berkeley: U of California P,
2000.

Branigin, William. "A Life of Exhaustion, Beatings and Isolation."
<u>Washington Post</u> 5 Jan. 1999: A6.

Bush, George W. "President Announces Initiatives to Human
Trafficking." Tampa Marriott Waterside Hotel, Tampa, FL. 16 July
2004. Online. 2 Apr. 2007 <http://www.whitehouse.gov/news/
releases/2004/07/20040716-11.html>.

Clarren, Rebecca. "Paradise Lost." <u>Ms.</u> Spring 2006: 35-41.

"Country Report — The United States." <u>The Protection Project</u>. 2002. 28
Apr. 2007 <http://www.protectionproject.org/projects.htm>.

Gallagher, Anne. "Human Rights and the New UN Protocols on
Trafficking and Migrant Smuggling: A Preliminary Analysis."
<u>Human Rights Quarterly</u> 23 (2001): 986-87.

Gittelsohn, John. "U.S. Sends Strong Message to Those Who Traffic in
Human Lives." <u>Global Issues: Responses to Human Trafficking</u> 8.2
(2003): 14-17. 2 Apr. 2007 <http://usinfo.state.gov/journals/itgic/
0603/ijge/ijge0603.pdf>.

Greenhouse, Steven. "Beatings and Other Abuses Cited at Samoan
Apparel Plant That Supplied U.S. Retailers." <u>New York Times</u> 6 Feb.
2001: A14.

Lelio, Marmora. <u>International Migration Policies and Programmes</u>.
Geneva: Intl. Organization for Migration, 1999.

"Made in the U.S.A."? <u>Clothing for J.C. Penney, Sears and Target Made
by Women Held under Conditions of Indentured Servitude at the
Daewoosa Factory in American Samoa</u>. New York: Natl. Labor

Brenner 13

Committee, 2001. 2 Apr. 2007 <http://www.nlcnet.org/campaigns/
    archive/samoa/Daewoosa_Report_1.shtml>.

National Labor Committee. "Photos Related to Daewoosa in American
    Samoa." 30 Apr. 2007 <http://www.nlcnet.org/campaigns/
    archive/samoa/Samoa_photogallery.shtml>.

Parks, Virginia. The Geography of Immigrant La3bor Markets: Space,
    Networks, and Gender. New York: LFB Scholarly Publishing, 2005.

Pier, Carol. Hidden in the Home: Abuse of Domestic Workers with Special
    Visas in the United States. New York: Human Rights Watch, 2001.

Ross, Andrew, ed. No Sweat: Fashion, Free Trade and the Rights of
    Garment Workers. New York: Verso, 1997.

"Treated Like Slaves": Donna Karan, Inc., Violates Women Workers'
    Human Rights. New York: Center for Economic and Social Rights,
    1999.

United Nations. Office on Drugs and Crime. Protocol to Prevent, Suppress
    and Punish Trafficking in Persons, Especially Women and Children,
    Supplementing the United Nations Convention against
    Transnational Organized Crime. New York: United Nations, 2000.

United States. Dept. of Justice. Report on Activities to Combat Human
    Trafficking: Fiscal Years 2001-2005. 24 Apr. 2007 <http://
    www.usdoj.gov/crt/crim/trafficking_report_2006.pdf>.

---. Dept. of State. Matrix of Some of the Major Trafficking Cases in the
    United States of the Last Eight Years. May 2003. 4 May 2007
    <http://www.state.gov/g/tip/>.

---. Trafficking in Persons Report. June 2004. 4 May 2007 <http://
    www.state.gov/documents/organization/34158.pdf>.

Van Impe, Kristof. "People for Sale: The Need for a Multidisciplinary
    Approach toward Human Trafficking." International Migration 1
    (2000): 114.

Photographs obtained from Web site

Three works from same government; hyphens substituted for name

|||||||||||||||||||||||||||||||||||||||||||||||||||||||||||||||||||||||||||||||||||

FOR THOUGHT, DISCUSSION, AND WRITING

1. After reviewing this chapter's discussion of paraphrasing and summarizing, select one of the sample essays that appear in Chapter 7, "Writing in the Disciplines: Making Choices as You Write." Choose a paragraph from the essay—one that strikes you as particularly interesting or informative. After reading this paragraph carefully, first write a paraphrase of it, and then summarize the same passage. Finally, write a paragraph explaining why your paraphrase and summary of this passage are effective.

2. Choose a topic that interests you. Using a Web search engine, do a general search on your topic, noting the number of hits that your search generates. Now develop a list of related terms, and use these to narrow your search. Run a keyword search for at least two items from this list, noting the number of hits for these searches. After reviewing suggestions for advanced searching provided by your search engine, conduct an advanced search. Take a few minutes to write a paragraph reflecting on this search. What was productive? Unproductive? What would you do differently if you needed to search on this topic again?

3. Using the search results from the previous activity, select two pages or sources that you located. Using the suggestions for evaluating Web sites provided in this chapter, assess the quality of the information presented on each site. Write one or two paragraphs of evaluation for each site.

|||||||||||||||||||||||||||||||||||||||||||||||||||||||||||||||||||||||||||||||||||

Writing in the Disciplines: Making Choices as You Write

Part I of *The Academic Writer* began by asking this question: What does it mean to be a writer in the twenty-first century? Despite the increasing prevalence and power of visual and multimedia texts, writing does indeed still matter. In fact, those with access to computer and online technologies are writing more than ever before, and in more diverse venues and media.

How can writers negotiate the opportunities and challenges of twenty-first century communication? They can draw upon their understanding of the writing process and of the rhetorical situation. As Chapter 1 explains, rhetoric is a practical art that enables writers to make effective choices within specific situations. When you analyze your rhetorical situation, you consider each of the four elements of rhetoric: writer, reader, text, and medium. In so doing, you approach writing as a problem-solving activity, where there is no one-size-fits-all solution. With each new situation, you draw on previous knowledge and experience and consider the needs and interests of your audience. You also address other aspects of your situation, such as the nature of the medium you're working in and the extent to which genres (or other elements of your situation) might limit or enable your work.

thinking rhetorically

Part II of *The Academic Writer* builds upon the rhetorical approach to writing conveyed in Part I. It applies this approach to the essential intellectual skills needed in college writing: the ability to analyze texts and contexts, make and support claims, and conduct research. One of the challenges you face as an academic writer is learning how to apply these skills in a wide range of courses — from philosophy to chemistry to psychology. This chapter will help you become familiar with the expectations and conventions of various academic disciplines. By learning how writing works in different fields, and by seeing examples of successful student writing in the humanities, sciences, social sciences, and business, you can become a successful academic writer in *all* of the courses you take in college.

You can use your knowledge of rhetoric and of the writing process to negotiate the demands of academic writing in a broad variety of disciplines. These demands can be significant — especially when you take courses outside of your major. A student majoring in biology who is used to scientific writing may be unsure and confused when she has to write an essay interpreting a poem for her Introduction to Poetry class. By thinking rhetorically about the nature and purpose of writing in the humanities, this student can gain confidence, skill, and flexibility as a writer—attributes that will prove very useful when she graduates and begins a career.

Thinking Rhetorically about Writing in the Disciplines

thinking
rhetorically

What does it mean to think rhetorically about writing in the disciplines? It means understanding that the differing textual conventions of various disciplines have evolved to meet the differing needs, interests, and goals of those who work in them. This understanding can help you draw on the rhetorical common sense that you have already developed as a reader, writer, speaker, and listener.

The conventions of academic writing have histories worth noting. For example, historians generally attribute the development of scientific writing to the rise of humanism and the scientific method during the Renaissance. Scientists such as Francis Bacon (1561–1626) emphasized the importance of reporting the results of experiments in clear and precise language, so that experiments could be replicated. Before that time, scientists often intentionally withheld crucial information about their projects. When in 1660 a group of scientists in Great Britain founded the Royal Society (a body that still exists, and whose official title is The Royal Society for the Improvement of Natural Knowledge), they worked to standardize methods for reporting scientific results. As science developed, practitioners formalized the textual conventions for scientific writing. The stability and predictability of these conventions played—and continue to play—an important role in the sciences.

As David Porush notes in *A Short Guide to Writing about Science*, "the basic outline of the scientific report has changed little in over a century" (8).[1] There is no need for it to change because the scientific report still meets the day-to-day needs of working scientists. As this example indicates, the textual conventions that inform scientific writing exist for a specific reason: They encourage effective and efficient communication among scientists.

Textual conventions in the humanities, too, have a history. One particularly important impetus for those conventions was the desire to interpret religious texts. Most of the world's great religions developed strong traditions of textual interpretation: Christians have long studied the Bible; Muslims,

---

[1]David Porush. *A Short Guide to Writing about Science.* New York: Harper, 1995.

the Koran; and Jews, the Torah. Over time, interpretive practices for reading religious texts were applied to secular works as well.

This tradition of textual interpretation is particularly important to such disciplines in the humanities as literature, philosophy, religious studies, and rhetoric—but it has influenced such other areas as history, music, and art. In diverse ways, all of these disciplines explore what it means to be human, either through the creative process or through analyzing or documenting human texts and experiences.

Whereas scientists work to achieve objective and reliable results that others can replicate, those in the humanities often study questions for which there is no definitive answer. What constitutes a just war? How can we best interpret Shakespeare's *The Tempest* or best understand the concept of free will? What were the most important causes of the Black Plague? Who is the better painter—Leonardo da Vinci or Michelangelo?

Scholars in the humanities take it for granted that there are multiple ways to approach any topic. Though they hope that their writing will lead to a broader understanding of their subject, they don't expect that their research will result in the kind of knowledge generated by the scientific method. Indeed, in the humanities, originality is valued over replicability. Rather than relying on predetermined formats as science scholars do, scholars in the humanities structure their writing according to the nature and content of their analysis.

This brief discussion of the development of textual conventions in the humanities and sciences emphasizes that rather than being arbitrary forms to be filled in, the textual conventions that characterize different academic disciplines are deeply grounded in their history, nature, and goals. It is important to remember, however, that even though disciplines in these two broad areas share a number of general assumptions and practices, variations do exist. Moreover, disciplines in the social sciences, such as psychology, sociology, economics, anthropology, communication, and political science, include elements of both the sciences and the humanities, as does much writing in business. In the broadest sense, then, analysis, argument, and research are central to all disciplines in the academy.

As a college student, you can better understand your teachers' expectations as you move from, say, a chemistry class to a course in art appreciation by thinking rhetorically about the subject matter, methodology, and goals of various disciplines. The questions on p. 186 can guide this analysis. In order to answer them, you'll need to read representative examples of writing from each field; your teacher can provide such examples. You may also wish to interview instructors from each field.

✳ bedfordstmartins.com/academicwriter
For a collection of dozens of sample student projects written for courses across the disciplines, go to **Re:Writing** *and then click on* **Model Documents Gallery**.

Questions for Analyzing Writing in the Disciplines

■ How would you characterize the overall style of writing in this discipline? Somewhat formal? Very formal?

■ What documentation style (such as MLA, APA, CBE, or *Chicago*) is used?

■ What constitutes appropriate and valid evidence in this discipline?

■ What role do quantitative and qualitative data play in this discipline? (Quantitative data include items that can be measured; qualitative data include items that can be systematically observed.)

■ What role does textual interpretation or other forms of interpretation (such as the interpretation of music or art) play in this discipline?

■ How does the writing use visual elements such as images, graphs, tables, charts, and maps? What role do headings and other elements of formatting play?

■ What types of texts do professionals in this discipline typically write?

■ What types of texts do students in this discipline typically write?

||||||||||||||||||||||||||||||||||||||||||||||||||||||||||||||||||||||||||||||||||||

FOR EXPLORATION

Take five minutes to write freely about your experience of creating texts in various disciplines. Are you more confident writing for some disciplines than others? Why? What questions seem most important to you as you anticipate writing in courses across the curriculum?

FOR COLLABORATION

Bring your response to the previous Exploration to class, and share it with a group of students. After each person has summarized his or her ideas, spend a few minutes noting shared experiences and questions. Be prepared to report your results with the class.

||||||||||||||||||||||||||||||||||||||||||||||||||||||||||||||||||||||||||||||||||||

Writing in the Humanities

In a general sense, those studying the humanities are attempting to determine what something means or how it can best be understood or evaluated. Thus textual interpretation is central. Depending upon their discipline, scholars in the humanities may read the same or similar texts for different analytical and interpretive purposes. An art critic may analyze paintings by the American folk artist Grandma Moses (1860–1961) to study her use of brush strokes and color, while a historian might study her work to learn more about life in rural America in the mid-twentieth century.

Given the important role that textual interpretation plays in the humanities, strong reading skills are essential. Chapter 8 provides strategies to strengthen your general critical reading skills (which will improve your performance in all the disciplines, not just the humanities).

Sample Student Essays in the Humanities

Here are two essays written by students in introductory humanities courses. The first one was written for an introductory philosophy class titled Great Ideas in Philosophy. The authors, Julie Baird and Stevon Roberts, were responding to the following questions on Descartes' *Meditations on First Philosophy*: *(1) What is Descartes' method of doubt, and how does he use it? (2) What kind of being is Descartes, and how does he establish his conclusion?* Note that this essay uses MLA documentation style, required for this course. For details on this style, see the MLA Documentation Guidelines section at the back of this book.

Julie Baird and Stevon Roberts
Professor Campbell
PHL 150
24 April 2007

Name,
instructor,
course number,
and date on left
margin, double-
spaced

Title centered

Introductory
paragraph gives
brief answer to
assignment's
questions

Addresses
method of
doubt — first
part of
assignment

Double-spaced
throughout

I Think I Am, I Think I Am

In Meditations on First Philosophy, Descartes introduces to us the
concepts of being and existence. Through his documented rationale,
we are able to share some conclusions about the kind of being that
Descartes establishes that he is. In the first meditation, he proposes
doubt as a key to decoding the mystery of truth. In his second
meditation, he refutes doubt for the existence of thought and therefore
concludes that he himself must exist in some form or other. It is then
that he begins to explore the nature of that form, consequently giving
us the opportunity to follow his logic and reach the same conclusion.

Descartes first wets his philosophical feet (and ours) by creating a
body of "knowledge" based on doubt. It is interesting to note that this
knowledge is really derived from lack of knowledge since Descartes
begins his meditations by discounting all of his previous knowledge
as potentially untrue. Descartes claims, "Whatever I have up till now
accepted as most true, I have acquired from either the senses or
through the senses. But from time to time I have found that the senses
deceive, and it is prudent never to trust completely those who have
deceived us even once" (12). This suggests that Descartes is already
preparing to divorce physical existence from a theoretical existence
that is characterized by a thinking mind. But he's not certain of his
existence at all up to this point.

In the second meditation, Descartes explores the possibility that
there might exist a deceptive entity whose sole purpose is to deceive
his senses. Descartes asserts that even if this were the case, the
existence of the demon deceiving him necessarily requires his own

Baird and Roberts 2

existence. He says, "I too undoubtedly exist, if he is deceiving me; and let him deceive me as much as he can, he will never bring about that I am nothing so long as I think I am something" (17). This lays the foundation for Descartes' assertion that he is a thinking being because he persuades himself of, if nothing else, this one thing.

Brief quotation supports answer to second part of assignment

However, Descartes still believes he lacks a sufficient understanding of his existence. He uses his prior meditation on doubt to reason that he is not merely a human body or thin vapor. Instead, he is "a thing that thinks. . . . A thing that doubts, understands, affirms, denies, is willing, is unwilling, and also imagines and has sensory perceptions" (19). Descartes illustrates these qualities by explaining to us the physical characteristics of wax. Because these physical properties can be altered by exposure to different physical environments, he calls them "accidental" properties. But the wax remains. Even though characteristics that can be perceived by the senses are all altered, the essence of the wax is unchanged. He feels that he is just like the wax in that he has intrinsic properties that are not influenced by external forces: His core being (like that of the wax) remains, despite potentially false sensory perceptions.

Ellipses in quotation indicate omission

Quotation and examples answer question, *What kind of being is Descartes?*

In the sixth and final meditation, Descartes further separates the mind from the body and ultimately decides that he is a thinking being who exists apart from the corporeal but is still intimately tied with the physical body. He says that material things are capable of existing (in theory) since they can be perceived clearly and distinctly. Descartes illustrates this concept with mathematics. He distinguishes between a pentagon, which can be both imagined and understood in "the mind's eye," and a chiliagon (a polygon with 1,000 sides), which might be understood but not imagined. He uses this comparison to illustrate the difference between the mind and the imaginative effort, suggesting

Comparison example lays out Descartes' logic

Baird and Roberts 3

that corporeal math exists in our minds as physical law, while imagination predicates a superreal soul apart from the mind, which is where Descartes believes he exists. His final step is to completely divorce this soul from his body in saying he is "distinct from [his] body and can exist without it" (54).

In following Descartes' progression of logic, it is easy to arrive at the conclusion about what kind of being Descartes believes he is. Descartes first recognizes the limitations of his physical being and establishes a body of knowledge based on empirical evidence. In so doing, he offers a caveat: There might exist a being whose purpose is to deceive his senses, in which case his own independent existence is unquestionably affirmed. With this confidence in his existence, he begins to explore the nature of that existence, explaining that any physical properties are merely "accidental" and that his true being exists apart from the physical world — but not completely. His core being (or soul) is still intimately tied with the physical body even though he can distinguish between them. Finally, Descartes arrives at the conclusion that he is a real, thinking being who exists apart from the entity that he had perceived via sensory experience.

Conclusion summarizes Descartes' steps, brings together answers to both parts of assignment

Baird and Roberts 4

Work Cited

Descartes, Rene. <u>Meditations on First Philosophy: With Selections from the Objections and Replies</u>. Trans. and ed. John Cottingham. Cambridge: Cambridge UP, 1996.

Julie and Stevon's teacher praised their writing, noting that they did an excellent job of addressing the questions he posed. In analyzing their rhetorical situation, Stevon and Julie realized that a careful reading of Descartes' work was essential, noting that:

> Our professor has emphasized the importance of our reading primary works in philosophy, rather than secondary textbooks. We realized that we needed to read Descartes' writing almost in the way we'd read a poem, looking carefully at what he says and doesn't say. Our assignment had a page limit, and our professor wanted us to focus more on analysis than on summary, so we picked only a few of the most important passages and gave a lot of attention to Descartes' style and meaning. In terms of our own writing, we focused mainly on being clear and concise.

(To see the guidelines Julie and Stevon were responding to, see Questions for Analyzing Your Rhetorical Situation, p. 44.)

Here is another essay, written for an in-class exam in an American history course. The author, Elizabeth Ridlington, was responding to the following question: *During his presidency, did Lincoln primarily respond to public opinion, or did he shape public opinion more than he responded to it?* Elizabeth's teacher specified that her response should take the form of an essay. In analyzing her rhetorical situation, Elizabeth commented that:

> My teacher phrased this as an either/or question, inviting a strong and clear position statement at the outset. Because this is a history class, I knew that I needed to provide evidence from primary documents we'd read, offering the kind of specific and concrete details that historians value. I also needed to incorporate material from the lectures. In thinking about how to present information, I knew it was important not just to provide evidence but also to explain the logic behind my choice of details. Doing this makes for a more coherent essay in which every paragraph supports my initial thesis statement. Finally, looking at events and actions from multiple perspectives is very important for historians, so I explained Lincoln's decisions in a variety of circumstances essentially as a series of mini-case studies.

Note that this essay was a response to a timed in-class exam question. Had Elizabeth been required to submit it as a formal essay for her history course, she would have had to cite her sources, using *Chicago*'s endnote and bibliography style. For details on this reference style, see *The Chicago Manual of Style*, 15th ed. (2003), or a special volume intended for student writers, *A Manual for Writers of Term Papers, Theses, and Dissertations*, 6th ed., by Kate L. Turabian.

Elizabeth Ridlington

Lincoln's Presidency and Public Opinion

This essay argues that Lincoln shaped public opinion more than he responded to it and examines the issues of military recruitment, Northern war goals, and emancipation as examples of Lincoln's interaction with public opinion.

> Introduction frames response, lists supporting points

At the start of the war, Lincoln needed men for the military. Because of this, he could hardly ignore public opinion. But even as he responded in various ways to public opinion, he did not significantly modify his policy goals. Lincoln's first call for seventy-five thousand soldiers was filled through militias that were under state rather than federal control. As the war progressed, the federal government took more control of military recruitment. The government set quotas for each state and permitted the enlistment of African American soldiers via the Militia Act. Kentucky, a slave state, protested, and Lincoln waived the requirement that blacks be enlisted so long as Kentucky still filled its quota. In so doing, Lincoln responded to public opinion without changing his policy goal. Another example of this strategy occurred when the first federal draft produced riots in New York City. When the riots occurred, Lincoln relented temporarily and waited for the unrest to quiet down. Then he reinstated the federal draft. Again, Lincoln responded to a volatile situation and even temporarily withdrew the federal draft. But he ultimately reinstated the draft.

> Multiple examples for first supporting point

Lincoln's efforts to shape public opinion in the North in favor of the war provide another example of his proactive stance. Whenever he discussed the war, Lincoln equated it with freedom and democracy. Northerners linked democracy with their personal freedom and daily well-being, and therefore Lincoln's linkage of the Union with democracy fostered Northern support for the war even when the conflict was bloody and Northern victory was anything but guaranteed. After the emancipation, Lincoln continued his effort to influence public opinion by connecting the abolition of slavery with democracy. The image of a "new birth of freedom" that Lincoln painted in his Gettysburg Address was part of this effort to overcome Northern racism and a reluctance to fight for the freedom of blacks.

> Second supporting point

The process that led to the emancipation provides perhaps the clearest example of Lincoln's determination to shape public opinion rather than simply respond to it. Lincoln's views on slavery were more progressive than those of many of his contemporaries. These views caused him personally to wish to abolish slavery. At the same time, Lincoln knew that winning the war was his highest priority. Consequently, retaining the border states early in the war was more important to Lincoln than emancipation, and for this reason he revoked Freemont's proclamation in the summer of 1861. In explaining this decision privately to Freemont, Lincoln admitted that he was concerned about public opinion in Kentucky since it would determine whether Kentucky stayed with the Union. However, in a letter that Lincoln knew might be made public, Lincoln denied that he had reacted to Kentucky's pressure and claimed that emancipation was not among his powers — a clear effort to gain public approval. Even when others such as Frederick Douglass (in a September 1861 speech) demanded emancipation, Lincoln did not change his policy. Not until July 1862 did Lincoln draft the preliminary emancipation proclamation. Rather than releasing it then, at the advice of his cabinet he waited for a time when it would have a more positive impact on public opinion.

Several primary sources cited to support third point

Lincoln realized that the timing of the Emancipation Proclamation was crucial. While he was waiting for an opportune time to release the document, Horace Greeley published his "Prayer of Twenty Million," calling on Lincoln to abolish slavery. Lincoln's response, a letter for publication, emphasized the importance of the Union and the secondary importance of the status of slavery. By taking this position, Lincoln hoped to shape public opinion. He wanted Northerners to believe that he saw the Union cause as foremost, so that the release of the proclamation would create as few racial concerns as possible. The Emancipation Proclamation was released on January 1, 1863. Once it was released, Lincoln stood by it despite strong public opposition. In 1864, when Democrats called for an armistice with the South, Lincoln stood by his decision to abolish slavery. He defended his position on military grounds, hoping voters would approve in the 1864 election.

Final section cites primary sources, gives dates

As the examples I have just discussed indicate, Lincoln could not ignore public opinion, and at times he had to respond to it. But when Lincoln did so, this was always part of a larger effort to shape public opinion and to ensure Union victory.

Conclusion restates thesis

These two essays are excellent examples of writing in the humanities. Both take clear positions that are grounded in the careful reading and interpretation of sources. Both provide evidence for their positions, and both explain why this evidence is important. The writers establish their credibility primarily through the content of their ideas, although their ability to express these ideas clearly and concisely is also important to their overall success.

It's no accident that both essays take the form of traditional print texts. If these students were writing longer essays, they might use such formatting features as bolding or italicizing words, providing headings, and so on. They might also include images or graphics. But brief student writing in the humanities often employs only the basic features of document design, such as the selection of font type, spacing, and margins, often specified by the instructor.

✳ bedfordstmartins.com/academicwriter
For additional sample student projects written for the humanities, go to **Re:Writing** *and then click on* **Model Documents Gallery**.

Writing in the Natural and Applied Sciences

Whatever their skill level, students in the humanities expect that writing will play a key role in their education. Those majoring in other areas, particularly the natural and applied sciences, sometimes assume otherwise. They are wrong. Here's what David Porush, author of *A Short Guide to Writing about Science*, tells students to expect if they enter the sciences:

> You will write to report your research. You will write to communicate with colleagues at other institutions. You will write to request financial support for your work. You will write to colleagues, managers, and subordinates in your own institutional setting. You will write instructions and memos, and keep lab notebooks. You might even write to explore your own ideas, theories, and speculations.

Porush's argument is supported by other scientists. When faculty members in the department of chemistry at Oregon State University developed a writing guide for their students, they had this to say about the importance of writing in their field.

> Is writing important in chemistry? Don't chemists spend their time turning knobs, mixing reagents, and collecting data? They still get to do those things, but professional scientists also make presentations, prepare reports, publish results, and submit proposals. Each of these activities involves writing.

Victoria McMillan, author of *Writing Papers in the Biological Sciences* (2006), likewise points out that "no experiment, however brilliant, can contribute to the existing fund of scientific knowledge unless it has been described to others working in the same field"[2] (1).

Because established formats encourage efficient communication and facilitate replication of experiments, scientists employ these formats whenever possible. As they do so, they pay particular attention to the effective presentation of data, often using figures, tables, images, and models. Similar attention to format and document design is important in student writing in the sciences.

Scientists write a variety of kinds of texts. Since maintaining and operating labs can be costly, scientists spend considerable time writing proposals to fund research projects. Most research proposals follow this format: title page, introduction, purpose, significance of the study, methods, timeline, budget, and references. The format for research reports and journal articles is generally as follows: title, author(s), abstract, introduction, literature review, materials and methods, results, discussion, and references.

Sample Student Essay in the Natural and Applied Sciences

Scientists value precision, clarity, and objectivity. The following essay, an undergraduate research proposal by Tara Gupta, demonstrates these traits. Note that Tara uses headings to mark the various sections of her proposal. She also uses the documentation style required by the Council of Science Editors. For details on this reference style, consult its handbook, *Scientific Style and Format: The CSE Manual for Authors, Editors, and Publishers*, 7th ed. (2006).

---

[2]Victoria McMillan, *Writing Papers in the Biological Sciences*, 4th ed. Boston: Bedford, 2006.

Field Measurements of
Photosynthesis and Transpiration
Rates in Dwarf Snapdragon
(*Chaenorrhinum minus* Lange):
An Investigation of Water Stress
Adaptations

Complete title,
specific and
informative

Tara Gupta

Proposal for a
Summer Research
Fellowship
Colgate University
February 25, 2003

Water Stress Adaptations 2

Introduction

Dwarf snapdragon (*Chaenorrhinum minus*) is a weedy pioneer plant found growing in central New York during spring and summer. The distribution of this species has been limited almost exclusively to the cinder ballast of railroad tracks[1] and to sterile strips of land along highways.[2] In these harsh environments, characterized by intense sunlight and poor soil water retention, one would expect *C. minus* to exhibit anatomical features similar to those of xeromorphic plants (species adapted to arid habitats).

However, this is not the case. T. Gupta and R. Arnold (unpublished) have found that the leaves and stems of *C. minus* are not covered by a thick, waxy cuticle but rather with a thin cuticle that is less effective in inhibiting water loss through diffusion. The root system is not long and thick, capable of reaching deeper, moister soils; instead, it is thin and diffuse, permeating only the topmost (and driest) soil horizon. Moreover, in contrast to many xeromorphic plants, the stomata (pores regulating gas exchange) are not found in sunken crypts or cavities in the epidermis that retard water loss from transpiration.

Despite a lack of these morphological adaptations to water stress, *C. minus* continues to grow and reproduce when morning dew has been its only source of water for up to five weeks (R. Arnold, personal communication). Such growth involves fixation of carbon by photosynthesis and requires that the stomata be open to admit sufficient carbon dioxide. Given the dry, sunny environment, the time required for adequate carbon fixation must also mean a significant loss of water through transpiration as open stomata exchange carbon dioxide with water. How does *C. minus* balance the need for carbon with the need to conserve water?

Shortened title and page number

Headings throughout help organize the proposal

Introduction states scientific issue, gives background information, cites relevant studies

Personal letter cited in parentheses, not included in references

Water Stress Adaptations 3

Purposes of the Proposed Study

The above observations have led me to an exploration of the extent to which *C. minus* is able to photosynthesize under conditions of low water availability. It is my hypothesis that *C. minus* adapts to these conditions by photosynthesizing in the early morning and late afternoon, when leaf and air temperatures are lower and transpirational water loss is reduced. During the middle of the day, its photosynthetic rate may be very low, perhaps even zero, on hot, sunny afternoons. Similar diurnal changes in photosynthetic rate in response to midday water deficits have been described in crop plants.[3,4] There appear to be no comparable studies on noncrop species in their natural habitats.

Thus, the research proposed here aims to help explain the apparent paradox of an organism that thrives in water-stressed conditions despite a lack of morphological adaptations. This summer's work will also serve as a basis for controlled experiments in a plant growth chamber on the individual effects of temperature, light intensity, soil water availability, and other environmental factors on photosynthesis and transpiration rates. These experiments are planned for the coming fall semester.

Methods and Timeline

Simultaneous measurements of photosynthesis and transpiration rates will indicate the balance *C. minus* has achieved in acquiring the energy it needs while retaining the water available to it. These measurements will be taken daily from June 22 to September 7, 2005, at field sites in the Hamilton, NY, area, using an LI-6220 portable photosynthesis system (LICOR, Inc., Lincoln, NE). Basic methodology and use of correction factors will be similar to that described in related studies.[5-7] Data will be collected at regular intervals throughout the daylight hours and will be related to measurements of ambient air

---

Purpose and scope of proposed study

CSE documentation, citation-sequence format

States significance of study

Connects study to future research projects

Methodology described briefly

Timeline

Water Stress Adaptations 4

temperature, leaf temperature, relative humidity, light intensity, wind velocity, and cloud cover.

Budget

Itemized budget gives details	
1 kg soda lime, 4-8 mesh	$70
(for absorption of CO_2 in photosynthesis analyzer)	
1 kg anhydrous magnesium perchlorate	$130
(used as desiccant for photosynthesis analyzer)	
SigmaScan software (Jandel Scientific Software, Inc.)	$195
(for measurement of leaf areas for which photosynthesis and transpiration rates are to be determined)	
Estimated 500 miles travel to field sites in own car @ $0.28/mile	$140
CO_2 cylinder, 80 days rental @ $0.25/day	$20
(for calibration of photosynthesis analyzer)	
TOTAL REQUEST	$555

Water Stress Adaptations 5

References

1. Wildrlechner MP. Historical and phenological observations of the spread of *Chaenorrhinum minus* across North America. Can J Bot 1983;61(1):179-87.

2. Dwarf Snapdragon [Internet]. Olympia (WA): Washington State Noxious Weed Control Board; [updated 2001 Jul 7; cited 2003 Jan 25]. Available from: http://www.wa.gov/agr/weedboard/weed_info/dwarf snapdragon.html

3. Boyer JS. Plant productivity and environment. Science. 1982; Nov6:443-8.

4. Manhas JG, Sukumaran NP. Diurnal changes in net photosynthetic rate in potato in two environments. Potato Res. 1988;31:375-8.

5. Doley DG, Unwin GL, Yates DJ. Spatial and temporal distribution of photosynthesis and transpiration by single leaves in a rainforest tree, *Argyrodendron peralatum*. Aust J Plant Physiol. 1988; 15(3):317-26.

6. Kallarackal J, Milburn JA, Baker DA. Water relations of the banana. III. Effects of controlled water stress on water potential, transpiration, photosynthesis and leaf growth. Aust J Plant Physiol. 1990;17(1):79-90.

7. Idso SB, Allen SG, Kimball BA, Choudhury BJ. Problems with porometry: measuring net photosynthesis by leaf chamber techniques. Agron. 1989;81(4):475-9.

Numbered references relate to citation order in text

Article from government site

Article in weekly journal

Article in journal

Before embarking on her grant proposal, Tara spent time analyzing her rhetorical situation. Here is her analysis:

> I am writing because I wish to persuade a committee to grant me funds for working on my scientific project. Because I want the readers (scientists) to notice my ideas and not the medium, and because I want to convince them of my scientific merit and training, I will use the traditional medium and style for scientists—a written research proposal. A research proposal follows a standard format. Hence, I would say that my role as a writer, and my product, is relatively fixed. In the end, I want readers to hear the voice of a fellow scientist who is hardworking, trustworthy, and a creative observer.
>
> To be persuasive, I need to understand the behaviors, motivations, and values of scientists. I expect the readers, as scientists, to immediately begin formulating questions and hypotheses as I present the background information—scientists instinctively do this. My job is to give them the BEST information to help them form the questions I would like them to be thinking about. In addition, it is important to include all logical steps in proceeding with my idea and background knowledge, especially since the scientists reading my proposal are not all in my research field and cannot fill in the information gaps. Nothing is more boring or painful for a scientist than reading something that has flawed logic which they have trouble following or understanding. I also need credibility, so I will have references for all background information.
>
> Scientists value communication that is succinct, concrete, logical, accurate, and above all, *objective*. For example, if I want to discuss the environmental conditions these plants live in, I will not write a subjective account of how I've grown up in this area and know how hot and dry it can be in the summer. Instead, I will present an objective account of the environmental conditions using specific language (location, temperatures, moisture). In science, the hardest information to write about is ambiguous information, since it can be difficult to be succinct, concrete, logical, accurate, or objective; though in the end, this ambiguity is where the next experiment is and where the real work is to be done.

In reading Tara's analysis, you might be surprised by how extensive and complex her thinking is. After all, scientists just follow the conventions of scientific writing, don't they? Tara's analysis is a powerful demonstration of the kind of rhetorical sensitivity that scientists draw upon when they write proposals, lab reports, and other scientific documents.

✳ bedfordstmartins.com/academicwriter
For additional sample student projects written for the natural and applied sciences, go to **Re: Writing** *and then click on* **Model Documents Gallery**.

Writing in the Social Sciences

The social sciences, disciplines such as sociology, psychology, anthropology, communications, political science, and economics, look toward both the sciences and the humanities. Many scholars in the social sciences address questions that interest humanities scholars also, but their methods of investigating these questions vary. Consider the topic of aging. An English professor might study several novels with elderly characters to see how they are represented. A philosopher might consider the moral and political issues surrounding aging and longevity. Social scientists might also address the topic of aging, but in different ways.

In general, social scientists explore questions through controlled methods, including (1) surveys and questionnaires, (2) experiments, (3) observation, (4) interviews, (5) case studies, and (6) ethnographic field work. Careful observation is central to all of these methods, for, like scientists, social scientists value the development of objective and reliable knowledge. As a result, they ground their arguments in quantitative data (data based on statistics) or qualitative data (data based on observations). An economist studying the effect of aging on earning power might gather statistics that enable him to generate a hypothesis about their relationship. A sociologist might use one or more surveys, interviews, and case studies to gain a nuanced understanding of the impact of aging on self-perception and self-esteem.

Writing is as important in the social sciences as it is in the natural and applied sciences and humanities. As Deidre McCloskey, internationally known economist and author of *Economical Writing* (2000), points out, a person trained in economics "is likely to spend most of her working life writing papers, reports, memoranda, proposals, columns, and letters. Economics depends much more on writing (and on speaking, another neglected art) than on the statistics and mathematics usually touted as the tools of the trade" (5).[1] In her book, McCloskey argues for the value of a rhetorical approach to writing in economics.

Because the social sciences look to both the sciences and the humanities, the forms of writing within the social sciences can be particularly varied. For example, a writing guide for political science students at Oregon State University lists the following types of assignments: summary, abstract, book report, reaction note, think piece, radio script, briefing note, journal, image analysis, agency analysis, book review, essay, essay-type exam, analytical case brief, research project for methodology, and research paper. A similar guide for sociology majors includes these assignments: theory paper, content paper, quantitative research paper, case study, and qualitative research paper.

---

[1]Deidre McCloskey, *Economical Writing*, 2nd ed. Long Grove: Waveland P, 2000.

Sample Student Essay in the Social Sciences

Here is an example of effective writing in the social sciences. Merlla McLaughlin wrote this essay for an upper-level Small Group Communication class. Merlla and a group of her peers had completed a substantial collaborative project on parking problems on campus. After completing the assignment, group members wrote individual essays describing what they had learned about small-group dynamics as a result of their project. Note that this essay uses APA documentation style, required for this course. For details on this reference style, see the APA Documentation Guidelines section at the back of this book.

Leadership Roles   1   Shortened title and page number, separated by five spaces

Leadership Roles in a Small-Group Project

Merlla McLaughlin

Professor Bushnell

Communications 302

February 23, 2006

Title and other information centered, double-spaced

Leadership Roles   2

Abstract
heading,
centered

Names of
authors given
as initials
and surnames

Double-spaced
without
indentation

Describes study
and key points

                              Abstract

Using the interpersonal communications research of J. K. Brilhart and
G. J. Galanes as well as that of W. Wilmot and J. Hocker, along with
T. Hartman's Personality Assessment, I observed and analyzed the
leadership roles and group dynamics of my project collaborators in a
communications course. Based on results of the Hartman Personality
Assessment, I predicted that a single leader would emerge. However,
complementary individual strengths and gender differences encouraged
a distributed leadership style, in which the group experienced little
confrontation. Conflict, because it was handled positively, was crucial
to the group's progress.

Leadership Roles in a Small-Group Project

Although classroom lectures provide students with volumes of
information, many experiences can be understood only by living
them. So it is with the workings of a small, task-focused group. What
observations can I make after working with a group of peers on a class
project? And what have I learned as a result?

Leadership Expectations and Emergence

The six members of this group were selected by the instructor; half were
male and half were female. By performing the Hartman Personality
Assessment (Hartman, 1998) in class, we learned that Hartman has
associated key personality traits with the colors red, blue, white, and
yellow (see Table 1). The assessment identified most of us as "Blues,"
concerned with intimacy and caring. Because of the bold qualities
associated with "Reds," I expected that Nate, our only "Red" member,
might become our leader. (Kaari, the only "White," seemed poised to
become the peacekeeper.) However, after Nate missed the first two

Table 1

Hartman's Key Personality Traits

| Trait | Color | | | |
category	Red	Blue	White	Yellow
Motive	Power	Intimacy	Peace	Fun
Strengths	Loyal to tasks	Loyal to people	Tolerant	Positive
Limitations	Arrogant	Self-righteous	Timid	Uncommitted

Note. Table is adapted from information found at *The Hartman
Personality Profile*, by N. Hayden. Retrieved February 16, 2006,
from http://students.cs.byu.edu/~nhayden/Code/index.php

Full title, centered

Questions frame focus of report

Heading, centered

APA-style parenthetical citation

Clear link to Table 1

Table displays information effectively and concisely

meetings, it seemed that Pat, who contributed often during our first three meetings, might emerge as leader. Pat has strong communications skills and a commanding presence, and displays sensitivity to others. I was surprised, then, when our group developed a *distributed style* of leadership (Brilhart & Galanes, 1998). The longer we worked together, however, the more I was convinced that this approach to leadership was best for our group.

As Brilhart and Galanes have noted, "distributed leadership explicitly acknowledges that the leadership of a group is spread among members, with each member expected to move the group toward its goal" (p. 175). These researchers divide positive communicative actions into two types: *task functions*, which affect a group's productivity, and *maintenance functions*, which influence the interactions of group members. One of the group's most immediate task-function needs was decision making, and as we made our first major decision — what topic to pursue — our group's distributed-leadership style began to emerge.

Decision-Making Methods

Our choice of topic — the parking services at Oregon State University (OSU) — was the result not of a majority vote but of negotiated consensus. During this decision-making meeting, several of us argued that a presentation on parking services at OSU would interest most students, and after considerable discussion, the other group members agreed. Once we had a topic, other decisions came naturally.

Roles Played

Thanks in part to the distributed leadership that our group developed, the strengths of individual group members became increasingly apparent. Although early in our project Pat was the key initiator and Nate largely an information seeker, all group members eventually took on these functions in addition to serving as recorders, gathering information, and working on

Defines key term

Section shows impartial discussion of group decision making; supports claim about leadership style

Headings help organize report

Additional observations support central claim

Leadership Roles   5

our questionnaire. Every member coordinated the group's work at some point; several made sure that everyone could speak and be heard, and one member was especially good at catching important details the rest of us were apt to miss. Joe, McKenzie, Kaari, and I frequently clarified or elaborated on information, whereas Pat, Kaari, and Nate were good at contributing ideas during brainstorming sessions. Nate, Joe, and McKenzie brought tension-relieving humor to the group.

Just as each member brought individual strengths to the group, gender differences also made us effective. For example, the women took a holistic approach to the project, looking at the big picture and making intuitive leaps in ways that the men generally did not. The men preferred a more systematic process. Brilhart and Galanes have suggested that men working in groups dominated by women may display "subtle forms of resistance to a dominant presence of women" (p. 98). Although the men in our group did not attend all the meetings and the women did, I did not find that the men's nonattendance implied male resistance any more than the women's attendance implied female dominance. Rather, our differing qualities complemented each other and enabled us to work together effectively.

Shifts to consider gender differences

Social Environment

As previously noted, most of our group members were Blues on the Hartman scale, valuing altruism, intimacy, and appreciation, and having a moral conscience (Hayden, "Blues"). At least three of the four Blues had White as their secondary color, signifying the importance of peace, kindness, independence, and sacrifice (Hayden, "Whites"). The presence of these traits may explain why our group experienced little confrontation and conflict. Nate (a Red) was the most likely to speak bluntly. The one time that Nate seemed put off, it was not his words but his body

Heading highlights further behavioral analysis

language that expressed his discomfort. This was an awkward moment, but a rare one given our group's generally positive handling of conflict.

Conclusion

Perhaps most important is the lesson I learned about conflict. Prior to participating in this group, I have always avoided conflict because, as Wilmot and Hocker (1998) have suggested, most people think "harmony is normal and conflict is abnormal" (p. 9). Now I recognize that some kinds of conflict are essential for increasing understanding among group members and creating an effective collaborative result. It was essential, for instance, that our group explore different members' ideas about possible topics for our project, and this process inevitably required some conflict. The end result, however, was a positive one.

Constructive conflict requires an open and engaging attitude among group members, encourages personal growth, and ends when the issue at hand is resolved. Most important for our group, such conflict encouraged cooperation (Wilmot & Hocker, 1998, pp. 47-48) and increased the group's cohesiveness. All the members of our group felt, for instance, that their ideas about possible topics were fully considered. Once we decided on a topic, everyone fully committed to it. Thus, our group effectiveness was enhanced by constructive conflict.

As a result of this project, I have a better sense of when conflict is — and isn't — productive. My group used conflict productively when we hashed out our ideas, and we avoided the kind of conflict that creates morale problems and wastes time. Although all groups operate somewhat differently, I now feel more prepared to understand and participate in future small-group projects.

Concluding section answers questions posed in introduction

Leadership Roles   7

References

Brilhart, J. K., & Galanes, G. J. (1998). *Effective group discussion* (9th ed.). Boston: McGraw-Hill.

Hartman, T. (1998). *The color code: A new way to see yourself, your relationships, and your life*. New York: Scribner.

Hayden, N. (n.d.). *The Hartman Personality Profile*. Retrieved February 16, 2006, from http://students.cs.byu.edu/~nhayden/Code/index.php

Wilmot, W., & Hocker, J. (1998). *Interpersonal conflict* (5th ed.). Boston: McGraw-Hill.

Heading centered

References begin new page, double-spaced throughout

Document from a Web site

First line of each entry at left margin; subsequent lines indent ½"

In reflecting on her experience writing this essay, Merlla had this to say:

In thinking about my rhetorical situation for this writing assignment, my final essay for a Small Group Communication class, I focused on the fact that this was my last opportunity to formally present the knowledge I had gained in class. Small Group Communication is a social science class that employs qualitative research methods, so in this paper I needed to demonstrate that I could use these methods. Because qualitative research strives for an impartial perspective that sets aside personal bias, I knew that my format and style had to reflect this preference. I also knew that I should draw upon as many of the behavioral analysis tools that we studied this term as possible to explain the emergence of leadership in our group and that I should describe specific behaviors, as well as trends, in our interactions. My main challenge in writing was to organize the essay around the analytical tools I used, rather than relying on a chronological organization. Since I'm more drawn to the humanities-oriented work in communications than the social science work, this is always an issue for me.

※ bedfordstmartins.com/academicwriter
For additional sample student projects written for the social sciences, go to **Re:Writing** *and then click on* **Model Documents Gallery**.

Writing in Business

Historians of business writing emphasize the role that the spread of literacy in the Middle Ages and the printing press in the Renaissance played in this history. According to Malcolm Richardson, a contributor to *Studies in the History of Business Writing* (1985), even before capitalism developed in Europe there were scribes and scriveners, who played a key role in both government and private communication. In the fourteenth century, what some historians believe to be the first business writing school opened in England. And in the sixteenth century, Angell Day's *The English Secretary or Method of Writing Epistles and Letters,* one of the earliest business communication texts (which at this time primarily took the form of letter writing), appeared.

The conventions that characterize modern business writing—particularly the preference for clear, concise, goal- and audience-oriented communication and an easy-to-read visual design—developed slowly but steadily. With the growth of the middle class and the increase of commerce, business persons needed to be able to communicate with both internal and external audiences. Basic forms of business writing, such as memos, letters, proposals, and reports, became more standard. As layers of management evolved and departments proliferated, written internal communication became increasingly important, as did changes in the technologies of communication. The typewriter and carbon paper (and, later, dictaphones and photocopiers) transformed the office up through the mid-twentieth century.

Developments in online, electronic, and digital communication are once again effecting powerful changes in business writing. Today's business writers communicate online, as well as in traditional print environments. They must be able to work effectively in teams, and they need to be able to respond to the demands of working in a global environment. But the essential characteristics of effective business writing remain grounded in basic issues of rhetorical sensitivity. When writing for business, it's especially important to consider the differing needs — and situations — of your readers. In many cases, you may need to consider readers spread geographically or across an organization chart, and even future readers.

Sample Student Memo for Business Writing

The following memo was written by Michelle Rosowsky and Carina Abernathy, two students in a business class. Their memo presents an analysis and recommendation to help an employer make a decision. As you read, notice how the opening paragraph provides necessary background information and clearly states the memo's purpose. Even if this memo is forwarded to others, its purpose will be clear. Michelle and Carina are also careful to follow the traditional memo design format and to use bold type to emphasize the most important information.

This assignment took the form of a case study. The students' teacher provided them with a series of hypothetical facts about a potential business transaction. Their job was to analyze this information, determine their recommendations, and communicate them in the most effective form possible.

❖ *Jenco* ❖

INTEROFFICE MEMORANDUM

To: ROSA DONAHUE, SALES MANAGER

Authors initial
next to their
names
From: MICHELLE ROSOWSKY & CARINA ABERNATHY,   *MR CA*
           SALES ASSOCIATES

Subject: TAYLOR NURSERY BID

Date: JANUARY 30, 2006

CC:

Paragraphs flush
left
As you know, Taylor Nursery has requested bids on a 25,000-pound order of private-label fertilizer. Taylor Nursery is one of the largest distributors of our Fertikil product. The following is our analysis of Jenco's costs to fill this special order and a recommendation for the bidding price.

Bold type
highlights the
most important
financial
information
The total cost for manufacturing 25,000 pounds of the private-label brand for Taylor Nursery is $44,075. This cost includes direct material, direct labor, and variable manufacturing overhead. Although our current equipment and facilities provide adequate capacity for processing this special order, the job will involve an excess in labor hours. The overtime labor rate has been factored into our costs.

Double-spaced
between
paragraphs
The absolute minimum price that Jenco could bid for this product without losing money is $44,075 (our cost). Applying our standard markup of 40% results in a price of $61,705. Thus, you could reasonably establish a price anywhere within that range.

Options
presented and
background
given
In making the final assessment, we advise you to consider factors relevant to this decision. Taylor Nursery has stated that this is a one-time order. Therefore, the effort to fill this special order will not bring long-term benefits.

Final
recommendation
Finally, Taylor Nursery has requested bids from several competitors. One rival, Eclipse Fertilizers, is submitting a bid of $60,000 on this order. Therefore, our recommendation is to slightly underbid Eclipse with a price of $58,000, representing a markup of approximately 32%.

Closing offers
further
assistance
Please let us know if we can be of further assistance in your decision on the Taylor Nursery bid.

In reflecting on their memo, Michelle and Carina commented that the first and most important step in their writing process involved analyzing both the information that they were given and their rhetorical situation.

> We had to first analyze the facts of the case to come up with an appropriate recommendation and then present the recommendation within the format of a typical business memo. Because it's written for a busy manager, we wrote the memo as concisely as possible so that the information would be available at a glance. We also put the most critical calculation, the manufacturing cost, at the beginning of the memo and in bold so that the manager could find it easily and refer back to it later if necessary. We go on to make a recommendation about a bidding price and then provide a few other relevant facts since the goal of the memo is to enable the manager to ultimately make her own decision. The succinctness of the memo also reflects our confidence in the analysis, which gives us a strong and positive *ethos* and helps establish our reliability and competence.

✳ **bedfordstmartins.com/academicwriter**
For additional student samples of business writing, go to **Re:Writing** *and then click on* **Model Documents Gallery***.*

|||||||||||||||||||||||||||||||||||||||||||||||||||||||||||||||||||||||||||||||||||||||||||||||

FOR THOUGHT, DISCUSSION, AND WRITING

1. Although you may not have determined your major area of study yet, you probably have some idea of whether you want to major in the humanities, social sciences, or sciences. Meet with a group of classmates who share your general interests. First make a list of the reasons you all find this area interesting. Then make a list of the writing challenges that students in this area face. Finally, choose two of these challenges and brainstorm productive ways that students can respond to them. Be prepared to share the results of your discussion with the entire class.

2. Write an essay in which you reflect on the reasons you are drawn to a particular discipline or general area of study. How long-standing is your interest in this discipline? What do you see as its challenges and rewards? (Before writing this essay, you might like to read Brandon Barrett's essay on his decision to major in chemistry. This essay appears on p. 57.)

3. Choose one of the student essays presented in this chapter, and analyze it to determine what features reflect the disciplinary preferences described in this chapter. Alternatively, choose an essay you have written for a class in the sciences, social sciences, or humanities and similarly analyze it. In studying either your own or an essay that appears in this chapter (or one of the examples on the book's companion Web site), be sure to consider its vocabulary, style, method of proof, and use of conventional formats.

|||||||||||||||||||||||||||||||||||||||||||||||||||||||||||||||||||||||||||||||||||||||||||||||

Strategies for Reading

Why—and how—do people read? Not surprisingly, they read for as many different reasons and in as many different contexts as they write. They read to gain information—to learn how to program their VCR, to decide whether to attend a movie or purchase a new product, or to explore ideas for writing. They read for pleasure—whether surfing the Web or enjoying a novel. They read to engage in extended conversations about issues of importance to them, such as ecology, U.S. foreign policy, or contemporary music. In all of these ways, people read to experience new ways of thinking, being, and acting.

Reading and writing are mutually reinforcing acts. The process of grappling with an essay for the first time—of attempting to determine where the writer is going and why—is similar to the process of writing a rough draft. When you reread an essay to examine the strategies used, or the arguments, you're "revising" your original reading, much as you revise a written draft. Because writing requires the physical activity of drafting, you may be more aware of the active role you play as writer than as reader. Reading is, however, an equally active process. Like writing, it is an act of *composing,* of constructing meaning through language and images.

Applying Rhetorical Sensitivity to Your Reading

Reading, like writing, is a *situated* activity. When you read, you draw not only on the printed words and images but on your own experiences as well. Whether you're reading traditional print or visually rich texts, you're making cultural, social, and rhetorical judgments about them as you engage them in a specific manner. The purposes you bring to your reading, the processes you use to scrutinize a text, your understanding of the significance of what you read—these and other aspects of your reading grow out of the relationship among writer, reader, text, and medium.

Some examples might help to clarify this point. Imagine two people sitting in a café reading and drinking tea. One person is reading an accounting textbook for a course she's taking; the other is reading a zine (an independently published poem, text, or magazine, sometimes featuring an intentionally crude design) he picked up on a whim. Both individuals are reading texts—but they are undoubtedly reading them in quite different ways. The accounting student has many reasons for believing the textbook is authoritative and therefore reads it slowly and with care. If asked what she's doing, she might say she's studying rather than reading. The person reading the zine, on the other hand, knows that zines represent a backlash against typical popular-culture magazines and that anyone with the time and inclination can produce one. Because a zine found in a café could be a well-written and thought-provoking reflection on a contemporary issue or a poorly written diatribe, this reader quickly skims the text and visuals to see if the topics are interesting and the writing worth reading. The differences between how these two people read reflect their purposes as well as their social and cultural understandings of the texts.

Another powerful influence on reading is genre. When we recognize that a text belongs to a certain genre—such as textbook, special-interest magazine, commercial Web site, or newspaper—we make assumptions about the form of the writing and about its purposes and subject matter. A businessperson reading a company's annual report understands that it is a serious document and that it must follow specific conventions, including those of standard written English. When he reads *Slam,* a magazine for basketball insiders, he brings quite different expectations to his reading. *Slam* uses a good deal of specialized jargon, including the street and hip-hop language of some urban African Americans. Even though the businessperson would find this language inappropriate in business writing, he not only accepts but enjoys its use in *Slam.* He would be outraged, however, if he identified an error of accuracy in a story, for he reads *Slam* to learn the kind of current news and obscure historical facts that serious fans crave.

‖‖

FOR EXPLORATION

Consider the different ways you read texts. Start by making a list of the different kinds of texts you read, such as nutritional labels, trade journals, newspaper editorials, graphic novels, and popular magazines. Then think about how your approach to these texts changes according to what they are and why you're reading them. For instance, do you read the introduction to a psychology text differently than a mystery novel or the sports page? Freewrite for five minutes about the reading strategies you already use.

‖‖

Questions for Conducting a Reading Inventory

Choose a particular text that interests you that is at least five to ten pages long. After reading the text, respond to the following questions.

- What were your initial thoughts about the text? Did you expect to find it easy or difficult? Interesting or boring? Were you looking forward to reading it, or were you reading it because a teacher or supervisor assigned it?

- How would you describe your reading process for this text? What story would you tell about your reading?

- Respond to one passage that is important to you and one passage that seems important to the author. Try to put yourself in the author's shoes. Do you think that the author would find your passage important? How important is the author's passage to you? What can you learn about the text and your reading of it by comparing the author's and your own expectations?

- What did this text remind you of? What question did it answer? What problem did it address? What was left unsaid? What did the text refuse to consider?

- What major questions do you have about this text? To what extent does the text attempt to address these questions? If it doesn't address your questions, why might this be the case? (You might be an undergraduate reading a text for specialists in a particular field, for instance.)

- What happens when you focus on your body's response to the text? How is your reading a performance? What can your body's response tell you about your experience of reading this text?

- How would you characterize your reading of this text — as a conversation? A lecture? Did your reading take you deeply into the text (as might be the case if you're reading an academic argument)? Or did it encourage you to relate your personal experience to the text (as might be the case if you're reading a poem)?

- What have you learned from undertaking this inventory?

You can strengthen your reading and writing skills by taking time to reflect on how you read various texts. Periodically you may want to inventory your reading process to gain valuable information about your strengths and limitations as a reader. This activity can also help you determine how best to approach unfamiliar texts. You can use the questions above to consider what you bring to the reading of a particular text, what the text brings to you, and where possible differences lie. The point of a reading inventory is not to determine if you are reading a text correctly. (If you read a poem that invites contemplation and interpretation in the same way that you read a chemistry textbook, however, there is a significant mismatch between what the text is bringing to you and what you are bringing to it.) Your goal should be to understand both the text and your reading of it.

NOTE FOR MULTILINGUAL WRITERS

If you have recently begun studying in an English-speaking environment, it may be challenging to interpret texts that require personal knowledge about American history, popular culture, literature, religion, or other topics. You may also bring different rhetorical and cultural expectations to your reading. To better understand how you approach reading, reflect on how your own linguistic and cultural background has influenced your expectations. It may be helpful to discuss these expectations with your teacher, your classmates, or a tutor in the writing center. You can also ask these people about unfamiliar references or expressions.

Becoming a Strong Reader

As a college student, you read many different kinds of texts for a wide variety of purposes. You may skim a magazine or surf the Web for fun. You may read a novel for pleasure and for its insight into human emotions. When you read a textbook for, say, your Introduction to Western Civilization class, you may read primarily for information. On other occasions, you read not simply to gain information but to engage in the process of inquiry. Professors David Bartholomae and Anthony Petrosky call this kind of reading "strong reading":

> Reading involves a fair measure of push and shove. You make your mark on a book and it makes its mark on you. Reading is not simply a matter of hanging back and waiting for a piece, or its author, to tell you what the writing has to say. In fact, one of the difficult things about reading is that the pages before you will begin to speak only when the authors are silent and you begin to speak in their place, sometimes for them — doing their work, continuing their projects — and sometimes for yourself, following your own agenda.
>
> — David Bartholomae and Anthony Petrosky, *Ways of Reading*

Strong readers evaluate their reading in terms of what they're able to *do* with a text. As they read, they engage in active dialogue with the author, posing questions and raising potential counterarguments. If you're like many students, you may feel more confident reading for information than engaging in a strong reading of an essay, advertisement, poem, political treatise, engineering report, or Web site. Yet gaining the ability to make your mark on a verbal or visual text is one of the most important goals of a college education. Such critical reading is intrinsically satisfying, for it enables you to engage in genuine inquiry. Strong reading leads to—and benefits—writing; one of the best ways to strengthen your writing ability is thus to become adept at strong reading.

Guidelines for Effective Reading

The following guidelines provide suggestions for reading a wide variety of print, online, and visual texts.

- *Be flexible.* Your purpose in reading should help you determine how to approach a text. If you are researching an essay on the homeless in urban centers in the Northeast, for instance, you might skim a number of print and online studies to become familiar with resources available on the subject. Once you have clearly defined your topic and purpose, you would begin reading in a more focused and critical manner.

- *Raise questions about the writer(s).* Who created this text? To what extent does the text call attention to the role of its author, editor, designer, or Webmaster? What did this person (or persons) hope the text would accomplish? What social, historical, cultural, economic, or political factors might have influenced its composition? How might those goals and factors have influenced the form, content, and look of the text?

- *Ask questions about the intended readers.* Are they a general audience? Specialists? Students? What role does the text invite readers to adopt as they read (study, surf, scan, or otherwise engage with) this text? Does the text assume considerable prior knowledge, or certain cultural or social understandings and preferences? Does it assume, for

(continued)

(continued)

instance, that readers won't read long passages of prose unless they include images or other design features? That readers will recognize a person whose photograph appears in an ad? That readers will share certain values and beliefs?

▪ *Look for clues about the text.* When was it published? What can you infer about the author's intentions? To inform? Entertain? Persuade? Does the text follow the conventions of an established genre? If not, how would you describe its organization?

▪ *Consider the medium* — where and how this text was published. Is it in a traditional print publication? In a more graphic form, such as a poster or advertisement? On the Web? Is the medium institutional? Business oriented? Personal? Formal or informal? How do visual elements (photographs, tables, design layout) contribute to its meaning? Is the form of publication static (like a book) or fluid (like a wiki or a message board)?

▪ *Read against the grain.* To read critically and actively, it sometimes helps to deliberately resist a text. For example, while reading an essay on immigration intended for a general audience, you might consider the essay from the perspective of a border patrol agent or from that of an illegal immigrant. How would those readers respond to the author's arguments and strategies? You might pay particular attention to issues or examples that the author *doesn't* mention. Or you might focus on how your own experience supports or doesn't support the author's arguments.

▪ *Work through difficulties with a text, identifying reason(s) it seems difficult,* and then turn these reasons into questions that you can use as you read. Rather than becoming frustrated when a writer dwells on an issue that seems unimportant to you, for instance, ask yourself why scholars in this field might find the issue worthy of attention.

▪ *Interact with the text.* Pose questions. Speculate about the implications of a line of argument. Look for gaps in the presentation of evidence or ideas. Use your personal experience to consider the issues raised by a text — and then imagine how someone different from you might approach these issues.

▪ *Be patient.* Just as the process of writing often requires rough drafts, so too can the process of reading require "rough readings." A text that on first reading seems difficult will often, on rereading, prove rewarding or more engaging.

Developing Critical Reading Skills

Reading critically means reading *actively*, reading not just to gather facts or information but to evaluate, analyze, appreciate, understand, and apply what you read. As a critical reader, you engage in a dialogue with the author and subject his or her arguments to careful examination. The following discussion presents a number of strategies for critical reading and provides an opportunity for you to apply these strategies to a specific text, an article that appeared in the September 2006 issue of *The Atlantic Monthly*.

PREVIEWING

When you preview a text, you survey it quickly to establish or clarify your purpose and context for reading, asking yourself questions such as those listed on p. 223. As you do so, recognize that print, online, and visual sources may call for different previewing strategies. With print sources, for instance, it's easy to determine the author and publisher. To learn the author of a homepage on the World Wide Web, however, you need to know how to read Web addresses and drill through sites. Whereas such print texts as scholarly journals and books have generally undergone extensive review and editing to ensure their reliability, this may not be the case with online sources, which can appear and disappear with alarming frequency. It may also be challenging to determine how accurate and trustworthy visually rich texts are. A photograph that appears in a national magazine has undoubtedly been screened for appropriateness, but it could also have been manipulated for effect (photographs in fashion magazines, for example, are routinely altered to hide cosmetic imperfections). Therefore, determining the accuracy, authority, and currency of online and visual resources can prove challenging.

NOTE FOR MULTILINGUAL WRITERS

All readers benefit from previewing texts, but if you are a multilingual reader and writer, you will find previewing particularly helpful. It will give you valuable information that can help you read the text efficiently and effectively. As you preview a text, be sure to formulate questions about specialized terms or about the text's general approach.

Questions for Previewing a Text

■ Where and when was this text published? If this text appears on the Web, how recently was it updated? What do this source and date suggest about the accuracy, authority, and currency of the text?

■ What, if anything, do you know about its author or creator?

■ What can you learn from the title?

■ How would you characterize the general design and presentation of words and images? Cluttered or spare? Colorful or subdued? Carefully organized or (apparently) randomly presented? Calm or busy? Traditional, contemporary, or cutting edge?

■ What can you learn by skimming this text? Is it divided into sections? If so, how do they appear to be organized? What links does a Web site provide? How useful do these links seem to be? Can you easily perceive the author's general approach? What predictions about this text can you make on the basis of a quick survey? What questions can you now formulate to guide your subsequent reading of this text?

■ What is your personal response to the text, based on this preview?

FOR EXPLORATION

Using the preceding questions, preview the article on pp. 224–25.

ANALYZING VISUAL ELEMENTS

When you read any kind of text, you need to be able to analyze its design and use of images and to understand the potentially powerful role that visual elements can play in written texts. Why? Perhaps the most important reason has to do with the increasingly pervasive role of images in modern life. Driving down the street, watching television, skimming a magazine — in these and other situations, we continually encounter images and texts — many of which are designed to persuade us to purchase, believe, or do certain things. Often these images can be a source of pleasure and entertainment. But given the persuasive intent of many images, critical readers will develop ways to not just "read" but "read into" them. The questions on p. 115 and the For Exploration box on p. 226 can help you analyze visual texts. For a fuller discussion of analyzing visuals and document design, see Chapter 11.

FIRST PRINCIPLES

The Height of Inequality

America's productivity gains have gone to giant salaries for just a few

BY CLIVE CROOK

In 1971, Jan Pen, a Dutch economist, published a celebrated treatise with a less-than-gripping title: *Income Distribution*. The book summoned a memorable image. This is how to think of the pattern of incomes in an economy, Pen said (he was writing about Britain, but bear with me). Suppose that every person in the economy walks by, as if in a parade. Imagine that the parade takes exactly an hour to pass, and that the marchers are arranged in order of income, with the lowest incomes at the front and the highest at the back. Also imagine that the heights of the people in the parade are proportional to what they make: those earning the average income will be of average height, those earning twice the average income will be twice the average height, and so on. We spectators, let us imagine, are also of average height.

Pen then described what the observers would see. Not a series of people of steadily increasing height—that's far too bland a picture. The observers would see something much stranger. They would see, mostly, a parade of dwarves, and then some unbelievable giants at the very end.

As the parade begins, Pen explained, the marchers cannot be seen at all. They are walking upside down, with their heads underground—owners of loss-making businesses, most likely. Very soon, upright marchers begin to pass by, but they are tiny. For five minutes or so, the observers are peering down at people just inches high—old people and youngsters, mainly; people without regular work, who make a little from odd jobs. Ten minutes in, the full-time labor force has arrived: to begin with, mainly unskilled manual and clerical workers, burger flippers, shop assistants, and the like, standing about waist-high to the observers. And at this point things start to get dull,

because there are so very many of these very small people. The minutes pass, and pass, and they keep on coming.

By about halfway through the parade, Pen wrote, the observers might expect to be looking people in the eye—people of average height ought to be in the middle. But no, the marchers are still quite small, these experienced tradespeople, skilled industrial workers, trained office staff, and so on—not yet five feet tall, many of them. On and on they come.

It takes about forty-five minutes—the parade is drawing to a close—before the marchers are as tall as the observers. Heights are visibly rising by this point, but even now not very fast. In the final six minutes, however, when people with earnings in the top 10 percent begin to arrive, things get weird again. Heights begin to surge upward at a madly accelerating rate. Doctors, lawyers, and senior civil servants twenty feet tall speed by. Moments later, successful corporate executives, bankers, stockbrokers—peering down from fifty feet, 100 feet, 500 feet. In the last few seconds you glimpse pop stars, movie stars, the most successful entrepreneurs. You can see only up to their knees (this is Britain: it's cloudy). And if you blink, you'll miss them altogether. At the very end of the parade (it's 1971, recall) is John Paul Getty, heir to the Getty Oil fortune. The sole of his shoe is hundreds of feet thick.

As Garrison Keillor ironically informs his listeners, not every child can be above average. But when it comes to incomes, the great majority can very easily be below average. A comparative handful of exceptionally well-paid people pulls the average up. As a matter of arithmetic, the median income—the income of the worker halfway up the income distribution—is bound to be less than average.

This is true in every economy, but in some more than others. Back when Pen

wrote his book, incomes were already more skewed in America than in Britain. Over the past thirty-five years, and especially over the past ten, that top-end skewness has greatly increased. The weirdness of the last half minute of today's American parade—even more so the weirdness of the last few seconds, and above all the weirdness of the last fraction of a second—is vastly greater than that of the vision, bizarre as it was, described by Pen.

Lately economists have been using new data to look more closely within the top decile of American incomes. What they've found is startling. Here are some results from Ian Dew-Becker and Robert Gordon of Northwestern University. Between 1966 and 2001, median wage and salary income increased by just 11 percent, after inflation. Income at the 90th percentile (six minutes from the end of the hour-long parade) increased nearly six times as much—by 58 percent. At the 99th percentile (the last thirty-six seconds), the rise was 121 percent. At the 99.9th percentile (3.6 seconds before the end), it was 236 percent. And at the 99.99th percentile (0.36 seconds, representing the 13,000 highest-paid workers in the American economy), the rise was 617 percent.

That is worth repeating: Over thirty-five years, the rise in wages and salaries in the wide middle of the income distribution was 11 percent. The rise in wages and salaries at the top of the income distribution was 617 percent.

This is (pretax) wage and salary income, not investment income. Many commentators attribute rising American inequality to growth in profits at the expense of salaries and wages. That's wrong: labor's share of national income does not seem to be trending up or down. What has changed is how much of labor's share goes to top earners. Since the mid-1970s, and especially since the mid-1990s, the dramatic rise in the share of national income earned by the very rich is due not to the strength of their investment portfolios but to their growing share of labor income.

7"

2'6"

10th percentile	35th percentile

Productivity growth has always been seen as perhaps the single most important indicator of rising, broad-based prosperity. But remarkable growth in top-end pay, together with the relative constancy of labor's overall share of income, has an obvious implication: the highest earners are now capturing most of the gain in national income caused by economy-wide productivity growth.

This is quite disturbing. Historically, rising productivity has been a tide that lifted nearly all boats. For more than twenty years during the long surge of productivity growth that followed the Second World War, median incomes in the United States rose as quickly as the highest incomes. This came to be regarded as normal—and, seen from a global vantage point, it still is. The dispersed benefits of high aggregate productivity are the reason why jobs of almost every kind pay better in rich countries than in poor ones.

Mechanics and hairdressers are paid far more in America than in Mexico, even though their individual productivity may not be that different in the two places; north of the border, workers share in the economy's higher overall productivity. A lot depends on whether this continues to be true. It is the very point that the new findings call into question.

The study by Dew-Becker and Gordon asks, "Where Did the Productivity Growth Go?" Over the past thirty-five years, that growth did not lift most boats, or even very many boats. Between 1966 and 2001, only 10 percent of American workers saw their incomes rise at least as fast as economy-wide productivity did. More astonishing still, according to the study's authors, from 1997 to 2001, the top 1 percent captured far more of the real national gain in wage and salary income than did the bottom 50 percent. And even within that highest percentile, the gains were heavily concentrated at the top.

Such extreme skewness is new. It suggests that a huge proportion of the economy's productivity gains are neither being passed on to consumers through lower prices—which would have the effect of raising real incomes very broadly—nor being distributed to investors as profit, nor even being used to raise the wages of most employees in industries seeing rapid productivity growth. Rather, they're being diverted to a comparative handful of employees.

Why is this happening? Nobody is sure, but Dew-Becker and Gordon suggest a combination of two things: for one small group, sports and media celebrities, income growth has come from a perfecting of the labor market; for a different group, top corporate executives, it has come from a breaking down (or even an overthrowing) of the market. Those two segments account for most of the 13,000 people in the 99.99th percentile—with total earnings of $83 billion in 2001.

A classic 1981 study by the late economist Sherwin Rosen worked out "The Economics of Superstars" and anticipated part of what has happened. The demand for stars in the sports and entertainment industries is such that small differences in talent cause disproportionate gaps in earnings. As technology puts stars in front of bigger audiences, their incomes multiply. Rosen could not have foreseen the media innovations of the past decade, but they have plainly given stars access to far more fans.

I find it interesting that there is no popular unease over the stupendous sums paid to Tiger Woods, or Eminem, or Tom Cruise. And, you might ask, why should there be? They are worth the price of the ticket, at least in the view of their audiences. If they are in demand worldwide, good luck to them. An economist would say the market is working.

The case of fat-cat chief executives arouses different feelings—as it should. In most cases, there is no audience-multiplication factor to account for the dramatic rise in CEO pay. If a Rosen-type process were at work, you would not expect to find that CEO pay had surged only in the United States (and to a lesser extent in Britain). Numerous widely reported cases of pay for no performance are also awkward to explain. When boards give big noncontractual severance packages to bosses fired for incompetence, you have to ask whether this second stratospheric zone of the labor market, unlike the superstar zone, is working properly.

Corporate-governance reforms that would help shareholders keep CEOs in check might do some good. If I'm skeptical, it's partly because shareholders already have some (admittedly limited) powers, and they usually let things slide. That might change if CEO pay continues to rise. At some point, the subdued "outrage constraint" that some corporate-governance activists wish to revive might kick in again. That would be a good thing.

Perhaps the CEOs' appetites can be curbed. Maybe the superstars will find that their audiences cannot widen without limit. And perhaps, if both those things happen, productivity growth will again raise incomes broadly, as it once did, and as it is supposed to. If not, how much longer before the dwarves get restless? ⚄

Clive Crook is a senior editor of The Atlantic.

INEQUALITY ON PARADE
The distribution of work income in the United States, 2001

The height of each figure is proportional to his or her salary and wages.
A worker of average income is assumed to be five feet ten.

(99.995th percentile) 933' ⟶
(99.95th percentile) 181' ⟶
(99.5th percentile) 49' ⟶
(97th percentile) 21'
13'9"
10'
5'9"
92.5th percentile
85th percentile
65th percentile

| | | | | | | | | | | | | | | | | | | | | | | | | | | | | | | | | | | | | | | | | | | | | | | | | | | | | | | | | | | | | | | | | | | | | | | | | | | | | | |

FOR EXPLORATION

Look again at the article by Clive Crook reprinted on pp. 224–25. Analyze its use of visuals according to the following questions, writing your responses to each question. Finally, write one or two paragraphs about what you have learned as a result of this analysis.

- ■ What is your general impression of the design and presentation of words and images in this text? Is the presentation cluttered or spare? Carefully organized or randomly presented? Calm or busy? Traditional, contemporary, or cutting edge?

- ■ What images or design features are important in this piece? Does it present a single dominant image or a variety of images? If the latter, how are these images related? What is your eye drawn to when you first look at this piece? Why?

- ■ In what ways do the design and presentation of words and images in this piece appeal to logic and to reason? To emotion? What role (if any) does the credibility of an organization or individual play?

- ■ What is the relationship between image and text? Does one predominate? Is their relationship explicit or implicit? Does the text function primarily to present information or to reinforce or extend — or even to subvert or undermine — the image?

- ■ If you were to translate the impact or message of the visual text into words, how would you describe it? What do you think the designers of this piece intended its visual impact to be? Do you believe that it achieves its intended impact? Why?

| | | | | | | | | | | | | | | | | | | | | | | | | | | | | | | | | | | | | | | | | | | | | | | | | | | | | | | | | | | | | | | | | | | | | | | | | | | | | | | |

✳ bedfordstmartins.com/academicwriter
For more advice and practice in analyzing visuals, go to **Re:Writing** *and then click on* **Visual Analysis**.

ANNOTATING

When you annotate a text, you highlight important words, passages, or images and write comments or questions that help you establish a dialogue with the text or remember important points. Some readers are heavy annotators, highlighting many passages and key words and filling the margins with comments and questions. Others annotate more selectively, preferring to write few comments and to highlight only the most important parts. In thinking about your own annotating strategies, remember that your purpose in reading should influence the way you annotate a text, whether that text includes print alone or combines words and visuals. You would annotate a text you're reading primarily for information differently than you would an essay you're reading for an assignment or a graphic novel you're reading for pleasure.

Many readers annotate directly on the text. If you have borrowed the text or prefer not to mark up your own copy, however, you can use sticky notes, a separate piece of paper, a photocopy, or a computer file to copy or highlight important passages and to write questions and comments.

How can you know the most effective way to annotate a text? The questions below can help you make appropriate choices as you read and annotate.

Questions for Annotating a Text

■ What is your purpose in reading this text? What do you need to annotate to accomplish this purpose?

■ Where does the writer identify the text's purpose and thesis (or main idea)?

■ What are the main points, definitions, and examples? Would it be useful to number the main points or make a scratch outline in the margin?

■ What questions does this text suggest to you?

■ What key words play an important role in the discussion? Does the text provide enough information so that you can understand these key words and appreciate their significance, or do you need further explanation?

■ What passages seem particularly crucial? What is your response to these passages?

■ What role, if any, do images and graphics play? Are they primary or secondary in creating meaning? Do they reinforce, challenge, or in other ways complicate the written words?

■ Do your personal experience and values or knowledge of the subject cause you to question the author's assertions, evidence, or method?

||||||||||||||||||||||||||||||||||||||||||||||||||||||||||||||||||||||||||||||||||

FOR EXPLORATION

Annotate the article on pp. 224–25 as if you expected to write an essay responding to it for your composition class.

||||||||||||||||||||||||||||||||||||||||||||||||||||||||||||||||||||||||||||||||||

SUMMARIZING

Never underestimate the usefulness of writing clear, concise summaries of texts. Writing a summary allows you to restate the major points of a book or essay in your own words. Summarizing is a skill worth developing, for it requires you to master the material you're reading and make it your own. Summaries can vary in length, depending on the complexity and length of the text. Ideally, however, they should be as brief as possible, certainly no longer than a paragraph or two. The guidelines below offer suggestions for writing your own summaries.

Guidelines for Summarizing a Text

- *Reread the material, trying to locate the main idea and the most important supporting points.* Start by skimming the text, focusing on the title, introduction, and conclusion. Look for an explicit statement of the author's argument and purpose: If one exists, paraphrase it; if the main idea is implied but not stated, try to express it in a sentence or two of your own.

- *Highlight or number the major points the author uses to support the main idea.* To find these, look for topic sentences, call-outs (boldface design elements used for emphasis), and illustrations. You might want to write those points down — in your own words — in a list or outline.

- *Identify how the major points relate to the main idea and to each other.* Before writing your summary, form a mental picture of how the author's argument is structured. Examine the introduction and conclusion for clues, and consider how headings and lists signal the organization and relative importance of ideas.

- *State the main idea and the major supporting points in your own words.* Write your summary in paragraph form, as briefly and clearly as you can. Stick to the main points and the most important ideas. Leave out examples and anecdotes, and don't try to mirror the author's organization.

(continued)

(continued)

■ *Resist the urge to quote or paraphrase sentences or phrases from the original text.* It may help to put the original out of sight and work from memory and notes, referring back to the text for accuracy only after you have drafted the summary.

■ *Be objective.* Your purpose is to distill the main idea and supporting points, not to record your reaction to the piece or to express your opinion of its merits.

|||||||||||||||||||||||||||||||||||||||||||||||||||||||||||||||||||||||||||||||||||||||||||

FOR EXPLORATION

Following the guidelines on pp. 228–29, write a one-paragraph summary of "The Height of Inequality: America's Productivity Gains Have Gone to Giant Salaries for Just a Few" (pp. 224–25).

|||||||||||||||||||||||||||||||||||||||||||||||||||||||||||||||||||||||||||||||||||||||||||

ANALYZING LINES OF ARGUMENT

Previewing, analyzing visuals, annotating, and summarizing can all help you determine the central points in a text. Sometimes the central argument is explicitly stated. In paragraphs 11 and 12 of "The Height of Inequality," for example, Clive Crook asserts that

> remarkable growth in top-end pay, together with the relative constancy of labor's overall share of income, has an obvious implication: the highest earners are now capturing most of the gain in national income caused by economy-wide productivity growth. This is quite disturbing.

Not all authors are so direct. Someone writing about the consequences of contemporary feminism for life in North America may raise questions rather than provide answers or make strong assertions. Whether an author articulates a clear position on a subject or poses a question for consideration, critical readers attempt to determine if the author's analysis is valid — if the author provides good reasons in support of a position or line of analysis.

The questions on p. 230 provide an introduction to analyzing the argument of a text. For a fuller discussion of this and related issues, see Part II, "Writing in College."

Questions for Analyzing a Text's Argument

■ What is the major claim or thesis of this text? Is it explicitly stated, or is it implicit, requiring you to read between the lines?

■ What interests or values may have caused the writer to develop this thesis? (Information about the writer from other sources, as well as clues from the writing itself, may help you determine this.)

■ What values and beliefs about the subject do you bring to your reading of this text? How might these values and beliefs affect your response to the writer's argument?

■ Does the writer define key terms? If not, what role do these unstated definitions play in the argument?

■ What other assumptions does the writer rely on in setting up or working through the argument? In texts on the Web, for instance, what choices and organizing principles do the links suggest?

■ What kinds of evidence does the writer present? Is the evidence used logically and fairly? Has the writer failed to consider any significant evidence, particularly evidence that might refute his or her claims?

■ What role, if any, do images and graphics play?

■ In what ways does the writer try to put the reader in a receptive frame of mind? Does the writer attempt to persuade the reader through inappropriately manipulative emotional appeals?

■ How does the writer establish his or her credibility? What self-image does the writer create?

NOTE FOR MULTILINGUAL WRITERS

The questions above reflect one approach that you can use to analyze a text's argument. If your first experience of reading is grounded in a language and culture other than English, some of these questions may strike you as odd. In many cultures, for instance, writers do not announce the major claim or thesis of their text; doing so may seem overly obvious. As you read these questions, then, consider the extent to which they are culturally grounded. Remember, too, that everyone can learn from cultural differences, so think about the preferences in argumentation that you bring from your home (or parents') culture. You, your classmates, and your teacher will all benefit if you discuss these differences in class.

||||||||||||||||||||||||||||||||||||||||||||||||||||||||||||||||||||||||||||||||

FOR EXPLORATION

Using the Questions for Analyzing a Text's Argument, analyze "The Height of In-equality: America's Productivity Gains Have Gone to Giant Salaries for Just a Few" (pp. 224–25). Be sure to answer all of the questions.

||||||||||||||||||||||||||||||||||||||||||||||||||||||||||||||||||||||||||||||||

Case Study: A Student Writer's Critical Reading

Here and throughout the rest of the chapters in Part III, we follow one student, Daniel Stiepleman, as he interacts with a text, explores ideas, and develops an essay for his first-year writing class. This case study should give you a clearer understanding of how reading, inventing, drafting, and revising work. Daniel was responding to an assignment that's common in first-year writing classes:

> Write a two- to three-page analytical essay responding to an image of your choice. Be sure to choose an image that involves significant interaction between the text and graphics. Your essay should focus on how the words and graphics work together to generate the image's meaning and impact. Consider your instructor and your classmates the primary readers of your essay.

Daniel's first step after receiving his assignment was to look for an image that interested him. While he was flipping through the magazine *The Atlantic Monthly*, a public service announcement (PSA) for the National Center for Family Literacy (NCFL) caught his eye. An aspiring English teacher, Daniel found the message of the PSA to be powerful, yet something that he couldn't quite put his finger on troubled him. In order to explore his initial response to the PSA, Daniel decided to annotate the text and image, using the Questions for Analyzing Visual Texts on p. 115 as a guide. See p. 232 for a reproduction of the PSA with Daniel's annotations.

Daniel's annotations are a good start at a strong reading of this visually rich text. He has begun to read against the grain and has noticed some details that he didn't catch at first, such as the way the layout and type style underscore the simplicity of the PSA's message. The text's line of argument seemed simple enough and was easy to summarize: Literacy improves lives. Like many readers, however, Daniel found that his reading raised more questions than it answered. The more he looked at his notes and re-examined the image and words, the more he wondered *why* simplicity was such a central part of the message. He also started to think about what the NCFL was trying

Daniel Stiepleman's Annotated Text

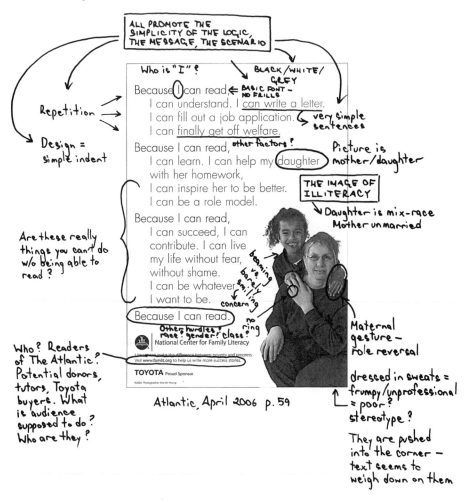

Atlantic, April 2006 p. 59

to accomplish with the PSA, and how other readers of *The Atlantic Monthly* might respond to it. And he still wasn't sure what it was about the message as a whole that troubled him.

As you can see, active reading is just one small part of academic writing. The following chapters follow Daniel as he uses strategies for invention, planning, drafting, and revising to better understand his response to the PSA and to express his ideas in writing.

FOR COLLABORATION

By comparing your responses to this chapter's Explorations with those of your peers, you can gain perspective on the effectiveness of your critical reading strategies. You can also better understand how different purposes and practices influence the reading of and responses to texts.

Bring your responses to the Explorations in this chapter to class. Meeting with a group, compare your responses. After doing so, work together to describe briefly the extent to which your responses are similar or dissimilar. Then discuss what these similarities and differences have helped you understand about the process of critical reading, coming to two or three conclusions to share with your classmates.

FOR THOUGHT, DISCUSSION, AND WRITING

1. Analyze the first chapter of two textbooks you are reading this term (including this one, if you like). Do these textbooks share certain textual conventions? How do you think the writers of these textbooks have analyzed their rhetorical situation? These textbooks are written for you and other students. How effective are they? How might they be more effective?

2. Pick a text that you have read recently (a traditional printed work, a visually rich text, or an electronic document of any length), and freewrite for five minutes about your experience of reading it. How did your rhetorical sensitivity affect the way you read it? To what extent did your expectations and previous experiences as a reader influence your interaction with the text? How would you approach it differently if you were to read it again?

3. Earlier in this chapter, you read "The Height of Inequality: America's Productivity Gains Have Gone to Giant Salaries for Just a Few" by Clive Crook (pp. 224–25). If you haven't already, use the questions and guidelines in this chapter to preview, annotate, summarize, and analyze Crook's argument. Then answer the following questions.

   ▪ As you skimmed this text, what were your expectations? To what extent did the form of the text and your knowledge of its original place of publication influence your expectations?

   ▪ After reading the text more carefully, what was your response? To what extent did this response represent a deepening of or shift from your earlier expectations?

   ▪ How did your own assumptions and values about labor issues and corporate pay scales influence your reading?

   ▪ How would you describe the author's stance or relationship with readers? What role does the text invite you to play as reader?

■ How did reading this text influence your own views about productivity and executive compensation?

■ What other observations about reading or about the subject of economic fairness did this text stimulate in you?

4. Choose one or two of the critical reading skills discussed in this chapter that you haven't used in the past, and try them as you work on a current reading assignment. If you have time, discuss this experiment with some classmates. Then write a brief analysis of which skills work best for you and why.

| | | | | | | | | | | | | | | | | | | | | | | | | | | | | | | | | | | | | | | | | | | | | | | | | | | | | | | | | | | | | | | | | | | | | | | | | | | | | | | | | | | | |

Strategies for Invention

Like many writers, you may feel that finding ideas to write about is the most mysterious part of the writing process. Where do ideas come from? How can you draw a blank one minute and suddenly know the right way to support your argument or describe your experience the next? Is it possible to increase your ability to think and write creatively? Writers and speakers have been concerned with questions such as these for centuries. The classical rhetoricians, in fact, were among the first to investigate the process of discovering and exploring ideas. The Roman rhetoricians called it *inventio,* for "invention" or "discovery." Contemporary writers, drawing on this Latin term, often refer to this process as *invention.*

In practice, invention usually involves both individual inquiry and dialogue with others. In working on a lab report, for example, you might spend most of your time writing alone, but the experiment you're writing about might have been undertaken by a group of students working together. Every time you talk with others about ideas, or consult print or online materials for information, you're entering into a conversation with others about your topic. All writers benefit from the support and insights of others.

The strategies discussed in this chapter aim to help you invent successfully, whether you're having a conversation with yourself as you think through and write about ideas, or whether you're working with classmates or friends. These methods can help you discover what you know—and don't know—about a subject. They can also guide you as you plan, draft, and revise your writing. Most writers find that some of the following methods work better for them than others. That's fine. Just be sure you give each method a fair chance.

Discovering Ideas

As a writer, you don't need to wait in frustration at your desk or computer for inspiration to strike. Successful writers are pragmatists. Understanding that different writing tasks call for different approaches, they develop a repertoire of strategies to find ideas and explore those ideas in writing.

Read this section with a writer's eye. Which of these strategies do you already use? Which ones could you use more effectively? What other strategies might extend your range or strengthen your writing abilities? As you read about and experiment with these strategies, remember to assess their usefulness based on your own needs and preferences as a writer and your particular writing situation.

✗NOTE FOR MULTILINGUAL WRITERS ✗

When you practice the methods of invention, you're focusing on generating ideas ✗not on being perfectly correct. There's no need to interrupt the flow of your ideas by stopping to edit your grammar, spelling, vocabulary, or punctuation. Feel free, in fact, to invent in your first or home language — or even to mix languages — if it increases your fluency and helps you generate ideas.

FREEWRITING

Freewriting is the practice of writing as freely as possible without stopping. It's a simple but powerful strategy for exploring important issues and problems. Here is a description of freewriting by Peter Elbow, the professor who created this technique:

> ✗ To do a freewriting exercise, simply force yourself to write without stopping for [a certain number] of minutes. . . . If you can't think of anything to write, write about how that feels or repeat over and over "I have nothing to write" or "Nonsense" or "No." If you get stuck in the middle of a sentence or thought, just repeat the last word or phrase till something comes along. The only point is to keep writing.
>
> — PETER ELBOW, *Writing with Power: Techniques for Mastering the Writing Process* ✗

Freewriting may at first seem *too* simple to achieve very powerful results, but in fact it can help you discover ideas that you couldn't reach through more conscious and logical means. Because it helps you generate a great deal of material, freewriting is also an excellent antidote for the nervousness many writers feel at the start of a project. It can also improve the speed and ease with which you write.

Freewriting is potentially powerful in a variety of writing situations. Writing quickly without censoring your thoughts can help you explore your personal experience, for example, by enabling you to gain access to images, events, and emotions that you've forgotten or suppressed. Freewriting can also help you experiment with more complex topics without having to assess the worthiness of individual ideas. See how one student used five minutes of freewriting to explore and focus her ideas for a political science paper on low voter turnout.

> I just don't get it. As soon as I could register I did — it felt like a really important day. I'd watched my mother vote and my sisters vote and now it was my turn. But why do I vote; guess I should ask myself that question — and why don't other people? Do I feel that my vote makes a difference? There have been some close elections but not all that many, so my vote doesn't literally count, doesn't decide if we pay a new tax or elect a new senator. Part of it's the feeling I get. When I go to vote I know the people at the polling booth; they're my neighbors. I know the people who are running for office in local elections, and for state and national elections — well, I just feel that I should. But the statistics on voter turnout tell me I'm unusual. I want to go beyond statistics. I want to understand *why* people don't vote. Seems like I need to look not only at research in political science, but also maybe in sociology. (Check journals in economics too?) I wonder if it'd be okay for me to interview some students, maybe some staff and faculty, about voting — better check. But wait a minute; this is a small college in a small town, like the town I'm from. I wonder if people in cities would feel differently — they might. Maybe what I need to look at in my paper is rural/small town versus urban voting patterns.

This student's freewriting not only helped her explore her ideas but also identified a possible question to address and sources she could draw on as she worked on her project.

LOOPING

Looping, an extended or directed form of freewriting, alternates freewriting with analysis and reflection. Begin looping by first establishing a subject for your freewriting; then freewrite for five or ten minutes. This is your first loop. After you have done so, reread what you have written. In rereading your freewriting, look for the center of gravity or "heart" of your ideas — the image, detail, issue, or problem that seems richest or most intriguing, compelling, or productive. Select or write a sentence that summarizes this understanding; this sentence will become the starting point of your second loop. The student who wrote about low voter turnout, for example, might decide to use looping to reflect on this sentence: "I want to understand *why* people don't vote." There is no predetermined number of loops that will work: Keep looping as many times as you like, or until you feel you've exhausted a subject.

When you loop, you don't know where your freewriting and reflection will take you; you don't worry about the final product. Your final essay might not even discuss the ideas generated by your efforts. That's fine; the goal in freewriting and looping is not to produce a draft of an essay but to discover and explore ideas, images, and sometimes even words, phrases, and sentences that you can use in your writing.

||||||||||||||||||||||||||||||||||||||||||||||||||||||||||||||||||||||||||||||||||||||

FOR EXPLORATION

Choose a question, idea, or subject that interests you, and freewrite for five or ten minutes. Then stop and reread your freewriting. What comments most interest or surprise you? Now write a statement that best expresses your freewriting's center of gravity, or "heart." Use this comment to begin a second loop by freewriting for five minutes more.

After completing the second freewriting, stop and reread both passages. What did you learn from your freewriting? Does your freewriting suggest possible ideas for an essay? Finally, reflect on the process itself. Did you find the experience of looping helpful? Would you use freewriting and looping in the future as a means of generating ideas and exploring your experiences?

||||||||||||||||||||||||||||||||||||||||||||||||||||||||||||||||||||||||||||||||||||||

Brainstorming

Like freewriting and looping, brainstorming is a simple but productive invention strategy. When you brainstorm, you list as quickly as possible all the thoughts about a subject that occur to you without censoring or stopping to reflect on them. Brainstorming can help you discover and explore a number of ideas in a short time. Not all of them will be worth using in a piece of writing, of course. The premise of brainstorming is that the more ideas you can generate, the better your chances will be of coming up with good ones.

Alex Osborn, the person generally credited with naming this technique, originally envisioned brainstorming as a group, not an individual, activity. Osborn believed that the enthusiasm generated by the group helped spark ideas. Group brainstorming can be used for a variety of purposes. If your class has just been assigned a broad topic, for instance, your group could brainstorm a list of ways to approach or limit this topic. Or the group could use an online discussion board, email listserv, or blog to generate possible arguments in support of or in opposition to a specific thesis. Use the guidelines on p. 239 to ensure a productive group brainstorming session.

There are other online resources available for brainstorming that you may find useful for group or solo brainstorming. This software, including Thinkature and Bubbl.us, allows you to brainstorm and diagram relationships between ideas or other pieces of information.

Guidelines for Group Brainstorming

- *Define the problem or issue to be addressed* at the start of your group session.
- *Appoint someone to act as a recorder.* This person can write down or save everyone's ideas so that they can be reproduced and distributed later.
- *Contribute freely and spontaneously to the discussion.* Don't stop to discuss or evaluate ideas; your goal is to generate as many ideas as possible.

Those who regularly write with teams or groups cite increased intellectual stimulation and improved quality of ideas as major benefits of brainstorming together, but solitary brainstorming can be just as productive. To brainstorm alone, take a few moments at the start to formulate your goal, purpose, or problem. Then list your ideas as quickly as you can. Include everything that comes to mind, from facts to images, memories, fragments of conversations, and other general impressions and responses. Then review your brainstorming list to identify the most promising or helpful ideas. You are the only one who needs to be able to decipher what you've written, so your brainstorming can be as messy or as organized as you like.

After freewriting about low voter turnout, for example, the student whose writing you read on p. 237 decided to brainstorm a possible list of reasons why people might not vote. Here is part of her list:

- Some people (young people?) mistrust politicians
- Alienated from the political process
- Many political issues are highly polarized—abortion, stem cells, war, drugs, death penalty, health care, etc.
- People in the middle may feel left out of the discussion
- Don't know enough about the issues—or the candidates—to decide
- "My vote won't make a difference"

Her brainstorming also raised several important questions:

- What role does voter registration play?
- Is the problem getting people to register—or getting registered voters to vote?

■ What's the connection between voting and other forms of community and civic engagement?

This student will need to explore her ideas further via both analysis and research, but her brainstormed list has raised important issues and questions for her to consider.

||||||||||||||||||||||||||||||||||||||||||||||||||||||||||||||||||||||||||||||||||

FOR EXPLORATION

Reread the freewriting you did earlier, and then choose one issue or question you'd like to explore further. Write a single sentence summarizing this issue or question, and then brainstorm for five to ten minutes. After brainstorming, return to your list. Put an asterisk (*) beside those ideas or images that didn't appear in your earlier freewriting. How do these new ideas or images add to your understanding of your subject?

||||||||||||||||||||||||||||||||||||||||||||||||||||||||||||||||||||||||||||||||||

CLUSTERING

Like freewriting, looping, and brainstorming, clustering emphasizes spontaneity. The goal of all four strategies is to generate as many ideas as possible, but clustering differs in that it uses visual means to generate ideas. Some writers find that it enables them to explore their ideas more deeply and creatively.

Start with a single word or phrase. If you're responding to an assigned topic, choose the word that best summarizes or evokes that topic. Write this word in the center of a page of blank paper and circle it. Now fill in the page by expanding on or developing ideas connected with this word. Don't censor your ideas or force your cluster to assume a certain shape. Simply circle your key ideas and connect them either to the first word or to other related ideas. Your goal is to be as spontaneous as possible. After clustering, you must distance yourself from the material you've generated so that you can evaluate it. In doing so, try to find the cluster's center of gravity—the idea or image that seems richest and most compelling.

The cluster on p. 241 was developed by student writer Daniel Stiepleman, whose critical reading of a public service announcement (PSA) appears in Chapter 8 (p. 232). As a future teacher, Daniel strongly agreed with the mission of the National Center for Family Literacy, but something about the PSA troubled him. He created a cluster on the word *illiteracy* to explore his response. After evaluating his cluster, Daniel realized that the causes and effects of illiteracy are more complicated than the PSA acknowledges—and that he had a promising topic for an essay.

Daniel Stiepleman's Cluster

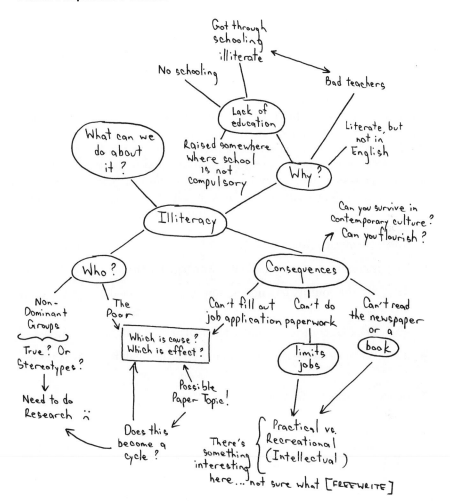

|||||||||||||||||||||||||||||||||||||||||||||||||||||||||||||||||||||||||||||||||||

FOR EXPLORATION

Reread the freewriting, looping, and brainstorming you have written thus far. Then choose one word that seems especially important for your subject, and use it as the center of a cluster. Without planning or worrying about form, fill in your cluster by branching out from this central word. Just include whatever comes to mind. Then take a moment to reflect on what you have learned.

|||||||||||||||||||||||||||||||||||||||||||||||||||||||||||||||||||||||||||||||||||

ASKING THE JOURNALIST'S QUESTIONS

If you have taken a journalism class or written for a newspaper, you know that journalists are taught to answer six questions in articles they write: *who, what, when, where, why,* and *how.* By answering these questions, journalists can be sure that they have provided the most important information about an event, issue, or problem for their readers. And because they probe several aspects of a topic, the journalist's questions can help you discover not just what you know about it, but also what you *don't* know — and thus alert you to the need for additional research.

You may find these questions particularly useful when describing an event or writing an informative essay. Suppose that your political science instructor has assigned an essay on the recent political conflict in Darfur, Sudan. Using the journalist's questions as headings, you could begin working on this assignment by asking yourself the following questions:

- *Who* is involved in this conflict?

- *What* issues most clearly divide those engaged in this dispute?

- *When* did the conflict begin, and how has it developed over the last few years?

- *Where* does the conflict seem most heated or violent?

- *Why* have those living in this area found it so difficult to resolve the situation?

- *How* might this conflict be resolved?

Although you might discover much the same information by simply brainstorming, using the journalist's questions ensures that you have covered all the major points.

|||||||||||||||||||||||||||||||||||||||||||||||||||||||||||||||||||||||||||||||||||||

FOR EXPLORATION

Using the journalist's questions, explore the subject that you have investigated in preceding Explorations in this chapter. (If you feel that you have exhausted this subject, feel free to choose a different topic.)

Once you have employed this method, take a few moments to reflect on this experience. To what extent did the strategy help you organize and review what you already know, and to what extent did it define what you still need to find out?

|||||||||||||||||||||||||||||||||||||||||||||||||||||||||||||||||||||||||||||||||||||

Exploring Ideas

The previous invention strategies have a number of advantages. They're easy to use, and they can help you generate a reassuringly large volume of material when you're just beginning to work on an essay. Sometimes, however, you may want to use more systematic methods to explore a topic. This is especially true when you've identified a potential topic but aren't sure that you have enough to say about it.

ASKING THE TOPICAL QUESTIONS

One of the most helpful methods for developing ideas is based on the topics of classical rhetoric. In his *Rhetoric,* Aristotle describes the topics as potential lines of argument, or places (*topos* in Greek means "place") where speakers and writers can find evidence or arguments. Aristotle defined twenty-eight topics, but the list is generally abbreviated to five: *definition, comparison, relationship, circumstance,* and *testimony.*

The classical topics represent natural ways of thinking about ideas. When confronted by an intellectual problem, we all instinctively ask such questions as these:

- What is it? (*definition*)

- What is it like or unlike? (*comparison*)

- What caused it? (*relationship*)

- What is possible or impossible? (*circumstance*)

- What have others said about it? (*testimony*)

Aristotle's topics build on these natural mental habits. The topical questions can help you pinpoint alternative approaches to a subject or probe one subject systematically, organizing what you know already and identifying gaps that require additional reading or research. Simply pose each question in turn about your subject, writing down as many responses as possible. You might also try answering the expanded list of topical questions on p. 244. These questions were proposed by Edward P. J. Corbett in *The Little Rhetoric and Handbook* (1982).

||||||||||||||||||||||||||||||||||||||||||||||||||||||||||||||||||||||||||||||||||||||||||||

FOR EXPLORATION

Use the topical questions on p. 244 to continue your investigation of the subject that you explored with the journalist's questions in the Exploration on p. 242. What new information or ideas do the topical questions generate? How would you compare these methods?

||||||||||||||||||||||||||||||||||||||||||||||||||||||||||||||||||||||||||||||||||||||||||||

Questions for Exploring a Topic

Questions about Physical Objects

- What are the physical characteristics of the object (shape, dimensions, materials, and so on)?
- What sort of structure does it have?
- What other object is it similar to?
- How does it differ from things that resemble it?
- Who or what produced it?
- Who uses it? For what?

Questions about Events

- Exactly what happened? (who? what? when? where? why? how?)
- What were its causes?
- What were its consequences?
- How was the event like or unlike similar events?
- To what other events was it connected?
- How might the event have been changed or avoided?

Questions about Abstract Concepts (e.g., democracy, justice)

- How has the term been defined by others?
- How do you define the term?
- What other concepts have been associated with it?
- What counterarguments must be confronted and refuted?
- What are the practical consequences of the proposition?

Questions about Propositions (statements to be proved or disproved)

- What must be established before the reader will believe it?
- What are the meanings of key words in the proposition?
- By what kind of evidence or argument can the proposition be proved or disproved?
- What counterarguments must be confronted and refuted?
- What are the practical consequences of the proposition?

RESEARCHING

You're probably already aware that many writing projects are based on research. The formal research paper, however, is not the only kind of writing that can benefit from looking at how others have approached a topic. Once you've explored your own thoughts, or even beforehand, a quick survey of published materials can give you a sense of the issues surrounding a topic, fill gaps in your knowledge, and spark new ideas and questions.

Chapter 6 covers the formal research process in detail. At the invention stage, however, loose, informal research is generally more effective. If you're interested in writing about skydiving, for example, you could pick up a copy of *Skydiving* magazine or spend a half hour or so browsing Web sites devoted to the sport to get a better feel for current trends and issues. Or, imagine that after freewriting and asking yourself the journalist's questions about the Americans with Disabilities Act (ADA) for a political science assignment, you find yourself wondering if President Franklin Delano Roosevelt's personal experiences with polio had any influence on accessibility legislation. By typing "FDR" and "disability" into a search engine, you discover that the first few hits emphasize Roosevelt's efforts to keep his wheelchair hidden from public view, even though he is now considered an inspiration for Americans with disabilities. Realizing that you're very interested in this shift in attitude, you decide to focus on the question of how the ADA has influenced public perceptions of disability. A few keystrokes have given you a valuable idea.

NOTE FOR MULTILINGUAL WRITERS

If you write in languages other than English, you may have learned other ways of discovering and exploring ideas, different from those discussed in this chapter. How are they different? If you have been educated in another culture, do the invention methods used in that culture reflect different rhetorical and cultural values? If there are significant differences, how have you dealt with them?

✳ bedfordstmartins.com/academicwriter
For more advice and resources for beginning informal research, go to **Re:Writing** *and then click on* **The Bedford Research Room**.

Sometimes the best way to develop and explore ideas is to write a very rough draft and see, in effect, what you think about your topic. This strategy, which is sometimes called *discovery drafting*, can work well as long as you recognize that your draft will need extensive analysis and revision.

Writing a discovery draft is a lot like freewriting, although the process tends to be more focused and usually takes more time. As you write, stick to your topic as best you can, but expect that your thoughts may veer off in unexpected directions. The goal is not to produce a polished—or even a coherent—essay, but to put your ideas into written form so that you can evaluate them. Once you have completed a discovery draft, you can use it to identify and fine-tune your most promising ideas, to clarify your goals, and to determine what remains to be done. In order to do so, you will need to distance yourself from your draft so you can look at it objectively.

Case Study: A Student Writer's Discovery Draft

Earlier in this chapter (see p. 241), you saw student writer Daniel Stiepleman's cluster on the topic of literacy for a paper responding to a public service announcement produced by the National Center for Family Literacy (reprinted on p. 232). In order to explore his thoughts more thoroughly, Dan wrote a discovery draft. Here is what he wrote.

> Literacy, often taken for granted, is a gift. The ability to read text not only offers opportunities for escape and entertainment, but gives access to ideas that challenge our own limited worldviews, thus allowing each of us to expand our understandings of our lives on our own terms, at our own pace. The generation of text allows for the further development and sharing of our own ideas with others, at a time when much of the world has lost reverence for oral traditions. Literacy is a gift.
>
> Several organizations exist to help share this gift, but they are underfunded and need help from the public. It is for this reason that groups like the National Center for Family Literacy (NCFL) print public service announcements (PSAs). Obviously these announcements, which appear in magazines and newspapers, are directed toward an educated and literate audience. The task of the men and women who design these advertisements is to convince readers to donate time and/or money toward the cause of literacy training.
>
> In my essay, I want to analyze a PSA that appeared in the April 2006 issue of <u>The Atlantic Monthly</u> magazine. This PSA uses both text and an

image to affect the emotions of the reader. The PSA consists of a series of "Because I can read" statements. The "I" is presumably the woman pictured with a young girl who seems to be the daughter mentioned in the advertisement, though they don't look that much alike. The woman pictured in the PSA stares directly at readers and explains some of the many real-world ways her life has improved because of literacy: "I can fill out a job application . . . I can help my daughter with her homework . . . I can be a role model." By using a first person narrator, the advertisement is, I think, very successful at adding an emotional element that can inspire people to want to help more illiterate Americans improve their lives. Even though some of the things that are stated in the PSA may not be necessarily linked with literacy, such as when she says, "I can contribute" (certainly there are ways she could contribute to society even without being literate), I think this flaw in the logic of the PSA is subtle enough that an American who is flipping through his or her magazine would probably not notice it.

After reviewing his discovery draft, Daniel realized that while it represented a good start on his essay, he still had considerable work ahead of him. Here's what Daniel wrote about this draft in his journal.

Now that I've got some distance from this draft, I can see that it really is just a starting point. Right at the end something clicked with me: a flaw in the logic of the PSA. I tried to dismiss it; I even thought about deleting it because it would be easier for me to write about the value of literacy. But the fact of the matter is that the logic behind this ad really is problematic. This is going to be harder to write about, but it's also a more interesting and provocative idea. I think that I need to rewrite with this idea (or something like it) as my thesis. I'm a little frustrated at having to start over, but the truth is that I probably wouldn't have noticed this problem with the PSA if I hadn't written this draft.

TROUBLESHOOTING

Troubleshooting is a simple but often productive means of identifying and resolving writing problems. It involves formally discussing work in progress with peers who respond with questions and advice — either in person or online. You will probably find group troubleshooting most productive in the early stages of writing, when you're still working out your ideas and determining your approach to your subject.

Guidelines for Troubleshooting

■ *Decide how much time to spend on each person's writing.* Appoint a timekeeper to enforce these limits. If you're working online, establish a time frame for group members to respond to queries.

■ *Begin by having the writer describe the issue or problem that he or she would like to discuss.* The writer should also identify questions for group response. These questions may be very general ("This is what I'm planning to do in my essay. Can you think of any problems I might run into?" "Do you have any suggestions about how I might develop my thesis?") or quite specific ("I've been able to think of two potential objections to my thesis. Can you think of others?" "I like these four ideas, but I don't think they fit together very well. What could I do?").

■ *Let the writer facilitate the resulting discussion.* If the writer needs a moment to write an idea down, he or she should ask the group to pause briefly. The writer should also feel free to ask group members to clarify or elaborate on suggestions.

■ *Respond to each writer's request for assistance as carefully and fully as possible.* Group members are helping you with your writing; you owe it to them to help with theirs.

■ *Practice good "netiquette" if your group is chatting online or compiling ideas in a discussion list.* Use subject lines to help list members identify the purpose and content of your messages, and keep your comments brief enough that they can be read on-screen easily. And remember that electronic messages may circulate in unexpected ways; don't write anything in anger or an attempt at humor that could cause you embarrassment later on.

FOR COLLABORATION

Meet with a group of classmates to discuss the methods of discovering and developing ideas. Begin by having group members briefly describe the advantages and disadvantages they experienced with these methods. (Appoint a recorder to summarize each person's statements.) Then, as a group, discuss your responses to these questions: (1) How might different students' preferences for one or more of these strategies be connected to different learning, composing, and cultural preferences? (2) What influence might situational factors (such as the nature of the assignment, or the amount of time available for working on an essay) have on the decision to use one or more of these strategies? Be prepared to discuss your conclusions with your classmates.

||||||||||||||||||||||||||||||||||||||||||||||||||||||||||||||||||||||||||||||||||

FOR THOUGHT, DISCUSSION, AND WRITING

1. Early in this chapter, you used freewriting, looping, brainstorming, clustering, and the journalist's questions to investigate a subject of interest to you. Continue your exploration of this topic by conducting some informal research and drawing on the topical questions. Then use the material you have gathered to write a discovery draft on your subject.

2. Observe a group of your classmates as they brainstorm (either in person or online), and make notes about what you see. It may be helpful to record how often each member of the group participates in the discussion, for example. Pay attention, too, to group dynamics. Is the group working effectively? Why or why not? What could group members do to interact more effectively? Summarize the results of your observations in a report addressed to the group. Be sure to suggest several ways that the group could work more effectively in the future.

3. Choose one of the strategies discussed in this chapter that you have not used in the past, and try it as you work on your current writing assignment. If you have time, discuss this experiment with some classmates. Then write a brief analysis of why this strategy did or did not work well.

||||||||||||||||||||||||||||||||||||||||||||||||||||||.|||||||||||||||||||||||||||||||||

Strategies for Planning and Drafting

Writing is a complex, dynamic process that challenges you to draw on all your resources and to be open to change as your thoughts — and your drafts — take unpredictable twists and turns. Although it can be intensely rewarding, writing is not easy for anyone. Even professional writers struggle, but they are willing to work through moments of frustration to achieve the insights that make writing worthwhile.

The processes of thinking and writing are too variable and situated to be reduced to rules or formulas. They do, however, involve several activities that you can understand, practice, and improve. The strategies discussed in this chapter can make the challenge of composing a draft more manageable. As you explore them, remember that different people have different composing styles and that many factors can affect the processes of planning and drafting, from the time available to the complexity of the writing task. No matter what your situation, however, the keys to successful writing are preparation and flexibility.

Understanding the Process of Planning

It may be helpful to think of planning as involving waves of play and work. When you're discovering and exploring ideas, for example, you're in a sense playing — pushing your ideas as far as you can without worrying about how useful they'll be later. Most people can't write an essay based on a brain-storming list or thirty minutes of freewriting, however. At some point, they need to settle down to work and formulate a plan for the project.

The planning activities described in this section generally require more discipline than the play of invention. Because much of the crafting of your essay occurs as a result of these activities, however, this work can be intensely rewarding.

ESTABLISHING A CONTROLLING PURPOSE

You can't establish a workable plan for your essay without having a tentative sense of the goals you hope to achieve by writing. These goals may change along the way, but they represent an important starting point for guiding your work in progress. Before you start to draft, then, try to establish a *controlling purpose,* sometimes called a working thesis, for your essay.

A controlling purpose reflects an essay's topic but differs from it in important ways. A controlling purpose reveals not just your topic but also the point you wish to make and the effect you wish to have on your readers. An effective controlling purpose narrows your topic, helps you organize your ideas, enables you to determine what you want to say and *can* say, helps you decide if you have enough information to support your assertions, and points to the most effective way to present your ideas.

A few examples may help clarify this concept. Suppose that you're writing a guest editorial for your campus newspaper. "What are you going to write about?" a friend asks. "The dining hall," you reply. You've just stated your topic, but this statement doesn't satisfy your friend. "What about the dining hall? What's your point?" "Oh," you say, "I'm going to argue that students should petition campus food services to offer more low-fat selections. The current menu is unhealthy." This second statement, which specifies both the point you want to make and its desired effect on readers, is a clearly defined controlling purpose. Further, because the newspaper editorial is an established genre with specific writing conventions, you know before you start that your argument will need to be brief, explicit, and backed up with concrete details.

A controlling purpose isn't always so clear-cut, however. An essay in response to an assignment on the national issue of obesity, for example, could go in many possible directions. You might be interested in drafting an argumentative essay persuading readers to boycott teen fashion magazines that promote an unrealistic image of thinness, or you might decide to write a personal account of your own struggles with weight, aiming both to amuse your readers and to encourage a broader acceptance of varied body types without arguing a specific point. Although both essays would address the same topic, they would have markedly different controlling purposes; as a result, they would demand very different approaches.

You can best understand and establish a controlling purpose by analyzing the elements of your rhetorical situation: writer, reader, text, and medium. This process (which is described in detail in Chapter 3) should give you a clearer understanding of both your reasons for writing and also the most appropriate means to communicate your ideas. In some cases, you may be able to analyze your rhetorical situation and establish a controlling purpose early in the writing process by asking yourself the questions on p. 252.

In many other instances, however, you'll have to think and write your way into understanding what you want to say.

A controlling purpose will help you structure your plan and guide your draft, but you should view it as preliminary, subject to revision. After you've worked on an essay for a while, your controlling purpose may evolve to reflect the understanding you gain through further planning and drafting. You may even discover that your controlling purpose isn't feasible. In either case, the time you spend thinking about your preliminary controlling purpose isn't wasted, for it enables you to begin the process of organizing and testing your ideas.

Questions for Establishing a Controlling Purpose

- What main point do you want to make in this essay? How does this main point relate to your purpose — to what you want your essay to *do* for readers?

- Who might be interested in reading this essay? How might readers' expectations influence its form and content?

- How can you structure your essay to communicate your ideas most effectively to readers?

- What kinds of examples and details will best support your main point? What kind of evidence will your readers find most persuasive?

- How realistic are your intentions, given your rhetorical situation, the assignment, and your time and length limitations?

- How will you accomplish your goals? Do you need to do additional reading? Talk with others? Spend more time discovering and exploring ideas? Write a discovery draft to see what you really think?

FOR EXPLORATION

For an essay that you are writing for this or another course, use the questions listed above to establish a controlling purpose. Then write a paragraph evaluating how your controlling purpose will influence the way you approach planning and drafting the essay.

FORMULATING A WORKABLE PLAN

Once you have established a controlling purpose, you should be able to develop a plan that can guide you as you work. As the discussion of differing composing styles in Chapter 2 indicates, people plan in different ways. Some develop detailed written plans; others rely on mental plans; others might freewrite and determine their goals by reflecting on their own written text.

As a college student, you will often find written plans helpful. Some writers develop carefully structured, detailed outlines. Others find that quick notes and diagrams are equally effective. Developing a plan — whether a jotted list of notes or a formal outline — is an efficient way to try out ideas and engage your unconscious mind in the writing process. In fact, many students find that by articulating their goals on paper or on-screen, they can more effectively critique their own ideas — an important but often difficult part of the writing process.

There is no such thing as an ideal one-size-fits-all plan. An effective plan is one that works for you. Plans are utilitarian, meant to be used — and revised. In working on an essay, you may draw up a general plan only to revise it as you write. Nevertheless, if it helps you begin drafting, your first plan will fulfill its function well.

Consider, for example, two students' actual plans. These plans differ significantly, yet each fulfilled the author's needs. The first is by Lisa DeArmand, a freshman majoring in business, for an informal essay reviewing three popular pizza parlors near campus. Lisa's plan is brief and simple. She had already decided that the most effective way to approach her essay would be to compare the three restaurants, and she had detailed notes, including interviews with students, parts of which she planned to incorporate in her essay. Because Lisa had such a clear mental image of what she wanted to say and how she wanted to say it, she didn't need a highly detailed written plan.

Lisa DeArmand's Plan

BOBBIE'S PIZZA	PIZZA-IN-A-HURRY	PIZZA ROMA
$12.50	$14.00	$18.50
close	coupons	best pizza!
limited hours	crust thin and soggy	unusual toppings
delivery charge	tastes like frozen pizza	two kinds of crust
pizza OK but not great	more toppings	spicy and mild sauces

Case Study: A Student Writer's Plan

Now consider the plan by Daniel Stiepleman, an education major, for his analysis of a public service announcement promoting literacy. He had already written a discovery draft (see p. 246) that helped him discover the point he wanted to make, but he wasn't sure how to proceed. Daniel described his controlling purpose and his rhetorical situation in these terms:

I am writing an analytical essay for my composition class. I want to convince my readers — my instructor and my classmates — that there are some disturbing assumptions behind the National Center for Family Literacy's public service campaign. If my readers are anything like I am, their first impressions will be that the ad must be good because it promotes literacy. I'm worried this will lead them to resist my argument that literacy isn't, as the ad implies, an easy solution to the problem of inequity. I've got to be convincing by using evidence, both from the text and from other sources.

How will I convince them of my argument? After all, I had to write my way to seeing it. Will it be more convincing to sound objective or passionate? I'm inclined to try the latter, but I know our instructor said that being objective is more convincing. Plus that may help it sound less like I'm arguing that the PSA's negative consequences are on purpose. I'll need to be careful in my description.

Daniel's task was more complex than Lisa's, so his plan needed to be more complex. He came up with a visual map that helped him imagine how his essay might be organized (see p. 255). It includes several questions he thought he should address, reminders to himself, definitions of terms, and general comments. He used his plan to further explore his ideas and to determine the best organization for his essay. Although probably no one but Daniel could develop an essay from the diagrams and notes he created, the plan fulfilled his needs — and that's what counts.

NOTE FOR MULTILINGUAL WRITERS

You may find it helpful to consider how your knowledge of multiple languages or dialects affects the way you formulate plans. Is it easier and more productive to formulate plans in your first or home language and then translate these plans into English? Or is it more helpful to formulate plans in English because doing so encourages you to keep North American rules and expectations in mind? You may want to experiment with both approaches so that you can determine the planning process that works best for you.

Daniel Stiepleman's Plan

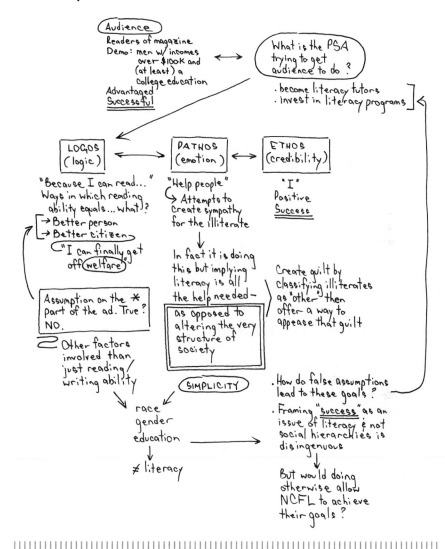

||||||||||||||||||||||||||||||||||||||||||||||||||||||||||||||||||||||||||||||||||||||||

FOR EXPLORATION

If you have ever created a plan for an essay or school project, what kinds of plans have you typically drawn up? Do you formulate detailed, carefully structured plans, or do you prefer less structured ones? Do you use diagrams or other visuals? Or do you just start writing? Use these questions to think about the plans you have (or have not) used in the past; then spend ten minutes writing about how you might develop more useful plans in the future.

||||||||||||||||||||||||||||||||||||||||||||||||||||||||||||||||||||||||||||||||||||||||

|||||||||||||||||||||||||||||||||||||||||||||||||||||||||||||||||||||||||||||||||||||||||||

FOR COLLABORATION

Meeting with a group of classmates, take turns reading your responses to the previous Exploration. Then work together to answer these questions. (Be sure to appoint a recorder.)

1. How often do you all develop written plans? What kinds of plans do you most often develop? How formal and detailed are they? Does anyone often use diagrams or other visual plans?

2. Did anyone suggest planning strategies that other members thought they might like to experiment with? If so, briefly describe these strategies and explain why they seem useful.

3. List three conclusions about planning that all group members can agree with. Make another list of at least three suggestions of ways to plan more efficiently and productively.

Be prepared to share the results of your discussion with the entire class.

|||||||||||||||||||||||||||||||||||||||||||||||||||||||||||||||||||||||||||||||||||||||||||

Developing Effective Strategies for Drafting

The British writer E. M. Forster once asked, "How can I know what I think until I see what I say?" By working through drafts of your work in progress, you gradually learn what you think about your subject. Although your process may begin with freewriting or brainstorming, drafting is the point in the process when you explore your ideas more fully and deeply. Drafting is important, for it is through drafting that you create a text that embodies your preliminary goals.

MANAGING THE DRAFTING PROCESS

When you sit down at your desk or computer to begin writing, it can be hard to imagine the satisfaction of completing a rough draft. Just picking up pen or pencil or beginning to type can seem daunting. Once you pass the initial hurdle of getting started, you'll probably experience the drafting process as a series of ebbs and flows. You may write intensely for a short period, stop and review what you've written, make a few notes about how to proceed, and then draft again more slowly, pausing now and then to reread what you've written. Drafting is a messy process that no two people approach the same way; indeed, even a single person will take different approaches at different times. All the same, the strategies discussed in this section can help make your process efficient and productive.

Overcoming Resistance to Drafting.   All writers experience some resistance to drafting; however, there are ways to overcome this resistance. Many writers rely on rituals to get started, such as clearing the writing space of clutter, gathering notes and other materials in a handy place, starting up a special playlist. Personal predispositions affect writing habits as well. Some people write best early in the morning; others, late at night. Some require a quiet atmosphere; others find the absence of noise distracting. Some find it easier to draft if they're doing something else at the same time; others shut down email and instant messaging so they can focus. Some writers work in fits and starts; others need to carve out large blocks of time. The trick is to figure out what works best for you.

Reading through early notes and plans is an effective way to begin a drafting session. If you've already spent time discovering and exploring ideas and making one or more tentative plans, you know that you're not starting from scratch. You may find yourself turning hasty notes and fragments into full sentences or grouping them into paragraphs — drafting before you know it.

Perhaps the best motivation is to remind yourself that a draft doesn't have to be perfect. Your initial goal should simply be to *get the words down.* If you can't think of a way to open your essay, for instance, don't try to do so; just begin writing whatever section you're ready to write.

Building Momentum.   The easiest way to produce a rough draft is to work at an even pace so that the momentum can help you move steadily toward your goal. Accept that your draft will be imperfect, even incomplete, and focus instead on putting your thoughts into words. By giving yourself permission to create a messy draft, you free yourself to explore ideas and discover what you want to say.

You'll naturally experiment with changes as you write, but don't try to correct or polish your writing in the drafting stage. Stopping to check spelling or grammar can interrupt your momentum and throw you off balance. Furthermore, it's easier to delete unnecessary or repetitive material when you revise than to add new material. If you can't quite articulate an argument or formulate an example, write yourself a note and keep drafting. When you return to your draft, you can fill in these gaps.

Like most writers, you'll probably experience moments of writer's block — times when the words won't come. But you don't have to bemoan your fate when this occurs. Instead, you can draw on a repertoire of block-busting strategies, including those suggested in the guidelines on p. 258, to get back on track.

Finally, be aware that most word processing programs offer a number of functions that can make writing easier and more productive. If you're drafting quickly and wish to maintain your momentum but also remember a question or an idea, for example, you can insert comments as you write and return

Guidelines for Overcoming Writer's Block

- *Lower your standards.* If you can't find the right words, get them down in any form you can. Write enough to remind yourself of the point you want to make; then move on.

- *Change strategies.* If you're stuck for ideas, stop trying to draft. Revise your written plan, or spend ten minutes freewriting or brainstorming. You might also try diagramming, clustering, or doodling instead.

- *Switch to a writing task that you can do.* If you can't determine how to make a particular point or explain an idea, turn to a different part of your essay or review some background material. Or switch to another project you need to complete.

- *Talk out your ideas.* Find a friend or family member to talk with. Begin by saying, "I've been trying to work on my essay, but I'm blocked. What I want to do is . . ."

- *Take a break.* Take a few minutes to describe the difficulty you're experiencing; then put your writing aside and do something that will give you satisfaction—exercising, cooking, whatever.

to them in a later drafting session. The guidelines on p. 259 offer suggestions for taking advantage of additional useful features. Be careful, however, not to let your computer's capabilities distract you from the task of drafting itself.

Keeping in Touch with Your "Felt Sense."   You attend to many things when you draft. You stop and reread; you reflect about your topic and assignment; you think about your readers. If you're an effective writer, you look at what you've written not just to see what's on the page but also what *might be* there. Writing about this kind of awareness, Professor Sondra Perl describes writers "keeping in touch with their *felt sense* as writers."

You might think of felt sense as inspiration—and it is, in the sense that many writers would find it difficult to articulate why they're writing a particular sentence or paragraph. The ability to develop felt sense doesn't require magical gifts, however. Writers develop felt sense when they are deeply immersed in their writing.

To develop and maintain your felt sense, you need to draft for long enough periods so that you can become immersed in your writing—an hour, minimally, but longer if possible. And as you write words, sentences, and paragraphs, keep one eye on such global issues as the extent to which your

Guidelines for Drafting on a Computer

- *Use the* WINDOW *or* SPLIT BAR *function* to work on multiple documents (or multiple versions of a single document) at the same time. You might, for example, place a freewrite, outline, or plan in one window and write your draft in the other. Or you might keep your introduction in view as you write later sections.

- *Use* CUT *and* PASTE *functions* to move items from one file to another or to move sections of text within a draft.

- *Use* TRACK CHANGE, COMMENT, *and* MARKUP *functions* to write notes or compare versions of a draft. Because changes appear on-screen but not in the printed text (or are easily removed with a single keystroke), these features allow you to interact with your own and others' writing without cluttering drafts with comments that must be deleted later.

- *Use the* SAVE AS *function* to take risks without endangering your original. If you decide while you're drafting that a paragraph isn't working, for example, you might change your mind later and regret deleting it. Give each new attempt at a draft a different name or number; this strategy makes it easy to revert to earlier versions.

- *Protect your work* by using the SAVE function frequently, making backup copies of your drafts, and printing hard copies.

draft responds to readers' needs and expectations. Reflecting on these concerns and jotting down notes are good ways to keep in touch with your felt sense.

Allowing Time for Incubation. Ideally, you'll come to a natural stopping point, a moment when you feel that you've solved a problem you've been wrestling with or concluded a section you've been working on. At this point, take a few moments to jot down notes about what you've accomplished as well as about what you still need to do. You may also wish to ask yourself a few questions: "What's the best transition here?" "Which examples should I use next?" If you're like many writers, your subconscious mind will present appropriate answers when you next sit down to draft.

Sometimes it helps to *stop* thinking consciously about your ideas and just let them develop in your mind while you relax, sleep, or occupy yourself with other projects. After this period of incubation, you'll often spontaneously recognize how to resolve a problem or answer a question. You can't draw on your mind's subconscious powers, however, if you don't build in time for incubation. And don't confuse incubation with procrastination. *Procrastination* means avoiding the writing process; *incubation* means recognizing and using the fluctuations of the process to advantage.

||||||||||||||||||||||||||||||||||||||||||||||||||||||||||||||||||||||||||||||||||||||||||||||

FOR EXPLORATION

How do you typically draft an essay? How long do your drafting sessions usually last? What do you do when you run into problems? Could one or more of the suggestions presented here enable you to draft more productively? How might you best implement these suggestions? Spend five or ten minutes freewriting in response to these questions.

FOR COLLABORATION

Meeting with a group of classmates, take turns reading your responses to the preceding Exploration. Then work together to answer these questions. (Be sure to appoint a recorder.)

1. How do group members overcome resistance to drafting? How long do drafting sessions typically last? How do group members keep in touch with their felt sense while drafting?

2. Did anyone suggest drafting strategies that others might like to try? Briefly describe any such strategies, and explain why you believe they might be useful.

3. List three conclusions about drafting with which all group members can agree. Make another list of at least three suggestions on how you can draft more efficiently and productively.

Be prepared to share the results of your discussion with your classmates.

||||||||||||||||||||||||||||||||||||||||||||||||||||||||||||||||||||||||||||||||||||||||||||||

Developing and Organizing Your Ideas

As you draft, you'll become more aware of what you have to say about a subject. Consequently, you'll also become increasingly engaged with issues of organization and structure. "What do I think about this subject?" becomes less important than "How can I best present my ideas to my readers?" This section suggests strategies for responding to the second question. These strategies are only suggestions; your use of them should be based on your understanding of your assignment, purpose, and rhetorical situation.

Using a Thesis Statement

North American readers quickly become irritated if they feel they're reading unorganized, disconnected prose or if their expectations about how a certain kind of writing should be organized are violated. For these reasons, sharing your controlling purpose with readers and providing cues about how you will achieve it is essential.

How to share your purpose most effectively depends on a number of factors. If you're working on a take-home essay exam for a history class or an analytical essay for a mass media class, for example, you may wish to include in your introduction a *thesis statement,* a single sentence (sometimes two) that states the main point of your essay, as opposed to just describing the topic. You may also preview the main lines of argument you'll use to support your position so that readers don't have to hunt for your main point. (Thesis statements are discussed in more detail in Chapter 5.)

Most readers expect to find a thesis statement in an academic essay, but in other situations, it may not be necessary or even desirable to include a specific indication of your intentions. If you're writing a personal essay about what the word *family* means to you, for example, you might decide that you don't want to articulate the main point of your essay in a single sentence. Instead, you might begin with an example that will create interest in your essay and show, rather than tell, what *family* means to you.

Whether or not you include a thesis statement, what's important is that you know your controlling purpose, and that readers can figure it out easily. As you work on your draft, having a thesis statement in mind — even if it's not expressed directly — will help you organize your thoughts; it will also help ensure that readers will stay with you.

thinking rhetorically

✳ bedfordstmartins.com/academicwriter

For more help developing a thesis statement for an academic project, go to **Re:Writing** *and then click on* **The Bedford Research Room**.

Developing Ideas

It's a good idea to begin each new drafting session by reviewing the material you've already generated, looking for ideas and details to add or develop more fully. Often in rereading these explorations and early drafts, writers realize that they've relied on words that have meaning for themselves but not necessarily for their readers. In her book *Problem-Solving Strategies for Writing in College and Community* (1996), Linda Flower calls them "code words." Learning to recognize and expand or "unpack" code words in your own writing can help you develop your ideas so that their significance is clear to readers.

Here is a paragraph from one student's freewriting about what the word *family* meant to her. While rereading her writing, she recognized a number of code words, which she underlined.

When I think of the good things about my family, Christmas comes most quickly to mind. Our house was filled with such <u>warmth and joy</u>. Mom was busy, but she was <u>happy</u>. Dad seemed less absorbed in his work. In the weeks before Christmas he almost never worked late at the office, and he often arrived with brightly wrapped presents that he would tantalizingly show us — before whisking them off to their hiding place. And at night we <u>did fun things together</u> to prepare for the big day.

Words like *warmth* and *joy* undoubtedly have many strong connotations for the writer; most readers, however, would find these terms vague. This writer realized that in drafting she would have to provide plenty of concrete, specific details to enable readers to visualize what she means.

NOTE FOR MULTILINGUAL WRITERS

You may find it helpful to organize — and perhaps even develop — some of your thoughts in your first or home language.

FOLLOWING TEXTUAL CONVENTIONS

When you draft, you don't have to come up with an organizational structure from scratch. Instead, you can draw on conventional methods of organization, methods that reflect common ways of analyzing and explaining information. Your subject may naturally lend itself to one or more methods of organization. Suppose that you're writing an essay about political and economic changes in Eastern Europe in the 1990s. Perhaps in your reading you were struck by the different responses of Russian and Czech citizens to economic privatization. You might draw on conventional methods of *comparing and contrasting* to organize your analysis. Or perhaps you wish to discuss the impact that severe industrial pollution in Russia could have on the development of a Western-style economy. After *classifying* the most prevalent forms of industrial pollution, you might discuss the consequences of this pollution for Russia's economy. In some cases, you may be able to use a single method of organization — such as *comparison*, *definition*, *cause and effect*, or *problem-solution* — to organize your entire essay. More often, however, you'll draw on several methods to present your ideas.

thinking
rhetorically

In considering how best to draw on conventional methods of organizing information, remember that you shouldn't impose them formulaically. Begin thinking about how to organize your writing by reflecting on your goals as a writer and your rhetorical situation. If your analysis suggests that one or more methods of organizing information represent commonsensical, logical ways of approaching your subject, use them in drafting. But remember, form should grow out of meaning and not be imposed on it.

||||||||||||||||||||||||||||||||||||||||||||||||||||||||||||||||||||||||||||||||||||||||

FOR THOUGHT, DISCUSSION, AND WRITING

1. Choose a writing assignment that you have just begun. After reflecting on your ideas, develop and write a workable plan. While drafting, keep a record of your activities. How helpful was your plan? Was it realistic? Did you revise your plan as you wrote? What can you learn about your writing process from this experience? Be prepared to discuss this experience with your class.

2. Interview someone who works in the field that you hope to enter after graduation, and ask the following questions about how he or she plans and drafts on-the-job writing.

   ▪ What kinds of plans do you typically construct?

   ▪ In what ways have electronic or other technologies influenced your planning and drafting strategies?

   ▪ Do you experience writing blocks? If yes, what block-busting strategies work best for you?

   ▪ How do your profession and work schedule influence your planning and drafting?

   ▪ How often do you write alone? As a member of a group or team?

   ▪ What advice about writing would you give to a student who hopes to enter this field?

   ▪ Write an essay summarizing the results of your interview.

3. Think of a time when you simply couldn't get started writing. What did you do to move beyond this block? How well did your efforts work—and why? After reflecting on your experience, write an essay (humorous or serious) about how you cope with writer's block.

||||||||||||||||||||||||||||||||||||||||||||||||||||||||||||||||||||||||||||||||||||||||

Strategies for Designing Pages and Screens

Until relatively recently, few writers concerned themselves with the visual look of a text. Although advertising copy, magazines and newspapers, and business and technical texts have long been influenced by design concerns, just twenty years ago most writers composed either in longhand or at the typewriter. Students were required to use specific margins, headings, and appropriate paper, and to follow other formatting rules. But these were the only visual elements that students needed to be concerned about.

Today's digital technologies allow communicators to make many more decisions about texts than they did in the past. Someone who wants to share her passion for black Labrador retrievers, for instance, could create an article, a Web site, a research paper, or a video about this popular breed. Each medium would require her to be as concerned with the visual as with the verbal, for in all of these media the verbal and visual are interdependent.

Personal computers opened up a new world of options for writers, who can now easily create headings and lists, print with color and multiple fonts, and develop sophisticated charts and graphs. With access to the Web, writers can easily (if not always legally) download or create texts, images, and audio or video clips and integrate them into their own writing. It is increasingly common for students to develop texts that take full advantage of these options.

Document design is fundamental to creating readable, clearly organized, and engaging texts. Your goal should be an appropriate final design, one that creates a consistent overall impression and that is most suitable for the kind of document you are creating. This chapter will help you answer basic questions about designing effective texts, online and in print. Note that your instructor may specify a particular document design or format. (If you're unsure about instructors' preferences, don't hesitate to ask.)

Looking at Design and the Rhetorical Situation

Questions about document design are, in fact, rhetorical questions—questions that depend on your rhetorical situation. For any writing project, you

|||||||||||||||||||||||||||||||||||||||||||||||||||||||||||||||||||||||||||||||||||

FOR EXPLORATION

How attuned are you to the visual elements in texts you read in print and online? Take a few moments to think about the many different texts that you read—from textbooks, magazines, newspapers, advertisements, and letters to Web sites, emails, and instant messages. How conscious are you of the ways that design elements and images influence your response to and understanding of a text? (How does a magazine or Web site intended for twenty-somethings, for instance, use visual elements to differentiate itself from one intended for a different readership?) Do you have strong preferences about such visual features as type font, color, and images? Take five minutes to freewrite in response to these questions.

|||||||||||||||||||||||||||||||||||||||||||||||||||||||||||||||||||||||||||||||||||||

NOTE FOR MULTILINGUAL WRITERS

Cultures have their own preferences about written texts, visual texts, and visual design principles. If you are an international student or come from an American community that uses a language other than English, you may have noticed that newspapers in your home country or home community look considerably different from most North American newspapers. These differences reflect cultural preferences about visual design.

Take a few moments to consider these differences. How might such design preferences influence your decisions as a writer of academic texts? Which elements of your home community's or culture's visual design preferences might enrich your academic writing, and vice versa?

should analyze your situation to make decisions about document design and other visual elements of communication.

thinking rhetorically

Imagine two students who are working on different projects. One student is taking an art history class: He's writing a twenty-page seminar paper on the nineteenth-century British artists who called themselves the Pre-Raphaelite Brotherhood. The second student, who's in an English class, is writing a four-page analysis of a poem by the contemporary American poet Mary Oliver. How should these students use visual elements in their writing? Both have access to online content and images (such as reproductions of paintings by various Pre-Raphaelites or photographs of Mary Oliver). But should they use these images?

A rhetorical response to these questions would consider the students' particular situations. Though they're writing different kinds of essays, both are writing *academic* essays, so any visual elements they use should reflect the seriousness and formality that characterize academic writing. Because ideas are central in academic writing, any image, chart, or other visual element should be essential to the intellectual richness and impact of the writing.

As you have perhaps already realized, both students need to use visual elements. Because the paper about the Pre-Raphaelites is long, headings will help orient readers to critical divisions within the paper. Even more important, however, is the role that reproductions of art by the Pre-Raphaelites could play in this student's analysis. Such reproductions would enable readers to understand and evaluate the student's analysis of various paintings without having to refer to other sources. The student might also include photographs of the Pre-Raphaelites themselves if he's sure that the photos will enrich his analysis—for example, if he's discussing the historical, cultural, or social role of this movement in nineteenth-century England.

The student writing on Oliver would also need to attend to visual elements, considering such issues as the use of white space, fonts, page numbers, and headings, which are important for any academic essay. But unless some aspect of the analysis requires visual support or clarification, this student probably wouldn't include photographs or other visuals. They would add little to the development of her ideas and might even distract readers.

As these examples suggest, a rhetorical approach to document design encourages you to ask questions about your reader, your text, your medium, and yourself. (See the Questions for Analyzing Your Rhetorical Situation on p. 44.)

✳ bedfordstmartins.com/academicwriter
For a tutorial on designing effective Web texts, go to **Re:Writing** *and then click on* **Designing for the Web**.

Understanding the Basic Principles of Design

Once you know the basic principles of document design, you can create accessible, inviting texts that share information, lead readers smoothly through your presentation, and achieve their purpose. Whether you're creating a print text or a digital or online text, certain fundamental design principles are essential: these include alignment, proximity, repetition, and contrast.

Guidelines for Thinking Rhetorically about Document Design

thinking rhetorically

■ *Consider your reader's expectations.* For a take-home midterm for a political science class, your reader — your teacher — probably expects you to submit a traditional, visually straightforward text. But if you're creating an honors thesis on the recent development of new techniques for groundwater purification, you might decide to include illustrations, tables, and graphs. Because you have worked intimately with your professors on this project, you can talk about design and format requirements with your committee members.

■ *Reflect on your own goals and strengths as the writer.* When you approach a writing assignment, consider your role and experience with design. How much authority do you have in this particular situation? How knowledgeable are you about the textual conventions that inform the kind of writing you're undertaking? How much do you know about various writing technologies that might visually enhance your text? And how much time do you have to take advantage of this knowledge?

■ *Gather information about textual conventions.* Textual conventions — the format and design standards for the kind of writing you're doing — play a role in your design decisions. Memos, for example, are formatted in certain ways, and they often include headings (see a sample memo on p. 214). In many of the sciences, tables and figures are common; other conventions include headings in lab reports and grant proposals. In traditionally text-based disciplines such as English and philosophy, tables are rarely used, and figures — photographs, graphs, and other images — are used infrequently. If you're unsure about the conventions for a particular discipline, take a conservative approach — or ask your teacher.

■ *Consider the requirements and limitations of your medium.* Think about the medium, whether you are working on a traditional text, such as a letter or a research essay, or something that requires more complex design choices, such as a Web site or set of PowerPoint slides. First, if the assignment doesn't specify a medium, consider whether the one you've chosen will appeal to readers and effectively convey your intended meaning. If the medium is assigned — a poster, for example — are there requirements about size or type of paper? If the medium is online, there are different issues to consider. For example, will your text require updates? Will you need to request permission to publish online any sources or visuals you've used? Also, consider practical issues such as costs and availability of necessary tools. Do you have access to — and skills for working with — the appropriate software? Do you need access to a high-speed Internet connection, color printer, scanner, or other hardware?

ALIGNMENT

This principle relates to the way words or visuals on a page or screen are lined up vertically or horizontally: flush left, flush right, or centered. Though your goal should be to maintain a clear, consistent alignment, you don't need to line up everything on the same side of the page; multiple columns in which each item is aligned within the column are fine, too. Be aware, however, that lack of alignment is a very common Web design problem; don't mix alignments within a design. Also pay special attention to the alignment of tables, charts, or other images so they're clearly linked to the text they support.

PROXIMITY

A page or screen makes effective use of the design principle of proximity when the relationships between text elements (such as headings, subheadings, and items in a list) and visual elements (such as captions and photos) are clear. Your goal should be to position related points, chunks of text, and visual elements together. An easy way to evaluate your text's use of proximity is to squint your eyes and see how the page or screen looks. Does your eye move logically from one part to another? If not, you'll want to work on the internal relationships, creating clearly defined chunks using headings, indentation, or white space.

REPETITION

This principle is important for creating a sense of coherence. A consistent design gives a unified look and helps guide readers through the text. One example of repetition is the practice of indenting paragraphs. Repetition can involve elements that are visual, verbal, or both. For example, you'll want to be consistent in the design of typefaces you choose, the placement and use of color, and the positioning of graphic elements, such as a navigational banner on a homepage.

CONTRAST

A page or screen effectively employs contrast when the design attracts the reader's eye and draws him or her in. Contrast helps organize and orient readers' interactions with a text, guiding the reader around the elements on a page and making the information accessible. Focal points play an important role in establishing contrast. A focal point—a point that the eye travels to first—may be an image, a logo, or a dominant set of words. You should design the rest of the page or screen so that the flow of information starts with this point. White space can also create effective contrast. Margins and double-spacing, or unused space around headings or graphics, for instance, frame the text and guide the reader through it.

Formatting and Layout

There are so many formatting and layout elements to consider when designing a document that it's sometimes hard to choose the best elements for a particular layout. There is no one right answer for all situations; what works well in one situation isn't necessarily appropriate in another. The following advice will help you make careful decisions, but remember that your assignment or the genre you're working in may have specific design requirements.

COLOR

Color can add visual appeal and impact, so it can play an important role in document design. When you write brochures, Web pages, newsletters, and similar documents, you may often employ color. When writing academic papers, however, you'll usually compose texts printed only in black ink. If you do plan to use color, see the guidelines below.

Guidelines for Using Color Effectively

- *Establish a plan.* How many colors will you use? Do you need to consider the costs of printing documents with color? What role do you want color to play in your overall design?
- *Use color to emphasize key elements of your text* — and do so consistently. If you're using color to emphasize subheads, for instance, use the same color for all of them.
- *Use color for only the most important elements.*
- *Use two — or at most three — colors.* Use a small number of colors for headings, graphics, images, or bullets, to avoid overwhelming or confusing readers.
- *Choose colors that will be legible and clear in your final product.* Colors can look different onscreen or in different browsers. (For example, headings may appear darker on-screen than when printed.) Test a print page to be certain color text and visuals are sharp.
- *Avoid colors that clash, and choose colors in combination that offer strong contrast.* Not all colors are equally legible when used for type. Generally use dark type on a light background; light type on a dark background offers strong contrast but can be more difficult to read. (There's an exception to this rule: when creating slides to be shown in a darkened room for an oral presentation.)

(continued)

(continued)

- *Be aware that certain colors may be hard for some readers to see comfortably.* Ask for feedback from representative readers.
- *If you are writing an academic essay, remember that color should only be used if it enhances the content and readability of your essay.* Check with your instructor if you are uncertain about the requirements of your assignment.

FONTS AND TYPEFACES

With computers, writers have a dazzling—but potentially bewildering—array of typefaces and sizes (or fonts) to choose from. How can you make the best use of them? For academic assignments, the easy-to-read 11 or 12 point type size is best:

This is 11 point Times New Roman.

This is 12 point Times New Roman.

But what if you're composing a brochure, newsletter, or Web site? You may want to use a variety of typefaces. First you should consider whether to use a *serif* or *sans serif* typeface for particular elements. Many readers find serif typefaces (such as the one used for the main text of this book) easier to read for printed texts and sans serif ones (such as Arial, Helvetica, or Verdana) easier to read online and for headings.

In some situations, you may want to consider using an unusual font such as **Impact** or Century Gothic to create a particular tone. Remember, though, that such typefaces (in a range of script, handwriting, or decorative styles) call attention to themselves and should be used sparingly. You'll probably want to limit yourself to two or at most three fonts in a document. If you shift fonts and sizes too often within a document, you'll distract readers from focusing on your text.

SPACING

Margins and the spacing of elements on a page are important for determining whether your text looks dense or readable. White space—in the margins, between paragraphs and sentences, and around visual or textual elements such as figures and lists—helps draw the reader's eye to the appropriate text or visual elements. For most academic writing, your text should be double-spaced, with one-inch margins and paragraphs indented one-half inch (or five spaces).

Some genres, including résumés, letters, and online texts, should be single-spaced, with no paragraph indents (use an extra line of space between paragraphs instead). With other genres, including brochures and flyers, you may want to choose different margins, use columns, or include additional white space around visual elements to draw attention to them and balance the visuals with the text. The choices you make for spacing will likely be determined by your instructor, your supervisor, or the conventions for your genre. Check the requirements of your assignment or course. See the examples in Chapter 7 for models of the formatting required by different disciplines.

PAGINATION

Academic assignments usually require you to follow the formatting and pagination rules of a particular style (MLA, APA, *Chicago,* CSE, and others), depending on the discipline. Often this involves putting the page number, the title or your name, and the date the text was produced on the first page and all subsequent pages. For MLA and APA style texts, put the page number in the upper right corner, one inch from the right edge and one-half inch from the top.

For online texts, the information that would appear on a printed page's header should appear in a navigation bar that unifies the electronic pages and makes it easy for users to locate parts of the text. Additional information that you can attach to each part of an online text includes your name, the date of publication, and links to the text's homepage.

If you haven't received specific information about how to handle the page number and other pagination information for your document, or if you aren't sure, check with your instructor.

✳ bedfordstmartins.com/academicwriter
  For more help creating effective layouts using your word processor, go to **Re:Writing** *and then click on* **Designing Documents with a Word Processor**.

Choosing Effective Headings

Headings help readers find the information they need because they structure a text into clear chunks. For longer print texts and for genres such as brochures and Web sites, headings help readers see the organization of the text. For some academic writing, there are required headings (*Works Cited* or *Abstract,* for example) and guidelines for their typeface and positioning. For texts where you have flexibility in choosing headings, you should consider wording, type size and style, and positioning.

WORDING

Make headings concise yet informative. They can be single nouns (*Literacy*), a noun phrase (*Literacy in Families*), a gerund phrase (*Testing for Literacy*), or a question or statement (*How Can Literacy Be Measured?*). Make all headings at the same level consistent throughout your text—for example, by using all single nouns or all gerund phrases. Avoid using headings that restate the name of the section of text (such as *Conclusion*).

Type Size and Style

For academic writing in MLA or APA style, headings need to be set in the same font as the rest of the text. For documents where you have some choice, you can distinguish headings by using color, bold or italics, and type size and style. Using only type, you might distinguish among levels using capitals, bold, and italics, as here:

FIRST-LEVEL HEADING

Second-Level Heading

Third-Level Heading

Positioning

Place headings consistently throughout your text. For academic texts following MLA style, headings should be aligned left, without additional space around them. For APA papers, center the first two levels of headings. For texts where you can choose the placement, centered headings are common for the first level; for secondary-level headings, you may indent, set flush left, or run them in to the text.

Using Visuals Effectively

Visuals can add to a text's persuasiveness. They're best used when a text truly *needs* them — that is, when they can present information more succinctly and clearly than words alone. Visuals fall into two broad categories: tables and figures. Tables summarize data, usually in clearly labeled horizontal rows and vertical columns. Figures include all other visuals: pie charts, line and bar graphs, drawings, diagrams, maps, photographs, and other illustrations. Whether you're using tables or figures, rhetorical common sense can help you make a number of important decisions.

Guidelines for Using Visuals Effectively

- *Use visuals only when they play a key role in communicating your ideas.* Never use visuals merely as decoration, particularly in academic writing.

- *In print texts, refer to the visual before it appears and explain its significance in the body of your text.* (A student who is writing about military deaths during the Vietnam War might introduce an important table by noting, "As Table 1 demonstrates, many more Vietnamese than American soldiers lost their lives during this war.") You may think that a visual's relevance to your discussion is obvious, but not all readers may find that to be the case.

- *Be sure to number and title all visuals.* Number and label tables and figures (photographs or other visuals) separately. Give a caption to visuals to relate their significance to your text. Label the parts of graphs and charts clearly.
- *Document all visual sources.* Cite the sources for all visuals and for data used in graphs. (See p. 340.)
- *Use visuals responsibly.* If you use visuals you haven't created yourself, take care to follow the conventions of copyright law. These laws allow for "fair use" of copyright-protected material if the material is used for a class and is not published (in print or on the Web). If you're reusing visuals online or plan to publish them, you'll need to request written permission. If you're downloading visuals, look for copyright notices and information about fair use. Many online sources of visuals allow you to download information without requesting permission. If there is no such statement on a site, you should email the site's Webmaster for permission. (See below for a sample permission request.)
- *Edit visuals ethically.* Take care not to mislead readers with any changes you make by cropping or otherwise altering a visual. Be clear in your text about how you have altered an image, and be sure that the edited image is an accurate representation of the subject.

Permission Request Email

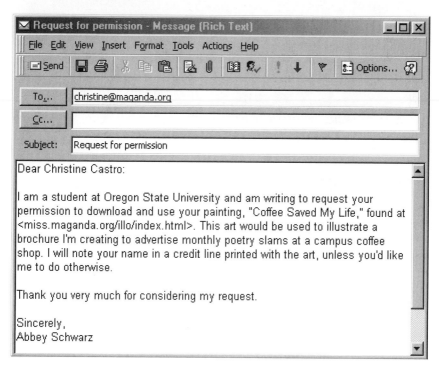

Remember that different situations call for different visuals. Use visuals that are appropriate to your situation and purpose.

Type of Visual		**Purpose**
Table		To convey detailed numerical information; to allow readers to make comparisons
Pie Chart		To display how a whole is divided; to show relationships among parts
Bar Graph or Line Graph	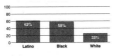	To call attention to relationships among data; to show change over time
Diagram or Drawing	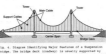	To call attention to details; to show processes
Map		To call attention to locations and spatial relationships
Photograph		To show people, objects, or an event; to convey an emotion or support an argument.

✳ bedfordstmartins.com/academicwriter

For more help creating effective visuals, go to **Re:Writing** *and then click on* **More Re:Writing** *to find* **Preparing Effective Charts and Graphs**.

| | | | | | | | | | | | | | | | | | | | | | | | | | | | | | | | | | | | | | | | | | | | | | | | | | | | | | | | | | | | | | | | | | | | | | | | | | | | | | | | | | | | | | | | | | | | | | |

FOR EXPLORATION

Review Alletta Brenner's research essay in Chapter 6 on human trafficking in the garment-manufacturing industry (pp. 169–81). As you reread this essay, pay particular attention to its visuals (two photographs). How do these visual elements contribute to her essay's effectiveness? How does Alletta follow the conventions of copyright law in acknowledging the sources of these visuals?

| | | | | | | | | | | | | | | | | | | | | | | | | | | | | | | | | | | | | | | | | | | | | | | | | | | | | | | | | | | | | | | | | | | | | | | | | | | | | | | | | | | | | | | | | | | | | | |

Making Effective Decisions about Design: Sample Documents

One way to learn how to make effective decisions about document design is to study the decision-making process that others have followed. Collected on pp. 275–78 are sample documents that make effective design moves, annotated with some tips to help you create your own documents.

Flyer

Distinct typefaces used in heading to differentiate important elements

The Craft of Writing Series Presents:

Bryan Ko

"Showing & Telling: Designing a Career in Picture Books"

April 19, 2006
4:00pm
Journey Room
Memorial Union

Central illustration draws attention and relates to speaker's topic

Bryan Ko is a recent OSU graduate and a passionate new author of picture books. He combines elements of Graphic Design with Fine Arts in his unique vision of children's literature. He graduated in 2005 from Oregon State University's Honors College with a Bachelor's Degree in Fine Arts. His undergraduate thesis, a picture book titled Eddie's World, is being considered for publication.

Bryan Ko joins us to share his experiences, his insights, and his vision with the OSU community and the public.

This event is free and open to the public.
Sponsored by The Center for Writing and Learning,
The Craft of Writing Series, and The Visiting Artists Series.

Boxed time and location information set off prominently

Related information grouped together

Brochure

Tall, narrow tri-fold design

Title in clear, prominent type

Clear, bold headings

Bulleted lists give questions to ask, steps to take

Questions to ask your local beach health monitoring official:

• Which beaches do you monitor and how often?

• What do you test for?

• Where can I see the test results and who can explain them to me?

• What are the primary sources of pollution that affect this beach?

What to do if your beach is not monitored regularly:

• Avoid swimming after a heavy rain.

• Look for storm drains along the beach. Don't swim near them.

• If the waters of your beach have been designated as a no-discharge zone for vessel sewage, check to see if boat pumpout facilities are available and working.

• Look for trash and such other signs of pollution as oil slicks in the water. These kinds of pollutants may indicate the presence of disease-causing microorganisms that may also have been washed into the water.

• If you think your beach water is contaminated, contact your local health or environmental protection officials. It is important for them to know about suspected beach water contamination so they can protect citizens from exposure.

• Work with your local authorities to create a monitoring program.

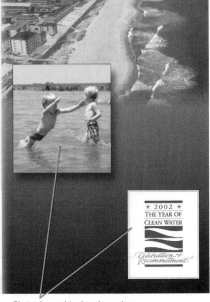

In celebration of the 30th anniversary of the Clean Water Act, EPA presents

Before You Go to the Beach...

Photos layered to draw in reader

First Page of a Web Text

Logo in distinctive font

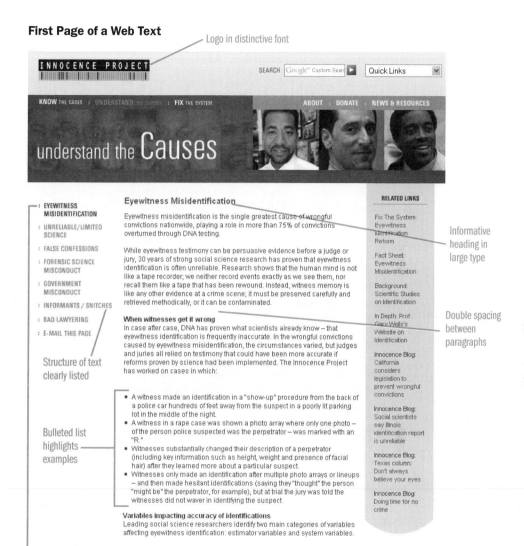

INNOCENCE PROJECT

SEARCH Google™ Custom Search ▶ Quick Links ▼

KNOW THE CASES ⁝ UNDERSTAND THE CAUSES ⁝ FIX THE SYSTEM

ABOUT ⁝ DONATE ⁝ NEWS & RESOURCES

understand the Causes

**: EYEWITNESS
MISIDENTIFICATION**

⁝ UNRELIABLE/LIMITED
SCIENCE

⁝ FALSE CONFESSIONS

⁝ FORENSIC SCIENCE
MISCONDUCT

⁝ GOVERNMENT
MISCONDUCT

⁝ INFORMANTS / SNITCHES

⁝ BAD LAWYERING

⁝ E-MAIL THIS PAGE

Structure of text
clearly listed

Eyewitness Misidentification

Eyewitness misidentification is the single greatest cause of wrongful
convictions nationwide, playing a role in more than 75% of convictions
overturned through DNA testing.

While eyewitness testimony can be persuasive evidence before a judge or
jury, 30 years of strong social science research has proven that eyewitness
identification is often unreliable. Research shows that the human mind is not
like a tape recorder; we neither record events exactly as we see them, nor
recall them like a tape that has been rewound. Instead, witness memory is
like any other evidence at a crime scene; it must be preserved carefully and
retrieved methodically, or it can be contaminated.

When witnesses get it wrong
In case after case, DNA has proven what scientists already know — that
eyewitness identification is frequently inaccurate. In the wrongful convictions
caused by eyewitness misidentification, the circumstances varied, but judges
and juries all relied on testimony that could have been more accurate if
reforms proven by science had been implemented. The Innocence Project
has worked on cases in which:

- A witness made an identification in a "show-up" procedure from the back of
  a police car hundreds of feet away from the suspect in a poorly lit parking
  lot in the middle of the night.
- A witness in a rape case was shown a photo array where only one photo —
  of the person police suspected was the perpetrator — was marked with an
  "R."
- Witnesses substantially changed their description of a perpetrator
  (including key information such as height, weight and presence of facial
  hair) after they learned more about a particular suspect.
- Witnesses only made an identification after multiple photo arrays or lineups
  — and then made hesitant identifications (saying they "thought" the person
  "might be" the perpetrator, for example), but at trial the jury was told the
  witnesses did not waver in identifying the suspect.

Variables impacting accuracy of identifications
Leading social science researchers identify two main categories of variables
affecting eyewitness identification: estimator variables and system variables.

Bulleted list
highlights
examples

RELATED LINKS

Fix The System:
Eyewitness
Identification
Reform

Fact Sheet:
Eyewitness
Misidentification

Background:
Scientific Studies
on Identification

In Depth: Prof.
Gary Wells's
Website on
Identification

Innocence Blog:
California
considers
legislation to
prevent wrongful
convictions

Innocence Blog:
Social scientists
say Illinois
identification report
is unreliable

Innocence Blog:
Texas column:
Don't always
believe your eyes

Innocence Blog:
Doing time for no
crime

Informative
heading in
large type

Double spacing
between
paragraphs

Color, used only in heading,
visuals and links

||||||||||||||||||||||||||||||||||||||||||||||||||||||||||||||||||||||||||||||||||||||||

FOR THOUGHT, DISCUSSION, AND WRITING

1. Look at the introductions to the three articles by Deborah Tannen presented in Chapter 3 on pp. 63–68. Chapter 3's discussion of these introductions touches on issues of document design, noting, for instance, that the article intended for the broadest audience uses the most fully developed visuals. But it doesn't discuss these visuals in depth. Drawing on the guidelines presented in this chapter, analyze the visual design of Tannen's documents and relate the elements of each design to the intended audience.

2. The textbook you're reading right now has, like most books, been designed by a team of editors, designers, and artists. The book's design uses elements such as type fonts and sizes, white space, headings, color, and visuals to increase the text's readability and effectiveness. Drawing on the principles of design discussed in this chapter and also on your own design preferences, write a paragraph in which you evaluate the design of this textbook. Conclude your analysis with one or two suggestions for improving the book's design in future editions.

3. For a community, church, civic, or other group project in which you are currently involved, develop a flyer, brochure, newsletter, or Web page that your group will use as an internal document or share with others. If you aren't currently involved in such a project, develop a document that relates to a project that interests you.

4. The following text, "Putin? Never Heard of Her," is from the July 2007 issue of *Wired* magazine. *Wired* is known for its cutting-edge page design, and in this piece the editors developed visuals to represent results from a recent study on Americans' knowledge of current events conducted by an independent research group. Read the text and examine the visuals carefully. In what ways are these visuals effective? What kind of information might be missing? Your instructor may ask you to write several paragraphs analyzing this page.

||||||||||||||||||||||||||||||||||||||||||||||||||||||||||||||||||||||||||||||||||||||||

Putin? Never Heard of Her.

Despite the Internet explosion, Americans remain woefully ill-informed.

More than a decade after the Internet went mainstream, the world's richest information source hasn't necessarily made its users any more informed. A new study from the Pew Research Center for the People & the Press shows that Americans, on average, are less able to correctly answer questions about current events than they were in 1989. Citizens who call the Internet their primary news source know slightly less than fans of TV and radio news. Hmmm ... maybe a little less Perez Hilton and a little more Jim Lehrer. —PATRICK DI JUSTO

Daily Show viewers are more up on current events than Fox News fans.

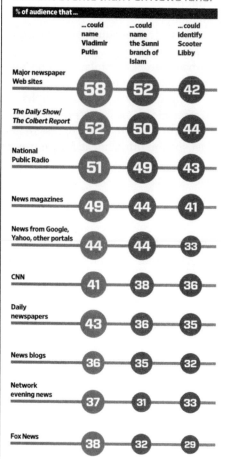

% of audience that ...

	...could name Vladimir Putin	...could name the Sunni branch of Islam	...could identify Scooter Libby
Major newspaper Web sites	58	52	42
The Daily Show/ The Colbert Report	52	50	44
National Public Radio	51	49	43
News magazines	49	44	41
News from Google, Yahoo, other portals	44	44	33
CNN	41	38	36
Daily newspapers	43	36	35
News blogs	36	35	32
Network evening news	37	31	33
Fox News	38	32	29

Americans now know less about politics than they did in 1989.

% of respondents who ...

	1989	2007
...could name the vice president	74	69
...could name their state's governor	74	66
...could name the president of Russia	47	36
...know whether the US has a trade deficit	81	68
...know which party controls the House	68	76
...know whether the chief justice is conservative	30	37
...could name the Speaker of the House		49
...could name the secretary of defense		21

Who knows less about the news? Pretty much everyone.

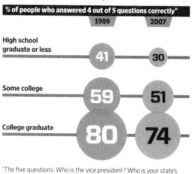

% of people who answered 4 out of 5 questions correctly*

	1989	2007
High school graduate or less	41	30
Some college	59	51
College graduate	80	74

*The five questions: Who is the vice president? Who is your state's governor? Does the US have a trade deficit or surplus? Which party controls the House of Representatives? Is the chief justice of the Supreme Court a liberal, moderate, or conservative?

Strategies for Revision

Revision challenges you to look at your work from a dual perspective: to read your work with your own intentions in mind, and also to consider your readers' perspectives. Although revision occurs throughout the writing process, you'll probably revise most intensively after completing a rough draft that articulates a preliminary statement of your ideas. Revising can be the most rewarding part of the writing process: It gives you the satisfaction of bringing your ideas to completion in an appropriate form.

This chapter focuses first on revision as a process, explaining how revision differs from editing, or correcting mistakes, and offering strategies for reading your work more objectively so that you can recognize strengths and weaknesses. Next the chapter describes strategies for revising effectively and efficiently and shows how you can use responses to work in progress to help establish priorities for revision. The last section offers ideas for improving your essay's structure and style.

Revising through Re-Vision

You can learn a great deal about revision just by considering the word itself. *Revision* combines the root word *vision* with the prefix *re-,* meaning "again." When you revise, you "see again": You develop a new vision of your essay's logic and organization or of the best way to improve the flow of a paragraph.

Revision is very different from editing, which generally occurs at the end of the writing process. When you edit, you're concerned mainly with correctness — with issues of grammar, punctuation, spelling, word choice, and sentence structure. Editing is the tidying up that concludes the writing process.

Unlike editing, revision is a process of discovery where much more than correctness is at stake. Because it generates growth and change, revision sometimes requires you to take risks. Often these risks are minor. If you attempt to fine-tune the details in a paragraph, for instance, you need spend only a little time and can easily revert back to the original version. Sometimes, however, when you revise, you make large-scale decisions with more significant consequences. You might conclude that a different organization is in order, decide to rework your thesis statement, or consider a new approach to

Guidelines for Revising Objectively

In order to revise your writing effectively, you need to be able to distance yourself from it. The following guidelines will help you develop the objectivity necessary for successful revision.

- *Plan at least a short break between writing and revising.* It's difficult to critique your rough draft when you've just finished composing it. Your own intentions are still too fresh for you to be able to read your words as they are, not as you intended them to be. Taking a break before revising can help you gain distance and objectivity.

- *Prepare mentally for a revising session.* Review your assignment and your rhetorical analysis before rereading your draft. As you do so, ask yourself the following questions:

  - What state is your draft in — how rough or near completion?
  - To what extent does your draft respond to the assignment and your rhetorical situation?
  - How well does your draft meet the goals you established for it?
  - What goals should you establish for this revising session, and how can you fulfill them? What should you work on first?

- *Revise from typed or printed copy.* Most people are less critical of hand-written or electronically displayed texts than they are of printed drafts. Thus you may find it helpful to type and print your essays as you write and revise. Once your words appear in print, you can see stylistic and organizational problems much more easily.

- *Try reading your work out loud.* When you read your own work silently, you unconsciously compensate to reflect your intentions. Reading it out loud (or asking someone else to read it to you) can help you hear problems that you might not otherwise detect. If you (or a reader) falter over a phrase or have to read a sentence several times before it makes sense, that may indicate a problem of style or logic.

|||||||||||||||||||||||||||||||||||||||||||||||||||||||||||||||||||||||||||||||||||||||

FOR EXPLORATION

Think back to earlier writing experiences. When, and for what reasons, have you revised your work rather than just edited it? How would you characterize these revision experiences? Were they satisfying? Frustrating? Why? Freewrite for five or ten minutes about these revision experiences.

|||||||||||||||||||||||||||||||||||||||||||||||||||||||||||||||||||||||||||||||||||||||

your topic altogether. Trying major changes such as these often requires rewriting or discarding whole sections of a draft, but a willingness to experiment can also lead to choices that make revising easier and less frustrating.

Asking the Big Questions: Revising for Focus, Content, and Organization

When you revise a draft, begin by asking the big, important questions — questions about how well your essay has responded to your rhetorical situation, and how successfully you've achieved the goals established by your controlling purpose. If you discover — as writers often do — that your essay hasn't achieved its original purpose or that your purpose evolved as you wrote, you'll want to make major changes in your draft.

EXAMINING YOUR OWN WRITING

From the moment you begin thinking about a writing project until you make your last revision, you must be an analyst and a decision maker. When you examine your work, you look for strengths to build on and weaknesses to remedy. Consequently, you must think about not just what is in your text but also what is *not* there and what *could be* there. You must read the part (the introduction, say, or several paragraphs) while still keeping in mind the whole. Asking the big questions first is a practical approach to revising. Furthermore, once you're confident that the overall focus, content, and organization of your essay are satisfactory, you'll be better able to recognize less significant but still important stylistic problems.

Questions for Evaluating Focus, Content, and Organization

Focus

- What do you hope to accomplish in this essay? How clearly have you defined — and communicated — your controlling purpose? (See pp. 250–52.)
- How well does your essay respond to your rhetorical situation? (See Chapter 3.) If it is an academic essay, does it fulfill the requirements of the assignment?
- Have you tried to do too much in this essay? Or are your goals too limited or inconsequential?
- How does your essay respond to the needs, interests, and expectations of your readers?

Content

- How effectively does your essay fulfill the commitment stated or implied by your controlling purpose? Do you need to develop it further?
- What supporting details and evidence have you provided? Do they relate clearly to your controlling purpose and to each other?
- What additional details, evidence, or counterarguments might strengthen your essay?
- Have you included any material that is irrelevant to your purpose?
- How could your introduction and conclusion be more effective?

Organization

- What overall organizational strategy does your essay follow?
- Does your essay follow the appropriate conventions for this kind of writing?
- What is the relationship between the organization of your essay and your controlling purpose? Is this relationship clear to readers? What cues have you provided to make the organization easy to follow?
- Have you tested the effectiveness of your organization by outlining or summarizing your draft?

|||||||||||||||||||||||||||||||||||||||||||||||||||||||||||||||||||||||||||||||||||||||||||||

FOR EXPLORATION

Use the Questions for Evaluating Focus, Content, and Organization above to evaluate the draft of an essay you are currently working on. Respond as specifically and as concretely as possible, and then take a few moments to reflect on what you have learned about your draft. Use your responses to make a list of goals for revising.

|||||||||||||||||||||||||||||||||||||||||||||||||||||||||||||||||||||||||||||||||||||||||||||

Case Study: A Student Writer's Evaluation of a Draft

What kinds of changes do writers make as they revise? Part III of this book follows one student, Daniel Stiepleman, as he develops an essay analyzing a visual text for his first-year writing class. This case study should give you a clearer understanding of how revision works.

Daniel decided early that he was interested in writing about a public service announcement (PSA) promoting literacy education, so he spent some time analyzing the PSA (see p. 232), clustering to find ideas (see p. 241), and writing a draft to get a better handle on why the words and images in the ad disturbed him (see pp. 246–47). Once he explored his ideas in writing, Daniel discovered a promising argument for his essay: A flaw in the logic of the PSA threatened to undermine its positive intentions. After analyzing his rhetorical situation (see p. 253) and putting together a plan (see p. 255), he wrote a more fully developed draft to explain this flaw to his readers and to convince them that although the ability to read and write is valuable, literacy cannot by itself solve the problem of poverty.

Note that for Daniel's first draft, he has not yet created the necessary Works Cited page and his in-text citations are incomplete.

Literacy, often taken for granted, is a gift. The ability to read text not only offers opportunities for escape and entertainment, but gives access to ideas that challenge our own limited worldviews, thus allowing each of us to expand our understandings of our lives on our own terms, at our own pace. The generation of text allows for the further development and sharing of our own ideas with others, at a time when much of the world has lost reverence for oral traditions. Literacy is a gift.

In recent years educational and other foundations have, in the print media especially, run literacy campaigns designed to persuade literate Americans to donate their time and/or money to the worthwhile cause of literacy education. These campaigns frequently create public service announcements (PSAs) to convey their message to the general public. One such PSA is produced by the National Center for Family Literacy (NCFL). Published in the April 2006 edition of the Atlantic Monthly magazine, the full-page advertisement essentially sets up a series of linked statements. It begins, "Because I can read," which is followed by a series of "I can . . ." statements, such as, "I can understand. I can write a letter. I can fill out a job application. I can finally get off welfare." At the bottom of the page is an invitation to help the person presented in this PSA and others like her get out of poverty by supporting the NCFL.

When I first read this PSA, I found it persuasive. But the more I thought about it, the more problematic the series of "I can" statements became. By asserting that the ability to read and write is tantamount to the ability to learn, be a role model, and contribute, the text also implies that people who are illiterate cannot learn, cannot be role models, and, worst of all, have nothing to contribute. Such persons, it seems, are utterly worthless without literacy.

The people reading the Atlantic Monthly are not illiterate. In fact, according to the magazine's Web site, the average reader of the Atlantic

<u>Monthly</u> is a man in his early fifties with a college degree and a median household income of over $130,000. The image incorporated into the NCFL's "Because I can read" PSA is certainly not that of the typical reader of the <u>Atlantic Monthly</u>. The image is of a woman with an approximately ten-year-old girl, presumably her daughter, who is significantly darker skinned. What's more, the woman is not wearing a wedding ring. The image of illiteracy, then, is a single mother with a mixed-race child.

Can literacy solve this woman's problems? American society is immensely stratified; 58% of black and 62% of Hispanic children live in low-income households, as opposed to only 25% of white children (NCCP). According to the 1999 U.S. Census data, black and Hispanic Americans ("Hispanic" was still classified as a race in the 1999 census data) are twice as likely as European Americans to be unemployed. Those who work have a weekly income far less than whites — over $100 a week less for blacks, and almost $200 a week less for Hispanics (United States Census Bureau).

The NCFL PSA suggests that being able to read will magically get the woman portrayed in the ad off of welfare. In reality, more highly educated black and Hispanic people are only slightly more likely to find work (as compared with equally educated whites) than their less-educated counterparts (United States Dept. of Education). Literacy does not equal social equality. Yet that is precisely what this PSA implies.

This PSA presents illiteracy as a problem of others who have not had the same advantages (role models, educational opportunities, membership in a dominant class or sex) as the readers. In so doing, it displays the inherent inequalities of our culture, but also offers an unrealistically simple solution to the problem — literacy. Given its purpose, the PSA is effective — but it is also a lie because it ignores the root causes of illiteracy. Granted, helping more Americans to become literate could be one step toward greater equality. So the question remains: Is the cumulative effect of this PSA harmful or good?

Using the Questions for Evaluating Focus, Content, and Organization on pp. 282–83, Daniel analyzed his draft and decided that his essay would be more effective if he made several important changes. Here is his analysis.

Focus: I think I do a good job of raising questions about the PSA. I wonder if I come on too strong, however. I also wonder if my focus is narrow and clear enough. I see that I don't write much about how the graphics and text interact. Our instructor specifically mentioned this in the assignment, so I need to pay more attention to that.

Content: I talk about how literacy affects income, and I think that's important. But looking back at the draft, I see that I don't really explain what other factors might cause a person to be poor. I suppose that means I'll have to do some research. I wonder, too, if I should include the PSA or describe it more thoroughly so that I can focus readers' attention on the parts of the PSA that are most important. I'd better go back to the PSA to decide which are the most important parts.

Organization: I'm not happy with my intro and conclusion. I kept the same introduction from my discovery draft mainly because I didn't want to worry about it. I'll need to change that. I like how I conclude with a question, but I wonder if it isn't more important to answer that question instead. There's still lots to do, but at least I can see that my ideas are taking shape.

Thanks to his analysis, Daniel has a clear sense of the next step in his writing process. He knows he has more work to do—but he also has a clear sense of direction and progress.

Benefiting from Responses to Work in Progress

You may write alone a good deal of the time, but writing needn't be a lonely process. You can draw on the responses of others to help you re-see your writing and to gain support. When you ask others to respond to your writing, you're asking for feedback so that you can see your writing in fresh and different ways.

Responses can take a number of forms. Sometimes you may find it helpful to ask others simply to describe your writing for you. You might, for example, ask them to summarize in their own words how they understand your main point or what they think you're getting at. Similarly, you might ask them what parts of your draft stood out for them, and what they felt was missing. On other occasions, you may find more analytical responses helpful. You might ask readers to comment on your essay's organization or how well it responds to their needs and interests. Finally, if you're writing an argumentative essay, you might ask readers to look for potential weaknesses in its structure or logic. To determine what kind of feedback will be most helpful, think commonsensically about your writing. Where are you in your composing process? How do you feel about your draft and the kind of writing you're working on? If you've just completed a rough draft, for instance, you might find descriptive feedback most helpful. After you've worked longer on the essay, you might invite more analytical responses.

As a student, you can turn to many people for feedback. The differences in their situations will influence how they respond; these differences should also influence how you use their responses. No matter who you approach for feedback, learn to distinguish between your writing and yourself. Try not to respond defensively to suggestions for improvement, and don't argue with readers' responses. Instead, use them to gain insight into your writing. Ultimately you are the one who must decide how to interpret and apply other people's comments and criticisms.

> ### NOTE FOR MULTILINGUAL WRITERS
>
> If you were educated in another culture, the process of revising through multiple drafts may be new to you. Revising—which involves looking at a draft for overall issues in content and organization as well as sentence-level errors and typos—will help you rework your writing to make sure it is as effective and clear as possible. Even if receiving (and giving) comments on drafts is new to you, be assured that the suggestions and questions from peer and other reviewers will lead to constructive collaboration.

RESPONSES FROM FRIENDS AND FAMILY MEMBERS

You can certainly ask the people close to you to respond to your writing, but you should understand their strengths and weaknesses as readers. One important strength is that you trust them. Even if you spend time filling them in, however, friends and family members won't understand the nature of your assignment or your instructor's standards for evaluation; they're also likely to be less objective than other readers. All the same, friends and family members can provide useful responses to your writing if you choose such respondents carefully and draw on their strengths as outsiders. Rather than asking them to respond in detail, you might ask them to give a general impression or a descriptive response. If their understanding of the main idea or controlling purpose of your essay differs substantially from your own, you've gained very useful information.

RESPONSES FROM CLASSMATES

Because your classmates know your instructor and the assignment as insiders, they can provide particularly effective responses to work in progress. Writing groups typically form strong bonds; participants genuinely want group members to do well and to develop as writers. Group members can also read your

Guidelines for Working with a Writing Group

Advice for Writers

- *Prepare for group meetings.* Carefully formulate the questions about your work that you most need to have answered.

- *Bring a legible draft to class.* Be sure to bring a working draft, not a jumble of brainstorming ideas, freewriting, and notes.

- *Explain your rhetorical situation.* If you are addressing a specific audience—members of a certain organization, for example, or readers of a particular magazine—be sure to let your classmates know.

- *Maintain your own authority as the writer.* Your fellow students' responses are just that: responses. Treat their comments seriously, for they are a potentially powerful indication of the strengths and weaknesses of your draft. But remember that you must always decide how to interpret these responses—what to accept and what to reject.

Advice for Readers

- *Follow the golden rule.* Respond to the writing of others as you would like them to respond to your own work.

- *Don't attempt to "play teacher."* Your job is not to evaluate or grade your classmates' writing but to respond to it.

- *Take your cue from the writer.* If he or she asks you to summarize an essay's main point, don't launch into an analysis of its tone or organization.

- *Give constructive comments.* The more specific and concrete your response is, the more helpful it will be.

||||||||||||||||||||||||||||||||||||||||||||||||||||||||||||||||||||||||||||||||||||||||||||||||||

FOR COLLABORATION

Think about responses to your work that you have received from classmates. Freewrite for five or ten minutes about these experiences, and then draw up a list of statements describing the kinds of responses that have been most helpful.

Meet with a group of your classmates. Begin by having each group member read his or her list. Then, working together, list all the suggestions for peer response. Have one student record all the suggestions and distribute them to everyone in the group for future use.

||||||||||||||||||||||||||||||||||||||||||||||||||||||||||||||||||||||||||||||||||||||||||||||||||

work more objectively than family members and friends can. Peers don't need to be experts to provide helpful responses. They simply need to be attentive, honest, supportive readers. To ensure that your writing group provides a helpful balance of support and criticism, follow the guidelines on p. 288.

RESPONSES FROM WRITING CENTER TUTORS

Many colleges and universities have writing centers staffed by undergraduate and graduate writing assistants or tutors. Tutors are not professional editors, nor are they faculty aides standing in for instructors who are unavailable or too busy to meet with students. Writing tutors are simply good writers who have been formally trained to *respond* to peers' work and to make suggestions for improvement.

Guidelines for Meeting with a Writing Tutor

- *Identify your goals before meeting with a tutor.* Reread your writing, and ask yourself what kind of help you need: Would you benefit most from a discussion of your essay's organization, an examination of a section of your draft, or some other activity?
- *Begin your conference by sharing your goals with your writing tutor.* You might also find it helpful to tell the writing tutor where you are in your process—in the early stages of drafting, for instance, or in the process of final editing.
- *Be realistic about what you can accomplish in the time available.* Recognize, as well, that the writing tutor's job is to respond and advise, not to correct or rewrite your draft.

RESPONSES FROM YOUR INSTRUCTOR

Because your instructor is such an important reader for your written assignments, you want to make good use of any written comments he or she provides.

Friends, family members, classmates, writing tutors, instructors—all can provide helpful responses to your writing. None of these responses, whether criticism or praise, should take the place of your own judgment, however. Your job is to *interpret* and *evaluate* these responses, using them along with your own assessment of your rough draft to establish goals for revising.

Guidelines for Using Your Instructor's Responses

- *Read your instructor's written comments carefully.* They are the clearest, most specific indication of how well you have fulfilled the assignment.

- *Read your instructor's comments more than once.* Read first to understand your instructor's general response to your writing. Then read the comments again several times, looking to establish priorities for revision.

- *Distinguish between local and global comments.* Local comments indicate specific questions, problems, or errors. For example, *awkward* is a local comment indicating a problem with a specific sentence. Global comments address broader issues, such as organization or the effectiveness of your evidence. The global comments in particular can help you set large-scale goals for revision.

- *Meet with your instructor if you don't understand his or her comments.* Even if you do understand the comments, you may wish to meet to discuss your plans for revision.

Case Study: A Student Writer's Revisions

When Daniel analyzed the first draft of his essay, he realized that while he had done a good job of exploring and raising questions about the PSA, his essay wasn't as effective as it could be. Daniel worried that he didn't provide enough evidence to convince readers that his argument was valid, and he was unhappy with his introduction and conclusion. He also realized that he didn't analyze how the words and graphics worked together to create meaning in the PSA. He revised his draft and shared it with members of his writing group for feedback. His second draft is presented here, with some of the group members' written comments. (Notice that his essay now has a title and that he has revised it in significant ways. This early draft includes some source citations, not yet in final, MLA form.)

Literacy in America: Reading between the Lines

Daniel Stiepleman

A woman and girl look straight at us. Their relationship to one another is unclear, but the girl, maybe ten, stands over the woman with a hand on her shoulder — she seems, unexpectedly perhaps, almost maternal. Huddled together in the lower right-hand corner,

Great opening!
–Parvin

they are cradled between a thin border and text. A series of connecting statements takes up the bulk of the page. "Because I can read," it begins in the opposite corner in simple, black font, which is followed, in slightly indented grey, by a series of "I can" statements: "I can understand. I can write a letter. I can fill out a job application. I can finally get off welfare." The call and response repeats: "Because I can read . . . Because I can read . . . Because I can read." This page, a public service announcement (PSA) by the National Center for Family Literacy (NCFL), appears in the <u>Atlantic Monthly</u> magazine. From its short diction to its basic design to its three-color scheme, everything about this ad reinforces the simplicity of its logic: "Because I can read, I can succeed." This simplicity is reassuring and hopeful, but it's more than that; it's deceptive.

> This is a really compelling description, and I like the idea that the simplicity of the design reflects the simplicity of the logic. But I'm having trouble imagining the design: Can you show a picture of it?
>
> –Eric

In order for the woman portrayed in this PSA to gain her worth through literacy, we are urged to accept that without reading and writing she is worthless. Asserting that once she learns to read, she can "learn . . . be a role model . . . [and] contribute," the PSA implies that people who cannot read or write cannot learn, cannot be a role model, and, worst of all, have nothing to contribute. It is here where both the simplicity and the logic of the NCFL's message begin to fall apart. The message becomes that people who are illiterate are worthless, and that must be why she is still on welfare. But perhaps even more astonishingly, literacy is supposed to magically solve her problems.

> It almost sounds like you're saying that the NCFL is deliberately insulting the people they help, but I don't think that's what you mean. Maybe you could start your essay by explaining what they're trying to do with the ad?
>
> –Kyong

This assertion ignores the systematic stratification of American society. Is illiteracy alone the reason why 58% of all black children and 62% of all Hispanic children in America currently live in poverty, while only 25% of white children do (National Center for Children in Poverty)? Will literacy training change the fact that, according to the 1999 U.S. Census data, black and Hispanic Americans are twice as likely as white Americans to be unemployed? Or that those who do work make an average of over $100 a week less than whites if they're black and almost $200 a week less if they're Hispanic? It seems unlikely that simply "Because I [or any illiterate person] can read . . . I can succeed." The NCFL's suggestion otherwise is an unfortunate confirmation of the great American myth that anyone can pull him- or herself up by the bootstraps through simple, concerted effort, with only his or her ability and desire standing as obstacles in the way.

> Good evidence. Are there similar statistics for women?
>
> –Parvin

> Where does this information come from?
>
> –Kyong

> I'm not sure I follow you. What are the other reasons? Why wouldn't being able to read help a person succeed? Maybe you could answer the questions that start the paragraph.
>
> –Eric

This PSA's potential for success relates directly to the degree to which it does not depict reality. The ad suggests that all the illiterate people in America need to achieve worth — based on its assumption that they are, without literacy, worthless — is to gain the ability to read and write; and it counts upon the readers' inexperience with both poverty and illiteracy to maintain its fiction. This is a safe bet as, according to the <u>Atlantic Monthly</u>'s Web site, the magazine's average reader is a man in his early fifties with a college degree and a median household income of over $130,000.

This sounds a little harsh.
–Eric

But the Census statistics portray a different image of America; it is a country in which the woman portrayed in the PSA will not so easily change her stake in the American dream. The injustice done by maintaining the myth of equal opportunity outweighs any good the NCFL can hope to accomplish with its ad. Looking at the woman more closely now, she seems somehow to know this. The girl is beaming, but there is a hesitance I see in the woman's smile. Am I projecting upon the image, or is there, in her face, concern? Her concern would be apt; she is shoved into the corner, held there, like so many Americans, beneath the weight of a text that would take the rich and daunting complexity of our multicultural society and give it short diction, basic design, and a three-color scheme. The illusion of simplicity.

This is a strong conclusion. But your overall argument might be more effective if you acknowledged the positive aspects of the ad — maybe in the introduction?
–Parvin

I love how you circle back to the image in your conclusion.
–Kyong

Daniel's second draft had many strengths, which members of his writing group acknowledge. But they had suggestions for improvement as well. A number of them commented on the evidence in paragraph 3, asking for more background on what Daniel meant by "the systematic stratification of American society." Several readers wanted to know more about the PSA's goals and suggested that Daniel's negative tone made his overall argument less convincing than it could be.

After Daniel contemplated his readers' responses, he thought about how he could improve his essay in a final draft. He recorded his reactions and ideas in his journal.

At first, I had some resistance to my writing group's comments. I've worked hard on this essay and taken it quite far, given my first draft. But after reading their comments and taking some time to think, I can see that they pointed out problems that I was just too close to my essay to see. Most important, I think I need to work some more on my tone so readers understand that I'm questioning the PSA's assumptions, not the value of literacy itself.

Several readers suggested that I include a new introductory paragraph that sets up the situation and explains what the PSA is trying to do. I thought quite a bit about this and tried out a few new paragraphs, but I kept coming back to the paragraph as it was. I really like this paragraph, so I decided to try to address their concerns by writing a new second paragraph.

Parvin commented that while I have evidence to support my claims, none of it cites the situation of women. Now that I think about it, this is odd. I'll check additional sources of information so I can include that.

The rest of the comments seem relatively minor — less revision than editing. I need to fix citations in the text and prepare the Works Cited page. Then I'll be really close to a final draft!

In reflecting on his group's responses, Daniel does a good job of taking their comments seriously while also holding to his own vision of his essay. It's not possible to show all the stages that Daniel's draft went through, for this process includes many scribbles, inserts, and crumpled papers. But the final draft demonstrates that his analysis of his readers' responses enabled him to truly revise his essay, to "see again" how he could most effectively make his point. Daniel's final draft begins on p. 294.

Stiepleman 1

Daniel Stiepleman
Professor Chang
English 1000
20 March 2007

Literacy in America: Reading between the Lines

A woman and girl look straight at us. Though they look nothing alike, they are apparently mother and daughter. The girl, maybe ten, stands over the woman with a hand on her shoulder; it is she who seems maternal. Huddled together in the lower, right-hand corner of the page, they are cradled between a thin border and text. This text, presumably the words of the woman pictured, takes up the bulk of the page. "Because I can read" begins in the upper left-hand corner in simple, black font. This is followed, in slightly indented grey, by a series of "I can" statements: "I can understand. I can write a letter. I can fill out a job application. I can finally get off welfare." The call and response repeats: "Because I can read . . . Because I can read . . . Because I can read."

> Because I can read,
>   I can understand. I can write a letter.
>   I can fill out a job application.
>   I can finally get off welfare.
> Because I can read,
>   I can learn. I can help my daughter
>   with her homework,
>   I can inspire her to be better.
>   I can be a role model.
> Because I can read,
>   I can succeed, I can
>   contribute. I can live
>   my life without fear,
>   without shame.
>   I can be whatever
>   I want to be.
> Because I can read.
>
> National Center for Family Literacy
> Literacy can make the difference between poverty and progress.
> Visit www.famlit.org to help us write more success stories.
> TOYOTA Proud Sponsor

When I came across this page in the Atlantic Monthly magazine (see Fig. 1), the image of the girl and the woman was what first caught my eye, but it was the repeated statement "Because I can read" that captured my imagination.

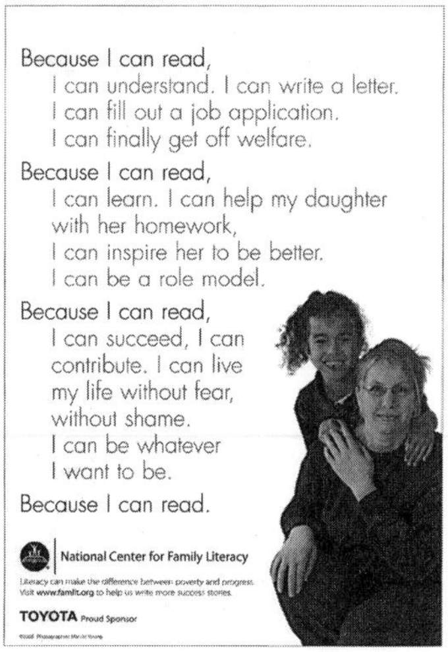

Fig. 1. NCFL Public Service Announcement. Atlantic Monthly, April 2006.

Stronger introduction focuses readers on the image being analyzed

New paragraph extends context

Copy of PSA included so readers can judge for themselves

Revised thesis statement is more balanced

Stiepleman 2

Its plainness was alluring. But as I read and reread the page, a public service announcement (PSA) designed to solicit donations of time and money for the National Center for Family Literacy (NCFL), I grew uncomfortable. The PSA, with its short diction, basic design, and black-and-white color scheme, reinforces the simplicity of its logic: "Because I can read, I can succeed." This simple message, though it promotes a mission I believe in, I fear does more harm than good.

The problem is with the underlying logic of this PSA. If we as readers believe the "Because I can read" statements, we must also believe that without literacy the woman in the PSA is worthless. Asserting that because a person can read, she "can learn . . . be a role model . . . [and] contribute," the PSA implies that people who cannot read or write cannot learn, cannot be role models, and, worst of all, have nothing to contribute to society. This is the real reason, the PSA suggests, why the woman portrayed in the photograph is still on welfare. But perhaps even more astonishing, literacy is supposed to be a quick fix for her problems.

This assertion ignores the systematic stratification of American society. Is illiteracy alone the reason why 60% of all black children and 61% of all Hispanic children in America currently live in poverty, while only 26% of white children do (National Center for Children in Poverty)? Will literacy training change the fact that, according to 1999 United States Census data, black and Hispanic Americans are twice as likely as white Americans to be unemployed? Or that those who do work make, on average, between $100 and 200 a week less than whites (406)? In the case of the woman pictured in the PSA, should literacy indeed lead her to a job, she is likely to make half as much money as a man with the same demographics who works in the same position (United States

New evidence added to strengthen argument

Sources are cited

Stiepleman 3

Less accusing
tone wins
readers over

Dept. of Education). It is not my intent to undermine the value of being able to read and write, but given the other obstacles facing the disadvantaged in America, it seems unlikely that simply because someone learns to read, he or she "can succeed."

New paragraph
provides
examples of
obstacles that
could prevent a
literate person
from succeeding

The benefits and opportunities for success extend well beyond a person's ability to fill out a job application. Race, class, and gender are powerful forces in our society, and the obstacles they present are self-perpetuating (Rothenberg 11-12). Even a well-educated person, if she is a minority or low-income, can find it overwhelmingly difficult to land a well-paying job with possibilities for advancement. The lack of simple things that middle-class readers of the Atlantic Monthly take for granted — the social connections of a network, the money for a professional wardrobe, a shared background with an interviewer — can cripple a job search. The NCFL's suggestion otherwise is an unfortunate reinforcement of the great American myth that anyone can pull him- or herself up by the bootstraps, with only his or her ability and desire standing as obstacles in the way.

Language is
more balanced

The PSA suggests that all the illiterate people in America need to achieve worth is the ability to read and write. But Americans disadvantaged by race, class, or gender will not so easily alter their position in our stratified culture. As long as we continue to pretend otherwise, we have no hope of changing the inequities that continue to be an inherent part of our society. For this reason, as much as I value this PSA's emphasis on the importance of literacy, I question its underlying logic.

Looking at the woman portrayed in the PSA more closely now, she seems somehow to know that her and her daughter's lives cannot improve so easily. Though the girl is beaming, there is a hesitance I see

Stiepleman 4

in the woman's smile and concern in her face. And it is apt; she is
shoved into the corner, held there, like so many Americans, beneath the
weight of a text that would take the rich and daunting complexity of
our multicultural society and give it the illusion of simplicity.

Stiepleman 5

Works Cited

National Center for Children in Poverty. Low-Income Children in the
United States. New York: Columbia, Mailman School of Public
Health, September 2006. 27 Feb. 2007 <http://www.nccp.org/
publications/pub_681.html>.

National Center for Family Literacy. Advertisement. Atlantic Monthly
Apr. 2006: 59.

Rothenberg, Paula S. Race, Class, and Gender in the United States: An
Integrated Study. 2nd ed. New York: St. Martin's, 1992.

United States. Census Bureau. "Labor Force, Employment, and Earnings."
Statistical Abstract of the United States: 1999. 5 Mar. 2007
<http://www.census.gov/prod/99pubs/99statab/sec13.pdf>.

---. Dept. of Education. Inst. of Education Science. Natl. Center for
Education Statistics. 1992 National Adult Literacy Survey. 2 Mar.
2007 <http://nces.ed.gov/naal>.

In the process of writing his essay, Daniel was able to articulate what was at first only a vague sense of unease about the National Center for Family Literacy PSA. As he moved from his first draft to the second, Daniel was able to identify why the ad concerned him. He clarified the problems with the PSA's logic in his third draft, while also attending more carefully to the interplay of words and graphics in the PSA.

Daniel's final draft, you will probably agree, develops an argument that is not only persuasive but also stylish. His tone is more even-handed, his paragraphs are more coherent, and his language is more polished. How did he do it? The fine-tuning that attends a final draft like Daniel's is a highly subjective process that varies from project to project and from writer to writer. Nonetheless, the tips in the following section offer some ideas that you can apply to revising for style in your own writing.

Keeping Your Readers on Track: Revising for Style

"Proper words in proper places" — that's how the eighteenth-century writer Jonathan Swift defined style. As Swift suggests, writing style reflects all of the choices a writer makes, from global questions of approach and organization to the smallest details about punctuation and grammar. When proper words *are* in proper places, readers are able to follow your ideas with understanding and interest. In addition, they probably have some sense of the person behind the words, the writer's presence.

Most writers concern themselves with style *after* writing a rough draft and determining that the essay's focus, content, and organization are effective. At this point, the writer can attend to style, making changes that enable readers to move through the writing easily and enjoyably.

ACHIEVING COHERENCE

Most writers are aware that paragraphs and essays need to be unified — that they should focus on a single topic. Writing is coherent when readers can move easily from word to word, sentence to sentence, and paragraph to paragraph. There are various means of achieving coherence. Some methods, such as *repeating key words and sentence structures* and *using pronouns*, reinforce or emphasize the logical development of ideas. Another method involves *using transitional words* such as *but, although*, and *because* to provide directional cues for readers.

The following introduction to "Home Town," an essay by the popular writer Ian Frazier, uses all of these methods to keep readers on track. The most important means of achieving coherence are italicized.

When glaciers covered much of northern Ohio, the land around Hudson, the town where I grew up, lay under one. *Glaciers* came and went several times, the most recent departing about 14,000 years ago. *When* we studied *glaciers* in an Ohio-history class in grade school, I imagined our *glacier* receding smoothly, like a sheet pulled off a new car. *Actually, glaciers* can move forward *but* they don't back up — *they* melt in place. *Most likely* the *glacier* above Hudson softened, *and* began to trickle underneath; rocks on its surface absorbed sunlight and melted tunnels into *it; it* rotted, *it* dwindled, *it* dripped, *it* ticked; *then it* dropped a pile of the sand and rocks *it* had been carrying around for centuries onto the ground in a heap. Hudson's landscape was hundreds of these little heaps — hills rarely big enough to sled down, a random arrangement made by gravity and smoothed by weather and time.

— Ian Frazier, "Home Town"

When you read your own writing to determine how to strengthen its coherence, use your common sense. Your writing is coherent if readers know where they have been and where they are going as they read. Don't assume that your writing will be more coherent if you simply sprinkle key words, pronouns, and transitions liberally throughout your prose. If the logic of your discussion is clear without such devices, adding them will only clutter up your writing.

Revision for coherence proceeds most effectively if you look first at large-scale issues, such as the relationship among your essay's introduction, body, and conclusion, before considering smaller concerns.

Guidelines for Revising for Coherence

- *Read your draft quickly to determine if it flows smoothly.* Pay particular attention to the movement from introduction to body and conclusion. How could you tighten or strengthen these connections?

- *Now read slowly, paying attention to the movement from paragraph to paragraph.* How do new paragraphs build on or connect with previous paragraphs? Would more explicit connections, such as transitions, help readers better understand your ideas?

- *Finally, read each paragraph separately.* How do your word choice and sentence structure help readers progress from sentence to sentence? Would repeating key words or using pronouns or adding transitions increase a paragraph's coherence?

FINDING AN APPROPRIATE VOICE

A writer's style reflects his or her individual taste and sensibility. But just as people dress differently for different occasions, so too do effective writers vary their style, depending on their rhetorical situation. As they do so, they are particularly attentive to the persona, or voice, they want to convey through their writing.

Sometimes writers present strong and distinctive voices. Here, for instance, is the beginning of an essay by the novelist Ken Kesey on the Pendleton Round-Up, a Northwest rodeo.

> My father took me up the Gorge and over the hills to my first one thirty-five years ago. It was on my fourteenth birthday. I had to miss a couple of days' school plus the possibility of suiting up for the varsity game that Friday night. Gives you some idea of the importance Daddy placed on this event.
>
> For this is more than just a world-class rodeo. It is a week-long shindig, a yearly rendezvous dating back beyond the first white trappers, a traditional powwow ground for the Indian nations of the Northwest for nobody knows how many centuries.
>
> — KEN KESEY, "THE BLUE-RIBBON AMERICAN BEAUTY ROSE OF RODEO"

Kesey's word choice and sentence structure help create an image of the writer as folksy, relaxed, and yet also forceful — just the right insider to write about a famous rodeo. In other situations, writers may prefer a less personal voice, as is often the case in informative writing — most textbooks, academic articles, newspapers, and the like.

If you think rhetorically, always asking questions about your rhetorical situation, you'll naturally consider such major stylistic issues as voice. The Questions for Analyzing Your Rhetorical Situation on p. 44 can help you determine the appropriate style for specific situations. You may also find it helpful to review the discussion of Aristotle's three appeals — *logos, pathos,* and *ethos* — on p. 55. By considering how much you wish to draw on appeals to reason *(logos)*, emotion *(pathos)*, and your own credibility as writer *(ethos)*, you will more easily determine your own voice and your relationship with readers.

thinking
rhetorically

REVISING FOR EFFECTIVE PROSE STYLE

The stylistic choices that you make as you draft and revise reflect not only your rhetorical awareness but also your awareness of general principles of effective prose style. Perhaps the easiest way to understand these principles is to analyze a passage that illustrates effective prose style in action.

Here is a paragraph from the first chapter of a psycholinguistics textbook. As you read it, imagine that you have been assigned to read the textbook for a course in psycholinguistics, an interdisciplinary field that studies linguistic behavior and the psychological mechanisms that make verbal communication possible.

> Language stands at the center of human affairs, from the most prosaic to the most profound. It is used for haggling with store clerks, telling off umpires, and gossiping with friends as well as for negotiating contracts, discussing ethics, and explaining religious beliefs. It is the medium through which the manners, morals, and mythology of a society are passed on to the next generation. Indeed, it is a basic ingredient in virtually every social situation. The thread that runs through all these activities is communication, people trying to put their ideas over to others. As the main vehicle of human communication, language is indispensable.
>   — HERBERT H. CLARK AND EVE V. CLARK, *Psychology and Language*

This paragraph, you would probably agree, does embody effective prose style. It's clearly organized and begins with a topic sentence, which the rest of the paragraph explains. The paragraph is also coherent, with pronouns, key words, and sentence patterns helping readers proceed. But what most distinguishes this paragraph, what makes it so effective, is the authors' use of concrete, precise, economical language and carefully crafted sentences.

Suppose that the paragraph were revised as follows. What would be lost?

> Language stands at the center of human affairs, from the most prosaic to the most profound. It is a means of human communication. It is a means of cultural change and regeneration. It is found in every social situation. The element that characterizes all these activities is communication. As the main vehicle of human communication, language is indispensable.

This revision communicates roughly the same ideas as the original paragraph, but it lacks that paragraph's liveliness and interest. Instead of presenting vivid examples — "haggling with store clerks, telling off umpires, and gossiping with friends" — these sentences state only vague generalities. Moreover, they're short and monotonous. Also lost in the revision is any sense of the authors' personalities, as revealed in their writing.

As this example demonstrates, effective prose style doesn't have to be flashy or call attention to itself. The focus in the original passage is on the *ideas* being discussed. The authors don't want readers to stop and think, "My, what a lovely sentence." But they do want their readers to become interested in and engaged with their ideas. So they use strong verbs and vivid, concrete examples whenever possible. They pay careful attention to sentence structure, alternating sequences of sentences with parallel structures with other, more varied sentences. They make sure that the relationships among ideas are clear. As a result of these and other choices, this paragraph succeeds in being both economical and emphatic.

Guidelines for Effective Prose Style

■ *Consider the context.* Decisions about structure and style, even about a single word, always depend upon how a passage fits within the work as a whole. To decide whether a sentence is awkward, for instance, you must look not just at that sentence but also at the surrounding paragraph.

■ *Vary the length and structure of your sentences.* An appropriate variety of sentence lengths and structures carries readers forward with a clear yet unobtrusive rhythm. Used sparingly, for example, short, simple sentences grab readers' attention—but presenting several of them in a row can be boring and repetitive. Similarly, longer, more complex sentences can give weight to important ideas, or they can test readers' patience. Try not to overuse the same sentence structures, such as parenthetical remarks, introductory phrases, or independent clauses connected with semicolons. Be alert to your habits, and make a conscious effort to inject more variety when you revise.

■ *Use language appropriate to your purpose and situation.* Effective writing usually interweaves the specific and the concrete with the abstract and the general. Specific, concrete words can give your writing power and depth. Such language isn't always appropriate, however. Sometimes you need to use abstract or general terms to convey your meaning, especially when writing about intellectual problems or ideas or emotions. Abstract words—like *patriotism, love,* and *duty*—refer to ideas, beliefs, relationships, conditions, and acts that you can't perceive with your senses. General words designate a group. The word *computer* is general; the word *iMac* identifies a specific machine within that group.

■ *Eliminate deadwood.* Readers can be impatient. They are reading for a reason—their reason, not yours—and they may become irritated by unnecessary words or flabby sentences. Words and phrases that add length to sentences without serving any rhetorical purpose are known as *deadwood,* and deadwood turns up in the drafts of even the most experienced writers. Make an effort to prune deadwood when you reread your drafts. Sometimes you can simply delete unnecessary words; in other cases, you may need to revise your sentence structure. Knowing whether words and sentences are necessary comes with practice and depends on an understanding of your goals. Words that aren't strictly necessary can enhance emphasis, rhythm, flow, or tone; the degree to which these are important to your writing is a question that can only be answered by considering your rhetorical situation and purpose.

Exploring your stylistic options—developing a style that reflects your understanding of yourself and the world and your feel for language—is one of the pleasures of writing. The guidelines on p. 303 describe just a few of the ways you can revise your own writing to improve its style.

||||||||||||||||||||||||||||||||||||||||||||||||||||||||||||||||||||||||||||||||||||

FOR THOUGHT, DISCUSSION, AND WRITING

1. To study your own revision process, number and save all your plans, drafts, and revisions for a paper that you're currently writing or have written recently. After you have completed the paper, review these materials, paying particular attention to the revisions you made. Can you describe the revision strategies that you followed and identify ways to improve the effectiveness of this process? Your instructor may ask you to write an essay discussing what you have learned as a result of this analysis.

2. Interview two students in your class about their revision strategies. How do their strategies reflect their preferred composing styles? (For more on composing styles see p. 31 in Chapter 2.) How are their strategies similar to and different from your own? How do these students feel about revising, and how do their feelings compare with your own? Can you apply any of their strategies to your own writing? What can you learn from these interviews? Your instructor may ask you to write an essay summarizing the results of your interviews.

3. From an essay you are currently working on, choose two or three paragraphs that you suspect could be more coherent or stylistically effective. Using this chapter's discussion as a guide, revise these paragraphs.

4. Read the essay by Clive Crook on p. 224 (or choose another essay in this book that interests you), and then answer the following questions.

   ■ How would you describe the general style of this essay? Write three or four sentences describing its style.

   ■ How would you describe the persona, or voice, conveyed by this essay? List at least three characteristics of the writer's voice, and then indicate several passages that exemplify these characteristics.

   ■ Find three passages that demonstrate the principles of effective prose style as discussed in this chapter. Indicate why you believe each passage is stylistically effective.

   ■ What additional comments could you make about the structure and style of this essay? Did anything about the style surprise you? Formulate at least one additional comment about the essay's structure and style.

||||||||||||||||||||||||||||||||||||||||||||||||||||||||||||||||||||||||||||||||||||

Writers' References

MLA Documentation Guidelines

The MLA recommends the following format for the manuscript of a re-search-based essay or project. It's always a good idea, however, to check with your instructor about formatting issues before preparing your final draft. For detailed guidelines on formatting a list of works cited, see p. 314. For a sample student essay in MLA style, see p. 169.

- *First page and title page*. The MLA does not require a title page. Type each of the following items on a separate line on the first page, beginning one inch from the top and flush with the left margin: your name, the instructor's name, the course name and number, and the date. Double-space between each item; then double-space again and center the title. Double-space between the title and the beginning of the text.

- *Margins and spacing*. Leave one-inch margins at the top and bottom and on both sides of each page. Double-space the entire text, including set-off quotations, notes, and the list of works cited. Indent the first line of a paragraph one-half inch, or five spaces.

- *Page numbers*. Include your last name and the page number on each page, one-half inch below the top and flush with the right margin.

- *Long quotations*. Set off a long quotation (more than four typed lines) in block format by starting it on a new line and indenting each line one inch, or ten spaces, from the left margin. Do not enclose the passage in quotation marks.

- *Headings*. MLA style allows, but does not require, headings. Many students and instructors find them helpful. (See Chapter 11 for guidelines on using headings.)

- *Visuals*. Place tables, photographs, drawings, charts, graphs, and other figures as near as possible to the relevant text. (See Chapter 11 for guidelines on incorporating visuals into your text.) Tables should have a label and number (*Table 1*) and a clear caption. The label and caption should be aligned on the left, on separate lines. Give the source information below the table. All other visuals should be labeled *Figure* (abbreviated *Fig.*), numbered, and captioned. The label and caption should appear on the same line, followed by the source information (see p. 169 for an example). Remember to refer to each visual in your text, indicating how it contributes to the point(s) you are making.

Directory to MLA style for in-text citations

1. Author named in a signal phrase, 308
2. Author named in a parenthetical reference, 309
3. Two or three authors, 309
4. Four or more authors, 309
5. Organization as author, 309
6. Unknown author, 309
7. Author of two or more works cited in the same project, 309
8. Two or more authors with the same last name, 310
9. Multivolume work, 310
10. Literary work, 310
11. Work in an anthology, 311
12. Sacred text, 311
13. Indirect source, 311
14. Two or more sources in one citation, 311
15. Entire work or one-page article, 311
16. Work without page numbers, 311
17. Electronic or nonprint source, 312

IN-TEXT CITATIONS

MLA style requires documentation in the text of an essay for every quotation, paraphrase, summary, or other material that must be cited. (For more advice about quoting, paraphrasing, and summarizing, see Chapter 6). In-text citations document material from other sources with both signal phrases and parenthetical references. Signal phrases introduce the material, often including the author's name. Parenthetical references direct readers to full bibliographic entries in a list of works cited at the end of the text.

Keep your parenthetical references short, but include enough information in the parentheses to allow readers to locate the full citation in the works-cited list. Place a parenthetical reference as near the relevant material as possible without disrupting the flow of the sentence. Note in the following examples *where* punctuation is placed in relation to the parentheses. Except for block quotations, place any punctuation mark *after* the closing parenthesis. If you're referring to a quotation, place the parenthetical reference *after* the closing quotation mark but *before* any other punctuation mark. For block quotations, place the reference one space after the final punctuation mark.

1. AUTHOR NAMED IN A SIGNAL PHRASE Ordinarily, you can use the author's name in a signal phrase that introduces the material and cite the page number(s) in parentheses. You may want to use the full name the first time you cite a source, but use just the last name for later references.

Herrera indicates that Kahlo believed in a "vitalistic form of pantheism" (328).

2. AUTHOR NAMED IN A PARENTHETICAL REFERENCE When you don't mention the author in a signal phrase, include the author's last name before the page number(s) in the parentheses. Use no punctuation between the author's name and the page number(s).

In places, Beauvoir "sees Marxists as believing in subjectivity" (Whitmarsh 63).

3. TWO OR THREE AUTHORS Use all the authors' last names in a signal phrase or parenthetical reference.

Gortner, Hebrun, and Nicolson maintain that "opinion leaders" influence other people in an organization because they are respected, not because they hold high positions (175).

4. FOUR OR MORE AUTHORS Use the names of all authors or the first author's name and *et al.* ("and others") in a signal phrase or parenthetical reference.

As Belenky, Clinchy, Goldberger, and Tarule assert, examining the lives of women expands our understanding of human development (7).

5. ORGANIZATION AS AUTHOR Give the organization's full name or a shortened form of it in a signal phrase or parenthetical reference.

Any study of social welfare involves a close analysis of "the impacts, the benefits, and the costs" of its policies (Social Research Corporation iii).

6. UNKNOWN AUTHOR Use the full title of the work or a shortened version in a signal phrase or parenthetical reference.

"Hype," by one analysis, is "an artificially engendered atmosphere of hysteria" ("Today's Marketplace" 51).

7. AUTHOR OF TWO OR MORE WORKS CITED IN THE SAME PROJECT If your list of works cited has more than one work by the same author, give the title of the work you are citing or a shortened version in a signal phrase or parenthetical reference.

Gardner shows readers their own silliness in his description of a "pointless, ridiculous monster, crouched in the shadows, stinking of dead men, murdered children, and martyred cows" (<u>Grendel</u> 2).

8. TWO OR MORE AUTHORS WITH THE SAME LAST NAME Include the author's first *and* last names in a signal phrase or first initial and last name in a parenthetical reference.

Children will learn to write if they are allowed to choose their own subjects, James Britton asserts, citing the Schools Council study of the 1960s (37-42).

9. MULTIVOLUME WORK In a parenthetical reference, note the volume number first and then the page number(s), with a colon and one space between them.

Modernist writers prized experimentation and gradually even sought to blur the line between poetry and prose, according to Forster (3: 150).

If you name only one volume of the work in your list of works cited, include only the page number in the parentheses.

10. LITERARY WORK Literary works are often available in many different editions. For a prose work, cite the page number(s) from the edition you used followed by a semicolon, and then give other identifying information that will lead readers to the passage in any edition. Indicate the act and/or scene in a play (*37; sc. 1*). For a novel, indicate the part or chapter (*175; ch. 4*).

Dostoyevsky's character Mitya wonders aloud about the "terrible tragedies realism inflicts on people" (376; bk. 8, ch. 2).

For a poem, instead of page numbers cite the part (if there is one) and line(s), separated by a period. If you are citing only line numbers, use the word *line(s)* in the first reference (*lines 33–34*).

Whitman speculates, "All goes onward and outward, nothing collapses, / And to die is different from what any one supposed, and luckier" (6.129-30).

For a verse play, give only the act, scene, and line numbers, separated by periods.

As <u>Macbeth</u> begins, the witches greet Banquo as "Lesser than Macbeth, and greater" (1.3.65).

11. WORK IN AN ANTHOLOGY For an essay, short story, or other piece of prose reprinted in an anthology, use the name of the author of the work, not the editor of the anthology, but use the page number(s) from the anthology.

> Narratives of captivity play a major role in early writing by women in the United States, as Silko demonstrates (219).

12. SACRED TEXT To cite a sacred text such as the Qur'an or the Bible, give the title of the edition you used, followed by location information, such as the book, chapter, and verse, separated by a period. In your text, spell out the names of books. In parenthetical references, use abbreviations for books with names of five or more letters (*Gen.* for *Genesis*).

> He ignored the admonition "Pride goes before destruction, and a haughty spirit before a fall" (New Oxford Annotated Bible, Prov. 16.18).

13. INDIRECT SOURCE Use the abbreviation *qtd. in* to indicate that you're quoting from someone else's report of a conversation, interview, letter, or the like.

> Arthur Miller says, "When somebody is destroyed everybody finally contributes to it, but in Willy's case, the end product would be virtually the same" (qtd. in Martin and Meyer 375).

14. TWO OR MORE SOURCES IN ONE CITATION Separate the information with semicolons.

> Some economists recommend that employment be redefined to include unpaid domestic labor (Clark 148; Nevins 39).

15. ENTIRE WORK OR ONE-PAGE ARTICLE Include the reference in the text without any page numbers or parentheses.

> Michael Ondaatje's poetic sensibility transfers beautifully to prose in The English Patient.

16. WORK WITHOUT PAGE NUMBERS If a work has no page numbers or is only one page long, you may omit the page number. If a work uses paragraph numbers instead, use the abbreviation *par.* (or *pars.*). If a parenthetical reference to a work with paragraph numbers includes the author's name, use a comma after the name.

> Whitman considered their speech "a source of a native grand opera" (Ellison, par. 13).

17. ELECTRONIC OR NONPRINT SOURCE Give enough information in a signal phrase or parenthetical reference for readers to locate the source in the list of works cited. Usually use the author or title under which you list the source. Specify a source's page, section, paragraph, or screen numbers, if numbered, in parentheses.

> Kilgore, the bloodthirsty lieutenant colonel played by Robert Duvall, declares, "I love the smell of napalm in the morning" (Apocalypse Now).

> As a Slate analysis has noted, "Prominent sports psychologists get praised for their successes and don't get grief for their failures" (Engber).

EXPLANATORY AND BIBLIOGRAPHIC NOTES

MLA style recommends explanatory notes for information or commentary that would not readily fit into your text but is needed for clarification or further explanation. In addition, MLA style permits bibliographic notes for citing several sources for one point and for offering thanks to, information about, or evaluation of a source. Use superscript numbers in the text to refer readers to the notes, which may appear as endnotes (typed under the heading *Notes* on a separate page after the text but before the list of works cited) or as footnotes at the bottom of the page (typed four lines below the last text line, first line indented one-half inch or five spaces).

SUPERSCRIPT NUMBER IN TEXT

> Stewart emphasizes the existence of social contacts in Hawthorne's life so that the audience will accept a different Hawthorne, one more attuned to modern times than the figure in Woodberry.[3]

NOTE

> [3]Woodberry does, however, show that Hawthorne was often an unsociable individual. He emphasizes the seclusion of Hawthorne's mother, who separated herself from her family after the death of her husband, often even taking meals alone (28). Woodberry seems to imply that Mrs. Hawthorne's isolation rubbed off onto her son.

Directory to MLA Style for works-cited entries

LIST OF WORKS CITED

A list of works cited is an alphabetical list of the sources you have referred to in your essay. (If your instructor asks you to list everything you have read as background, call the list *Works Consulted*.) Here are some guidelines for preparing such a list:

- Start your list on a separate page after the text of your essay and any notes.

- Continue the consecutive numbering of pages.

- Center the heading *Works Cited* an inch from the top of the page; don't underline or italicize it or enclose it in quotation marks. Double-space between the heading and the first entry, and double-space the entire list.

- Start each entry flush with the left margin, and indent subsequent lines one-half inch or five spaces.

- List your sources alphabetically by author's (or editor's) last name. If the author is unknown, alphabetize the source by the first word of the title, disregarding *A*, *An*, or *The*.

The sample works-cited entries that follow observe MLA's advice to underline words that are often italicized in print. If you wish to use italics instead, first check with your instructor.

BOOKS

The basic format for a works-cited entry for a book is outlined on pp. 316–17. For an online book, see p. 330.

1. ONE AUTHOR

Winchester, Simon. <u>The Meaning of Everything: The Story of the Oxford English Dictionary</u>. New York: Oxford UP, 2003.

2. TWO OR THREE AUTHORS Give the first author listed on the title page, last name first; then list the name(s) of the other author(s) in regular order, with a comma between authors and the word *and* before the last one.

> Martineau, Jane, Desmond Shawe-Taylor, and Jonathon Bate. <u>Shakespeare in Art</u>. London: Merrill, 2003.

3. FOUR OR MORE AUTHORS Give the first author listed on the title page, followed by a comma and *et al.* ("and others"), or list all the names, since the use of *et al.* diminishes the importance of the other contributors.

> Lupton, Ellen, Jennifer Tobias, Alicia Imperiale, Grace Jeffers, and Randi Mates. <u>Skin: Surface, Substance, and Design</u>. New York: Princeton Architectural, 2002.

4. ORGANIZATION AS AUTHOR Give the name of the group listed on the title page as the author, even if the same group published the book.

> Getty Trust Publications. <u>Seeing the Getty Center/Seeing the Getty Gardens</u>. Los Angeles: Getty Trust Publications, 2000.

5. UNKNOWN AUTHOR Begin the entry with the title, and list the work alphabetically by the first word of the title after any initial *A*, *An*, or *The*.

> <u>New Concise World Atlas</u>. New York: Oxford UP, 2003.

6. TWO OR MORE BOOKS BY THE SAME AUTHOR(S) Arrange the entries alphabetically by title. Include the name(s) of the author(s) in the first entry, but in subsequent entries, use three hyphens followed by a period.

> Lorde, Audre. <u>A Burst of Light</u>. Ithaca: Firebrand, 1988.
>
> ---. <u>Sister Outsider</u>. Trumansburg: Crossing, 1984.

If you cite a work by one author who is also listed as the first coauthor of another work you cite, list the single-author work first, and repeat the author's name in the entry for the coauthored work. Also repeat the author's name if you cite a work in which that author is listed as the first of a different set of coauthors. In other words, use three hyphens only when the work is by *exactly* the same author(s) as the previous entry.

7. EDITOR Treat an editor as an author, but add a comma and *ed.* (or *eds.*).

> Wall, Cheryl A., ed. <u>Changing Our Own Words: Essays on Criticism, Theory, and Writing by Black Women</u>. New Brunswick: Rutgers UP, 1989.

SOURCE MAP: Citing Books Using MLA Style

Take information from the book's title page and copyright page (on the reverse side of the title page), not from the book's cover or a library catalog.

(1) *Author.* List the last name first, followed by a comma, the first name, and the middle initial (if given). Omit titles such as *MD, PhD,* or *Sir;* include suffixes after the name and a comma (*O'Driscoll, Gerald P., Jr.*). End with a period.

(2) *Title.* Underline or (if your instructor permits) italicize the title and any sub-title; capitalize all major words. End with a period.

(3) *City of publication.* If more than one city is given, use the first one listed. For foreign cities that may be unfamiliar to your readers, add an abbreviation of the country or province (*Cork, Ire.*). Follow it with a colon.

(4) *Publisher.* Give a shortened version of the publisher's name (*Harper* for *HarperCollins Publishers; Harcourt* for *Harcourt Brace; Oxford UP* for *Oxford University Press*). Follow it with a comma.

(5) *Year of publication.* Consult the copyright page. If more than one copyright date is given, use the most recent one. End with a period.

For a book by one author, use the following format:

Last name, First name. <u>Title of book</u>. City: Publisher, Year.

A citation for the book on p. 317 would look like this:

AUTHOR, LAST
NAME FIRST   TITLE AND SUBTITLE, UNDERLINED

Twitchell, James B. <u>Living It Up: America's Love Affair with Luxury</u>. New York:

Simon, 2002. ——————— PUBLISHER'S CITY AND NAME,
YEAR OF PUBLICATION

—— DOUBLE-SPACE; INDENT ONE-HALF INCH OR FIVE SPACES

For more on using MLA style to cite books, see pp. 314–21. (For guidelines and models for using APA style, see pp. 349–52.)

LIVING IT UP

America's Love Affair with *Luxury*

James B. Twitchell

For Liz

SIMON & SCHUSTER
NEW YORK   LONDON   TORONTO
SYDNEY   SINGAPORE

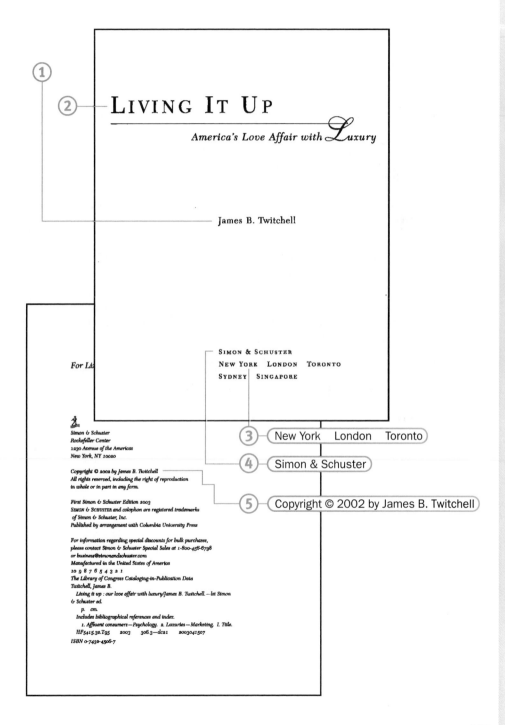

New York   London   Toronto

Simon & Schuster

Copyright © 2002 by James B. Twitchell

Simon & Schuster
Rockefeller Center
1230 Avenue of the Americas
New York, NY 10020

First Simon & Schuster Edition 2003
SIMON & SCHUSTER and colophon are registered trademarks
of Simon & Schuster, Inc.
Published by arrangement with Columbia University Press

For information regarding special discounts for bulk purchases,
please contact Simon & Schuster Special Sales at 1-800-456-6798
or business@simonandschuster.com
Manufactured in the United States of America
10 9 8 7 6 5 4 3 2 1
The Library of Congress Cataloging-in-Publication Data
Twitchell, James B.
   Living it up : our love affair with luxury/James B. Twitchell. — 1st Simon
& Schuster ed.
   p.   cm.
   Includes bibliographical references and index.
   1. Affluent consumers—Psychology. 2. Luxuries—Marketing. I. Title.
   HF5415.32.T95   2003   306.3—dc21   2003041507
ISBN 0-7432-4506-7

8. AUTHOR AND EDITOR If you have cited the body of the text, begin with the author's name. Then list the editor(s), introduced by *Ed.* ("Edited by"), after the title.

> James, Henry. <u>Portrait of a Lady</u>. Ed. Leon Edel. Boston: Houghton, 1963.

If you have cited the editor's contribution, begin with the name(s) of the editor(s), followed by a comma and *ed.* (or *eds.*). Then list the author's name, introduced by *By*, after the title.

> Edel, Leon, ed. <u>Portrait of a Lady</u>. By Henry James. Boston: Houghton, 1963.

9. WORK IN AN ANTHOLOGY OR CHAPTER IN A BOOK WITH AN EDITOR List the author(s) of the selection or chapter; its title; the title of the book in which the selection or chapter appears; *Ed.* and the name(s) of the editor(s); the publication information; and the inclusive page numbers of the selection or chapter.

> Komunyakaa, Yusef. "Facing It." <u>The Seagull Reader</u>. Ed. Joseph Kelly.
>   New York: Norton, 2000. 126-27.

If the selection was originally published in a periodical and you are asked to supply information for this original source, use the following format. *Rpt.* is the abbreviation for *Reprinted*.

> Byatt, A. S. "The Thing in the Forest." <u>New Yorker</u> 3 June 2002: 80-89. Rpt.
>   in <u>The O. Henry Prize Stories 2003</u>. Ed. Laura Furman. New York:
>   Anchor, 2003. 3-22.

For inclusive page numbers up to 99, note all digits in the second number. For numbers above 99, note only the last two digits and any others that change in the second number (*115–18, 1378–79, 296–301*).

10. TWO OR MORE ITEMS FROM AN ANTHOLOGY Include the anthology itself in your list of works cited. If the title page uses the term *compiler(s)* rather than *editor(s)*, use the abbreviation *comp.* (or *comps.*) instead of *ed.* (or *eds.*).

> Walker, Dale L., ed. <u>Westward: A Fictional History of the American West</u>.
>   New York: Forge, 2003.

Also list each selection separately by its author and title, followed by a cross-reference to the anthology. Alphabetize all entries.

> Estleman, Loren D. "Big Tim Magoon and the Wild West." Walker 391-404.
> Salzer, Susan K. "Miss Libbie Tells All." Walker 199-212.

11. TRANSLATION Begin the entry with the author's name, and give the translator's name, preceded by *Trans.* ("Translated by"), after the title.

> Hietamies, Laila. <u>Red Moon over White Sea</u>. Trans. Borje Vahamaki. Beaverton, OR: Aspasia, 2000.

If you cite a translated selection from an anthology, add *Trans.* and the translator's name before the title of the anthology.

> Horace. <u>The Art of Poetry</u>. Trans. Smith Palmer Bovie. <u>The Critical Tradition: Classic Texts and Contemporary Trends</u>. Ed. David H. Richter. 2nd ed. Boston: Bedford, 1998. 68-78.

12. BOOK IN A LANGUAGE OTHER THAN ENGLISH If necessary, you may provide a translation of the book's title in brackets. You may also choose to give the English name of a foreign city in brackets.

> Benedetti, Mario. <u>La borra del café [The Coffee Grind]</u>. Buenos Aires: Sudamericana, 2000.

13. EDITION OTHER THAN THE FIRST Add the information, in abbreviated form, after the title.

> Walker, John A. <u>Art in the Age of Mass Media</u>. 3rd ed. London: Pluto, 2001.

14. MULTIVOLUME WORK If you cite only one volume, give the volume number after the title, using the abbreviation *Vol.* You may give the number of volumes in the complete work at the end of the entry, using the abbreviation *vols.*

> Ch'oe, Yong-Ho, Peter Lee, and William Theodore De Barry, eds. <u>Sources of Korean Tradition</u>. Vol. 2. New York: Columbia UP, 2000. 2 vols.

If you cite two or more volumes, give the number of volumes in the complete work after the title.

> Ch'oe, Yong-Ho, Peter Lee, and William Theodore De Barry, eds. <u>Sources of Korean Tradition</u>. 2 vols. New York: Columbia UP, 2000.

15. PREFACE, FOREWORD, INTRODUCTION, OR AFTERWORD Begin with the author of the item and the item title (not underlined, italicized, or in quotation marks). Then give the title of the book and the book's author (preceded by the word *By*) or editor (preceded by *Ed.*). If the same person wrote or edited both the book and the cited item, use just the last name after *By* or *Ed.* List the page numbers of the item at the end of the entry.

Atwan, Robert. Foreword. <u>The Best American Essays 2002</u>. Ed. Stephen Jay
    Gould. Boston: Houghton, 2002. viii-xii.

16. ENTRY IN A REFERENCE WORK   List the author of the entry, if known. If
no author is identified, begin with the title. For a well-known reference
work, just note the edition number and year of publication, or designate the
edition by its year of publication. If the entries in the work are in alphabetical
order, you need not give volume or page numbers. (For an electronic version
of a reference work, see p. 331.)

"Hero." <u>Merriam-Webster's Collegiate Dictionary</u>. 11th ed. 2003.

Kettering, Alison McNeil. "Art Nouveau." <u>World Book Encyclopedia</u>. 2002 ed.

17. BOOK THAT IS PART OF A SERIES   Cite the series name as it appears on
the title page, followed by any series number.

Nichanian, Marc, and Vartan Matiossian, eds. <u>Yeghishe Charents: Poet of the</u>
    <u>Revolution</u>. Armenian Studies Ser. 5. Costa Mesa: Mazda, 2003.

18. REPUBLICATION   To cite a modern edition of an older book, add the
original publication date, followed by a period, after the title.

Scott, Walter. <u>Kenilworth</u>. 1821. New York: Dodd, 1956.

19. PUBLISHER'S IMPRINT   If a book is published under a publisher's imprint (indicated on the title page), hyphenate the imprint and the publisher's
name.

Gilligan, Carol. <u>The Birth of Pleasure: A New Map of Love</u>. New York:
    Vintage-Random, 2003.

20. BOOK WITH A TITLE WITHIN THE TITLE   Do not underline or italicize the
title of a book within the title of a book you are citing. Enclose in quotation
marks the title of a short work within a book title, and underline or italicize it
as you do the rest of the title.

Mullaney, Julie. <u>Arundhati Roy's</u> The God of Small Things: <u>A Reader's Guide</u>.
    New York: Continuum, 2002.

Rhynes, Martha. <u>"I, Too, Sing America": The Story of Langston Hughes</u>.
    Greensboro: Morgan, 2002.

21. SACRED TEXT   To cite individual published editions of sacred books,
begin with the title. If a specified version is not part of the title, list the ver-

sion after the title. If you are not citing a particular edition, do not include sacred texts in the works-cited list.

PERIODICALS

The basic format for a works-cited entry for a periodical article appears on pp. 322–23.

22. ARTICLE IN A JOURNAL PAGINATED BY VOLUME Follow the journal title with the volume number in arabic numerals.

> Gigante, Denise. "The Monster in the Rainbow: Keats and the Science of Life." PMLA 117 (2002): 433-48.

23. ARTICLE IN A JOURNAL PAGINATED BY ISSUE If each issue begins with page 1, put a period and the issue number after the volume number.

> Zivley, Sherry Lutz. "Sylvia Plath's Transformations of Modernist Paintings." College Literature 29.3 (2002): 35-56.

24. ARTICLE THAT SKIPS PAGES When an article skips pages, give only the first page number and a plus sign.

> Tyrnauer, Matthew. "Empire by Martha." Vanity Fair Sept. 2002: 364+.

25. ARTICLE WITH A TITLE WITHIN THE TITLE Enclose in single quotation marks the title of a short work within an article title. Underline or italicize the title of a book within an article title.

> Frey, Leonard H. "Irony and Point of View in 'That Evening Sun.'" Faulkner Studies 2 (1953): 33-40.

26. ARTICLE IN A MONTHLY MAGAZINE Put the month (or months, hyphenated) before the year. Abbreviate months other than *May*, *June*, and *July*. Do not include volume or issue numbers.

> Fonda, Daren. "Saving the Dead." Life Apr. 2000: 69-72.

27. ARTICLE IN A WEEKLY MAGAZINE Include the day, month, and year in that order, with no commas between them. Do not include volume or issue numbers.

> Gilgoff, Dan. "Unusual Suspects." US News and World Report 26 Nov. 2001: 51.

(1) *Author.* List the last name first, followed by a comma, the first name, and the middle initial (if given). Omit titles such as *MD, PhD,* or *Sir;* include suffixes after the name and a comma (*O'Driscoll, Gerald P., Jr.*). End with a period.

(2) *Article title.* Enclose the title and any subtitle in quotation marks, and capital-ize all major words. The closing period goes inside the closing quotation mark.

(3) *Periodical title.* Underline or italicize the periodical title (excluding any initial *A, An,* or *The*), and capitalize all major words. For journals, give the volume number; if each issue starts with page 1, include the issue number as well.

(4) *Date of publication.* For journals, list the year in parentheses, followed by a colon. For monthly magazines, list the month and year. For weekly magazines and newspapers, list the day, month, and year.

(5) *Inclusive page numbers.* For page numbers up to 99, note all digits in the second number. For numbers above 99, note only the last two digits and any others that change in the second number (*115–18, 1378–79, 296–301*). In-clude section letters for newspapers. End with a period.

For a journal article, use the following format:

Last name, First name. "Title of article." <u>Journal</u> Volume number (year): Page
    number(s).

For a newspaper article, use the following format:

Last name, First name. "Title." <u>Newspaper</u> Date, Edition (if any): Section number
    (if any): Page number(s) (including section letter, if any).

For a magazine article, use the following format:

Last name, First name. "Title of article." <u>Magazine</u> Date: Page number(s).

A citation for the magazine article on p. 323 would look like this:

AUTHOR, LAST
NAME FIRST   ARTICLE TITLE AND SUBTITLE, IN QUOTATION MARKS

Conniff, Richard. "Counting Carbons: How Much Greenhouse Gas Does Your
          PERIODICAL TITLE, UNDERLINED   DATE   INCLUSIVE PAGE NUMBERS

    Family Produce?" <u>Discover</u> Aug. 2005: 54-61.   DOUBLE-SPACE
          INDENT ONE-HALF INCH OR FIVE SPACES

For more on using MLA style to cite periodical articles, see pp. 321–24. (For guide-lines and models for using APA style, see pp. 352–55.)

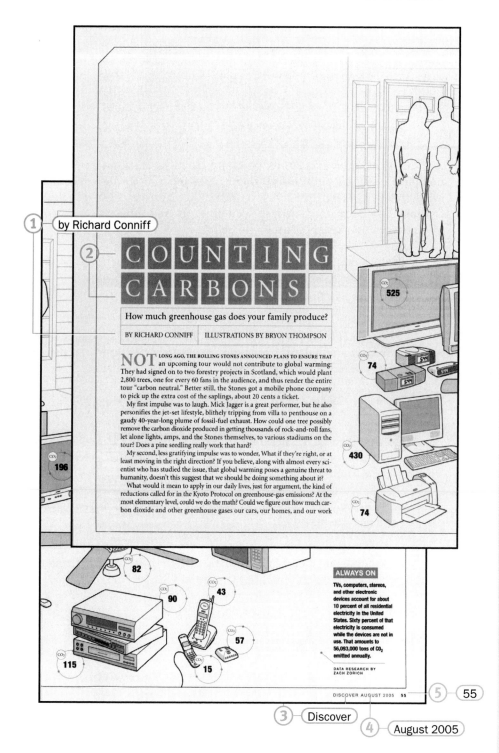

by Richard Conniff

COUNTING CARBONS

How much greenhouse gas does your family produce?

BY RICHARD CONNIFF   ILLUSTRATIONS BY BRYON THOMPSON

NOT LONG AGO, THE ROLLING STONES ANNOUNCED PLANS TO ENSURE THAT an upcoming tour would not contribute to global warming: They had signed on to two forestry projects in Scotland, which would plant 2,800 trees, one for every 60 fans in the audience, and thus render the entire tour "carbon neutral." Better still, the Stones got a mobile phone company to pick up the extra cost of the saplings, about 20 cents a ticket.

My first impulse was to laugh. Mick Jagger is a great performer, but he also personifies the jet-set lifestyle, blithely tripping from villa to penthouse on a gaudy 40-year-long plume of fossil-fuel exhaust. How could one tree possibly remove the carbon dioxide produced in getting thousands of rock-and-roll fans, let alone lights, amps, and the Stones themselves, to various stadiums on the tour? Does a pine seedling really work that hard?

My second, less gratifying impulse was to wonder, What if they're right, or at least moving in the right direction? If you believe, along with almost every scientist who has studied the issue, that global warming poses a genuine threat to humanity, doesn't this suggest that we should be doing something about it?

What would it mean to apply in our daily lives, just for argument, the kind of reductions called for in the Kyoto Protocol on greenhouse-gas emissions? At the most elementary level, could we do the math? Could we figure out how much carbon dioxide and other greenhouse gases our cars, our homes, and our work

ALWAYS ON

TVs, computers, stereos, and other electronic devices account for about 10 percent of all residential electricity in the United States. Sixty percent of that electricity is consumed while the devices are not in use. That amounts to 56,093,000 tons of CO_2 emitted annually.

DATA RESEARCH BY
ZACH ZORICH

28. ARTICLE IN A NEWSPAPER After the author and title of the article, give the name of the newspaper as it appears on the front page but without any initial *A*, *An*, or *The*. For locally published newspapers, add the city in brackets after the name if it is not part of the name. Then give the date and the edition (if listed), followed by a colon, a space, the section number or letter (if listed), and the page number(s). If the article does not appear on consecutive pages, give the first page followed by a plus sign.

> Bernstein, Nina. "On Lucille Avenue, the Immigration Debate." New York
>   Times 26 June 2006, late ed.: A1+.

29. ARTICLE IN A COLLECTION OF REPRINTED ARTICLES First give the citation for the original publication. Then give the citation for the collection in which the article is reprinted. Insert *Rpt. in* ("Reprinted in") between the two citations. Use *Comp.* to identify the compiler. *Ed.* and *Trans.* are other common abbreviations used in citing a collection.

> Quindlen, Anna. "Playing God on No Sleep." Newsweek 2 July 2001: 64. Rpt.
>   in The Best American Magazine Writing 2002. Comp. Amer. Soc. of
>   Magazine Eds. New York: Perennial, 2002. 458-62.

30. EDITORIAL OR LETTER TO THE EDITOR Use the label *Editorial* or *Letter*, not underlined, italicized, or in quotation marks, after the title or, if there is no title, after the author's name, if given.

> Magee, Doug. "Soldier's Home." Editorial. Nation 26 Mar. 1988: 400-01.

31. REVIEW List the reviewer's name and the title of the review, if any, followed by *Rev. of* and the title and author, director, or other creator of the work reviewed. Then add the publication information.

> Franklin, Nancy. "Dead On." Rev. of Deadwood, by David Milch. New Yorker
>   12 June 2006: 158-59.

32. UNSIGNED ARTICLE Begin with the article title, alphabetizing the entry according to the first word after any initial *A*, *An*, or *The*.

> "Performance of the Week." Time 6 Oct. 2003: 18.

ELECTRONIC SOURCES

Electronic sources such as Web sites differ from print sources in the ease with which they can be—and frequently are—changed, updated, or even eliminated. In addition, the various electronic media do not organize their works the same way. For these reasons, as the *MLA Handbook for Writers of Research Papers* notes, "References to electronic works . . . must provide more information than print citations generally offer."

The most commonly cited electronic sources are documents from Web sites and databases. The entry for such a source may include up to five basic elements, as in the following list, but must always include the last two:

■ *Author.* List the last name first, followed by a comma and the first name, and end with a period. If no author is given, begin the entry with the title.

■ *Title.* Enclose the title and subtitle of the document in quotation marks unless you're citing an entire site or an online book, both of which should be underlined or italicized. Capitalize all major words, and end with a period inside the closing quotation marks.

■ *Print publication information.* Give any information the document provides about a previous or simultaneous publication in print, using the guidelines on pp. 314–24.

■ *Electronic publication information.* List all of the following items that you can find, with a period after each one: the title of the site, underlined or italicized, with all major words capitalized; the editor(s) of the site, preceded by *Ed.*; the version number of the site, preceded by *Vers.*; the date of electronic publication or of the latest update, with the month, if any, abbreviated except for *May*, *June*, and *July*; and the name of any sponsoring institution or organization. (The sponsor's name usually appears at the bottom of the site's home page.)

■ *Access information.* Give the most recent date you accessed the source, abbreviating months as noted above; the URL enclosed in angle brackets; and a period after the closing bracket. In general, give the complete URL, including the opening *http, ftp, gopher, telnet,* or *news.* If the URL is very long and complicated, however, substitute the URL of the site's search page instead. If the site does not provide a usable URL for individual documents, and citing the search page is inappropriate, give the URL of the site's home page. To help readers find the document through links on the home page, do the following: After the URL of the home page, give the word *Path* and a colon, and then list the sequence of links. Use semicolons between the links and a period at the end. Whenever a URL will not fit on one line, break it only after a slash; do not add a hyphen at the break.

Further guidelines for citing electronic sources can be found in the *MLA Handbook for Writers of Research Papers* and online at www.mla.org.

33. ARTICLE FROM AN ONLINE DATABASE OR A SUBSCRIPTION SERVICE The basic format for citing a work from a database appears on pp. 328–29. For a work from an online database, provide all of following elements that are available: the author's name (if given); the title of the work in quotation marks; any print publication information; the name of the online database, underlined or italicized; the name of its editor (if any), preceded by *Ed.*; the date of the most recent revision; and the name of any organization or institution with which the database is affiliated. End with the date of access and the URL, in angle brackets.

> "Bolivia: Elecciones Presidenciales de 2005." <u>Political Database of the Americas</u>. 1 Feb. 2007. Georgetown U and Organization of Amer. States. 13 July 2007 <http://pdba.georgetown.edu/Elecdata/Bolivia/pres05.html>.

For a work from a library subscription service, after the information about the work give the name of the database, underlined or italicized, if you know it; the name of the service; the library; the date of access; and the URL of the service's home page, if you know it.

> Gordon, Andrew. "It's Not Such a Wonderful Life: The Neurotic George Bailey." 54.3 (1994): 219-33. <u>American Journal of Psychoanalysis</u>. EBSCOhost. City U of New York, Graduate Center Lib. 26 Oct. 2003 <http://www.epnet.com>.

For a work from a personal online subscription service such as America Online, follow the guidelines in this chapter for the appropriate type of work. End the entry with the URL of the specific work or, if it is long and complicated, the URL of the service's search page. If, however, the service supplies no URL or one that is not accessible to others, you need to provide other access information at the end of the entry. Depending on the service's retrieval system, give either the word *Keyword* followed by a colon and the keyword you used or the word *Path* followed by a colon and the sequence of links you followed, separated with semicolons.

> "Steps in Reading a Poem." AOL's Academic Assistance Center. 11 Feb. 2004. Path: Reading & Learning; Poetry; Analysis and Interpreting Poetry.

> Weeks, W. William. "Beyond the Ark." <u>Nature Conservancy</u> Mar.-Apr. 1999. America Online. 2 Apr. 1999. Keyword: Ecology.

34. WORK FROM A WEB SITE For a visual overview of citing a work from a Web site, see pp. 328–29. Include all of the following elements that are available: the author; the title of the document; the name of the Web site, underlined or italicized; the name of the editor, if any; the date of publication or the latest update; the name of the institution or organization associated with the site; the date of access; and the document's URL.

"Hands Off Public Broadcasting." <u>Media Matters for America</u>. 24 May 2005. Media Matters for America. 31 May 2005 <http://www.mediamatters.org/items/200505240001>.

Stauder, Ellen Keck. "Darkness Audible: Negative Capability and Mark Doty's 'Nocturne in Black and Gold.'" <u>Romantic Circles Praxis Series</u>. Ed. Orrin Wang. 2003. 28 Sept. 2003 <http://www.rc.umd.edu/praxis/poetics/stauder/stauder.html>.

For a personal Web site, include the name of the person who created the site; the title, underlined or italicized, or (if there is no title) a description such as *Home page*; the date of the last update, if given; the access information; and the URL.

Lunsford, Andrea A. Home page. 27 Mar. 2003. 17 May 2007 <http://www.stanford.edu/~lunsfor1/>.

35. ENTIRE WEB SITE Follow the guidelines for a specific work from the Web, but begin with the title of the entire site and the names of the editor(s), if any.

<u>Electronic Poetry Center</u>. Ed. Charles Bernstein, Kenneth Goldsmith, Martin Spinelli, and Patrick Durgin. 2003. Poetics Program/Dept. of Media Study, SUNY Buffalo. 26 Sept. 2003 <http://wings.buffalo.edu/epc/>.

<u>Weather.com</u>. 2007. Weather Channel Interactive. 13 Mar. 2007 <http://www.weather.com>.

36. ACADEMIC COURSE OR DEPARTMENT WEB SITE For a course site, include the name of the instructor, the title of the course, a description such as *Course home page*, the dates of the course, the department name, the institution, and the access information.

Lunsford, Andrea A. Memory and Media. Course home page. Sept.-Dec. 2002. Dept. of English, Stanford U. 13 Mar. 2007 <http://www.stanford.edu/class/english12sc>.

For a department site, give the department name, a description such as *Dept. home page*, the institution, and the access information.

English. Dept. home page. Amherst Coll. 5 Apr. 2007 <http://www.amherst.edu/~english>.

SOURCE MAP: Citing Articles from Databases Using MLA Style

Libraries pay for services—such as InfoTrac, EBSCOhost, ProQuest, and Lexis-Nexis—that provide access to huge databases of electronic articles.

(1) *Author.* List the last name first.

(2) *Article title.* Enclose the title and any subtitle in quotation marks.

(3) *Periodical title.* Underline or italicize it. Exclude any initial *A, An,* or *The.*

(4) *Volume number.* Also list the issue number if appropriate.

(5) *Date of publication.* Give the year for journals; the month and year for monthly magazines; the day, month, and year for weekly magazines and newspapers.

(6) *Inclusive page number(s).* Include section letters for newspapers, if relevant. If only the first page number is given, follow it with a hyphen, a space, and a period.

(7) *Name of the database.* Underline or italicize the name.

(8) *Name of the subscription service, if available.* Here, it is InfoTrac.

(9) *Name of the library where you accessed the article.* Also list the city and, if necessary, an abbreviation for the state (*Burnt Hills, NY*).

(10) End with the date you accessed the article and a brief URL for the database.

For an article from a database, use the following format:

[Citation format for article in a journal, magazine, or newspaper—see pp. 321–24]. Name of database. Name of service. Library name, Location. Date accessed <Brief Web address>.

A citation for the article on p. 329 would look like this:

CITATION INFORMATION FOR THE ARTICLE

Wallace, Maurice. "Richard Wright's Black Medusa." Journal of African

NAME OF DATABASE, UNDERLINED

American History 88.1 (2003): 71- . Expanded Academic ASAP.

SERVICE   LIBRARY LOCATION   ACCESS DATE   BRIEF URL

InfoTrac. Boston Public Lib., Boston. 27 July 2007 <http://

infotrac.galegroup.com>.

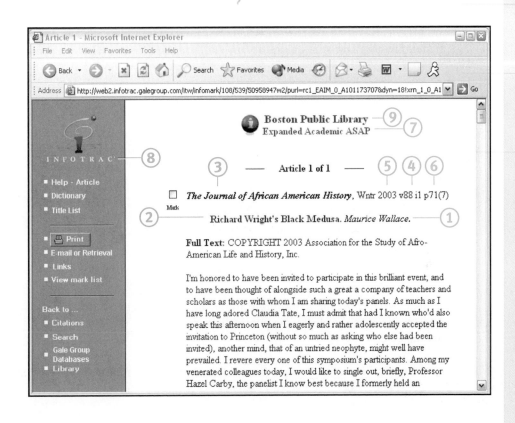

For more on using MLA style to cite articles from databases, see pp. 325–26. (For guidelines and models for using APA style, see p. 357.)

37. WEB LOG (BLOG)   For an entire Web log, give the author's name; the title of the Web log; the description *Web log*; the date of the most recent update; the sponsor of the site, if any; the date of access; and the URL. (Because the MLA currently provides no guidelines for documenting a blog, these models are based on MLA guidelines for Web sites and short works from Web sites.)

> Atrios. Eschaton. Web log. 27 June 2006. 27 June 2006 <http://
> www.atrios.blogspot.com/>.

For a post or comment on a Web log, give the author's name; the title of the post or comment, if any; the description *Web log post* or *Web log comment*; and the publication and access information.

> Parker, Randall. "Growth Rate for Electric Hybrid Vehicle Market Debated."
> Web log post. FuturePundit. 20 May 2005. 24 May 2007 <http://
> www.futurepundit.com/archives/002783.html>.

38. ONLINE BOOK   Cite an online book as you would a print book (see models 1–21). After the print publication information (city, publisher, and year), if any, give the electronic publication information, the date of access, and the URL.

> Euripides. The Trojan Women. Trans. Gilbert Murray. New York: Oxford UP,
> 1915. 12 Oct. 2003 <http://www.sacred-texts.com/cla/eurip/
> trojan.htm>.

Cite a part of an online book as you would a part of a print book (see models 9 and 15). Give the available print and electronic publication information, the date of access, and the URL of the part.

> Riis, Jacob. "The Genesis of the Gang." The Battle with the Slum. New York:
> Macmillan, 1902. Bartleby.com: Great Books Online. 2000. 31 Mar. 2007
> <http://www.bartleby.com/175/9.html>.

39. ONLINE POEM   Include the poet's name and the title of the poem, followed by the print publication information for the poem (if applicable). End with electronic publication information, the date of access, and the URL.

> Dickinson, Emily. "The Grass." Poems: Emily Dickinson. Boston, 1891.
> Humanities Text Initiative American Verse Project. Ed. Nancy Kushigian.
> 1995. U of Michigan. 6 Jan 2006 <http://www.hti.umich.edu>.

40. ARTICLE IN AN ONLINE JOURNAL, MAGAZINE, OR NEWSPAPER Cite the article as you would an article from a print journal, magazine, or newspaper (see models 22–28). End with the total number of pages, paragraphs, parts, or other sections, if numbered; the date of access; and the URL.

> Burt, Stephen. "The True Legacy of Marianne Moore, Modernist Monument." Slate 11 Nov. 2003. 12 Nov. 2003 <http://slate.msn.com/id/2091081/>.

> Gallagher, Brian. "Greta Garbo Is Sad: Some Historical Reflections on the Paradoxes of Stardom in the American Film Industry, 1910-1960." Images: A Journal of Film and Popular Culture 3 (1997): 7 pts. 7 June 2007 <http://imagesjournal.com/issue03/infocus.htm>.

> Shea, Christopher. "Five Truths about Tuition." New York Times Online 9 Nov. 2003. 11 Nov. 2003 <http://www.nytimes.com/2003/11/09/edlife/1109SHT.html>.

41. ONLINE EDITORIAL OR LETTER TO THE EDITOR Include the word *Editorial* or *Letter* after the author (if given) and title (if any). End with the name of the Web site, the date of electronic publication, the date of access, and the URL.

> "The Funding Gap." Editorial. Washingtonpost.com 5 Nov. 2003. 9 Nov. 2003 <http://www.washingtonpost.com/wp-dyn/articles/A1087-2003Nov5.html>.

> Piccato, Pablo. Letter. New York Times Online 9 Nov. 2003. 9 Nov. 2003 <http://www.nytimes.com/2003/11/09/opinion/L09IMMI.html>.

42. ONLINE REVIEW Cite an online review as you would a print review (see model 31). End with the name of the Web site, the date of electronic publication, the date of access, and the URL.

> O'Hehir, Andrew. "The Nightmare in Iraq." Rev. of Gunner Palace, dir. Michael Tucker and Petra Epperlein. Salon 4 Mar. 2005. 24 May 2007 <http://www.salon.com/ent/movies/review/2005/03/04/gunner/index.html>.

43. ENTRY IN AN ONLINE REFERENCE WORK Cite the entry as you would an entry from a print reference work (see model 16). End with the sponsor and access information.

> "Tour de France." Encyclopaedia Britannica Online. 2006. Encyclopaedia Britannica. 21 May 2006 <http://www.britannica.com>.

You may need to browse other parts of a site to find some elements, and some sites may omit elements. Uncover as much information as you can.

① *Author of the work.* List the last name first, followed by a comma, the first name, and the middle initial (if given). End with a period. If no author is given, begin with the title.

② *Title of the work.* Enclose the title and any subtitle of the work in quotation marks.

③ *Title of the Web site.* Give the title of the entire Web site, underlined or italicized. Where there is no clear title, use *Home page* without underlining or italicizing it.

④ *Date of publication or latest update.* Give the most recent date.

⑤ *Name of the sponsoring organization.* The sponsor's name often appears at the bottom of the site's home page.

⑥ *Access information.* Give the most recent date you accessed the work. Give the complete URL, enclosed in angle brackets. If the URL is very long and complicated, give the URL of the site's search page instead. If the URL will not fit on one line, break it only after a slash, and do not add a hyphen.

For a work from a Web site, use the following format:

Last name, First name. "Title of work." <u>Title of Web site</u>. Date of publication or latest update. Sponsoring organization. Date accessed <Web address>.

A citation for the work on p. 333 would look like this:

AUTHOR OF WORK,
LAST NAME FIRST   *TITLE AND SUBTITLE OF WORK, IN QUOTATION MARKS*

Jangfeldt, Bengt. "Joseph Brodsky: A Virgilian Hero, Doomed Never to

TITLE OF WEB SITE, UNDERLINED   *DATE OF PUBLICATION OR LAST UPDATE*   *SPONSORING ORGANIZATION*

Return Home." <u>Nobelprize.org</u>. 7 Sept. 2004. Nobel Foundation.

ACCESS DATE   *URL*

4 May 2005 <http://nobelprize.org/literature/jangfeldt/index.html>.

For more on using MLA style to cite Web documents, see pp. 324–35. (For guidelines and models for using APA style, see pp. 356–62.)

① by Bengt Jangfeldt

② Joseph Brodsky: A Virgillian Hero, Doomed Never to Return Home

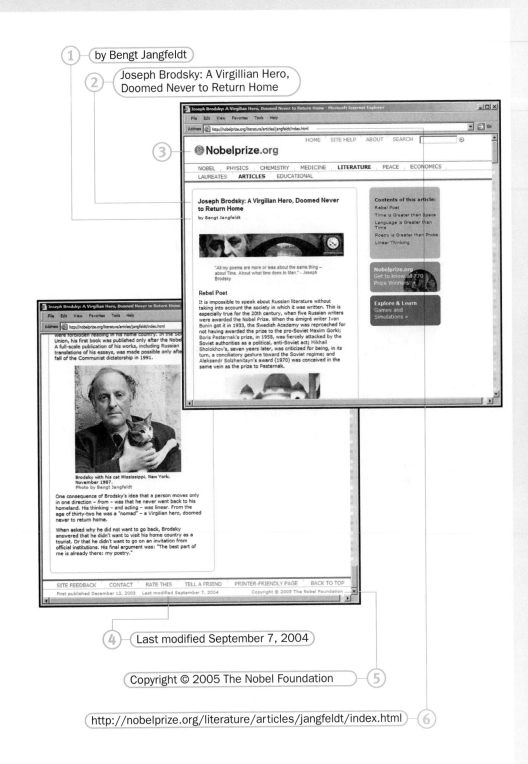

③

④ Last modified September 7, 2004

⑤ Copyright © 2005 The Nobel Foundation

⑥ http://nobelprize.org/literature/articles/jangfeldt/index.html

44. ENTRY IN A WIKI Because wiki content is collectively edited, do not include an author. Include the title of the entry; the name of the wiki; the date of the latest update; the sponsor of the wiki, if any; access information; and the URL. Check with your instructor before using a wiki as a source. (The MLA does not provide guidelines on citing wikis; this model is based on the MLA's guidelines on citing short works from Web sites.)

> "Fédération Internationale de Football Association." <u>Wikipedia</u>. 27 June
>   2006. Wikimedia Foundation. 27 June 2006 <http://en.wikipedia.org/
>   wiki/FIFA>.

45. POSTING TO A DISCUSSION GROUP Begin with the author's name; the title of the posting, in quotation marks; the description *Online posting*, not underlined or italicized or in quotation marks; and the date of posting. For a listserv posting, then give the name of the listserv; the date of access; and the URL of the listserv, the email address of its moderator, or (preferably) the URL of an archival version of the posting.

> Daly, Catherine. "Poetry Slams." Online posting. 29 Aug. 2003. SUNY Buffalo
>   Poetics Discussion List. 1 Oct. 2003 <http://listserv.acsu.buffalo.edu/
>   archives/poetics.html>.

For a newsgroup posting, end with the date of access and the name of the newsgroup in angle brackets, with the prefix *news*.

> Stonehouse, Robert. "Repeated Words in Shakespeare's Sonnets."
>   Online posting. 27 July 2003. 24 Sept. 2003
>   <news:humanities.lit.authors.shakespeare>.

46. EMAIL Include the writer's name; the subject line, in quotation marks; a description of the message that mentions the recipient; and the date of the message. (MLA style hyphenates *e-mail*.)

> Harris, Jay. "Thoughts on Impromptu Stage Productions." E-mail to the
>   author. 16 July 2006.

47. REAL-TIME COMMUNICATION In citing a posting in a real-time forum, include all of the following information that is available: the name(s) of any speaker(s) you are citing; a description of the event; its date; the name of the forum; the access date; and the URL. Always cite an archival version of the posting if one is available.

> Hong, Billy. Billy's Final Draft: Homeless Essay. 14 Oct. 2003. LinguaMOO.
>   12 Nov. 2003 <http://lingua.utdallas.edu:7000/25871/>.

48. COMPUTER SOFTWARE OR VIDEO GAME Include the title, underlined or italicized, version number (if given), and publication information. If you're citing downloaded software, replace the publication information with the date of access and the URL.

> The Sims 2. Redwood City: Electronic Arts, 2004.

> Web Cache Illuminator. Vers. 4.02. 12 Nov. 2006 <http://www.tucows.com/
> adnload/332309_126245.html>.

49. PERIODICALLY REVISED CD-ROM For a periodically revised CD-ROM, begin with the author, title, and any available print publication information. Then give the term *CD-ROM*, the name of the company or group producing it, and the electronic publication date (month and year, if available).

> Ashenfelter, Orley, and Kathryn Graddy. "Auctions and the Price of Art."
> Journal of Economic Literature 41.3 (2003): 763-87. CD-ROM. Amer.
> Economic Assn. Sept. 2003.

50. SINGLE-ISSUE CD-ROM Cite a CD-ROM like a book if it is not regularly updated. Add the term *CD-ROM* and, if appropriate, the number of the electronic edition, release, or version. If you're citing only a part of the source, indicate which part and end with the numbers of the part, if provided.

> Cambridge Advanced Learner's Dictionary. CD-ROM. Cambridge: Cambridge UP,
> 2003.

51. MULTIDISC CD-ROM If the CD-ROM includes more than one disc, include the term *CD-ROM* and either the total number of discs (*3 discs*) or, if you used material from only one, the number of that disc.

> IRIS: Immigration Research Information Service, LawDesk. CD-ROM. Disc 2.
> Eagon, MN: West, 2003.

OTHER SOURCES (INCLUDING ONLINE VERSIONS)

If an online version is not shown here, use the appropriate model for the source and then end with the date of access and the URL.

52. REPORT OR PAMPHLET Cite a report or pamphlet by following the guidelines for a print or an online book.

> Allen, Katherine, and Lee Rainie. Parents Online. Washington: Pew Internet
> and Amer. Life Project, 2002.

Environmental Working Group. <u>Dead in the Water</u>. 2006. Environmental
Working Group. 24 Apr. 2006 <http://www.ewg.org/reports/deadzone/>.

53. GOVERNMENT PUBLICATION Begin with the author, if identified. Otherwise, start with the name of the government, followed by the agency and any subdivision. Use abbreviations if they can be readily understood. Then give the title. For congressional documents, cite the number, session, and house of Congress (using *S* for Senate and *H* or *HR* for House of Representatives); the type (*Report, Resolution, Document*) in abbreviated form; and the number of the material. If you cite the *Congressional Record*, give only the date and page number(s). Otherwise, end with the publication information. For print versions, the publisher is often the Government Printing Office (GPO). For online versions, include as much publication information as you can find and end with the date of access and the URL.

Gregg, Judd. <u>Report to Accompany the Genetic Information Act of 2003</u>. US
108th Cong., 1st sess. S. Rept. 108-22. Washington: GPO, 2003.

Kinsella, Kevin, and Victoria Velkoff. <u>An Aging World: 2001</u>. US Bureau of
the Census. Washington: GPO, 2001.

United States. Environmental Protection Agency. Office of Emergency and
Remedial Response. <u>This Is Superfund</u>. Jan. 2000. 16 Aug. 2002
<http://www.epa.gov/superfund/whatissf/sfguide.htm>.

54. PUBLISHED PROCEEDINGS OF A CONFERENCE Cite proceedings as you would a book. If the title doesn't include enough information about the conference, add necessary information after the title.

Cleary, John, and Gary Gurtler, eds. <u>Proceedings of the Boston Area
Colloquium in Ancient Philosophy 2002</u>. Boston: Brill Academic, 2003.

55. UNPUBLISHED DISSERTATION OR THESIS Enclose the title in quotation marks. Add the label *Diss.*, the school, and the year the work was accepted. If you are citing a thesis, use a label such as *MA thesis* (or whatever is appropriate) instead of *Diss.*

LeCourt, Donna. "The Self in Motion: The Status of the (Student) Subject in
Composition Studies." Diss. Ohio State U, 1993.

56. PUBLISHED DISSERTATION Cite a published dissertation as a book, adding the identification *Diss.* and the university. If the dissertation was published by University Microfilms International, end the entry with *Ann Arbor: UMI*, the year, and the UMI number.

Yau, Rittchell Ann. <u>The Portrayal of Immigration in a Selection of Picture Books Published since 1970</u>. Diss. U of San Francisco, 2003. Ann Arbor: UMI, 2003. 3103491.

57. DISSERTATION ABSTRACT To cite the abstract of a dissertation using *Dissertation Abstracts International (DAI)*, include the *DAI* volume, year (in parentheses), and page number.

Huang-Tiller, Gillian C. "The Power of the Meta-Genre: Cultural, Sexual, and Racial Politics of the American Modernist Sonnet." Diss. U of Notre Dame, 2000. <u>DAI</u> 61 (2000): 1401.

58. UNPUBLISHED OR PERSONAL INTERVIEW List the person interviewed, and then use the label *Telephone interview, Personal interview*, or *E-mail interview*. End with the date(s) the interview took place.

Freedman, Sasha. Personal interview. 10 Nov. 2006.

59. PUBLISHED OR BROADCAST INTERVIEW List the person interviewed and then the title of the interview. If the interview has no title, use the label *Interview* and name the interviewer, if relevant. Then identify the source.

Ebert, Robert. Interview with Matthew Rothschild. <u>Progressive</u>. Aug. 2003. 5 Oct. 2003 <http://www.progressive.org/aug03/intv803.html>.

Taylor, Max. "Max Taylor on Winning." <u>Time</u> 13 Nov. 2000: 66.

To cite a broadcast interview, end with information about the program and the date(s) the interview took place.

Revkin, Andrew. Interview. <u>Fresh Air</u>. Natl. Public Radio. WNYC, New York. 14 June 2006.

60. UNPUBLISHED LETTER Cite a published letter as a work in an anthology (see model 9). If the letter is unpublished, follow this form:

Anzaldúa, Gloria. Letter to the author. 10 Sept. 2002.

61. MANUSCRIPT OR OTHER UNPUBLISHED WORK Begin with the author's name and the title or, if there is no title, a description of the material. Then note the form of the material (such as *ms.* for *manuscript* or *ts.* for *typescript*) and any identifying numbers assigned to it. End by giving the name and location of the library or research institution housing the material, if applicable.

Woolf, Virginia. "The Searchlight." Ts. Ser. III, Box 4, Item 184. Papers of
Virginia Woolf, 1902-1956. Smith Coll., Northampton.

62. LEGAL SOURCE To cite a legal case, give the name of the case, the
number of the case (using the abbreviation *No.*), the name of the court, and
the date of the decision.

Eldred v. Ashcroft. No. 01-618. Supreme Ct. of the US. 15 Jan. 2003.

To cite an act, give the name of the act followed by its Public Law (*Pub. L.*)
number, the date the act was enacted, and its Statutes at Large (*Stat.*) cata-
loging number.

Museum and Library Services Act of 2003. Pub. L. 108-81. 25 Sept. 2003.
Stat. 117.991.

63. FILM, VIDEO, OR DVD If you cite a particular person's work, start the
entry with that person's name. In general, start with the title, underlined or
italicized; then name the director, the distributor, and the year of release.
Other contributors, such as writers or performers, may follow the director. If
you cite a video or DVD instead of a theatrical release, include the original
film release date (if relevant) and the label *Videocassette* or *DVD*.

Moore, Michael, dir. Bowling for Columbine. 2002. BowlingforColumbine.com.
30 Sept. 2005 <http://www.bowlingforcolumbine.com/media/clips/
index.php>.

Spirited Away. Dir. Hiyao Miyazaki. Perf. Daveigh Chase, Suzanne Pleshette,
and Jason Marsden. 2001. DVD. Walt Disney Video, 2003.

Water. Dir. Deepa Mehta. Fox Searchlight, 2006.

64. TELEVISION OR RADIO PROGRAM In general, begin with the title of the
program, underlined or italicized. Then list any important contributors
(narrator, writer, director, actors); the network; the local station and city, if
any; and the broadcast date. To cite a particular person's work, begin the
entry with that name. To cite a particular episode, begin with the episode
title, in quotation marks.

Box Office Bombshell: Marilyn Monroe. Writ. Andy Thomas, Jeff Schefel, and
Kevin Burns. Dir. Bill Harris. Narr. Peter Graves. A&E Biography. Arts and
Entertainment Network. 23 Oct. 2002.

"The Fleshy Part of the Thigh." The Sopranos. Writ. Diane Frolov and Andrew
Schneider. Dir. Alan Taylor. HBO. 2 Apr. 2006.

Komando, Kim. "E-mail Hacking and the Law." <u>WCBS Radio</u>. WCBS, New York. 28 Oct. 2003. 11 Nov. 2003 <http://wcbs880.com/komando/local_story_309135535.html>.

65. SOUND RECORDING Begin with the name of the person or group you wish to emphasize (such as the composer, conductor, or band). Then give the title of the recording or musical composition; the artist(s), if appropriate; the manufacturer; and the year of issue. If you are not citing a compact disc, give the medium (such as *MP3* or *LP*) before the manufacturer. If you are citing a particular song or selection, include its title, in quotation marks, before the title of the recording. If you are citing a piece of instrumental music (such as a symphony) that is identified *only* by form, number, and key, do not underline, italicize, or enclose it in quotation marks.

Fountains of Wayne. "Bright Future in Sales." <u>Welcome Interstate Managers</u>. S-Curve, 2003.

Grieg, Edvard. Concerto in A minor, op. 16. Cond. Eugene Ormandy. Philadelphia Orch. LP. RCA, 1989.

Sonic Youth. "Incinerate." <u>Rather Ripped</u>. MP3. Geffen, 2006. 18 June 2006 <http://www.sonicyouth.com/alt-main/rippedpop.html>.

66. MUSICAL COMPOSITION When you are *not* citing a specific published version, first give the composer's name, followed by the title. Underline or italicize the title of an opera, a ballet, or a piece of instrumental music that is identified by name.

Mozart, Wolfgang Amadeus. <u>Don Giovanni</u>, K527.

Mozart, Wolfgang Amadeus. Symphony no. 41 in C major, K551.

Cite a published score as you would a book. If you include the date when the composition was written, do so immediately following the title.

Schoenberg, Arnold. <u>Chamber Symphony No. 1 for 15 Solo Instruments, Op. 9</u>. 1906. New York: Dover, 2002.

67. LECTURE OR SPEECH List the speaker, the title in quotation marks, the name of the sponsoring institution or group, the place, and the date. If the speech is untitled, use a label such as *Lecture* or *Keynote speech*.

Colbert, Stephen. Speech. White House Correspondents' Association Dinner. Washington Hilton, Washington, DC. 29 Apr. 2006. 20 May 2006 <http://video.google.com/videoplay?docid=-869183917758574879>.

Eugenides, Jeffrey. Lecture. Portland Arts and Lectures. Arlene Schnitzer
    Concert Hall, Portland, OR. 30 Sept. 2003.

68. LIVE PERFORMANCE List the title, other appropriate details (composer, writer, performer, or director), the place, and the date. To cite a particular person's work, begin the entry with that name.

Anything Goes. By Cole Porter. Perf. Klea Blackhurst. Shubert Theater, New
    Haven. 7 Oct. 2003.

69. PODCAST Include all of the following that are relevant and available: the speaker, the title of the podcast, the title of the program, the word *Podcast*, the host or performers, the title of the site, the date of posting, the site's sponsor, access information, and the URL. (Because the MLA currently provides no guidelines for documenting a podcast, this model is based on MLA guidelines for a short work from a Web site.)

"Seven Arrested in U.S. Terror Raid." Morning Report. Podcast. Host
    Krishnan Guru-Murthy. 4 Radio. 23 June 2006. Channel 4. 28 June 2006
    <http://www.channel4.com/news/podcasts/morning_report/mp3s/
    2006/06/23_mr.mp3>.

70. WORK OF ART OR PHOTOGRAPH List the artist or photographer; the work's title, underlined or italicized; the name of the museum or other location; and the city. Add the publication information if you did not see the work in person. If you want to include the date the work was created, add it after the title.

Chagall, Marc. The Poet with the Birds. 1911. Minneapolis Inst. of Arts.
    6 Oct. 2003 <http://www.artsmia.org/collection/search/
    art.cfm?id=1427>.

Kahlo, Frida. Self-Portrait with Cropped Hair. 1940. Museum of Mod. Art,
    New York.

71. MAP OR CHART Include the label *Map* or *Chart*.

Australia. Map. Perry-Casteñeda Library Map Collection. 4 Nov. 2003
    <http://www.lib.utexas.edu/maps/australia/australia_rel99.jpg>.

California. Map. Chicago: Rand, 2002.

72. CARTOON OR COMIC STRIP List the artist's name; the title (if any) of the cartoon or comic strip, in quotation marks; the label *Cartoon* or *Comic strip*; and the usual publication information.

Johnston, Lynn. "For Better or for Worse." Comic strip. 30 June 2006.
20 July 2006 <http://www.fborfw.com/strip_fix/archives/001879.php>.

Lewis, Eric. "The Unpublished Freud." Cartoon. New Yorker 11 Mar. 2002: 80.

73. ADVERTISEMENT Include the label *Advertisement* after the name of the item or organization being advertised.

Microsoft. Advertisement. Harper's Oct. 2003: 2-3.

Microsoft. Advertisement. New York Times Online 11 Nov. 2003. 11 Nov. 2003
<http://www.nytimes.com/>.

APA Documentation Guidelines

The following formatting guidelines are adapted from the APA's recommendations for preparing manuscripts for publication in journals. However, check with your instructor before preparing your final draft. For detailed guidelines on formatting a list of references, see p. 347. For a sample student essay in APA style, see p. 205.

- *Title page.* Center the title, and include your name, the course name and number, the instructor's name, and the date. In the top right-hand corner, type a short version of the title (fifty characters or fewer, including spaces), skip five spaces, and type the number 1; the page number should be at least one inch from the right side.

- *Margins and spacing.* Leave margins of at least one inch at the top and bottom and on both sides of the page. Do not justify the right margin. Double-space the entire text, including headings, set-off quotations, content notes, and the list of references. Indent the first line of each paragraph one-half inch (or five to seven spaces) from the left margin.

- *Short title and page numbers.* Type the short title and page number in the upper right-hand corner of each page, in the same position as on the title page.

- *Long quotations.* For a long, set-off quotation (one having more than forty words), indent it one-half inch (or five to seven spaces) from the left margin and do not use quotation marks. Place the page reference in parentheses one space after the final punctuation.

- *Abstract.* If your instructor asks for an abstract with your paper — a one-paragraph summary of your major thesis and supporting points—it should go on a separate page immediately after the title page. Center the word *Abstract* about an inch from the top of the page. Double-space the text of the abstract, and begin the first line flush with the left margin. APA recommends that an abstract not exceed 120 words.

- *Headings.* Headings are used within the text of many APA-style papers. In papers with only one or two levels of headings, center the main headings; italicize the subheadings and position them flush with the left margin. Capitalize all major words; however, do not capitalize articles, short prepositions, or coordinating conjunctions unless they are the first word or follow a colon.

- *Visuals.* Tables should be labeled *Table*, numbered, and captioned. All other visuals (charts, graphs, photographs, and drawings) should be labeled *Figure*, numbered, and captioned with a description and the source information. Remember to refer to each visual in your text, stating how it contributes to the point(s) you are making. Tables and figures should appear near the relevant text; check with your instructor for guidelines on placement of visuals.

IN-TEXT CITATIONS

APA style requires parenthetical references in the text to document quotations, paraphrases, summaries, and other material from a source (see Chapter 6). These citations include the year of publication and correspond to full bibliographic entries in the list of references at the end of the text. Note that APA style generally calls for past-tense signal verbs (*Baker showed*) in literature reviews or when describing a past action that occurred at a definite time. Use the present perfect tense (*Baker has shown*) for actions or conditions that are ongoing or didn't happen at a specific time. Use the present tense to discuss results (*the second experiment corroborates*) or widely accepted information (*researchers agree*).

Directory to APA style for in-text citations

1. AUTHOR NAMED IN A SIGNAL PHRASE In most instances, use the author's name in a signal phrase to introduce the cited material, and place the date, in parentheses, immediately after the author's name. For a quotation, the page number, preceded by *p.*, appears in parentheses after the quotation.

> As Fanderclai (2001) observed, older siblings play an important role in the development of language and learning skills.

> Chavez (2003) noted that "six years after slim cigarettes for women were introduced, more than twice as many teenage girls were smoking" (p. 13).

For electronic texts or other works with paragraph numbers but no page numbers, use the paragraph number preceded by the ¶ symbol or the abbreviation *para.*

> Weinberg (2000) has claimed that "the techniques used in group therapy can be verbal, expressive, or psychodramatic" (¶ 5).

If paragraph numbers are not given, cite the heading and number of the paragraph in that section, if any: (*Types of Groups section, para. 1*). For a long, set-off quotation (one having more than forty words), place the page reference in parentheses one space after the final punctuation.

2. AUTHOR NAMED IN A PARENTHETICAL REFERENCE When you do not mention the author in a signal phrase in your text, give the author's name and the date, separated by a comma, in parentheses at the end of the cited material.

> One study found that 17% of adopted children in the United States are of a different race than their adoptive parents (Peterson, 2003).

3. TWO AUTHORS Use both names in all citations. Join the names with *and* in a signal phrase, but use an ampersand (&) instead in a parenthetical reference.

> Babcock and Laschever (2003) have suggested that many women do not negotiate their salaries and pay raises as vigorously as their male counterparts do.

> A recent study has suggested that many women do not negotiate their salaries and pay raises as vigorously as their male counterparts do (Babcock & Laschever, 2003).

4. THREE TO FIVE AUTHORS List all the authors' names for the first reference.

Safer, Voccola, Hurd, and Goodwin (2003) reached somewhat different conclusions by designing a study that was less dependent on subjective judgment than were previous studies.

In subsequent references, use just the first author's name plus *et al.* ("and others").

Based on the results, Safer et al. (2003) determined that the apes took significant steps toward self-expression.

5. SIX OR MORE AUTHORS Use only the first author's name and *et al.* ("and others") in every citation, including the first.

As Soleim et al. (2002) demonstrated, advertising holds the potential for manipulating "free-willed" consumers.

6. CORPORATE OR GROUP AUTHOR If the name of the organization or corporation is long, spell it out the first time you use it, followed by an abbreviation in brackets. In later references, use the abbreviation only.

FIRST CITATION   (Centers for Disease Control and Prevention [CDC], 2006)

LATER CITATIONS   (CDC, 2006)

7. UNKNOWN AUTHOR Use the title or its first few words in a signal phrase or in parentheses. Italicize a book or report title; place an article title in quotation marks.

The school profiles for the county substantiate this trend (*Guide to secondary schools*, 2003).

8. TWO OR MORE AUTHORS WITH THE SAME LAST NAME If your list of references includes works by different authors with the same last name, include the authors' initials in each citation.

G. Jones (2001) conducted the groundbreaking study on teenage childbearing.

9. TWO OR MORE WORKS BY AN AUTHOR IN A SINGLE YEAR Assign lowercase letters (*a, b,* and so on) alphabetically by title, and include the letters after the year.

Gordon (2004b) examined this trend in more detail.

10. TWO OR MORE SOURCES IN ONE PARENTHETICAL REFERENCE List sources by different authors in alphabetical order by authors' last names, separated by semicolons; list works by the same author in chronological order, separated by commas.

(Cardone, 2004; Lai, 2002)

(Lai, 2000, 2002)

11. SPECIFIC PARTS OF A SOURCE Use abbreviations (*chap.*, *p.*, *para.*, and so on) in a parenthetical reference to name the part of a work you are citing.

Mogolov (2003, chap. 9) has argued that his research yielded the opposite results.

12. EMAIL AND OTHER PERSONAL COMMUNICATION Cite any personal letters, email messages, electronic postings, telephone conversations, or interviews with the person's initial(s) and last name, the identification *personal communication*, and the date. Do not include personal communications in the reference list.

R. Tobin (personal communication, November 4, 2005) supported his claims about music therapy with new evidence.

13. ELECTRONIC DOCUMENT To cite an entire Web site, include its address in parentheses in your text (http://www.gallup.com); you don't need to include it in your list of references. Otherwise, cite a Web or electronic document as you would a print source, using the author's name and date; indicating the chapter or figure, as appropriate; and giving a full citation in your list of references. To cite a quotation, include the page or paragraph numbers.

In her report, Zomkowski stressed the importance of "ensuring equitable access to the Internet" (2003, para. 3).

CONTENT NOTES

APA style allows you to use content notes to expand or supplement your text. Indicate such notes in the text by superscript numerals ([1]). Type the notes themselves on a separate page after the last page of the text, under the heading *Footnotes*, which should be centered at the top of the page. Double-space all entries. Indent the first line of each note one-half inch (or five to seven spaces), but begin subsequent lines at the left margin.

The age of the children involved in the study was an important factor in the selection of items for the questionnaire.[1]

[1]Marjorie Youngston Forman and William Cole of the Child Study Team provided great assistance in identifying appropriate items for the questionnaire.

LIST OF REFERENCES

The alphabetical list of all the sources cited in your document is called *References*. (If your instructor asks that you list everything you have read as background—not just the sources you cite—call the list *Bibliography*.) Here are guidelines for preparing a list of references:

- Start your list on a separate page after the text of your document but before any appendices or notes. Identify each page with the short title and page number, continuing the numbering of the text.

- Type the heading *References*, neither italicized nor in quotation marks, centered one inch from the top of the page.

- Double-space, and begin your first entry. Unless your instructor suggests otherwise, do not indent the first line of each entry, but indent subsequent lines one-half inch or five to seven spaces. Double-space the entire list.

- List sources alphabetically by authors' (or editors') last names. If the author is unknown, alphabetize the source by the first major word of the title, disregarding *A*, *An*, or *The*. If the list includes two or more works by the same author, see the examples on pp. 352 and 353. APA style specifies the treatment and placement of four basic elements—author, publication date, title, and other publication information.

- *Author.* List all authors' last names first, and use only initials for first and middle names. Separate the names of multiple authors with commas, and use an ampersand (&) before the last author's name.

- *Publication date.* Enclose the date in parentheses. Use only the year for books and journals; use the year, a comma, and the month or month and day for magazines; use the year, a comma, and the month and day for newspapers. Do not abbreviate.

- *Title.* Italicize titles and subtitles of books and periodicals. Do not enclose titles of articles in quotation marks. For books and articles, capitalize only the first word of the title and subtitle and any proper nouns or proper adjectives. Capitalize all major words in a periodical title.

- *Publication information*. For a book, list the city of publication (and the country or postal abbreviation for the state if the city is unfamiliar), a colon, and the publisher's name, dropping any *Inc.*, *Co.*, or *Publishers*. For a periodical, follow the periodical title with a comma, the volume number (italicized), the issue number (if appropriate) in parentheses and followed by a comma, and the inclusive page numbers of the article. For newspaper articles and for articles or chapters in books, include the abbreviation *p.* ("page") or *pp.* ("pages") before the page numbers.

The sample entries that start on p. 349 use a hanging indent format, in which the first line aligns on the left and the subsequent lines indent one-half inch or five to seven spaces. This is the customary APA format for final copy, including student papers.

Directory to APA style for references

BOOKS

The basic format for a reference-list entry for a book is outlined on pp. 350–51.

1. ONE AUTHOR

Lightman, A. P. (2002). *The diagnosis.* New York: Vintage Books.

2. TWO OR MORE AUTHORS

Walsh, M. E., & Murphy, J. A. (2003). *Children, health, and learning: A guide to the issues.* Westport, CT: Praeger.

3. CORPORATE OR GROUP AUTHOR

Committee on Abrupt Climate Change, National Research Council. (2002). *Abrupt climate change: Inevitable surprises.* Washington, DC: National Academies Press.

Use the word *Author* as the publisher when the organization is both the author and the publisher.

Resources for Rehabilitation. (2003). *A woman's guide to coping with disability.* London: Author.

4. UNKNOWN AUTHOR

National Geographic atlas of the Middle East. (2003). Washington, DC: National Geographic Society.

5. EDITOR

Dickens, J. (Ed.). (1995). *Family outing: A guide for parents of gays, lesbians, and bisexuals.* London: Peter Owen.

6. SELECTION IN A BOOK WITH AN EDITOR

Burke, W. W., & Nourmair, D. A. (2001). The role of personality assessment in organization development. In J. Waclawski & A. H. Church (Eds.), *Organization development: A data-driven approach to organizational change* (pp. 55-77). San Francisco: Jossey-Bass.

SOURCE MAP: Citing Books Using APA Style

Take information from the book's title page and copyright page (on the reverse side of the title page), not from the book's cover or a library catalog.

(1) *Author.* List all authors' last names first, and use only initials for first and middle names. Separate the names of multiple authors with commas, and use an ampersand (&) before the last author's name.

(2) *Publication year.* Enclose the year of publication in parentheses.

(3) *Title.* Italicize the title and subtitle. Capitalize only the first word of the title and the subtitle and any proper nouns or proper adjectives.

(4) *City of publication.* List the city of publication (and the country or state abbreviation if the city is unfamiliar) followed by a colon.

(5) *Publisher.* Give the publisher's name, dropping any *Inc., Co.,* or *Publishers.*

For a book by one author, use the following format:

Last name, initial(s). (Year). *Title of book: Subtitle.* City: Publisher.

A citation for the book on p. 351 would look like this:

AUTHOR'S LAST NAME AND INITIAL   YEAR OF PUBLICATION   TITLE AND SUBTITLE, ITALICIZED

Tsutsui, W. (2004). *Godzilla on my mind: Fifty years of the king of monsters.*

PUBLISHER'S CITY AND NAME

New York: Palgrave Macmillan.

DOUBLE-SPACE; INDENT ONE-HALF INCH OR FIVE TO SEVEN SPACES

For more on using APA style to cite books, see p. 349–52. (For guidelines and models for using MLA style, see pp. 314–21.)

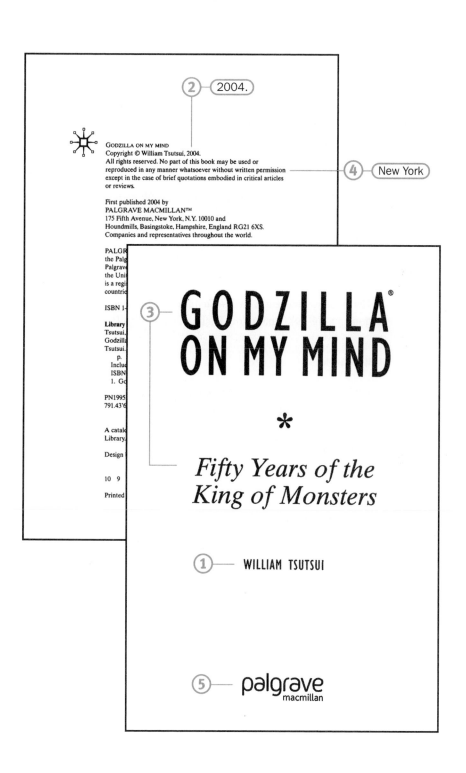

(2)—(2004.)

(4)—(New York)

First published 2004 by
PALGRAVE MACMILLAN™
175 Fifth Avenue, New York, N.Y. 10010 and
Houndmills, Basingstoke, Hampshire, England RG21 6XS.
Companies and representatives throughout the world.

PALGR
the Palg
Palgrave
the Unit
is a regi
countrie

ISBN 1-

Library
Tsutsui,
Godzilla
Tsutsui.
    p.
  Inclu
  ISBN
  1. Go

PN1995
791.43'6

A catalo
Library.

Design

10 9

Printed

GODZILLA®
ON MY MIND

(3)

*

*Fifty Years of the
King of Monsters*

(1)— WILLIAM TSUTSUI

(5)— palgrave
macmillan

Al-Farabi, A. N. (1998). *On the perfect state* (R. Walzer, Trans.). Chicago: Kazi.

Moore, G. S. (2002). *Living with the earth: Concepts in environmental health science* (2nd ed.). New York: Lewis.

Barnes, J. (Ed.). (1995). *Complete works of Aristotle* (Vols. 1-2). Princeton, NJ: Princeton University Press.

10. ARTICLE IN A REFERENCE WORK If no author is listed, begin with the title.

Dean, C. (1994). Jaws and teeth. In *The Cambridge encyclopedia of human evolution* (pp. 56-59). Cambridge, England: Cambridge University Press.

Piaget, J. (1952). *The language and thought of the child.* London: Routledge & Kegan Paul. (Original work published 1932)

12. TWO OR MORE WORKS BY THE SAME AUTHOR(S) List two or more works by the same author in chronological order (if the works appear in a single year, see model 21). Repeat the author's name in each entry.

Goodall, J. (1999). *Reason for hope: A spiritual journey*. New York: Warner Books.

Goodall, J. (2002). *Performance and evolution in the age of Darwin: Out of the natural order*. New York: Routledge.

PERIODICALS

The basic format for a reference-list entry for an article in a periodical is outlined on pp. 354–55.

O'Connell, D. C., & Kowal, S. (2003). Psycholinguistics: A half century of monologism. *The American Journal of Psychology, 116,* 191-212.

14. ARTICLE IN A JOURNAL PAGINATED BY ISSUE

Hall, R. E. (2000). Marriage as vehicle of racism among women of color. *Psychology: A Journal of Human Behavior, 37*(2), 29-40.

15. ARTICLE IN A MAGAZINE

Ricciardi, S. (2003, August 5). Enabling the mobile work force. *PC Magazine, 22,* 46.

16. ARTICLE IN A NEWSPAPER

Faler, B. (2003, August 29). Primary colors: Race and fundraising. *The Washington Post*, p. A5.

17. EDITORIAL OR LETTER TO THE EDITOR

Zelneck, B. (2003, July 18). Serving the public at public universities [Letter to the editor]. *The Chronicle Review*, p. B18.

18. UNSIGNED ARTICLE

Annual meeting announcement. (2003, March). *Cognitive Psychology, 46,* 227.

19. REVIEW

Ringel, S. (2003). [Review of the book *Multiculturalism and the therapeutic process*]. *Clinical Social Work Journal, 31,* 212-213.

20. PUBLISHED INTERVIEW

Smith, H. (2002, October). [Interview with A. Thompson]. *The Sun*, pp. 4-7.

21. TWO OR MORE WORKS BY THE SAME AUTHOR IN THE SAME YEAR List the works alphabetically by title, and place lowercase letters (*a*, *b*, and so on) after the dates.

Shermer, M. (2002a). On estimating the lifetime of civilizations. *Scientific American, 287*(2), 33.

Shermer, M. (2002b). Readers who question evolution. *Scientific American, 287*(1), 37.

SOURCE MAP: Citing Articles from Periodicals Using APA Style

(1) *Author.* List all authors' last names first, and use only initials for first and middle names. Separate the names of multiple authors with commas, and use an ampersand (&) before the last author's name.

(2) *Publication date.* Enclose the date in parentheses. For journals, use only the year. For magazines and newspapers, use the year, a comma, the month (spelled out), and the day of the month if given.

(3) *Article title.* Do not italicize or enclose article titles in quotation marks. Capitalize only the first word of the article title and subtitle and any proper nouns or proper adjectives.

(4) *Periodical title.* Italicize the periodical title (and subtitle, if any), and capitalize all major words.

(5) *Publication information.* Follow the periodical title with a comma, and then give the volume number (italicized) and, without a space in between, the issue number (if given) in parentheses.

(6) *Page numbers.* Give the inclusive page numbers of the article. For newspapers only, include the abbreviation *p.* ("page") or *pp.* ("pages") before the page numbers. End the citation with a period.

For a basic periodical article, use the following format:

Last name, First initial. (Year, month day [or year alone for journal]). Title of article. *Title of Periodical, Volume number* (Issue number), Page number(s).

A citation for the magazine article on p. 355 would look like this:

AUTHORS' LAST NAMES, FIRST INITIALS   PUBLICATION DATE   ARTICLE TITLE, FIRST WORD CAPITALIZED

Tyre, P., & Staveley-O'Carroll, S. (2005, August 8). How to fix school lunch.

PERIODICAL TITLE, ITALICIZED   PAGE NUMBERS

Newsweek, 146(6), 50-51.

VOLUME NUMBER, ITALICIZED; ISSUE NUMBER

DOUBLE-SPACE; INDENT ONE-HALF INCH OR FIVE TO SEVEN SPACES

For more on using APA style to cite periodicals, see pp. 352–55. (For guidelines and models for using MLA style, see pp. 321–24.)

By Peg Tyre and Sarah Staveley-O'Carroll

HEALTHY CHOICE:
Jamie Oliver
serves up lunch

How to Fix School Lunch

Celebrity chefs, politicians and concerned parents are joining forces to improve the meals kids eat every day.

BY PEG TYRE AND SARAH STAVELEY-O'CARROLL

FOR JORGE COLLAZO, EXECUTIVE chef for the New York City public schools, coming up with the perfect jerk sauce is yet another step toward making the 1.1 million schoolkids he serves healthier. In a little more than a year, he's introduced salad bars and replaced whole milk with skim. Beef patties are now served on whole-wheat buns. Until recently, "every piece of chicken the manufacturers sent us was either breaded or covered in a glaze," says Collazo. Brandishing the might of his $125 million annual food budget, he switched to plain cutlets and asked suppliers to come up with something healthy—and appealing—to put on his [menu]. [One supplier's] offering. The [new version] [tasted good?] and doesn't have trans fats. Too salty, he says with a grimace. Within minutes, the supplier is hard at work on a lower-sodium version.

A cramped public-school test kitchen might seem an unlikely outpost for a food revolution. But Collazo and scores of others across the country—celebrity chefs and

lunch ladies, district superintendents and politicians—say they're determined to improve what kids eat in school. Nearly everyone agrees something must be done. Most school cafeterias are staffed by poorly trained, badly equipped workers who churn out 4.8 billion hot lunches a year. Often the meals, produced for about $1 each, consist of breaded meat patties, french fries and overcooked vegetables. So the kids buy muffins, cookies and ice cream instead—or they feast on fast food from McDonald's, Pizza Hut and Taco Bell, which is available in more than half the schools in the nation.

Vending machines packed with sodas and candy line the hallways. "We're killing our kids" with the food we serve, says Texas Education Commissioner Susan Combs.

As rates of childhood obesity and diabetes skyrocket, public-health officials say schools need to change the way kids eat. It won't be easy. Some kids and their parents don't know better. Home cooking is becoming a forgotten art. And fast-food companies now spend $3 billion a year on television ads aimed at children. Along with reading and writing, schools need to teach kids what to eat to stay healthy, says culinary innovator Alice Waters, who is introducing gardening and fresh produce to 16 schools in California. It's a golden opportunity, she says, "to affect the way children eat for the rest of their lives." Last year star English chef Jamie Oliver took over a school cafeteria in a working-class suburb of London. A documentary about his work shamed the British government into spending $500 million to revamp the nation's school-food program. Oliver says it's the United States' turn now. "If you can put a man on the moon," he says, "you can give kids the food they need to make them lighter, fitter and live longer."

Changing school food takes time. More than a decade ago, when local restaurateur Lynn Walters lobbied school-board members in Santa Fe, N.M., to provide kids with

TOP TO BOTTOM: JULIAN MAKEY—REX FEATURES; PHOTOGRAPH BY LAUREN FLEISHMAN FOR NEWSWEEK

RETHINKING 'CHOICE': The pro-*Roe* forces brace for battle

COVER: Photograph by Mark Allen Johnson—ZUMA

Newsweek (**ISSN 0028-9604**), August 8, 2005, Volume CXLVI, No. 6. Newsweek publishes an issue weekly, except when combined issues are published which count as two issues (currently in August and December) and when, from time to time, an additional special issue may be published. A one-year subscription (52 issues) is U.S. $41.08 and Canadian $61.88 a year. In the U.S. send subscription inquiries to Newsweek, P.O. Box 5571, Harlan, IA 51593-1871. In Canada: Newsweek, Inc., P.O. Box 4087, Postal Station A, Toronto, ON M5W2K1. Canada Post International Publications Mail (Canadian Distribution) Sales Agreement No. 40051822. Canadian GST No. 123-321-301. All changes of address: **800-634-6850**. All other inquiries: **800-631-1040**. Unless otherwise indicated by source or currency designation, all terms and prices are applicable in the U.S. only and may not apply in Canada. Copyright © 2005 Newsweek, Inc. All rights reserved. 251 West 57th Street, New York, NY 10019-1894. Richard M. Smith, Chairman and Editor-in-Chief; Stephen Fuzesi Jr., Chief Counsel and Secretary. Periodicals postage paid at New York, NY, and at additional mailing offices. **POSTMASTERS: send address changes to Newsweek, P.O. Box 5972, Harlan, IA 51593-1072.** Printed in U.S.A. We may make a portion of our mailing list available to a select group of companies whose products or services may be of interest of you. If you would prefer that we not disclose your personal information for this purpose, please contact subscriber services by mail, phone or e-mail at nwsub@newsweek.com. Your choice will not affect the cost of your service.

ELECTRONIC SOURCES

The *Publication Manual of the American Psychological Association*, Fifth Edition, includes guidelines for citing various kinds of electronic resources, including Web sites; articles, reports, and abstracts; some types of online communications; and computer software. Updated guidelines are maintained at the APA's Web site (www.apa.org).

The basic entry for most sources accessed via the Internet should include the following elements:

- *Author*. Give the author's name, if available.

- *Publication date*. Include the date of electronic publication or of the latest update, if available. Use *n.d.* ("no date") when the publication date is unavailable.

- *Title*. List the title of the document or subject line of the message, neither italicized nor in quotation marks.

- *Publication information*. For articles from online journals, newspapers, or reference databases, give the publication title and other publishing information as you would for a print periodical.

- *Retrieval information*. For most Internet sources, type the word *Retrieved* followed by the date of access, a comma, and the word *from*. End with the URL or other retrieval information and no period. If the URL will not fit on one line, break it after a slash or before a period and do not add a hyphen. For listserv or newsgroup messages and other online postings, type *Message posted to*, followed by the name of the list or group and the URL of the group or its archive.

22. ARTICLE IN AN ONLINE PERIODICAL If the article also appears in a print journal, no retrieval statement is required; instead, include the label *[Electronic version]* after the article title.

> Steedman, M., & Jones, G. P. (2000). Information structure and the syntaxphonology interface [Electronic version]. *Linguistic Inquiry, 31,* 649-689.

However, if the online article differs from the print version (for example, if page numbers are not indicated) or did not appear in print, include the date of access and the URL.

> Lou, L., & Chen, J. (2003, January). Attention and blind-spot phenomenology. *Psyche, 9*(2). Retrieved March 22, 2003, from http://psyche.cs.monash.edu.au/v9/psyche-9-02-lou.html

23. ARTICLE OR ABSTRACT FROM A DATABASE (See pp. 358–59 for the basic format for citing an article from a database.) Give the information as you would for a print document. List the date you retrieved the article and the name of the database. If you are citing an abstract, use the notation *Abstract retrieved*. End with the document number in parentheses, if appropriate.

> Crook, S. (2003). Change, uncertainty and the future of sociology. *Journal of Sociology, 39*(1), 7-14. Retrieved January 10, 2004, from Expanded Academic ASAP database (A101260213).

> Hayhoe, G. (2001). The long and winding road: Technology's future. *Technical Communication, 48*(2), 133-145. Retrieved September 22, 2001, from ProQuest database.

> McCall, R. B. (1988). Science and the press: Like oil and water? *American Psychologist, 43*(2), 87-94. Abstract retrieved July 13, 2007, from PsycINFO database (1988-18263-001).

24. DOCUMENT FROM A WEB SITE (See pp. 360–61 for the basic format for citing a work from a Web site.) Include information as you would for a print document, followed by information about its retrieval. If no author is identified, give the title of the document followed by the date (if available).

> DotComSense: Commonsense ways to protect your privacy and assess online mental health information. (2000, January). *APA Monitor, 31*, 32. Retrieved January 25, 2001, from http://helping.apa.org/dotcomsense/

To cite an entire Web site, give its address in a parenthetical reference but do not include it in your list of references.

25. CHAPTER OR SECTION OF A WEB DOCUMENT After the chapter or section title, type *In* and give the document title, with identifying information, if any, in parentheses. End with the date of access and the URL.

> Salamon, Andrew. (n.d.). War in Europe. In *Childhood in times of war* (chap. 2). Retrieved April 11, 2005, from http://remember.org/jean

26. EMAIL MESSAGE OR REAL-TIME COMMUNICATION Do not include entries for email messages or real-time communications (such as IMs) in the list of references; instead, cite these sources in your text as forms of personal communication (see in-text model 12 on p. 346).

SOURCE MAP: Citing Articles from Databases
Using APA Style

Libraries pay for services—such as InfoTrac, EBSCOhost, ProQuest, and Lexis-Nexis—that provide access to large databases of electronic articles.

(1) *Author.* If available, include the author's name as you would for a print source. List all authors' last names first, and use only initials for first and middle names. Separate the names of multiple authors with commas, and use an ampersand (&) before the last author's name.

(2) *Publication date.* Enclose the date in parentheses. For journals, use only the year. For magazines and newspapers, use the year, a comma, the month (spelled out), and the day of the month if given.

(3) *Article title.* Do not italicize or enclose article titles in quotation marks. Capitalize only the first word of the article title and the subtitle and any proper nouns or proper adjectives.

(4) *Periodical title.* Italicize the periodical title (and subtitle, if any), and capitalize all major words.

(5) *Publication information.* Follow the periodical title with a comma, and then give the volume number (italicized) and, without a space in between, the issue number (if given) in parentheses.

(6) *Page numbers.* Give inclusive page numbers of the article. For newspapers, include abbreviation *p.* ("page") or *pp.* ("pages") before the page numbers.

(7) *Retrieval information.* Type the word *Retrieved* (or *Abstract retrieved*, for abstracts), followed by the date you retrieved the article and the name of the database.

(8) *Document number.* Provide a document number (sometimes called an article or accession number), if available, and end the citation with a period.

For a journal article retrieved from a database, use the following format:

Last name, First initial. (Year). Title of article. *Title of Journal, Volume number* (Issue number), Page number(s). Retrieved Month day, year, from Database name (Document number, if available).

A citation for the article on p. 359 would look like this:

AUTHORS' LAST NAMES, INITIALS   YEAR OF PUBLICATION   ARTICLE TITLE AND SUBTITLE, FIRST WORD OF EACH CAPITALIZED

Chory-Assad, R. M., & Tamborini, R. (2004). Television sitcom exposure and

PERIODICAL TITLE, ITALICIZED

aggressive communication: A priming perspective. *North American*

VOLUME NUMBER, ITALICIZED, AND ISSUE NUMBER, IF GIVEN   PAGE NUMBERS   RETRIEVAL DATE

Journal of Psychology, 6(3), 415-422. Retrieved August 8, 2005,

DATABASE NAME   DOCUMENT NUMBER

from Academic Search Premier (15630823).

DOUBLE-SPACE; INDENT ONE-HALF INCH OR FIVE TO SEVEN SPACES

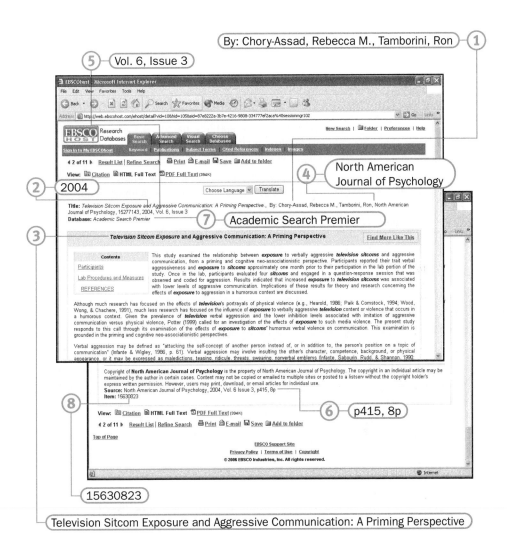

By: Chory-Assad, Rebecca M., Tamborini, Ron — (1)

(5) — Vol. 6, Issue 3

(2) — 2004

(4) — North American Journal of Psychology

(7) — Academic Search Premier

(3)

(8)

(6) — p415, 8p

15630823

Television Sitcom Exposure and Aggressive Communication: A Priming Perspective

For more on using APA style to cite articles retrieved from databases, see p. 357. (For guidelines and models for using MLA style, see pp. 325–26.)

(1) *Author.* If available, include the author's name as you would for a print source. List all authors' last names first, and use only initials for first and middle names. Separate the names of multiple authors with commas, and use an ampersand (&) before the last author's name. In some cases, the site's host or sponsoring organization may be the author. If no author is identified, begin the citation with the title of the document or Web site.

(2) *Publication date.* Include the date of Internet publication or latest update, if available. Use *n.d.* ("no date") when the publication date is unavailable.

(3) *Title.* Do not italicize or enclose document titles in quotation marks. Capitalize only the first word of the title and subtitle and any proper nouns or proper adjectives.

(4) *Retrieval information.* Type the word *Retrieved* followed by the date of access, a comma, and the word *from*. End with the URL and no period.

For a document found on a Web site with one author, use the following format:

Last name, First initial. (Internet publication date). Title of document. Retrieved Month day, year, from URL

A citation for the Web document on p. 361 would look like this:

NAME OF AUTHOR OR SPONSOR   INTERNET PUBLICATION DATE   TITLE OF DOCUMENT

African Economic Research Consortium. (2005, May 27). International

migration: Friend or foe of Africa's economic development? Retrieved

RETRIEVAL DATE   URL

August 25, 2006, from http://www.aercafrica.org/news/newsarticle

.asp?newsid=39

DOUBLE-SPACE; INDENT ONE-HALF INCH OR FIVE TO SEVEN SPACES

For more on using APA style to cite works from Web sites, see 356–62. (For guidelines and models for using MLA style, see pp. 324–25.)

④ http://www.aercafrica.org/news/newsarticle.asp?newsid=39

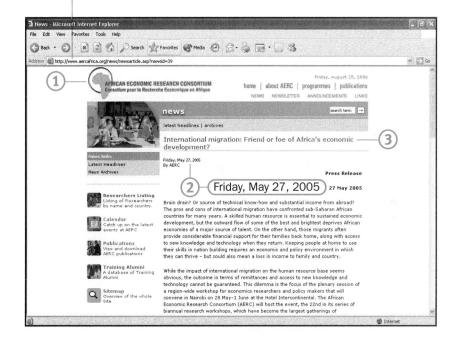

27. ONLINE POSTING List an online posting in the reference list only if the message is retrievable from a mailing list's archive. Give the author's name and the posting's date and subject line. Include other identifying information in square brackets. For a listserv message, include both the name of the list and the URL of the archived message.

> Troike, R. C. (2001, June 21). Buttercups and primroses [Msg 8]. Message posted to the American Dialect Society's electronic mailing list, archived at http://listserv.linguistlist.org/archives/ads-l.html

For a newsgroup posting, end with the name of the newsgroup. (If the author's real name is unavailable, include the screen name.)

> Wittenberg, E. (2001, July 11). Gender and the Internet [Msg 4]. Message posted to news://comp.edu.composition

28. SOFTWARE OR COMPUTER PROGRAM

> PsychMate [Computer software]. (2003). Pittsburgh, PA: Psychology Software Tools.

OTHER SOURCES (INCLUDING ONLINE VERSIONS)

29. GOVERNMENT PUBLICATION

> Office of the Federal Register. (2003). *The United States government manual 2003/2004*. Washington, DC: U.S. Government Printing Office.

For an online government document, add the date of access and the URL.

> U.S. Public Health Service. (1999). *The surgeon general's call to action to prevent suicide*. Retrieved November 5, 2003, from http://www.mentalhealth.org/suicideprevention/calltoaction.asp

30. DISSERTATION ABSTRACT If you use *Dissertation Abstracts International* (*DAI*), include the *DAI* volume, issue, and page number. If you use the UMI digital dissertation service, include the UMI number in parentheses but with no period at the end of the entry.

> Bandelj, N. (2003). Embedded economies: Foreign direct investment in Central and Eastern Europe. *Dissertation Abstracts International, 64* (03), 1083. (UMI No. 3085036)

31. UNPUBLISHED DISSERTATION

Leverenz, C. A. (1994). *Collaboration and difference in the composition classroom*. Unpublished doctoral dissertation, Ohio State University, Columbus.

32. TECHNICAL OR RESEARCH REPORT
Give the report number, if available, in parentheses after the title.

McCool, R., Fikes, R., & McGuinness, D. (2003). *Semantic web tools for enhanced authoring* (Report No. KSL-03-07). Stanford, CA: Knowledge Systems Laboratory.

33. CONFERENCE PROCEEDINGS

Mama, A. (2001). Challenging subjects: Gender and power in African contexts. In *Proceedings of Nordic African Institute Conference: Rethinking power in Africa*. Uppsala, Sweden, 9-18.

34. PAPER PRESENTED AT A MEETING OR SYMPOSIUM, UNPUBLISHED
Cite the month of the meeting if it is available.

Jones, J. G. (1999, February). *Mental health intervention in mass casualty disasters*. Paper presented at the Rocky Mountain Region Disaster Mental Health Conference, Laramie, WY.

35. POSTER SESSION

Barnes, Young, L. L. (2003, August). *Cognition, aging, and dementia*. Poster session presented at the 2003 Division 40 APA Convention, Toronto, Ontario, Canada.

36. FILM, VIDEO, OR DVD

Moore, M. (Director). (2003). *Bowling for Columbine* [Motion picture]. United States: MGM.

37. TELEVISION PROGRAM, SINGLE EPISODE

Imperioli, M. (Writer), & Buscemi, S. (Director). (2002). Everybody hurts [Television series episode]. In D. Chase (Executive Producer), *The Sopranos*. New York: HBO.

The Avalanches. (2001). Frontier psychiatrist. On *Since I left you* [CD].
   Los Angeles: Elektra/Asylum Records.

Acknowledgments

Picture Credits

Joe Rosenthal, Associated Press, February 23, 1945. **Chapter 6: 148,** © 2007 Google. **149,** © Merlin Information Services. **150, 151,** © 2007 LexisNexis. **169, 170,** Courtesy National Labor Committee. **Chapter 8: 232,** Courtesy National Center for Family Literacy. **Chapter 11: 274** (pie chart) Energy Information Administration, U.S. Department of Energy, (bar graph) © 2007 The Trustees of Columbia University in the City of New York for its National Center for Children in Poverty, (map) U.S. Census Bureau. **277,** © Innocence Project. **Chapter 12: 294,** Courtesy National Center for Family Literacy.

Index